INDEPENDENT VERIFICATION AND VALIDATION

NEW DIMENSIONS IN ENGINEERING

Editor
RODNEY D. STEWART

SYSTEM ENGINEERING MANAGEMENT
Benjamin S. Blanchard

NONDESTRUCTIVE TESTING TECHNIQUES
Don E. Bray (Editor)
Don McBride (Editor)

LOGISTICS ENGINEERING
Linda L. Green

NEW PRODUCT DEVELOPMENT: DESIGN AND ANALYSIS
Ronald E. Kmetovicz

INDEPENDENT VERIFICATION AND VALIDATION:
A LIFE CYCLE ENGINEERING PROCESS FOR QUALITY SOFTWARE
Robert O. Lewis

DESIGN TO COST
Jack V. Michaels
William P. Wood

OPTIMAL INVENTORY MODELING OF SYSTEMS:
MULTI-ECHELON TECHNIQUES
Craig C. Sherbrooke

COST ESTIMATING, SECOND EDITION
Rodney D. Stewart

PROPOSAL PREPARATION, SECOND EDITION
Rodney D. Stewart
Ann L. Stewart

INDEPENDENT VERIFICATION AND VALIDATION

A Life Cycle Engineering Process for Quality Software

ROBERT O. LEWIS

A Wiley–Interscience Publication
JOHN WILEY & SONS, INC.
New York • Chichester • Brisbane • Toronto • Singapore

In recognition of the importance of preserving what has been
written, it is a policy of John Wiley & Sons, Inc., to have books
of enduring value published in the United States printed on
acid-free paper, and we exert our best efforts to that end.

Library of Congress Cataloging in Publication Data:

Lewis, Robert O., 1938–
    Independent verification and validation: a life cycle engineering
process for quality software / Robert O. Lewis.
      p. cm. — (New dimensions in engineering)
    Includes index.
    ISBN 0-471-57011-7
    1. Computer software—Verification. 2. Computer software—
Validation. I. Title. II. Series.
QA76.76.V47L48 1992
005.1'4—dc20   92-7792

Printed in the United States of America
10 9 8 7 6 5 4 3 2 1

To Carolyn and Lyla

CONTENTS

DETAILED CONTENTS

EDITOR'S PREFACE

Software is becoming a larger and larger part of high-technology processes, products, projects, and services as we move through the 1990s and into the 21st century. Independent Verification and Validation is a comprehensive and up-to-date text that covers the most vital part of software development. Many of the principles involved also apply to computer hardware and to the even broader fields of science and engineering. Cost-efficient development of high-quality work activities and work outputs in this age of high technology requires a life cycle approach to software and hardware verification and validation. Bob Lewis has been working in this field for many years, and his text represents a major step forward in technology transfer from those traditionally advanced arenas to the commercial, industrial, and academic sectors of the science and engineering community. This reference is a must for any person or organization involved in software or software-related activities. We welcome this new author and new text to the New Dimensions in Engineering series.

RODNEY D. STEWART
Series Editor

AUTHOR'S PREFACE

Independent verification and validation (IV&V) as we know it today dates back to the early 1970s when the U. S. Army sponsored the first significant such IV&V program for the Safeguard Anti-Ballistic Missile System. This program pushed IV&V from a fledgling stage to being a mature systems and software engineering discipline. Until then, IV&V was mostly free-form, not very independent, often started too late to be really effective, and was sometimes even performed by the very people who were developing the system. The Safeguard program, with a development staff of well over 2,000 people for several years, provided the fertile field upon which verification methods, tools, and techniques could be developed, tested, and fine-tuned. It was from this effort that IV&V became well known within the Department of Defense and the aerospace communities as an accepted method of ensuring better quality, performance, and reliability of critical systems.

By the mid- to late 1970s, IV&V was rapidly becoming popular and in some cases was required by the military services, especially for systems that had a high cost of failure and hence were able to justify the small added cost of IV&V. As it turns out, in almost every case where IV&V is properly applied, its cost is offset by a reduction in reported problems and latent errors and a much higher level of user satisfaction compared to similar systems that do not have IV&V programs. "Satisfaction" is admittedly subjective, but there also are several case studies that demonstrate cost savings because of IV&V of up to double the IV&V investment. In many of these instances, the savings came from having an expert second opinion when deciding whether or not to fund change proposals and when developing alternative solutions.

Toward the end of the 1970s, I got inspired enough to develop a 40-hour training course, which I then taught all around the country for the next several years, and I got very involved with setting up and participating in IV&V programs for my employer. At the same time, I wrote the original manuscript for this book and used it extensively in my courses, but I held up publishing it because I wanted to further verify and validate its concepts, processes, and conclusions. It was a case of practicing what I was preaching. I was also quite curious about what impact Ada, fourth-generation languages (4GLs), and the proliferation of software tools that were emerging in the marketplace would have on IV&V; in essence, would these things eliminate the need for having a third party review, inspect, analyze, and evaluate the evolving software and hardware products?

I can unequivocally say that IV&V is just as necessary and important today as it ever was. Can total quality management (TQM) replace IV&V? Can a computer-aided software engineering (CASE) tool, support environment, or highly structured methodology supplant IV&V? The answer is absolutely no. Have these developments changed the form, focus and application of IV&V? The answer is definitely yes. Because systems continue to become more complex, solving larger problems in less time with greater fidelity and accuracy, the demands on IV&V increase as well. The 1991 U. S. Strategic Defense ("Star Wars") Initiative System addresses an engagement problem at least three orders of magnitude larger and more difficult than its predecessor system of 20 years ago—from hundreds of objects to hundreds of thousands of objects.

Although IV&V is not limited to software alone, it focuses there, where the biggest payoff occurs. The study of and application of IV&V depends upon having a solid understanding of the system life cycle and, more specifically, of the software development process, a major part of that life cycle. The reason for this is that IV&V has a dependent relationship with the software development process. You can have software development without IV&V, but you cannot have IV&V without a software project to support it. Therefore, a good part of the early chapters of this book are devoted to ensuring that the reader thoroughly understands the software development process.

The reader must also be reminded that IV&V did not begin life as a systematized scientific method with its own well-defined set of rules, tools, and practices; it evolved and is still evolving, more or less in step with software development practices and technologies, from which it was born. It is clearly a product of the fallibility of the software design process itself and the cognizance of men with vision, who recognized that external, third-party forces could be introduced to fortify that process. Thus, IV&V can be very loosely defined as an external augmentation to the many discrete subprocesses that occur during the development of a system. The immediate question that comes to mind is, "If it is so good, why not build it into the process?" The fallacy of this reasoning is best revealed by a series of somewhat obvious questions. Should the meat inspector work for the packing house? Should the bank examiner work for the bank? Should an auditor work for the company being audited? Should IV&V be built into the development process? The answer to all of the above is an emphatic no. The objectivity derived from organizational independence, the perspective of being the first user of the system, and the goal of quality, not quantity and schedule, are some of the most important attributes of IV&V.

There is a natural tendency to orient discussions of IV&V to government-sponsored development efforts—for the Department of Defense (DOD), Social Security

Administration, Federal Aviation Administration (FAA), National Aeronautics and Space Administration (NASA), communications and navigation systems, etc.— since most programs have come out of these organizations. This book is, therefore, based primarily upon a government life cycle model and software development process, because both are so well-defined and regulated, in addition to being the most complex examples available. This in no way implies that the use of IV&V in the industrial, commercial, and institutional sectors is less effective; in fact, quite the contrary. Thus, throughout the book, parallels are drawn between the government's and private sector's way of developing systems, since I believe that IV&V has significant contributions to make to both sides. Some of the world's largest software-intensive systems are indeed nongovernmental, which affords an excellent opportunity for IV&V to make its impact in mostly virgin territory.

The organization of this book is based on approximately 15 years of teaching IV&V and related courses. This experience has convinced me that; (1) IV&V must be studied in the context of the development process that it is supporting, and (2) the material must be multilevel to support the widest possible reader base. Thus, with the hope of making this book as useful as possible, I have divided it into four parts, which progress from a high-level tutorial to the details of planning, implementation, and operation.

Part I is intended to provide a broad understanding of IV&V concepts and to introduce the unique vocabulary. As such, Part I can serve as a manager's overview as well as the prerequisite for the other parts for those who are interested in a more in-depth understanding and who will possibly implement or procure IV&V services.

Part II provides an in-depth study of each key IV&V discipline. It focuses on the products, processes, techniques, and tools—both manual and automated—that make IV&V an efficient and effective discipline.

Part III discusses the application of IV&V from the time of procurement to the operational period of the system. It contains suggestions for scoping and staffing, cost–benefit analysis, development of effective IV&V plans, performance measurement, descriptions of typical products, a synopsis of the Software Engineering Institute (SEI) contractor evaluation methodology, and a comparison of IV&V to quality assurance.

Part IV provides case studies based on actual experiences. These are intended to serve as examples of the wide range of applications possible with IV&V. The actual systems are disguised where necessary to protect all parties' (software and system developer, IV&V contractor and the customer) sensitive elements from unwanted disclosure.

Throughout this book, I refer to the one who designs and implements the system and its software as *the developer* and, when appropriate, as *the development contractor*. I refer to the procurer of the system, of software, and of IV&V as *the customer*. Some government agencies like to call themselves *the developer*, but in this book I call them *the customer*.

IV&V can be performed by an organic (internal) resource already in place and supported by the customer or it can be a contracted service. The approach is basically the same either way, except that a procurement action and contract result in the latter case. Therefore, I simply refer to IV&V in most cases, without making any distinction between organic or contracted services.

The U. S. Department of Defense made significant changes to its acquisition management policies, effective February 23, 1991. This book acknowledges the new names for key items, new documents, and changes to the acquisition cycle. It will take some time for all of the standards to react to these name changes, so I will primarily use the older common names, adding the new names when necessary to avoid confusion. Specifically, the name changes that had the largest impact pertain to the DOD development phases, as follows:

- Concept definition (CD) phase is now officially concept exploration and definition (CE&D).
- Demonstration and validation (Dem/Val) phase is unchanged, although it is also known as "advanced development" by some agencies.
- Full-scale (engineering) development (FSD or FSED) is now officially "engineering and manufacturing development (E&MD)."

These new guidelines canceled over 60 directives, instructions, and memoranda that pertained to this subject and initiated over 100 new ones. The controlling and implementing instructions are as follows:

- U. S. Department of Defense Directive (DODD) 5000.1, "Major and Non-Major Acquisition Programs," February 23, 1991.
- U. S. Department of Defense Instruction (DODI) 5000.2, "Defense Acquisition Management Policies and Procedures," February 23, 1991.
- U. S. Department of Defense Manual DOD 5000.2-M, "Defense Acquisition Management Document and Reports," February 23, 1991.

ROBERT O. LEWIS

FOREWORD

"One of the keys to a successful independent verification and validation (IV&V) program is how the IV&V personnel interface with development personnel," Robert Lewis notes. In order for that interface to be successful, it is necessary for both the developer and the IV&V agent to know how to properly interact. For the frequent case of U.S. government projects, the government program office must equally understand the interaction. Lewis's book, *Independent Verification and Validation: a Life Cycle Engineering Process for Quality Software* provides an outstanding tutorial and precise outline of how that interaction can successfully be accomplished; it serves the needs not only of the IV&V agent, but also of the developer and government program office personnel. In addition, it places the interaction in the context of the full system development life cycle, simultaneously providing a tutorial for the life cycle along with the IV&V interface activities.

The book is primarily oriented toward those who are performing or will accomplish the IV&V function. After an introductory overview of concepts and introduction of vocabulary, it provides an in-depth study of each IV&V discipline. It addresses the aspects of the job that the IV&V specialist must understand: products, processes, techniques, and tools. Along the way, it gives valuable hints, tips, and specific guidance for interaction with the developer and the program management office. The book is equally valuable for the system developer, giving insight into why IV&V is valuable, how it can help the developer to produce better product, and what actions should be taken to make the interface effective. Finally the book is valuable—even mandatory—reading for personnel in the program management office; these are the people who are responsible for contracting for IV&V, managing the developer–IV&V interface, and ultimately providing an effective system for operational use. By addressing the key issues of IV&V and providing case-study style examples of appropriate IV&V activities and interactions, the book gives ample guidance for the establishment and effective management of the IV&V function and its interaction with the developer.

For all three players in the development process, the book's concise representation of the life cycle's activities is an effective summary of literally thousands of pages of government documentation related to systems development, and it can ensure a common viewpoint of the stages and activities of each of the players during the process. Its discussion of scoping/staffing, development of plans, description of typical products, and measurement of performance will remove some of the mystery of what can and should be done as part of IV&V; this continues to further the effective interface between all the players in the system's development. An important final step is that the book shows how the software process maturity levels of the Software Engineering Institute interact with and cause modifications to the IV&V process.

In summary, the book is an effective overview of the software development process for major systems, and it is an effective detailed tutorial on how to conduct IV&V in the context of that process. It is valuable for the IV&V specialist, the system's software developer, and the program management office.

KEN SHUMATE
Hughes Aircraft Company

PART I

COMPENDIUM OF INDEPENDENT VERIFICATION AND VALIDATION CONCEPTS

1

THE WHAT AND WHY OF INDEPENDENT VERIFICATION AND VALIDATION

1.1 WHY IS INDEPENDENT VERIFICATION AND VALIDATION NEEDED?

1.1.1 First, Let's Examine the Underlying Problem

Everyone who has ever been associated with software projects even peripherally realizes how difficult it has always been to exactly match the developed product to the users' needs and how software "bugs" seem to surface at the worst possible times. Software problems have postponed Space Shuttle launches, scrambled the Strategic Air Command, snarled rail and commuter traffic, disrupted communications, and even occasionally have messed up our credit and bank accounts. Software engineering has often been accused of being a mixture of science and art which, it turns out, is a pretty accurate depiction. To say the least, software development is definitely an inexact process, which is strongly influenced by the personalities, abilities, and experience of the people doing it. Herein lies much of the problem. No two people given the same problem would ever possibly design and code the same precise software solution, so software is as complicated and varied as the combined cognitive strategies from all the people who contribute to it. Place a few hundred software developers on a project, give them a tight schedule, and you begin to see why there are problems no matter how carefully you manage and orchestrate the team. Realizing these things, the government, academia, and industry that comprise the "high tech" community have created a complex infrastructure to deal with them. There are regulations and standards, tools and techniques, special languages and databases, specific curricula, management strategies, methodologies and paradigms, and almost countless writings on the subject. All this has helped in varying degrees, but it has yet to solve the problem. Some experts believe that having a single language, common hardware architectures and operating systems, and tightly controlled methods are the answer, but to expect real standardization in software development is like asking everyone to think and act just alike. In addition, part of the continued difficulty is that customer expectations for system performance continue to increase greatly, whether for missile systems, insurance database query systems, or automatic teller machines. In addition, the customer or user very often has even more difficulty expressing the requirements than he or she did when systems were simpler. Thus, through the years there has actually been a significant compounding of the problem of developing adequate requirements. Not many years ago, the computers that ran the software were the big shortcoming, plagued by lack of memory, low throughput, and poor reliability—but no more! The problem is now more than ever the software.

Now that we are at the core of the problem, what can be done to help alleviate this predicament and build better (and cheaper) software-driven systems? To be somewhat trite, the solution lies in two places: First, a conscientiously applied program of software hygiene wherein development is closely controlled and forced to follow one of the thorough and complete development paradigms, whether automated or not (Yourdon–DeMarco, Martin, Warnier–Orr, Jackson, Hatley–Pirbhai, Ward–Mellor, or whatever). At least that puts everyone on the job in the same frame of reference and makes integration and reuse of the parts more efficient. Out of those mentioned, there is probably no "best method"; it is a matter of what works most effectively for your applications. This discussion takes for granted that the rest of the infrastructure is in place for quality assurance, configuration and data management, etc. There are numerous computer-aided software engineering (CASE) tools that incorporate an adequate development paradigm and that are very cost-effective through enhanced productivity and error reduction. But a word of warning, don't rush out and buy a CASE tool with the idea that it is going to solve all your problems. It will not and, in fact, it brings with it some of its own issues like hardware proliferation and networking, database management, version control, and–the big ones initially—training and mindset adjustments. If your staff is familiar with doing things a certain way, it is very, very hard to sway them toward the new way. So the first set of solutions can be characterized as what can be done from inside the development organization, which we call *the internal domain*.

1.1.2 Independent Verification and Validation: A Practical, Cost-Effective Solution

Now let us consider the second set of solutions, that of the external domain, through which energy can be directed to influence, fortify, and enhance the internal domain. This external process is called *independent verification and validation* (IV&V). Although this book is directed primarily at the external realm, the reader must fully understand the system and software development cycles and the fact that IV&V must get and stay in sync with them to be effective. In fact, IV&V should go along with the development effort in a symbiotic—even mutualistic—relationship wherein both parties share and participate to the mutual benefit of each. To give you a couple of simple analogies, why does a skilled surgeon require an attending doctor to look over his shoulder and why does an insurance carrier want a second opinion before approving serious surgery? I have also posed the following question many times in seminars and classes: "Would you want to trust your life to a system that could have had this second-opinion action and didn't?" This is what IV&V is all about. If the risk of failure for whatever reason is significant, IV&V is the answer. It will not solve every problem and does no magic, but if you want to feel that you did everything within reason to improve and mature the product, IV&V is the answer. IV&V is objective, adds perspectives that the developer does not have, brings along its own set of tools and analytical techniques, becomes the first outside user of the system, discovers design flaws and coding errors, and greatly enhances the testing, to name a few of the more obvious features. As this book unfolds, the reader will be exposed to the full complement of IV&V attributes and principles. The reader must also be reminded that IV&V has to be studied in the context of the software development cycle and that it must be attached to a development job; by itself it is merely a collection of tools, techniques, and methods that can serve no useful purpose. Software development can exist without IV&V, but the converse is not true.

1.2   ESSENTIAL DEFINITIONS

There are a few definitions and concepts that must be understood with certainty before going any farther because they explain and define the core concept of IV&V and the system and software processes with which it interacts.

1.2.1   How Systems Are Developed: The System Life Cycle

The term *system life cycle (SLC)* describes the span of time from its conception through the useful life of a system. All systems regardless of size are built using this evolutionary process. The SLC is also known as the *system development life cycle (SDLC)*; however, this book uses the simpler and shorter of the two designations. Although there is wide agreement among the technical community that this cycle is an accurate description of the tasks that must be accomplished and is thus inviolable, there is disagreement regarding the number of discrete steps and their names that comprise it. The SLC model chosen for Figure 1-1 uses the most common names and is the simplest possible form that shows all of the major phases. The *concept phase* typically involves the process of creation, filtering of ideas, feasi-

Figure 1-1   The simplest possible system life cycle.

bility studies, tradeoffs concerning cost and performance objectives, statements of operational concepts and capabilities, ultimate purpose and mission, and user considerations. The *development phase* transforms the concept into a firm set of requirements followed by a formal design. The design is then implemented, which means it is coded if software or fabricated if hardware. The parts are then integrated, tested, and fixed until sufficient confidence exists that the system is ready for use; then it enters the *operational phase* until eventually decommissioned.

1.2.2   Inside the System Life Cycle Is the Development Cycle

The development phase of the SLC is of particular interest in the study of IV&V because it describes the development cycle (or process) that encompasses those activities that relate directly to producing a product or system. Figure 1-2 shows how this cycle fits within the SLC and uses the simplest possible names for each phase. The *requirements phase* transforms the required operational capabilities into a definition of a suitable system; identifies and defines its subsystems; and allocates functions, performance objectives, and physical constraints and attributes to each subsystem relative to the total system. After the requirements are sufficiently refined and as complete as possible, the *design phase* can begin. Design is the translation of the functions that the system is required to perform into the necessary logical, mathematical, and physical processes. This translation is manifested in the diagrams, pictorials, schematics, flowcharts, screens, menus, specifications, materials, and algorithms that provide the detail needed for implementation. The *implementation phase* covers fabrication of hardware, coding for software, and training for the human subsystem. The *integration and testing phase* combines the parts and tests the system to determine whether all the requirements are met, with the assumption that if they are, the system will satisfy its mission objectives. The proof of how well the system performs over time can of course only be gained through operation.

1.2.3   Independent Verification and Validation Defined

IV&V has been the subject of widely differing interpretations ranging from code checking and test support to more elaborate processes that parallel each phase of the development effort. It is the latter process that offers the most payoff in thorough requirements and design verification aimed at preventing otherwise costly errors,

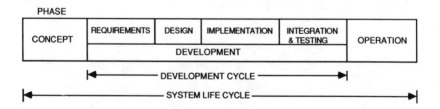

Figure 1-2   The development cycle, viewed as part of the system life cycle.

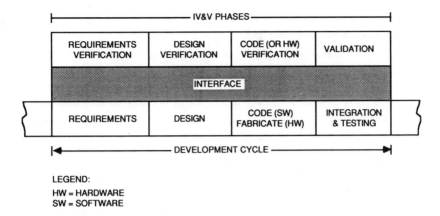

Figure 1-3 The IV&V phases shown in association with the development cycle.

omissions, and inadequacies from ever reaching the coding stage. Thus, this book strongly advocates the full cycle, in-phase approach. A study that I conducted several years ago [8] showed that errors in requirements cost on the average 36 times more to fix if allowed to go undetected until the integration and testing phase. There are numerous other studies discussed by Dr. Barry Boehm in his book on Software Engineering Economics [1] that agreed with this conclusion. Another point of contention is how to characterize each IV&V phase. The definitions that follow and the methodology in this book are based on my experience in teaching, consulting, and performing on numerous IV&V programs. I believe that they represent the consensus of government standards as well as practices in the private sector. This methodology includes the IV&V phases shown in Figure 1-3 linked to their associated development phases. Thus, there are three verification phases and one validation phase defined. There are a few sources that talk about such things as "requirements validation," but that rather corrupts the original definition, which dates back about 20 years. The first two definitions that follow are composites, followed by definitions of each individual phase.

Independent Verification and Validation (IV&V) is a series of technical and management activities performed by someone other than the developer of a system to improve the quality and reliability of that system and to assure that the delivered product satisfies the user's operational needs. When applied to the computer software of a military system, the definition found in U.S. Air Force Regulation 800–14 further refines the definition of IV&V as, *"The process of determining that the computer program was developed in accordance with the stated specification and satisfactorily performs, in the mission environment, the function(s) for which it was designed."* [26]. Neither of these definitions is in itself quite sufficient to convey the entire concept, but rather provides the general thesis that IV&V augments the existing development process with the overall goal of product improvement.

- *Verification is an iterative process aimed at determining whether the product of each step in the development cycle (a) fulfills all the requirements levied on it by the previous step and (b) is internally complete, consistent, and correct enough to support the next phase.*

- *Validation is the process of executing the software to exercise the hardware and comparing the test results to the required performance.*

Comprehensive validation ensures that all requirements are adequately tested and that the results can be repeated whenever necessary to support recalibration and rebaselining of the system after changes are installed. Revalidation can be used throughout the life of the system to maintain configuration and operational integrity.

Because the software element of complex systems is generally more difficult to specify, design, and test than the hardware, the main focus of this book is on software IV&V. It does not, however, limit the application of IV&V to the software alone since it is impossible to do so. The functional interactions of the software, hardware, and even the human in the loop are the ultimate concerns of IV&V.

1.2.4   Variations in Development Practices: The Acquisition Cycle

There are variations to the life and development cycles that have not yet been touched on. Those presented so far have been the ordinary variety that satisfy most situations, but it is necessary to look at the other cases to understand some of the major differences. Therefore, the book presents three typical examples and illustrates the acquisition steps involved.

In-House Development.   This is the simplest acquisition model. Typically, it begins when one department in a company needs a new system or modification to an existing system. They contact the data-processing (DP) department and set up a meeting with the users, managers, DP experts, and finance people to formalize the request. Assuming that the internal DP group has the resources, skills, charter, and mandate to do the job, an agreement is reached and the effort begins. Figure 1-4 is a simplified example of this acquisition process. Additional staff, vendor software and/or hardware may be required, depending on the size and complexity of the effort. Note that our straightforward SLC and development models satisfy the needs of this type of system or software acquisition. A formal contract between the parties is usually not required.

Commercial Development.   The most typical commercial development jobs are those in which the customer does not have all of the resources, skills, or desire to be

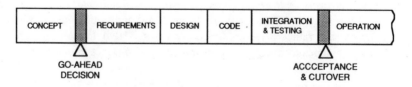

Figure 1-4   In-house development acquisition model.

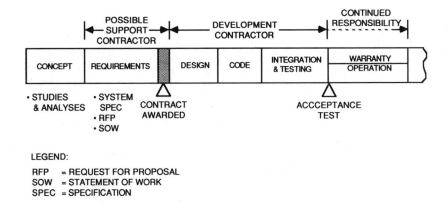

Figure 1-5 Commercial development acquisition model.

his or her own developer and wants to let a contract for the system development. This presents the big problem of describing to would-be bidders exactly what he or she wants built. This problem is so acute that there are companies who make a good living just writing the system specifications, statements of work, and requests for proposals for these kinds of customers. Regardless of who writes this bid package, the customer's goal is to have a contractor perform the development effort. The acquisition model as shown in Figure 1-5 reflects the addition that the system specification is provided by the customer; it also indicates that the contractor must run a formal and comprehensive acceptance test before getting all of his money. If the system is fairly complex and expensive, it is common to find a warranty clause to place certain liabilities on the contractor for a period of time after operational status is reached. Thus, the key things to remember about this model are that the requirements are usually not the responsibility of the development contractor; the development contractor will, however, have to demonstrate the performance of the system before getting paid (in full). Otherwise, the development cycle follows pretty much the same sequence as the in-house model.

Government Development. There are government development efforts that look just like the one expressed for commercial efforts, but those are not the ones that we need to talk about here. Instead, we want to look at a complex example. The U.S. Department of Defense (DOD) spends billions of dollars annually on software-intensive systems. These efforts range from real-time weapons systems and very large logistical databases to personnel and even hospital systems. Incidentally, there are thousands of pages of regulations and DOD/Military Standards that control and govern the development of these systems. Because it is possible for these individual systems to cost hundreds of millions of dollars and they must perform as intended, the government wanted to reduce development risk to a minimum so it uses a variation of the SLC model. As noted in the preface to this book, on February 23, 1991, DOD made significant changes to the life cycle model, renamed phases, and altered many directives and policies. These new names are reflected throughout this

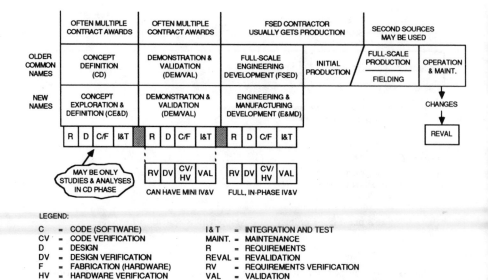

Figure 1-6 U.S. government development acquisition model, giving old and new phase names.

book, but because many other DOD standards in use will take considerable time to be revised, I have included both the new and older common names for such things as the names of the major phases. The government development acquisition model, shown in Figure 1-6, can have up to three development phases known as follows:

- (new) *Concept exploration and definition (CE&D) phase,* also called (the old common name) *concept definition (CD)* or other minor variations of that name, which imply early prototyping and/or studies and analyses
- (unchanged) *Demonstration and validation (Dem/Val) phase,* also sometimes called *advanced development (AD)*
- (new) *Engineering and manufacturing development (E&MD) phase,* also called (the old common name) *full-scale (engineering) development (FSD or FSED)*, or sometimes *ED* for short.

It is intuitively obvious that a system developed in this manner will come much closer to meeting all its performance and operational goals and will mature more gracefully than one which you rush out and build the first try, *but* (and it is a big "but") each cycle takes a certain minimum time based on the formality of the process. This means that if you actually build an operating prototype during CD, it will (most likely) take about two years. Then if you build a Dem/Val prototype and put it through any kind of comprehensive evaluation, that will take two or three years. On the plus side, these early systems are often commissioned by the government as multiple awards, so there is a performance competition between multiple designs and the contractor with the best prototype wins the follow-on FSD contract and usually initial production as well. On the negative side, FSD takes another three to five years. These are average times. Typically, big systems take 10 years (or more) to develop. This also assumes that the federal budget is kind to the system in question and that procurements go without a hitch, not a very likely scenario. There should be a better and more reliable way to build systems without doing them several times. Not only that, but it is highly unlikely that you can envision the operational environment 10 years hence so that you can write down a set of comprehensive software and hardware requirements that will not change. Our experience shows us that change is inevitable—and the longer the cycle time, the greater the change. Part of the answer to this problem is to build highly adaptable or multipurpose systems, but that drives the cost up too. Are we stuck? Perhaps partly. Hardware modularity and building-block concepts where such things as standard processors, common input/output (I/O) bus devices and designs, and standard interfaces and protocols allow the designer to go to off-the-shelf components and quickly assemble a system from pretested parts are giant steps in the right direction. Is there a software counterpart? It is coming, but it is not here yet; CASE tools, reusable software libraries, standard languages like Ada, better database systems, and common user-friendly graphical interfaces all help a great deal. As I pointed out very early in this book, the software problem is much more subject to variation and personality effects than the hardware problem. Meanwhile and for the foreseeable future, IV&V offers an efficient and effective way to reduce the development time and risk, improve the quality of the products, and better satisfy the users. I do not think that future systems can afford to take 10 years or more from concept to fielding; to do so will mean they are hopelessly obsolete long before the first production model ever becomes operational. System developers need to rethink the basic processes involved and endeavor to really streamline the acquisition process.

1.3 ADDITIONAL PERSPECTIVES ON INDEPENDENT VERIFICATION AND VALIDATION

1.3.1 How Independent Verification and Validation Interfaces with Development

One of the keys to a successful IV&V program is how the IV&V personnel interface with development personnel. In the case where both parties are contractors and there is a government project (or program) office, IV&V should document and route its verification and validation results, requests for data and documents, etc., to the project office and refrain from direct interaction or interface with the other contractor. If the government requests meetings or expressly approves direct interaction and information exchange, it is best if the other contractor's representatives are also present. It should be understood that one contractor seldom if ever has the rights to make requests of the other unless it is so specified in the terms and conditions of both contracts. Routine deliveries and exchanges can be handled by requests, but make certain such exchanges are approved in the contract. This simple act can avoid a lot of blame and accusations later on, especially if a scheduled event is missed. I will discuss this and other hints for a successful IV&V program in Chapter 12.

1.3.2   When Should an Independent Verification and Validation Program Begin?

IV&V can be characterized somewhat by its entry point into the development phase of the system that is supports.

Full, In-Phase IV&V. The most comprehensive of all possible IV&V efforts is performed in parallel with the system development and spans as much of the life cycle as possible. The terms "full, in-phase" are used because they are the least ambiguous and controversial of all descriptors found in the literature. It is necessary to further restrict the definition of full, in-phase IV&V by two qualifications: (1) IV&V must start no later than the requirements phase of full-scale development and (2) it must continue long enough to include acceptance testing of the system. This form of IV&V is by far the most effective in terms of cost savings to the development program since it detects defects as they occur and attempts to improve the processes that cause them.

Partial IV&V. Anytime IV&V begins after the requirements phase has been completed, the term partial IV&V can be applied. It must be noted that all the influence the IV&V group could and would otherwise have on the establishment and verification of requirements becomes an after-the-fact retrospective activity, and cost savings from discovery of requirement imperfections are thus less than optimal. The term "in-phase" becomes somewhat ambiguous with partial IV&V, since the first thing the IV&V group must do is go back and verify the earlier phases (e.g., requirements). Once the IV&V activity catches up and begins to run in sync with development, the terms "partial, in-phase" IV&V could apply, but are seldom used.

Endgame IV&V. Endgame IV&V, somewhat characteristic of added test and integration resources, is far less cost-effective and requires the IV&V group to perform much of its analysis by looking at what has already occurred. Although it can still involve limited requirements and design documentation analysis, the emphasis shifts to concentrate on the results of testing and hence it is highly validation-oriented. Although the benefits of third-party independent testing and test analysis are many, IV&V is most effective and efficient when applied from the beginning of the development program, more than compensating the procurer for dollars expended through early discovery of problems, weaknesses, and errors.

Audit-Level IV&V. This is a barebones effort wherein a customer calls in IV&V to "audit" the plans, procedures, practices, and emerging products for adequacy, correctness, compliance to standards, etc. Many times it is done as a quick fix of a program that is beginning to develop symptoms that something is going wrong. Just how effective this form of IV&V is in the long term is questionable, since once the auditors leave, things tend to revert to the original way of doing things. On the other hand, if the IV&V audit introduces a new method, such as a comprehensive CASE tool, or helps the developers better understand an important process or paradigm, then the results can be extremely beneficial and cost-effective. Audit-level IV&V can be as short as a few weeks, using a "tiger team" that goes in and digs out the necessary information. It is a job for IV&V experts who understand the domain in which they are performing. It is extremely desirable to have follow-up audits to ensure that the remedies are being followed. Case studies G and H in Part IV of this book deal with audit-level IV&V programs. Additional perspectives are given in Chapter 13 on the cost-effectiveness of the various forms of IV&V programs.

1.4   RULES FOR JUDGING INDEPENDENT VERIFICATION AND VALIDATION AUTHENTICITY

1.4.1   Statement of the Rules

It is my experience that some of the past misunderstanding surrounding IV&V has resulted from incorrectly defined and applied efforts that were called IV&V but were in reality either only a portion of what the purist would describe as IV&V or were simply misnamed programs. Thus, I have developed a set of six rules, which I have tested for 15 years to help promote a more universally acceptable set of criteria for judging the authenticity of an IV&V program. These rules are sufficiently broad in scope to accommodate all of the possible design and development variables, at the same time providing a general framework for the selection and application of specific methods, tools and techniques to match the particular job requirement. IV&V should always be viewed as an adaptive process, which is tailored to fit each application.

Rule 1: IV&V must be an independent, third-party activity.

Rule 2: IV&V must be an overlay, not an integral part of the development cycle; it is an added-value concept.

Rule 3: IV&V must report to and owes its fundamental allegiance to the customer, not the developing contractor or organization.

Rule 4: Although it may share the development tools and data, IV&V must also provide its own tools and disciplines apart from those used in development.

Rule 5: Although flexible in terms of its starting point, IV&V must *verify* each phase relative to itself and to its adjacent phases.

Rule 6: IV&V must provide a means of *validating* all testable software performance requirements.

Violation of any of the above rules should result in a serious examination of IV&V planning, organization, and methodology, with the idea of correcting the deficiency as quickly as possible. In the past, there have been programs called IV&V that seriously corrupted the above-listed concepts and may have left a false impression as to what IV&V is all about.

1.4.2 Supporting Arguments

Rule 1 must be considered in terms of available resources within the customer sphere of influence. One obvious choice is to obtain a separate contractor who has a history of successful IV&V programs, is in no way involved with the project's hardware or software procurements, and who has no other conflict of interest or vested interest. A second choice is to obtain the services of a qualified organization from outside the developer's group and establish them in this role; however, this organization must be able to satisfy the other five rules.

Rule 2 is so stated to avoid the misunderstanding between the term "validation" often used in defining the second stage of the acquisition life cycle and the term "validation" used in IV&V. In the former case, validation is the conceptual proof that the preliminary system design is ready to proceed into full-scale engineering development and is indeed a part of the overall system life cycle and is not in any way associated with IV&V. In the latter case, validation is a specific set of activities that occurs during testing (and integration on larger systems) to ensure that system and software performance requirements are satisfied. Because IV&V is characteristically an additional resource allocated to a development effort, it is thought of as an overlay, which should never impede or interfere with the development effort. IV&V is a piggyback activity that goes largely where the development program leads it.

Rule 3 dictates that the program office (developing agency) or customer serves as the buffer though which the IV&V organization requests data and documents and reports its evaluation and analysis results back to the developing contractor or organization. This rule maintains the proper IV&V objectivity with the developer and prevents complaints of interference and impact caused by IV&V. Conversely, it keeps the two groups from forming too close a relationship, which could compromise the impartiality and independence of IV&V. For years, I have characterized this relationship as mildly adversarial, but no more so than the customer's relationship to the developer, since IV&V is really an extension of the customer's resources and represents his or her interests.

Rule 4 implies that the organization selected to perform IV&V has a defined methodology and a set of tools and techniques that are complementary, not identical, to those used by the developer. In this way, synergistic rather than redundant effects can be derived. This rule does not preclude the sharing of models, simulations, CASE tools, databases, and analysis aids, which will tend to better distribute their cost over the entire program.

Rule 5 pertains to verification activities that are fundamentally the complementary activities aligned to the development cycle phases. For example, design verification parallels the design phase; code verification parallels the coding phase, etc. Although each phase of development and its corresponding IV&V activities can be thought of as having a unique character, they are by no means autonomous and have to be considered a continuous flow, transitioning from phase to phase. Thus, a comprehensive verification discipline maintains its perspective in terms of what has already occurred, its current state, and by logical implications is able to predict ahead at least into the near term to forecast risks and suggest redirection of future effort.

Rule 6 is directed at validation activities that are test- and demonstration-oriented. Validation is essentially that part of IV&V that looks back at the software requirements and determines through testing that they are (or are not) satisfied by observable and measurable system-performance indicators. Successful validation implies that the system will meet its operational life cycle design commitments. The term "certification" is sometimes associated with this activity to further attest (usually in writing) to the quality and suitability of the system to perform its mission. Because of legal ramifications associated with this activity, few if any IV&V organizations are willing to guarantee someone else's work to this degree. Conversely, if you water down the interpretation of the term "certification", does it serve any useful purpose? Thus, certification is not emphasized in this book's overall IV&V methodology.

These rules are in themselves insufficient to describe an IV&V program, but rather they are an effective means of authenticating or disqualifying a program. They have little to do with the quality and application of methodology, which are the primary subjects of the remainder of this book.

1.5 FREQUENTLY ASKED QUESTIONS ABOUT INDEPENDENT VERIFICATION AND VALIDATION

1.5.1 Which Programs Need Independent Verification and Validation?

This is the most frequently asked and most difficult to answer question about IV&V. Just as with the definition of IV&V, which is admittedly complex, the answer to this question must be couched in a series of statements that qualify the answer. But before going further, I vividly recall a question posed to me by a military officer. He asked with a sneer, "Why do we need IV&V on this (man-rated space vehicle) program?" My answer, in the form of another question, was simple enough, "Would you be willing to fly aboard the first mission without it?" He mumbled something and looked away.

I had gotten his attention, as you might guess, so I then answered the first question something like this: "You must do everything possible to ensure the safety of your crew and the success of your program. If you cannot absolutely establish via the prime contractor the necessary level of confidence, then hire a third-party (IV&V) contractor to double-check everything the prime does, gain added perspective through complementary analysis and testing, ensure that the requirements of the system are met, and know that as the unexpected occurs (and it will) additional resources are available to help solve the difficult and often subtle problems."

The extreme case? Perhaps, but nonetheless quite expressive of the point to be made. Broadly speaking, it can be said that IV&V should be required for the following:

- Real-time critical software (and systems) that must work the first time and every time
- Programs having critical outputs that cannot be verified every run
- Programs having a high cost of failure in human life, national security, or money
- Software for which the cost of error detection through operational use exceeds the cost of IV&V
- Software for which the cost of maintenance and modification exceeds the cost of IV&V.

1.5.2   What Size Program Needs Independent Verification and Validation?

A second frequently asked question pertains to size. It usually goes something like this, "Are some jobs too small for IV&V, and if so, where is this threshold?" An analogy will help answer this question. It is fairly obvious that a mom-and-pop grocery store does not need an independent auditor, just an accountant or book-keeper. So the answer is "yes," some jobs are too small or inconsequential for IV&V. The difficult part of this issue is one of establishing the proper threshold, and here the issue becomes cloudy. The answer is best determined by the criticality of the thing being developed as opposed to attempting to decide by size alone. No doubt the nuclear surety and arming of an intercontinental ballistic missile is controlled by a small set of software programs and some clever hardware protection devices, but because of the extremely critical nature of this "code," IV&V would be essential. On the other hand, a life insurance company may have an enormous database and a large number of programs to access this information, but no one could die from a minor software bug, no great economic loss could occur, no mission could be jeopardized. Thus, size can play a part, but criticality is by far the greater influence on the decision to have or not to have IV&V. You be the judge.

1.5.3   Will Quality Assurance Do the Same Job as Independent Verification and Validation?

This question goes something like this, "I already have a great quality assurance (QA) group in house. In fact, we have a total quality management (TQM) program where everyone gets in the loop. Isn't IV&V just a redundant effort?" On the surface, this appears to be a valid question and no doubt is the genuine concern of many a large prime contractor who sinks a significant budget each year into doing his or her own "housekeeping." Again, the answer is one of perspective, of vested interest, and of bias. Only an extremely courageous person would criticize on his or her own company, and that is sometimes the kind of decision that has to be made. Most likely the company's QA representatives try diligently to force everyone to follow the rules, practices, and regulations that allow the company to "meet the specification and letter of the contract." This is all well and good, but it simply is not enough. The customer, being just as fallible as the developer, cannot always specify exactly what he or she needs in advance, so contract procurement packages and deliverable definitions are never perfect.

The worst-case scenario goes something like this: The contractor who wins the job by bidding too low delights in finding loopholes, omissions, and errors in the specifications. These give the contractor the opportunity to recover his losses through change orders. Thus, quite often because the contractor is successfully able to mask what he or she is really doing in the early stages, while living up to the letter of the contract, the customer proceeds with false sense of security until the system is ready for acceptance. (Sometimes it doesn't get this far, but let's simplify the example.) Then the system simply fails to meet some of its performance goals or users' needs. The obvious remedy is to perform just enough redesign and "patching" to add or correct the features and functions that are missing or done incorrectly. An overrun in cost and schedule ensues. This has happened so often in software development that it is the rule rather than the exception.

The QA group is too close to the problem to have a truly objective perspective and is often too understaffed to accomplish the analysis and corrective action to fix the more complex problems. Although QA helps, it simply cannot do what IV&V can. If it could, IV&V would never have evolved. QA is a very necessary mechanism to keep the internal rigor enforced in an organized fashion, but it isn't independent; it is inbred and internally controlled. If it steps beyond its boundaries, it gets rebuffed. The whistle-blower is seldom looked on as a hero by his fellow-workers.

Suffice it to say the QA and IV&V efforts are not redundant; they are in fact quite complementary. Remember that *QA enforces internal rigor and IV&V enforces external rigor.* QA answers to the same bosses (even if way up the line) that are developing the product, while IV&V answers to the customer. And finally, while QA may uncover problems, it seldom can force changes, whereas good IV&V always seeks the most effective solutions and pushes where necessary to ensure their inclusion.

I feel an obligation to mention the exception in which the QA organization does take an active part in the solution. In such cases, the organizational structure invariably places the QA manager at the same level as the software or product development manager, which provides sufficient authority and independence to the QA group to exercise the necessary corrective actions. When this type of organization (as cited in Rule 1, Section 1.4.1) exists, it is possible to blend a number of IV&V techniques into the QA function, forming a sort of hybrid operation which works very successfully, especially in the non-DOD environment where the company develops products for direct sale. More detail on this subject can be found in Section 14.2.

The reader should also appreciate that QA is not the only form of internal rigor that enhances and aids the development process. Such things as modern design and coding practices, top-down design, special requirements and design languages, and tools that automate the designer's and programmer's environment and automate the testing process have all made significant contributions toward more reliable and maintainable software.

1.6   KEYS TO A SUCCESSFUL IV&V PROGRAM: HAVING THE "RIGHT STUFF"

The experience gained from performing and examining numerous IV&V programs performed by others indicates that there are four primary factors that strongly affect the success of an IV&V program. These are having the right people, procedures, tools, and products at the right time. Although this section only introduces each one to the reader, they are discussed in much greater detail in appropriate sections throughout the book.

1.6.1   The Right People

The stereotypical IV&V person is characterized as a self-starter with an abiding desire for quality. These traits may well be the most important, since the performer of IV&V must be inquisitive, able to quickly grasp and perceive what the system should do, and then able to project solutions in cases where the system is failing. It is not generally a job for someone who has never worked on the development side of the problem. He or she must be attuned to the difficulties and realities of development and must have an understanding of how to constructively change the outcome without being offensive or dictatorial. Thus, it requires mature people who understand the domain they are working in as well as the IV&V methodology and application.

- A generaliz...
- A trend analysis depi...   of the v...   related ba...
Step 12. A determination of the va...   will be related ba...   and operato...
will be made. Each PR will be related ba...   procedure, and operato...
occurred. The test script, procedure, a genuine specification defici...
where the PR reflects a genuine specification of the record.
and description shall be entered into the record.
Step 13. Determination of which problem reports require conversion to a change
recommendation and eventual ECP will be made. This judgment is based upon
the technical analysis of the problem report and may result in modifications to the
specifications (and other system documentation such as operator handbooks an
...intenance manuals) or a modification to the software proper. This determin
...lso be provided to the SQA organization.
...esults from the problem report, IV&V will recomme
... its system impact and also suggest its catego
... modification to the software und
...ed as "test-only" chan
...and later aft

1.6.2   The Right Procedures

Pragmatism is the key issue here. The IV&V approach must have an overall discipline that guides and controls the activities at each phase of the program. This discipline has to be sufficiently broad so that it is not affected by the unique factors of a particular project or by the developer's paradigm and engineering environment. This enables the IV&V approach to be optimized, regardless of the size of the effort, to direct the maximum forces on the early recognition and ultimate solutions of problems.

1.6.3   The Right Tools

Today's development organizations—even within the same large aerospace company—can vary widely across the tools spectrum from using no automated tools to having a fully automated software support environment. IV&V would like to do two

TOOLS

primary things regarding the developer's tools: one, share the tools and especially the output and databases when it makes sense to do so, and two, select IV&V tools that complement those of the developer. As a general rule, if the developer has none, then IV&V should select the most comprehensive tools possible and invest heavily in their use. If the developer has a good set of tools, IV&V can possibly share as just mentioned, but should also be prepared to introduce tools that examine other perspectives and dimensions of the software not touched by the development set. The other goal in the tool arena is to select tools that provide continuity across more than one phase whenever possible. This goes along with the idea that software development is more of a continuum than a discrete set of abrupt steps. Certainly the latest paradigms of rapid prototyping, spiral models, software first, and recursive design have left the older "waterfall" model exposed to a great deal of criticism. I personally think the waterfall model is adaptable to virtually any development situation with a little creative interpretation and, therefore, can be made to work. Several of these other models are cyclical versions of the waterfall model. The biggest problem is often convincing the customer that tailoring of the model is in the best interest of the development program. Until and unless DOD changes the development cycle with its predefined key reviews and milestones as imposed by many hundreds of standards and regulations that are based on the waterfall model, I think we will just have to continue to make the best of it.

1.6.4 The Right Products

IV&V products are designed for high visibility, responsiveness, and unambiguous presentation. Experience has shown repeatedly that near-immediate communication of problem awareness to the customer is one of the most effective actions that can be taken by the IV&V group. Thus, a pipeline is advocated through which informal communiques are passed, with formal follow-up to ensure that the problem and analysis reports include the disposition and status for all such issues affecting the system. The style and presentation media of the IV&V documentation are deliber-

PRODUCTS

REQUIREMENTS VERIFICATION · DESIGN VERIFICATION P1 · DESIGN VERIFICATION P2 · ALGORITHM ANALYSIS · CODE VERIFICATION · TEST ANALYSIS · DATABASE ANALYSIS · IV&V TEST PLAN · VALIDATION · IV&V NOTEBOOK · SPECIAL STUDIES · MEETINGS & ACTIONS

ately chosen to provide visibility and understanding. The products are designed to provide a chronological history of the program, life-cycle traceability, and in-depth evaluation of each critical element of the program.

1.7 CHAPTER SUMMARY

- Despite the many automated software tools and support environments and emphasis from management on such things as total quality management, the software development process is partly art and partly science and tends to reflect the personality of its developers, which leads to numerous problems large and small.
- Although the tools and techniques have improved greatly over the years, the complexity of the problems that the software is expected to solve also has increased; thus, the situation is not really much better than before.
- Since the solution to the software crisis seems as elusive as ever, the idea of reinforcing and augmenting the process from outside the development organization is quite appropriate and falls in step with the popular philosophy of having an expert second opinion whenever some critical decision must be made. Independent verification and validation (IV&V) is the name given this engineering discipline.
- To thoroughly understand and appreciate what IV&V is all about requires a good working knowledge of the system life cycle and the development cycle since IV&V links up with and supports these cycles.
- IV&V defines a verification step matching the first three of the four main phases of the software development cycle—requirements verification, design verification, and code verification. Validation, on the other hand, tests the software and ultimately the system to ensure that the performance requirements are satisfied.
- Because of the differences in customers and the way they do business, development efforts range from simple in-house projects to complex contract awards from government agencies and commercial customers. The term *acquisition cycle* or *acquisition model* is used to describe this process of procurement and development. The most complex such model is that of the U.S. Department of Defense (DOD), which often goes through as many as three successive development programs on major systems.
- IV&V is a highly flexible and adaptive process that must be adjusted to the peculiarities of each development effort to which it is applied.

1.8 WHAT COMES NEXT

Before refining and expanding the definition of IV&V, a more detailed look at how systems, and especially their software, are developed is necessary so that the reader can develop a better appreciation of how IV&V fits into the process. Therefore, the next chapter will describe the development cycle in two significant examples. The discussion begins with what can be called the basic development process, intended to help the novice as well as the accomplished engineer or analyst to better understand the process. This model is very general and uses the most common names available for the products and processes to benefit the widest possible readership. Once that is mastered, a typical DOD Military Standard (MIL-STD) development model is presented, which describes the processes, all the deliverables, formal reviews and audits, and the control and management structure. The remainder of the book will assume that the reader has a reasonable knowledge of these processes and understands the terms.

2
HOW SYSTEMS ARE DEVELOPED

Perhaps the most important concept introduced in Chapter 1 is that IV&V is an overlay, which brings externally controlled and initiated forces to bear on system and software quality factors. To fully understand how this augmentation is applied, it is necessary to probe further into the processes involved in developing systems. Therefore, this chapter is dedicated to describing how systems are developed, with emphasis on the software. It covers both the commercial and U.S. Department of Defense (DOD) life-cycle models (LCMs), as well as the DOD acquisition model.

2.1 AN IN-DEPTH LOOK AT THE COMMERCIAL LIFE CYCLE MODEL

This section is devoted to the common form of the software life cycle, which is used throughout the commercial, industrial, institutional, and even governmental communities when a single development effort is appropriate and military standards (MIL-STDs) or other government standards are not mandated. The book refers to this model as the *commercial life cycle*. This "plain vanilla" model can be followed whether the job is being performed by an in-house team or a contractor. Although the model works for jobs of all sizes, this discussion assumes an effort that is significant enough to require formal specifications and program reviews at each key point as well as appropriate levels of configuration management, quality assurance, and program management. Figure 2-1 shows this model with both in-house and contractor configurations. To simplify the drawing, the documentation and support activities are only shown once, but relate equally to either model except as noted, namely, the request for proposal (RFP) and statement of work (SOW) are not required for in-house development. This figure introduces many new terms which will be touched on here and then discussed in detail in the remainder of this section.

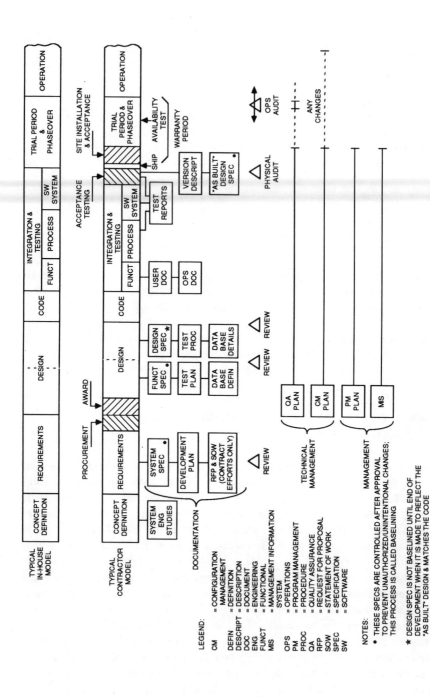

Figure 2-1 Commercial life cycle model.

24

When comparing the two configurations of this model, the most obvious differences occur because when a contractor is considered, several things have to be added. As just mentioned, it is essential that the customer provide a system specification, RFP, and SOW as the fundamental items of a procurement package. If the company or agency lacks the experience or skills to generate these documents, an outside contractor can be hired to help. This contractor should not be allowed to bid the development effort, but could be a candidate for IV&V if other conditions are met (refer to Section 11.1). The more sophisticated commercial customers will also produce a development plan, which discusses such things as the target hardware, development standards to be followed, programming language and compiler of choice, operating system, support tools, development environment, and other systems that may interface with the new system. The customer should always hold an internal review to discuss the plans, system specification, the RFP package before advertising the opportunity. If the customer went outside the parent organization for help earlier, it may be prudent to use the same contractor to help evaluate the proposals.

Once the award is made, the two models look alike throughout the rest of development until final testing, when it is good business to have an acceptance test for contractor-built software systems. Very often the contractor will develop the system in its own facility. In these cases, acceptance is twofold, requiring a repeat of enough of the factory acceptance test to ensure that the system is working correctly after being installed at site. Some customers even require that an availability test be run wherein the system must operate normally for some number of hours, days, weeks, etc. without a failure. The elapsed time clock gets set back to zero every time a problem surfaces that hampers use of the system. The customer may require a warranty usually for up to one year, wherein the contractor must fix any faults that occur free of charge.

Returning to the development activities, the key documents from the requirements phases have been already discussed, so moving to the design phase finds that most developers acknowledge that this is a two-step process. The first part produces a functional specification, a test plan and a database definition (for systems with significant database requirements). A review is held to ensure that the documents are adequate and that the program is on track. The second part of the design phase deals with the detailed design and usually produces at least a design specification, test procedures and details of the database. Most methodologies call the design specification produced at this time the "code to" document. Much later, when the system is being accepted, an audit is held to ensure that this document has kept pace with the code and that it then reflects the "as-built" design. This document is sometimes renamed the *software product specification* when it is updated and baselined at the end of development.

Baselining is a configuration management term that implies that the item is placed under formal control so that it cannot be changed without going through a formal review process. That review is performed by a configuration control board (CCB) composed of key project personnel usually under the leadership of the project manager.

No later than the beginning of the integration and testing (I&T) phase, a user's manual is produced. Some systems may also require an operator's manual and, if so, it likewise is produced in this timeframe. Test reports are written to document what happens during the various subphases of I&T. Quality assurance (QA) should oversee these reports to make sure that they are accurate and complete. Finally, almost at the end of the testing, a record of the software version numbers and dates, etc. is prepared by configuration management (CM) to ensure that the customer receives the product being tested and only that product. In software, this is a nontrivial problem. Some years ago a Fortune 500 company called to ask for help. They had fielded over 100 systems, all slightly different, and had no earthly idea what customer had what version of what software. They did not know what configuration management meant. It was costly and time-consuming to fix.

Note also that there are two types of activities that run through all of the development phases: Technical management and program management. The distinction between the two is based on the type of work involved. Both QA and CM are basically technical jobs but contribute strongly to the overall management of the software products, so they are classified as technical management activities. Program management activities, which typically involve planning, scheduling, direction and control, resource administration, budgeting, status monitoring, contract administration and the like and are usually supported by some form of management information system (MIS), are classified as management tasks. These activities are shown in Figure 2-1 as stopping at the end of development, except for CM which essentially lies dormant until changes are needed. Because it is CM that archives all the source code and baselined documents, it must be reactivated whenever changes are desired. Even when this function is performed by the contractor during development, all necessary code, documents, and records are transitioned to the new owner's CM organization when operation begins. Large changes to an operational system may indeed activate all the support activities because much of the development cycle may have to be repeated.

This section now expands upon the definition of each development cycle phase by describing the attributes, processes, and major products of each in much more detail.

2.1.1   Requirements Phase for the Commercial Life Cycle Model

This phase, as the name implies, deals with all kinds of requirements—system, software, hardware, and human in the loop. It assumes that some form of conceptual activity took place, which determined the feasibility and reasonableness of the system to be developed. The results of this earlier work may or may not have been very formal. Figure 2-2 shows a typical set of activities and products of this phase. In the private sector, it is possible to reach the requirements stage with a memo or even a handshake between members of the two organizations, one that wants the system and the other that agrees to develop it. The other extreme is found in big comprehensive efforts where a great deal of formal proof of concept work including modeling, analytical studies, simulations, and even limited prototypes are developed to prove feasibility before committing development funding. This early work is usually called *systems engineering and analysis* and when adequately documented serves as an excellent source for system requirements formalized in this phase. A representative example of the activities of the concept phase is included on Figure 2-2.

The requirements phase usually produces two documents. The first is called the *system specification,* which is a collection and ordering of requirements from all appropriate sources—users, customers, overseers, interacting systems, etc. The second is the *development plan.* The system specification describes such things as intended use, performance requirements, physical characteristics, external interfaces, environment, safety, materials, human engineering, logistics, and personnel requirements. A lot of engineering analysis and judgment goes into this document, so it is very difficult to produce without some inconsistencies, conflicting requirements, incomplete statements, etc. A number of computer-aided software engineering (CASE) tools have appeared in the marketplace to address the inadequacies of system specifications. These have helped, but so far none solve the total problem. Part of the fallibility of the entire requirements process is that the people writing them do not always know exactly what they need the system to do, so they give "educated guesses," or worse yet, simply make up numbers or describe features just so the statements look complete. This results in ambiguous requirements that cannot be implemented as written. Need I say more?

Once the system specification has matured to a point that all parties feel it is adequate, it should be approved and baselined. The specification is thus controlled from that time forward to prevent unauthorized changes from being made to it. If two (or more) parties are involved with building the system, this specification forms a very significant part of the contract (regardless of how formal) between the developer and the customer. When IV&V is included, it forms a very important part of that contract as well.

The system specification will typically contain a series of functional block or data flow diagrams that define and relate the functional groupings and interfaces among them. This representation is loosely referred as *the system architecture* and it may be modeled and even simulated to confirm the feasibility of this early design as well as its gross performance and operational characterization. It should be at a level that all of the main processes and functions that the system is expected to have are defined; but note that the system specification makes very little distinction between whether a function is implemented in hardware, software, or a mix of the two. The system specification also concerns itself with how the system will be operated, maintained, and supported logistically. If the system is expected to interface with other systems, then compatibility and interoperability will also be important concerns.

The development plan is the other important document that should be generated at this time. This is especially vital when the effort is to be performed by a contractor since this document describes the environment in which the system should be developed to best match the needs, existing facilities, and operational concerns of the customer. The kind of information that needs to be in a development plan is

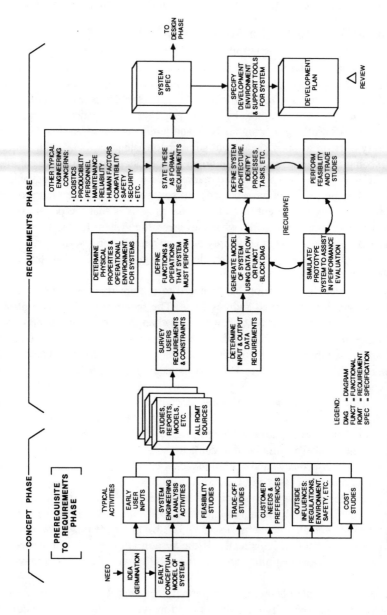

Figure 2-2 Activities and products of requirements phase for the commercial life cycle model.

given in outline form in Table 2-1. The list is not absolute and should be used only as a guide in generating a tailored plan to suit the individual needs of each specific program. The government has created a document commonly called a computer resource management plan (CRMP) or computer resource life-cycle management plan (CRLCMP) (pronounced cril'comp), which accompanies many requests for proposals (RFPs) to guide contractors in these matters. In turn, the proposing contractors develop their own development plans aimed at closely matching the guidelines given in the CRMP. The coordination provided by these plans helps build new systems that are as compatible as possible with existing systems.

2.1.2 Design Phase for the Commercial LCM Life Cycle Model

This phase normally consists of two parts, preliminary design and detailed design. This two-step process enables an orderly expansion of detail to occur from the process and task level (packages or main routines), which are the intermediate

---

TABLE 2-1. Types of Information Needed in a Development Plan

Organizational overview
Description of existing facilities
Anticipated additions to facilities to support new system
Interfacing systems and common data requirements
Compatibility requirements
Operational overview
Software development and engineering practices[a]
    Development standards and conventions
    Computer language and compiler
    Operating system
    Naming conventions
    Preferred development methodology
    Development environment
    Software tools
Configuration management practices
Quality assurance
Libraries
    Software
    Data
    Documentation
Program management
    Responsibility and authority
    MIS
    Monitoring and reporting practices
    Cost/performance reporting
Requirements for IV&V

---

[a]Customer may require that contractor provide this information in the proposal to best match the other stated requirements.

building blocks, to the software unit level (subroutines). Figure 2-3 shows the main processes and products of the design phase.

Preliminary Design. This step performs two very important functions. First, it identifies, decomposes, and allocates the requirements from the system specification into a functional level specification(s). Second, it transitions these requirements into an intermediate level design. The generation and organization of documents at this level can get tricky because it is desirable to separate hardware and software functionality. In cases where the hardware is general purpose and no special fabrication is required, its functional description can be handled as a separate section of a combined functional specification. When this is not the case and significant amounts of special hardware are to be developed, a separate hardware functional specification is usually generated. In any case, the primary concern of this book is the software part of the functional specification.

The act of generating a functional level specification for each mid-level component (process or task) is something of a recursive process, which can be aided by rapid prototyping and a number of CASE tools that support decomposition and structured analysis. This level concerns itself with relating requirements to intermediate level software components and how these components behave and interact. The intermediate design emerges from this process when the physical and logical interfaces are defined and the data flow through the system is determined. The document should also contain estimates on sizing, timing, and throughput requirements for that part of the system as well as recommended methods for testing and confirming the performance requirements. By this time, the "originating requirements" from the system specification are now accompanied by a large number of "derived requirements" spawned from inside the functional specification as it is being generated. These are needed to fully describe the software (or hardware) at this level.

On large programs, a number of plans are generated during the preliminary design phase to aid in the control and management of the products, and formal reviews are held to monitor and control the program at reasonable intervals. Other important documents produced during the preliminary design step are the *test plan* and the *database definition document,* assuming the system has a significant database component. The test plan describes such things as the test environment and facilities, test classes and levels, qualification methods, data collection and analysis requirements, test reporting, and organizational responsibilities. It is advisable for the test plan to link to the requirements which it covers. Additional detail on generation of the test plan is included in Section 2.1.4. Systems that have a significant database component may benefit greatly from having a separate document to cover the selection, definition, and design of database-related elements. This is especially true if one of the many commercial database management systems (DBMSs) is used as the nucleus of the database.

The goal of this first half of the design phase is to complete the logical design of all of the components, not to go all the way to the unit or subroutine level just yet;

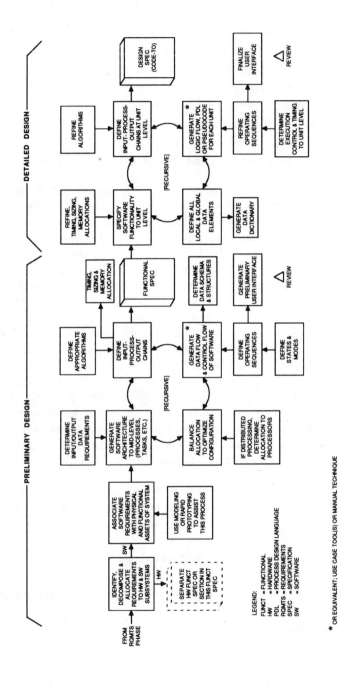

Figure 2-3 Design phase for the commercial life cycle model.

PRELIMINARY DESIGN ———— DETAILED DESIGN

FROM ROMTS PHASE

IDENTIFY, DECOMPOSE & ALLOCATE REQUIREMENTS TO HW & SW SUBSYSTEMS

SEPARATE HW FUNCT SPEC OR SECTION IN THIS FUNCT SPEC

ASSOCIATE SOFTWARE REQUIREMENTS WITH PHYSICAL AND FUNCTIONAL ASSETS OF SYSTEM

USE MODELING OR RAPID PROTOTYPING TO ASSIST THIS PROCESS

DETERMINE INPUT/OUTPUT DATA REQUIREMENTS

GENERATE SOFTWARE ARCHITECTURE TO MID-LEVEL (PROCESSES, TASKS, ETC.)

BALANCE ALLOCATION TO OPTIMIZE CONFIGURATION

IF DISTRIBUTED PROCESSING, DETERMINE ALLOCATION TO PROCESSORS

[RECURSIVE]

DEFINE APPROPRIATE ALGORITHMS

DEFINE INPUT-PROCESS-OUTPUT CHAINS

GENERATE * DATA FLOW & CONTROL FLOW OF SOFTWARE

DEFINE OPERATING SEQUENCES

DEFINE STATES & MODES

TIMING, SIZING & MEMORY ALLOCATION

FUNCTIONAL SPEC

DETERMINE DATA SCHEMA & STRUCTURES

GENERATE PRELIMINARY USER INTERFACE

REVIEW

REFINE, TIMING, SIZING, MEMORY ALLOCATIONS

SPECIFY SOFTWARE FUNCTIONALITY TO UNIT LEVEL

DEFINE ALL LOCAL & GLOBAL DATA ELEMENTS

GENERATE DATA DICTIONARY

[RECURSIVE]

REFINE ALGORITHMS

DEFINE INPUT-PROCESS-OUTPUT CHAINS AT UNIT LEVEL

GENERATE * LOGIC FLOW, PDL OR PSEUDOCODE FOR EACH UNIT

REFINE OPERATING SEQUENCES

DETERMINE EXECUTION CONTROL & TIMING TO UNIT LEVEL

DESIGN SPEC (CODE-TO)

FINALIZE USER INTERFACE

REVIEW

LEGEND:
FUNCT = FUNCTIONAL
HW = HARDWARE
PDL = PROCESS DESIGN LANGUAGE
ROMTS = REQUIREMENTS
SPEC = SPECIFICATION
SW = SOFTWARE

* OR EQUIVALENT; USE CASE TOOL(S) OR MANUAL TECHNIQUE

SW

HW

that is the role of detailed design. Preliminary design typically calls for the following types of activities:

- Selection and/or generation of appropriate algorithms
- Definition of the modes and states of the software and system
- Generation of data and control flow at the intermediate level
- Definition of data structures and schema
- Generation of sizing and memory allocations
- Preliminary designs of the user interface
- Generation of a timing template for the software
- A formal review to comment on and approve the preliminary design.

Detailed Design. This step is somewhat similar to the process just discussed, except that the amount of detail is amplified and now goes all the way to the bottom of the design chain to the software units—subroutines and the like. It is customary for this level of design to be documented in some form of design specification that, when completed initially is referred to as the "code-to" version. This document is the programmer's roadmap and guide. It becomes a working document that is kept in sync with the evolving code so that when the system is completely tested, the design specification matches what was actually built. The document is then called the "as-built" version and may have its name changed to the *product specification,* since it is representative of the product as it is delivered. It really does not matter very much what it is called in the commercial world, so this section leaves the name unchanged, but acknowledges the change from code-to to as-built status. It is here also that a much closer embrace with the operating system and the hardware is to be expected since several of the concerns now deal with finite timing of each process or task, interrupts and their effects on data integrity, error control and recovery, checkpointing, initialization, task scheduling, etc. Database details can be documented in a separate document or included in the design specification. It is an essential practice to develop a complete data dictionary defining each data element as the design occurs.

The goal, of course, is to have a complete design that will support coding with minimum changes and unresolved loose ends. Detailed design calls for the following types of activities:

- Refined algorithms (early testing in this phase may be desirable)
- Comprehensive error handling
- Complete logic flow or textual equivalent; i.e., pseudocode, program design language, etc.
- Complete I/O data element definition
- Definition of all required data structures
- Local and global data requirements
- Designs for the user interface (including screens, menus, etc.)
- Comprehensive data dictionary

- Refined unit-level timing, sizing, and memory budgets
- A formal review to comment on and approve the detailed design.

This phase has long been fraught with difficulty, mostly resulting from inadequate and incomplete execution. Many times developers do not finish their designs before attempting to code the software or fabricate the hardware. The effects are worse in software because the choices are much more infinite and varied. Software prepared before design is complete tends to be very inconsistent and subject to change and has numerous "bugs" resulting from poorly defined interfaces, underdeveloped algorithms, erroneous logic, and unnecessarily redundant functions. Properly selected and applied CASE tools offer significant improvements because they enforce more complete design and automate such things as diagramming, consistency checking, data structure transformation, logic error detection, simulation, and so on. But a word to the wise, CASE tools do not solve all the problems associated with software design.

Regardless of the mechanisms and tools used to get through the process, the ultimate goal of this phase is to provide a graceful translation from the symbolic and logical levels to the physical level, just short of actually coding in the computer language of choice. In fact, the ultimate stopping point for design is at pseudocode (or equivalent), accompanied by the list of things that a comprehensive detailed design process provides—detailed data definitions and formats, timing and sequence charts for all tasks, complete input and output forms and formats, complete user interface definition, etc. that are so complete that "a stranger could code from them."

During the evolution of the detailed design, the detailed test procedures are generated. They cover complete test setup, test case, data, script, pass–fail criteria, and recording and reporting requirements for each discrete test. Test-procedure generation is discussed in detail in Section 2.1.4.

2.1.3 Code Phase for the Commercial Life Cycle Model

The code phase implements the detailed design in some form of programming language. Most coding today is done in higher-order languages; however, that choice is really a function of the application, customer's preference, and possibly mandates imposed on the organization. Although coding may appear to be a straightforward process, the decision of which convention to follow can have far-reaching consequences. Figure 2-4 shows the three popular coding options—top-down, bottom-up, and what I call "middle-out." Top-down, as the name implies, involves coding the software starting at the top of the architectural hierarchy and stubbing out all the functionality that is not implemented in actual code. A stub is an abbreviated procedure to allow complete definition of the software architecture. It can be called, may perform a simple operation, and then returns control to the caller using a consistent set of arguments. This skeleton takes time to build and usually requires a complex, realistic driver to stimulate the software. Also when you add features, you retest the whole system, which is good, but very time-consuming and processing-intensive. Integration occurs throughout the coding process, so the dis-

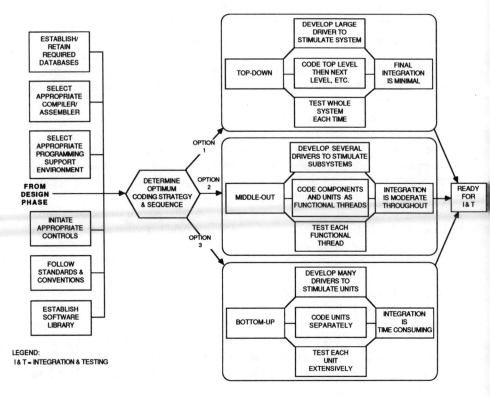

Figure 2-4 Code phase for the commercial life cycle model, showing 3 options.

tinction between coding and the integration and testing phases is very vague and recursive. Bottom-up coding, on the other hand, means that all the lowest level units (subroutines, etc.) are coded and unit-tested with their own simple little drivers. Then all the parts are integrated, which is usually a big effort. I prefer the middle-out approach, wherein the core functions of the software are developed first, to provide a functioning system. This core usually involves basic capabilities of the user interface, database, and limited input and output processing. It then incrementally adds features and functions based on criticality, user needs, implementation risk and difficulty, etc. The term "thread" is used by Michael Deutsch [3] and others to describe these sets of capabilities that get coded and added in this manner. Table 2-2 is included to address the more obvious pros and cons of each coding approach. Remember that the selection of the coding technique is very organization- and application-dependent. It also affects how IV&V is applied since the drivers and availability of code for verification differ widely depending on the approach. More about that in Chapter 7.

Now that you understand that there are several ways to develop code, it is also important to consider the support mechanisms that need to be in place as well. First and foremost is the selection and installation of the appropriate compiler (or as-

TABLE 2-2. Comparison of Coding Implementation Approaches

Advantages	Disadvantages
Top-down	
Software executes early and often	Stubs are required
Good visibility of total software architecture	Difficult to eliminate redundancies at lowest levels
Interfaces are defined early	Testing overhead is large
Data structures are defined early	Forces hardware decisions early
Integration is distributed by level throughout implementation	Big complex driver is expensive and difficult to maintain
Big complex driver provides consistency in testing	Testing at workstation level difficult to coordinate
Error handling in software easier to incorporate	Bug propagation hard to control
Easier memory management	
Middle-out	
Software executes early	Forces hardware decisions early
Critical parts can be developed early	Several drivers are required; could cause inconsistencies
Core functionality is developed early	Growth in data and structures may be difficult to control
Moderately complex drivers are needed	Overall sizing allocations confirmed late in program
Integration is incremental and only moderately difficult	Adding functions may disturb CPU loading and process scheduling
Stubs are not required	
Incremental releases are possible	Frequent changes to global data definitions difficult to manage
Works well with DBMS SQL	Interfaces may be moderately difficult to control
Enable users to be involved early	
Bottom-up	
High risk/critical units are coded and unit tested early	System execution comes late
	Integration can be very difficult
Units can be replaced early with little impact on system	Many drivers required; could cause inconsistencies
Unit testing requires simple drivers, hardware decision can come late	Interfaces undergo frequent changes
	System level testing is difficult
General purpose routines can be consistently defined	Sizing and allocations confirmed very late, can cause unexpected hardware growth
User interface can be developed incrementally and in any order	User interface operational very late
Tuning the system occurs at lowest levels	

DBMS SQL, database management system standard query language; CPU, central processing unit.

sembler) and the programming support environment. Support environments have changed dramatically over the last 25 years from flow-chart templates and keypunch machines to terminals and big mainframes and then on to personal computers (PCs) and workstations that often have more computing power than the old mainframes. In addition to excellent compilers and companion debuggers for all the common higher-order languages, there are also programmer's toolboxes that contain the necessary software tools to do such things as edit, print, format, path check, variable check, reference check, and monitor execution.

The move away from centralized data processing (DP) to networked distributed facilities has brought with it some new problems in managing distributed databases, software libraries and version control, licensing of support software, and saving and maintaining the artifacts of coding and testing. The coding phase also must acknowledge and follow the standards, conventions, and practices set forth earlier in the program. In addition, software and data libraries are required to manage and control the evolution of the software products.

Traditionally, when code has been successfully unit-tested, it is released to the integration and testing activity. If pure top-down implementation occurs, this process happens as each horizontal level is traversed, coded, and unit-tested. In bottom-up, it happens when enough units are ready to be combined to execute and perform a given function. In this case as well as with middle-out implementation, integration is much more vertical than in top-down and can occur more or less randomly anywhere in the architecture.

2.1.4   Integration and Testing Phase for the Commercial Life Cycle Model

This fourth and final phase is tailored to match the kind of software being developed and the manner in which it is being implemented and integrated. For example, if the system being developed is primarily software and is to be installed on noncustom hardware, then the highest level system tests are basically software. Conversely, where significant amounts of specially built hardware are involved, it is appropriate to test the software and then the system. In both cases, the relationships between the key specifications and the types and levels of tests are as shown in Figure 2-5. This figure provides a generalized model of the test hierarchy followed by most developers. That is, testing almost invariably starts with discrete functions—"press a key and get a response." This is followed by a gradual build up of capabilities—"press a button, watch a chain of responses." The order of integration of software and the order of testing need to be coordinated closely. Notice that the test criteria for system level tests come from the system specification, criteria for software high-level tests come from the functional specification, and criteria for lower level software come from the design specification. On the right side of Figure 2-5, the types of tools that are most often used in testing are shown. They range from the very simple at the unit level to such things as static analyzers and then dynamic code analyzers (discussed in detail in Chapter 8) at the process level. As the software system reaches full-blown proportions, it is usually best to begin testing it as a complete entity, which requires some sort of testbed (usually a host computer with

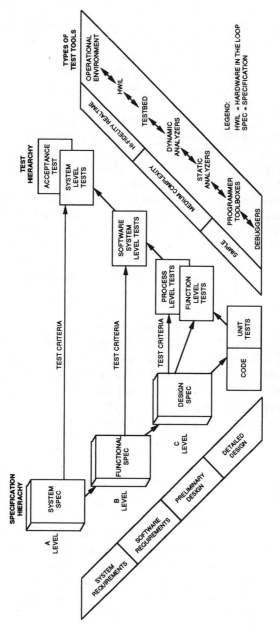

Figure 2-5 Correlation between specifications and tests—commercial life cycle model.

instrumentation), target hardware, or at least a representative system, which will behave like the ultimate target machine. The use of hardware in the loop (HWIL) means that hardware elements of the final system are introduced into the test environment to add realism and credibility to the testing. Normally, high-level testing requires that the input be run at the same rate and volume that the operational environment will provide, so this is dubbed a "high-fidelity real-time test environment." Systems that are time-critical in nature should be tested in this manner to ensure that they do not "break" or "crash" the first time that a stressing load is encountered. The ability of the test environment to overload and otherwise stress the system should always be provided.

The major activities of the integration and testing phase are illustrated in Figure 2-6. Notice that one of the early determinations is selection and specification of the optimum test strategy for the particular software and system being built. As the *test plan* is written (usually much earlier in the program), decisions relating to the test support must be made. The tools, instrumentation, recording, drivers, and environment, including hardware configuration and location, must be selected. In addition, the testable requirements are examined to characterize the kinds of testing that will be necessary to thoroughly demonstrate all the capabilities, and then the individual tests are developed and defined for the *test procedures document*. These are typically done on a per function, per process and per subsystem basis, culminating in the overall software and system level tests. Such things as the test setup and conditions, test case, script, I/O data, recording, and data reduction will be stated for each test. The software test article must be controlled and known to the tester. When the test is finally run and the results are known, they are fed back to the designers and coders for analysis and possible changes if "bugs" were detected. All problems are not "hard" errors; the most elusive and difficult to find are such things as erratic or poor performance, slightly incorrect calculations, and lost data. In any case, it is customary to collect and document the results in formal reports, the number of which greatly depends on the size of the job and the customer's needs. QA should monitor and control all testing very closely and is usually charged with the responsibility of archiving all important test data.

2.2   AN IN-DEPTH LOOK AT A DEPARTMENT OF DEFENSE LIFE CYCLE MODEL

Systems developed for the U.S. Department of Defense (DOD) are invariably developed in accordance with a large family of regulations, directives, policies, military standards (MIL-STDs) and DOD standards (DOD-STDs). These efforts are so commonplace that they have become known as MIL-STD or MIL-spec developments. The most common (and popular) current standard imposed for software projects at the time this book was written was DOD-STD-2167A [24]. This standard references and incorporates several other related standards that cover configuration control (MIL-STD-480, MIL-STD-481 and MIL-STD-482) [19, 20, 21]; specification practices (MIL-STD-490) [22]; engineering management (MIL-STD-499) [12];

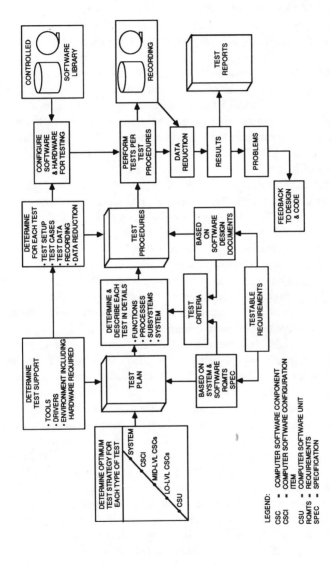

Figure 2-6 Integration and testing phase for the commercial life cycle model.

LEGEND:

CSC = COMPUTER SOFTWARE CONPONENT
CSCI = COMPUTER SOFTWARE CONFIGURATION ITEM
CSU = COMPUTER SOFTWARE UNIT
RQMTS = REQUIREMENTS
SPEC = SPECIFICATION

technical reviews and audits (MIL-STD-1521) [13]; and software quality assurance (DOD-STD-2168) [25]. Their latest revision level is denoted by a letter suffix. (For example, MIL-STD-490A supersedes MIL-STD-490.) The development cycle model imposed by DOD-STD-2167A is shown in Figure 2-7. The phase names are dictated by the standard. The reader is encouraged to look back at Figure 2-1 near the beginning of this chapter and compare the commercial model to the DOD model. In fact, if you have not read that section first, you should do it now because it discusses many common concepts, which are not repeated here to avoid redundancy.

Most of the differences between the two models are in nomenclature, not content; however, there is one significant philosophical difference in the specification structure. In the commercial model, the middle-level software functional specification (B-level spec) is a two-part document. The first part deals with capturing and expressing the software requirements and the second part presents the preliminary design. In DOD-STD-2167A, the equivalent document is called the software requirements specification (SRS) and is only a requirements document. Also, it is prepared in the requirements phase. The design specification (C-level spec) in the commercial model is a monolithic document; whereas, the software design document (SDD) in DOD-STD-2167A is a two-part book that is actually prepared at two distinct times and each part is published separately.

Other differences between the commercial and DOD models are in the formality of the process, control mechanisms, and the number of documents produced. The names of these documents are self-explanatory and do not require individual discussion. The center of Figure 2-7 identifies the "development configuration," which is the name for the contractor's internal configuration-controlled software (source code) and documentation (software design document or SDD), which evolves during development. There are a number of formal technical reviews and audits imposed by the standards, which help ensure good visibility into the development process. Configuration management (CM) within DOD (and most other organizations as well) is traditionally a three-part process—configuration identification, configuration (and change) control, and configuration status accounting. Sometimes auditing is added as a fourth CM activity. Configuration identification organizes the software into computer software configuration items (CSCIs) and hardware into hardware configuration items (HWCIs), establishes unique names and identifiers for these items, and designates key documents as specification baselines. Configuration control invokes formal procedures on key physical products that prevent changes of any kind from occurring without the knowledge and consent of the "approving" authority. This authority will vary depending upon the severity of the anticipated change and the artifacts that will be affected by it. This activity establishes configuration control boards (CCBs) at appropriate levels to oversee this process. Configuration status accounting provides the recordkeeping for any and all change proposals, change orders, waivers, deviations, and problem reporting. As indicated in Figure 2-7, CM continues throughout the useful life of the product although it transitions back to become the customer's responsibility once operational status is reached.

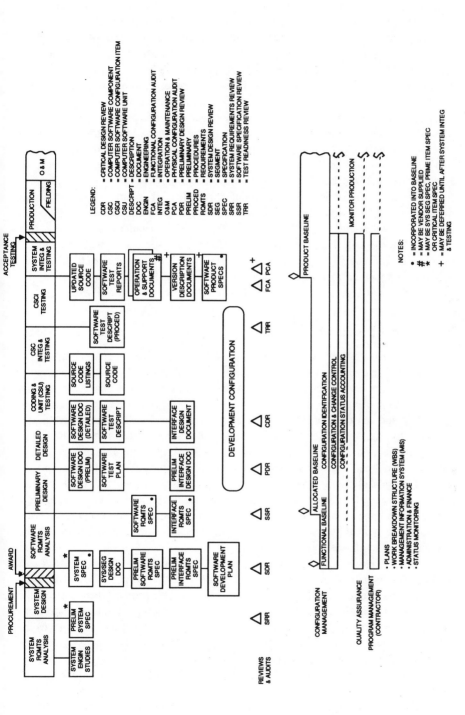

Figure 2-7 U.S. Department of Defense (DOD) life cycle model.

41

Software quality assurance is conducted under the guidance of DOD-STD-2168 [25], which provides for a comprehensive program of monitoring, control, review, and evaluation throughout the development cycle and can be extended into production to ensure that the software "copies" are correct for the given installation and application. Program management on DOD-sponsored efforts is usually quite comprehensive. In order to support the stringent customer reporting required and to provide timely and informative data to all levels of management, most development organizations incorporate some form of management information system (MIS). Most DOD contract efforts are organized by a work breakdown structure (WBS) according to MIL-STD-881A [23], which first hierarchically decomposes the job into work categories and then into conveniently sized work packages for ease of planning, scheduling, budgeting, and status monitoring.

There will of course be variations in this DOD life cycle model, depending upon the particular application. Because variations are frequently encountered, there is a tailoring guide, Handbook DOD-HDBK-287/286 [15], available to assist in this process. Simple tailoring is provided by deleting nonapplicable sections and requirements from the Data Item Directive (DID), which defines the contents of each deliverable document. Complex tailoring interprets the DID and adapts it to best fit the situation and program needs via instructions in the statement of work.

2.2.1 Requirements Phase for the Department of Defense Life Cycle Model

The requirements phase for the DOD life cycle model, like its counterpart in the commercial life cycle model, deals with all kinds of requirements—system, software, hardware, and human. It assumes that a formal concept phase, or perhaps even an earlier development prototyping effort, took place which determined the feasibility and reasonableness of the system to be developed. This model is not sensitive to exactly where it is used in the total system evolution; that will be covered in Section 2.3, which deals with the DOD Acquisition Process. Suffice to say, this model can be used sequentially up to three times in a DOD program: for concept (exploration and) definition (CD), for demonstration/validation (Dem/Val), and for full-scale (engineering and manufacturing) development (FSD). (The new names for the phases include the words in parentheses.) To reduce confusion to a minimum, a typical full-scale development, contractor-performed effort will be assumed for this discussion.

Figure 2-8 shows a typical set of activities and products of this phase. Most government-sponsored efforts invest a great deal in the formal proof of concept including models, analytical studies, simulations, and even prototypes to prove the system's feasibility before committing development funding. A representative example of these prerequisite activities is included to indicate some of the sources for the requirements that end up in the System Specification. Weapon systems, for example, often have a long list of external requirements, which come from outside the acquisition manager's domain. It is customary for the customer to produce and include the preliminary system specification in the procurement package. The winning contractor is then tasked to finalize this document based on the conditions

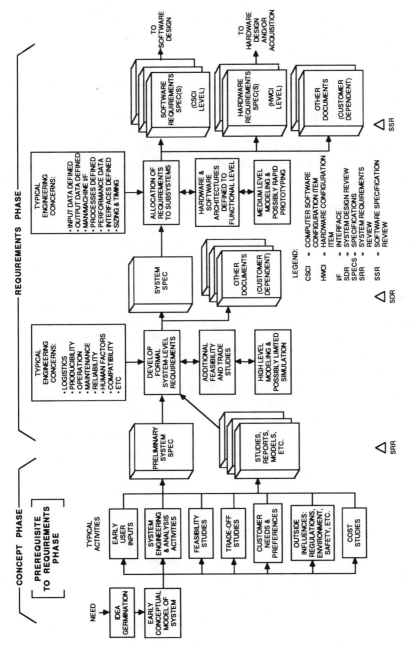

Figure 2-8 Requirements phase for the Department of Defense life cycle model.

43

stated in the contract and additional systems engineering work, which often includes more high-level simulation and modeling, feasibility and trade studies, and inclusion of such things as logistics, safety, security, human engineering, maintainability and reliability objectives, and operational criteria. The system specification is also called the *Type-A specification* or simply the *A spec*. MIL-S-83490 [18] defines the A,B,C family of specifications.

Because it is not an acceptable practice to go from this high-level document (the system specification) directly to design, a second set of requirements documents at the functional level is required. Here things begin to get more complicated because it is traditional to divide the development process into its major functional groupings. Fairly modest systems can be documented by a *hardware prime item* (*requirements*) *specification* (PIS) and a *software requirements specification* (*SRS*). If, however, the system is very complex and/or has dissimilar functional groupings, separate specifications for each group are recommended. These groups are called "configuration items (CIs)" in the trade and are managed and developed as entities. Thus, there are hardware CIs (HWCIs) and computer software CIs (CSCIs), as mentioned earlier. They have their own version identifiers, are compiled or assembled into a single item, etc. Complex systems can have several CSCIs and HWCIs.

Other common names found in government standards for this class of specifications include: software development specification, software performance specification, and Type B specifications (B1 for hardware, B5 for software, and other B-numbered documents for special purposes) and prime item development specification (for hardware). This book uses the DOD-STD-2167A [24] designation "software requirements specification (SRS)" as the preferred name.

The act of generating a requirements specification for each CSCI and HWCI requires that the requirements contained in the system specification be "decomposed" into logically grouped parts and allocated to software and hardware components. In software, these components are typically high-level processes or tasks; they are known in the DOD software community as *computer software components* (*CSCs*). In hardware, components are subsystems, assemblies, boards, etc. This decomposition is something of a recursive process, which can be aided by rapid prototyping and a number of CASE tools that support decomposition and structured analysis. The SRS level document concerns itself with relating requirements to components, how these components behave and interact, what the physical and logical interfaces look like, and what data are required to flow through the system. The document should also contain estimates on sizing, timing, and throughput requirements for that part of the system as well as recommended methods for testing and confirming the performance requirements. At this level of system definition, the number of software configuration items (CSCIs) and hardware configuration items (HWCIs) are firmly established and the next level of components (with their insides treated as black boxes) are described in terms of their interaction, behavior, and physical and logical arrangement. By this time, the "originating requirements" from the system specification are now accompanied by a large number of "derived requirements" spawned from inside the SRS as they are generated. In addition, an interface requirements specification (IRS), system/segment design document (SSDD), and software development plan (SDP) are also normally produced during this period.

2.2.2   Design Phase for the Department of Defense Life Cycle Model

This phase normally consists of two parts, preliminary and detailed design. This two-step process enables an orderly expansion of detail to occur from the computer software components (CSCs), which are the intermediate building blocks, to the computer software unit (CSU) level. Figure 2-9 shows the main processes and products of the design phase. The first part of the process is called *preliminary design;* the second is called *detailed design.*

Preliminary Design. This step is an intermediate-level representation of the software which describes all of the components (CSCs) in the context of the entire configuration item (CSCI), as well as how these components interact and interface with each other. A few examples may help in understanding this concept: If the CSCI is an accounting system, then the first-level CSCs would typically be receivables, payables, inventory, payroll, etc. If the CSCI is a guided missile, then these CSCs could be the seeker, navigation subsystem, propulsion, warhead, etc. Thus, the goal of this first half of the design phase is to complete the logical design of all of these components, not to go all the way to the unit or subroutine level just yet; that is the role of detailed design. Preliminary design typically calls for the following types of activities:

- Selection and/or generation of appropriate algorithms
- Definition of the modes and states of the software
- Generation of control flow at the CSC level
- Definition of input/output (I/O) data requirements
- Generation of data flow at the CSC level
- Definition of data structures and schema
- Generation of sizing and memory allocations
- Preliminary designs of the user interface
- Generation of timing budgets at the CSC level
- A formal preliminary design review (PDR) to comment on and approve the preliminary design.

Detailed Design. This step is similar to the process just discussed, except that the amount of detail is increased and now goes all the way to the bottom of the design chain to the computer software units (CSUs)—subroutines and the like. Since many DOD systems must operate in real time, it is very important to deal with finite timing of each process, interrupts and their effects on data integrity, error control and recovery, initialization, task scheduling, etc. The goal, of course, is to have a

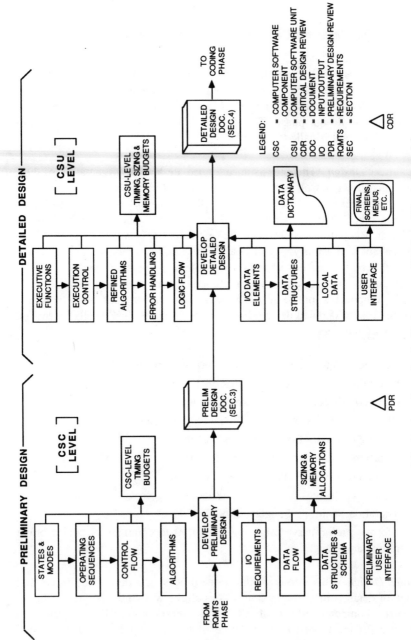

Figure 2-9 Design phase for the Department of Defense life cycle model.

LEGEND:

CSC = COMPUTER SOFTWARE COMPONENT
CSU = COMPUTER SOFTWARE UNIT
CDR = CRITICAL DESIGN REVIEW
DOC = DOCUMENT
I/O = INPUT/OUTPUT
PDR = PRELIMINARY DESIGN REVIEW
RQMTS = REQUIREMENTS
SEC = SECTION

46

complete design that will support coding with minimum changes and no unresolved loose ends. Detailed design calls for the following types of activities:

- Complete specification of the executive functions
- Execution control mapping
- Refined algorithms (early testing in this phase may be desirable)
- Comprehensive error handling
- Complete logic flow or textual equivalent; ie, pseudocode, program design language, etc.
- Complete I/O data element definition
- Definition of all required data structures
- Local and global data requirements
- Designs for the user interface (including screens, menus, etc.)
- Comprehensive data dictionary
- Refined CSU-level timing, sizing, and memory budgets
- A formal critical design review (CDR) to comment on and approve the detailed design.

It is customary for both levels of design to be documented in a *Software Design Document (SDD)*. DOD-STD-2167A [24] allows the same document to grow from preliminary design, as recorded in Section 3, by later adding the detailed design portion as Section 4 and republishing the document. This serves to keep all the design detail in one place and simplifies the cross-referencing problem. This class of software design specifications is also known as a *Type-C5 specification, design specification, and Part 1 and 2 development specification* in other MIL-STDs.

The ultimate stopping point for design is at the logic flow or pseudocode level (or equivalent) accompanied by the list of things that a comprehensive detailed design process provides: detailed data definitions and formats, complete interface definitions, detailed algorithms, timing sequence charts for all tasks, complete input and output forms and formats, complete user interface definition including screens, menus, etc.

2.2.3 Code Phase for the Department of Defense Life Cycle Model

The code phase, diagrammed in Figure 2-10, implements the detailed design in some form of programming language. Although most coding today is done in higher-order languages (HOLs) like Fortran, COBOL, Pascal, C, and Ada, that choice is really a function of the application, customer's preference, and possibly mandates imposed on the organization. Ada is the language of choice in the U.S. DOD at the time that this book was written and waivers are required to use another language. As we discussed in the previous section dealing with the commercial life cycle model, coding conventions greatly affect the manner and order in which software is implemented. Also in that earlier section, Table 2-1 listed the pros and

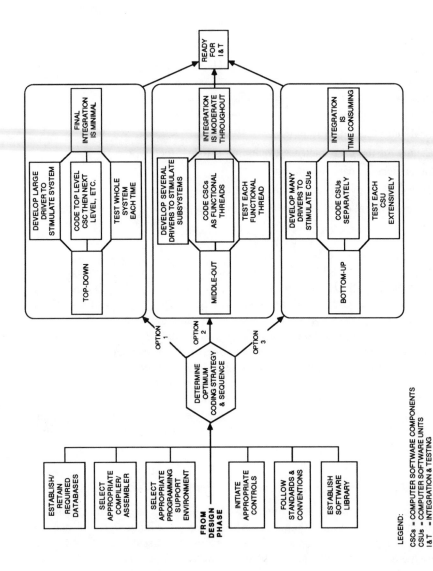

LEGEND:

CSCs = COMPUTER SOFTWARE COMPONENTS
CSUs = COMPUTER SOFTWARE UNITS
I&T = INTEGRATION & TESTING

Figure 2-10 Code phase for the Department of Defense life cycle model.

cons the three popular options: "top-down, bottom-up" and what I called "middle-out." Top-down, as the name implies, involves coding the software starting at the top of the architectural hierarchy and stubbing out the necessary functionality. Stubbing is described in Section 2.1.3. This executable structure takes time to build and requires a complex driver to stimulate the software. Also every time you add features, the whole system gets retested, which is good, but very time-consuming and resource-intensive. Integration occurs throughout the coding process, so the distinction between coding and the integration and testing phases gets very vague and recursive. The developer may have to hold multiple critical design reviews (CDRs) to approve the design for each level incrementally before proceeding with the coding.

Bottom-up coding, on the other hand, means that all the lowest level units (subroutines, etc.) are coded and unit-tested with their own little simple drivers. Then functionality is added at higher and higher levels and the parts are integrated, which is usually a big effort that grows in complexity as the end nears. I prefer the middle-out approach, wherein the core functions of the software are developed first to provide a functioning system. This core usually involves basic capabilities of the user interface, database, input and output processing, and then incrementally adds features and functions based on criticality, user needs, implementation risk and difficulty, etc. The term "thread" is used by Michael Deutsch [3] and others to describe these sets of capabilities that get coded and added in this manner.

Now that you understand that there are several ways to develop code, it is also important to consider the support mechanisms that need to be in place as well. First and foremost is the selection and installation of the appropriate compiler (or assembler) and the programming support environment. The coding phase must acknowledge and follow the standards, conventions, and practices set forth earlier in the program. In addition, software and data libraries are required to manage and control the evolution of the software.

Traditionally, when code has been successfully unit-tested, it is released to the integration and testing activity, which is often a separate organization in large companies. If pure top-down implementation occurs, this process happens as each horizontal level is traversed, coded, and tested. In bottom-up, it happens when enough units are ready to be combined to execute and perform a demonstrable function. In this case, as well as with middle-out implementation, integration is much more vertical than in top-down. Regardless of the coding approach, most complex systems are integrated and tested in a serial fashion often called *incremental builds*.

2.2.4 Integration and Testing Phase for the Department of Defense Life Cycle Model

Integration and testing is tailored to some extent to match the kind of software being developed and the manner in which it is being implemented and integrated. If the system being developed is primarily software and is to be installed on non-custom hardware, then the highest level system tests are basically software. Conversely, where significant amounts of specially built hardware are involved, it is appropriate to test the software and then the system, as in the case of virtually all military "embedded computer systems." In both cases, the relationships between the key specifications and the types and levels of tests are as shown in Figure 2-11, which is the DOD-STD-2167A version of Figure 2-5, which appeared earlier in this chapter. Notice that the test criteria for system level tests comes from the system specification, criteria for software CSCI-level tests from the software requirements specification (SRS), and for computer software component (CSC)-level tests from the software design document (SDD). Also on Figure 2-11, notice that the types of tools range from the very simple at the computer software unit (CSU) level to such things as static and then dynamic code analyzers (discussed in detail in Chapters 7 and 8, respectively) at the CSC level. As the CSCI reaches full-blown proportions, it is usually best to begin testing it as a complete entity, which requires a testbed (usually a host with special tools and instrumentation), target hardware, or at least a representative system which will behave like the ultimate target machine. The use of hardware in the loop (HWIL) means that hardware elements of the final system are introduced into the test environment to add realism and credibility to the testing. High-level testing requires that the input be run at the same rate and volume as the operational environment will provide, so this is dubbed a "high-fidelity real-time test environment." Systems that are time-critical in nature should be tested in this manner to ensure that they do not "break" or "crash" the first time a stressing load is encountered. The ability of the test environment to overload and stress the system should always be considered.

The major activities of the integration and testing phase are illustrated in Figure 2-12. Notice that one of the early determinations is selection and specification of the optimum test strategy for the particular software and system being built. As the *software test plan* (*STP*) is written (usually much earlier in the program), decisions relating to the test support must be made. The tools, instrumentation, recording, drivers, and environment, including hardware configuration and location, must be selected. In addition, the testable requirements are examined to characterize the kinds of testing that will be necessary to thoroughly demonstrate all the capabilities, and then the individual tests are developed and defined for the *software test descriptions* (*STD*) document. These are done on a per-function basis (typically by low-level CSCs and CSUs); a per-process basis (typically by mid-level CSCs); and a per-subsystem basis (typically by high-level CSCs); this culminates in the overall CSCI and system level tests. Such things as the test setup and conditions, test case, script, I/O data, recording, and data reduction will be stated for each test. The software test article must be controlled and known to the testers.

There are three types of testing that occur in most DOD contracts [11]. These are defined as follows:

- *Contractor Tests*. This category includes all the contractor-specified and -run tests.
- *Developmental Tests*. These are tests specified by the government and usually run by the contractor to ensure that all system objectives are met.

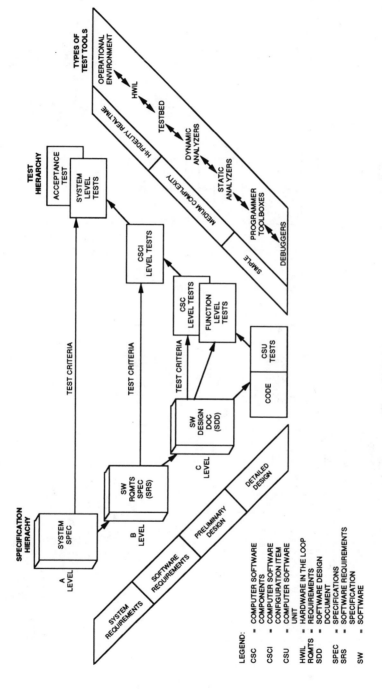

Figure 2-11 Correlation between specifications and tests—Department of Defense life cycle model.

51

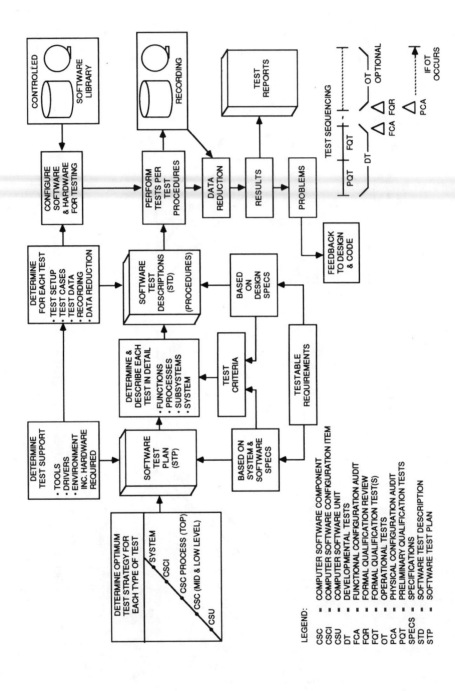

Figure 2-12 Integration and testing phase for the Department of Defense life cycle model—major activities.

LEGEND:

CSC = COMPUTER SOFTWARE COMPONENT
CSCI = COMPUTER SOFTWARE CONFIGURATION ITEM
CSU = COMPUTER SOFTWARE UNIT
DT = DEVELOPMENTAL TESTS
FCA = FUNCTIONAL CONFIGURATION AUDIT
FQR = FORMAL QUALIFICATION REVIEW
FQT = FORMAL QUALIFICATION TEST(S)
OT = OPERATIONAL TESTS
PCA = PHYSICAL CONFIGURATION AUDIT
PQT = PRELIMINARY QUALIFICATION TESTS
SPECS = SPECIFICATIONS
STD = SOFTWARE TEST DESCRIPTION
STP = SOFTWARE TEST PLAN

- *Operational Tests.* These are tests specified by the government that include the user community in a series of realistic demonstrations to determine mission and operational suitability. Not all systems require operational testing.

Developmental tests include what the contractor and government jointly designate as preliminary qualification tests (PQT) and formal qualification tests (FQT) as well as any other special tests deemed necessary. PQT are typically contractor-run tests, the customer can come in and witness them and/or ask for the test package. These give a good measure of progress and build confidence as the effort proceeds. When the system is sufficiently mature, the contractor will hold the test readiness review (TRR) and begin running CSCI-level tests. These culminate in the formal qualification tests with the customer present and possibly with an independent test and evaluation team. In either case, IV&V becomes another analysis asset during these test and may run some independent validation tests during this period as well. FQTs are usually a series of comprehensive demonstrations that verify the CSCI performance against what was specified in the requirements specifications. A functional configuration audit (FCA) is held to compare the specifications to the measured and observed performance of the system and deficiencies are recorded. Any failures from the testing will be repaired and testing will be repeated until the results are acceptable. The formal qualification review (FQR) is held to dispose of and close any and all deficiencies in the testing and documentation. The physical configuration audit (PCA) is held after a successful disposition of all open items from the FQR to ensure that all of the system artifacts are present and correctly designated and marked for delivery and that no superfluous items are present. It is during this period that the code-to software design document for each CSCI is converted to an as-built software product specification to form the "product baseline." If there is a series of operational tests, the PCA (and sometimes the FQR) is postponed until after these are complete.

2.3   A GLOBAL LOOK AT THE DEPARTMENT OF DEFENSE ACQUISITION CYCLE

Most DOD systems that are eventually targeted for production follow the traditional acquisition model shown in Figure 2-13. The goal of this process is to evolve systems in an orderly fashion that will ensure high-quality products, encourage competition, reduce risk, and hopefully control cost. Three out of four is not too bad! The model shows three major development phases initiated and separated by major milestones designated MS0, I, II, and III. The streamlined acquisition model shown at the bottom of the figure can cut the total development period roughly in half. In theory, a program must pass each milestone to enter into the next phase of development. The traditional acquisition cycle will be discussed first, since it is the most common and the most complex.

Traditional Acquisition Cycle. That there are new names (discussed below) for two of the phases resulting from the latest revisions to DOD Directive 5000.1 [14] and

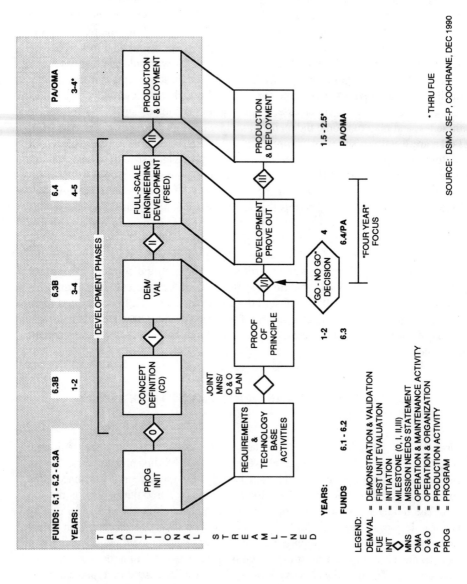

Figure 2-13 Department of Defense acquisition process—comparison of traditional and streamlined models.

its companion instructions DODI 5000.2 and 5000.2-M [16, 17]. Our present book continues to use the older common names, while recognizing the new names, with the new additional words shown in parentheses for clarification when necessary. No doubt, it will be years before the new names will be widely accepted, and the ripple effects will be felt throughout DOD for years to come since thousands of standards, policies, and related publications have now been made obsolete by this single act. If it had really helped anything, I could understand doing it, but I feel it is a colossal waste of money and time to make something simple and straightforward that everyone understood into something more difficult. Not only that, but the term "manufacturing" does not well describe the software development process or cases where off-the-shelf hardware is used to host systems, which is a very common trend and growing. They should have let well enough alone. Specifically, the name changes that had the largest impact are as follows:

- The concept definition (CD) phase is now officially concept exploration and definition (CE&D)
- Full-scale (engineering) development (FSD or FSED) is now officially engineering and manufacturing development (E&MD).

In addition, these revisions altered the milestone passage criteria and changed many of the documents that must be prepared by the program and project offices, making obsolete over 60 documents and creating over 100 new ones. Table 2-3 shows the names of the documents required at each phase for a (major) acquisition, acquisition category I (ACAT I) program. The highest level DOD programs are designated ACAT ID and involve more than $300 million in development and $1.8 billion in procurement costs in constant 1990 FY dollars. Less costly programs generally require less phase transition documentation. To find out exactly what is required for a specific program, you are urged to refer to DOD 5000:1, DOD 5000.2, and DOD 5000.2-M [14, 16, 17].

Figure 2-13 includes the type of funding commonly used for each phase, although there are exceptions where carryover funds can be used in the next phase. Typical years of duration also are included.

Streamlined Acquisition Cycle. This approach, shown in the bottom half of Fig 2-13, is designed to greatly speed up the development of systems when the increased risk is justified by the necessity to provide a rapidly fielded new system or to introduce new technology into an existing system. Typical risks include immature technology, single-source availability, incomplete process development, limited environmental testing/knowledge, and new tooling requirements. The streamlined acquisition cycle can have other variations depending upon the amount of non-developmental items (NDI) included in the design and the willingness of the customer and user community to arrange the acquisition cycle to purposely delay the infusion of immature technologies or processes until a preplanned product improvement (P3I) program can introduce them in a more reasonable timeframe. Planning for identified improvements in the state of the art scheduled for later release can

TABLE 2-3. Documents Required for Milestone Reviews (Acquisition Category I Programs)

Document ×: Prepared by PM/Military Dept. √: Prepared by OSD Staff	Milestone					Required by Congress
	0	I	II	III	IV	
Mission Need Statement (MNS)	×					
Operational Requirements Document (ORD)		×	×	×	×	
System Threat Assessment Report (STAR)		×	×	×	×	
Integrated Program Summary (IPS)		×	×	×	×	
Program Life Cycle Cost Estimate		×	×	×	×	
Acquisition Program Baseline (APB)		×	×	×	×	yes
Test & Evaluation Master Plan (TEMP)		×	×	×	×	yes
Manpower Estimate Report (MER)			×	×		yes
LRIP Report for Naval Vessels and Satellites			×			yes
Live Fire Test & Evaluation Waiver			×			yes
Competitive Prototyping Strategy (CPS) Waiver		×				yes
Independent Cost Estimate (ICE)		×	×	×	×	yes
Cost & Operational Effectiveness Analysis (COEA)		×	×	×	×	
Early Operational Assessment Report			×			
Operational Test & Evaluation Report				×		yes
Development Test & Evaluation Report			×	×		
Defense Intelligence Agency (DIA) Report	√	√	√	√	√	
Joint Requirements Oversight Council (JROC) Report		√	√	√	√	
Integrated Program Assessment (IPA)		√	√	√	√	
Independent Cost Estimate (ICE) Report		√	√	√	√	yes
Live Fire Test & Evaluation Report				√		yes
Beyond Low Rate Initial Production (LRIP) Report				√		yes
Acquisition Decision Memorandum (ADM)	√	√	√	√	√	

Source: DSMC, SE-P, Cochrane, Dec 1990
OSD, Office Secretary Defense; PM, Program Manager

keep the developing system from becoming obsolete by the time it is deployed. Successful execution of a P3I program requires careful initial systems analysis and planning to ensure that all subsystem interfaces and configurations are adequately specified, controlled, and managed to gracefully accept the later insertion of new-technology items. Currently, DOD has several important initiatives designed to reduce risk as well as cost on future programs; these initiatives support decisions to use the streamlined acquisition cycle. These include reusable software libraries, standard highly transportable languages centered on Ada, government-sponsored CASE tools and support environments, contractor evaluations (via the Software Engineering Institute as discussed in Chapter 15), and use of NDI hardware and software (especially things like database management systems, windows, application generators, and the like).

With this cursory understanding of the DOD acquisition process, the book now focuses on the traditional three-phased approach as shown in Figure 2-14. This figure emphasizes the unique characteristics of each phase, stressing the increase in formality and development thoroughness as the products pass from phase to phase.

2.3.1   Concept (Exploration and) Definition

Programs that pass Milestone 0 enter either concept study or concept development, which can consist of a prototype system. In hardware, this was called the "breadboard prototype" and the circuits were many times built on real wooden breadboards. When I was at Bell Labs 20 years ago you could still get breadboards from the stock room. In software, this level "prototype" is often only representative of features and functions that the final product might have, but little attention is given the finite details as long as the feasibility of the product can be demonstrated by using the prototype. There are two types of government tests—developmental (DT I) and operational tests (OT 1)—that can be used to calibrate the quality and suitability of the prototype to perform its mission. These tests are also called *developmental test and evaluation* (DT&E) and *operational test and evaluation* (OT&E) in some of the services. Figure 2-14 lists the typical characteristics of the software and the processing environment. There can be two or more contractors each developing a prototype.

If a formal development process is not considered necessary, then systems engineering studies and analyses are performed in place of building an actual physical prototype. These are often supported by simulations and modeling of the theoretical system. The documentation that is produced during this phase is seldom done to the MIL-STDs except for the system specification, but it needs to be sufficient to get the program into the next phase. One of the primary goals of this phase is to produce an adequate system specification to define the functional baseline and to support entry into the Dem/Val program. There is also a large amount of planning, cost analysis, and special documentation required just to get through the milestone. Major programs are usually reviewed at the highest levels of the Defense Department to keep them in sync with national goals and policies, federal budget constraints, and the dynamics of their mission and intended use.

2.3.2   Demonstration and Validation

Assuming that the program has passed Milestone 1, a procurement action is held to compete the demonstration and validation (Dem/Val) program. Here again, multiple awards are commonplace but are usually limited to two competitors. A pro-

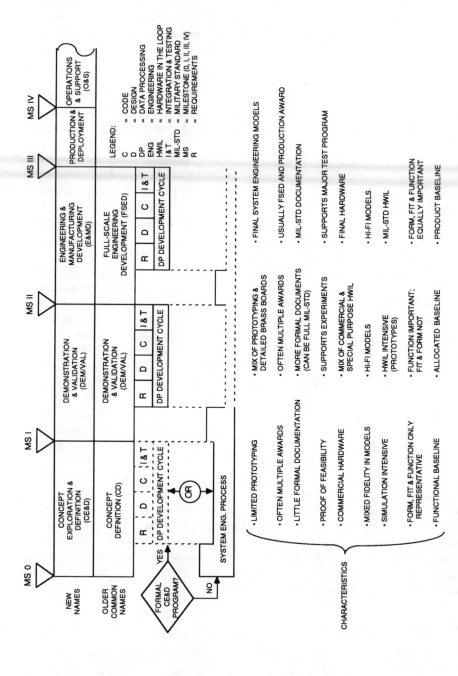

Figure 2-14 Key activities of the traditional Department of Defense acquisition cycle phase.

totype built at this level is called the "brassboard" in hardware, which implies metal bending, limited fabrication, wire-wrapped boards, etc. The function is now very important, but the final fit and form can be less than optimal. In this phase, the DP hardware is usually a mix of commercial and special-purpose components. Performance needs to be very representative of the final system in order to demonstrate that the system is ready to go into full-scale engineering development. This performance is confirmed or denied through a series of government tests—DT II and OT II (or DT&E II and OT&E II). Documentation is now mostly MIL-STD, but is tailored to less-than-optimal levels and the development cycle is MIL-STD, but at a reduced level of enforcement. This means that the 2167A model (or other, as appropriate) discussed in Section 2.2 will be followed, but there can be shortcuts taken; technical reviews have a different emphasis than they do later on. Here the primary interests are to see which of the competing systems is better than the other and in what ways, and if the overall mission goals and performance objectives can be met by either or both competing systems.

A primary goal of this phase is to produce the hardware and software requirements specifications for each configuration item that are good enough to begin preliminary design of the FSED version once the program passes Milestone II. When approved, these documents define the "allocated baseline." When this form of sequential iteration of the DOD development cycle occurs, the requirements phase of engineering development (ED) all but disappears. It will be there only long enough to confirm or modify the baselines per the new contract, hold a software specification review (SSR), and begin preliminary design in earnest. This has an adverse effect on IV&V unless the Dem/Val program has had its own IV&V program. Assuming that one of IV&V's major cost benefits is early and timely detection of faulty requirements, then the IV&V program may start behind the power curve.

When it is necessary to field systems in the least possible time, the streamlined version of the classic three-phase acquisition cycle can be executed. As mentioned at the beginning of this section, there are several versions of this model, all of which accomplish about the same thing. In one configuration, the government combines CD and Dem/Val into a single step, which combines Milestones I and II; this is probably the most common form. Another combines Dem/Val and FSED and sometimes early production articles into a maturation phase. In this case, Milestones II and III would be combined. As you may have guessed, it is always the exceptions that make the rules when it come to the acquisition process. Just how time-critical the program is to DOD has a lot to do with the configuration of the acquisition process model that is ultimately used.

2.3.3 Full-Scale Engineering (and Manufacturing) Development

As previously mentioned, inclusion of a Dem/Val phase greatly reduces the risk of the full-scale engineering development (FSED) phase but should not be considered a panacea since there is a greater tendency to ignore detail and become overconfident after a prototype system is built and successfully tested. When the size of a system increases linearly, there is a nearly exponential rise in development difficulty. This has been attributed to many factors, not the least of which are human interfaces and interactions, organization structure, and communication problems, but nonetheless the phenomenon is real. Therefore, even with a successful Dem/Val phase completed, the smart developer remains wary.

The usual sequence for FSED finds the approved and baselined system specification and hardware and software requirements specifications supplied as part of the procurement package so that all competing contractors in effect bid to these documents. After award, the first major activity of the winning contractor is to ensure that these documents are totally compliant with the specifics of the FSED contract. If there were only preliminary software and hardware requirements specifications produced from Dem/Val, the FSED program will have to refine and finalize them as one of its first tasks. When these B-level specifications are finally approved, they are placed under formal configuration control to serve as the "allocated" baseline of the system and can no longer be changed without approval from the configuration control board (CCB).

The remainder of full-scale engineering development follows the process described in Section 2.2, which evolves through the two-step design sequence, coding, and integration and testing. The contractor's tests cover all the basic and buildup testing required to debug, integrate, and demonstrate the system to the government. The developmental testing (DT III or, as it is sometimes called, DT&E III) series are government-designated tests intended to verify and eventually certify the performance of the FSED system. The preliminary qualification tests of DT III are normally run by the contractor with limited government monitoring. The formal qualification test (FQT) portion, however, usually involves the government agency and/or its test organization with some "hands on" participation. Finally, the operational tests (OT III or OT&E III), if included, stress the operational aspects of the system, are generally scripted to represent a realistic operational load, scenario, and environment, and are normally performed with test evaluation and user agencies. The reader is reminded that the IV&V contractor should have the opportunity to participate in the developmental tests and as such becomes the first user of the system. Through this earlier experience, IV&V can also be very effective as an asset for operational testing (OT III). As stated previously, one of the last steps in FSED is to convert the code-to software design documents to as-built software product specifications to form the "product baseline."

2.3.4 Production (and Deployment) Phase

Production of a DOD system can only begin after the Defense Acquisition Board (DAB) for major Acquisition Category ID (ACAT ID) systems or the Component Head or Acquisition Executive for lesser programs approves it and funds are allocated. This decision can take at least two forms: One, the full-rate production can begin immediately or two, an initial or low-rate production can occur followed by additional testing (DT/OT IIIa) to verify that the initial systems meet the required mission performance and operational specifications. IV&V is not directly concerned with the production process itself; our only interest is when the system is changed, for whatever reason. The magnitude of the change determines whether IV&V should be reapplied and to what extent. The IV&V database and analyst's notebooks collected and developed throughout FSED form a valuable source for assessing the impact of the proposed change and identify the documentation, software, and tests necessary to rebaseline the system.

2.3.5 Operation and Support Phase

The operation and support (O&S) period, also called operation and maintenance (O&M), represents the operational life of the system. It is almost as sure as taxes that if the system is useful, it will eventually be changed. The venerable B-52 and F-111 aircraft are two of the classics that come to mind, the IBM 360/370 computer another, the Nike-Hercules and Hawk missile systems still others—all systems that had or have an operational life of 25 or more years. The point in all this nostalgia is that good systems are worth maintaining even when significant retrofits are involved. The IV&V contractor should not only assist the developing agency in establishing a strong in-house capability, but can help to safely maintain and archive the necessary records, software, documents, and database to support revalidation or even more extensive IV&V if needed whenever changes occur during the operational life of the system. Thus, there is a valuable role for IV&V in postdeployment software support (PDSS), but practically speaking, it is unlikely to occur unless through some form of organic assets within the command or government organization, where the practice is becoming more and more common.

2.4 CHAPTER SUMMARY

- Variations in the ways in which systems are built in the commercial world and the Department of Defense (DOD) make it necessary to understand the differences between both processes and, hence, the effects that they will have on IV&V.
- The commercial life cycle model is generic and, therefore, common to virtually all industrial, institutional, and governmental nondefense development efforts. With a little adaptation, it can be used to develop any type of software.
- The DOD model incorporates this generic model, but goes much further in establishing rigorous control, management, and direction through a very large collection of regulations, standards, policies, procedures, and infrastructure.
- The DOD model shows marked improvement over the commercial model in the consistent structure and thoroughness of the specifications and support documentation, design completeness, and in the formality and organization of testing, to name three areas.

- There are arguments on both sides of the issue of just how much structure and control is really necessary. Some of the largest software systems in the world are nondefense and were built and fielded without the benefit of MIL-STDs.
- By the mid-1980s, DOD recognized that the proliferation of regulations and standards had gone too far and initiated a couple of things to reverse this trend: The endorsement of Ada as the standard language and use of DOD-STD-2167A [24] as the standard software development practice.
- Things like CASE tools, de facto standards for operating systems, telecommunications standards, common user interfaces, and database management systems (DBMSs) have all equally helped both defense and nondefense developers. Despite these things, software for big systems remains a problem of international proportions.
- DOD established a phased approach to developing complex software-intensive systems called the DOD acquisition cycle. It calls for up to three successive development cycles, which typically produce correspondingly more sophisticated prototypes with each iteration to reduce risk, ensure mission suitability, encourage competition and technology advancement, and control cost.
- The major disadvantage to the phased approach is that it adds several years to the fielding of a system, which can counter many of the otherwise beneficial results. I personally believe that the engineering technology exists today to build systems in a much more time- and cost-efficient manner. I also acknowledge that schedule compression always increases program risk, making IV&V even more important and necessary than ever.

2.5 WHAT COMES NEXT

Now that the reader has a fundamental knowledge of the different forms of the development cycle and how systems are acquired by DOD, the book can devote its attention much more exclusively to IV&V. The fundamentals of development must be understood because IV&V overlays that process, uses and examines the products, evaluates the subordinate processes, and provides continuous course correction. The next chapter starts with a life cycle overview of IV&V based on the DOD model, which is more comprehensive and therefore more appropriate than the others. Once this is thoroughly explored, the other extreme is described, wherein an IV&V program for an in-house development is discussed.

3

A LIFE CYCLE OVERVIEW OF INDEPENDENT VERIFICATION AND VALIDATION

The most frequent users of independent verification and validation (IV&V) thus far have been defense systems, so it is only appropriate to begin the life cycle tour using the DOD-STD-2167A [24] model as the framework. This model has a moderate level of complexity, being simpler than its predecessor DOD-STD-2167 and more complete and less ambiguous than the commercial model. I especially like the manner in which 2167A handles the software requirements specification as an artifact of the requirements phase and then provides a two-part software design document to complement the development process as closely as possible. IV&V works with this model very nicely.

No life cycle tour would be complete if it did not include a look at a typical IV&V application at the other end of the spectrum—the in-house development environment. Thus, the chapter concludes with a characterization of a typical in-house software IV&V effort based on actual observations.

3.1 INDEPENDENT VERIFICATION AND VALIDATION ACROSS THE DEPARTMENT OF DEFENSE ACQUISITION CYCLE

3.1.1 Possible Configurations

In several places in the first two chapters I have reminded the reader that the U.S. Department of Defense (DOD) acquisition cycle is a somewhat flexible mechanism used to procure and build systems that are usually targeted for production and/or deployment. The ability to adapt this cycle to the needs of any program makes the process difficult to describe in absolute terms, so a discussion of the options seems to be the best way to convey the points that need to be made. Figure 3-1 illustrates

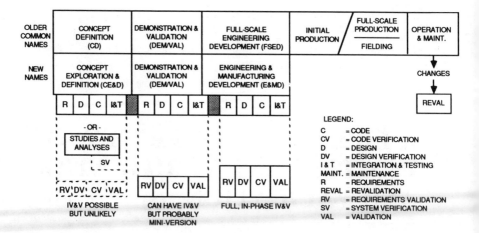

Figure 3-1 Acquisition life cycle with independent verification and validation.

the process in simplified form. As we mentioned earlier in the book, not all systems go through the classical three-phased approach. Phases can be combined or reduced in scope when more rapid development is necessary. Therefore, IV&V has to react to this flexibility by mimicking the needs and configuration of the development effort.

3.1.2 Independent Verification and Validation During Concept (Exploration and) Definition

When a concept definition (CD) phase occurs as a series of engineering studies and analyses, there are usually not enough artifacts or structure to support a traditional IV&V effort. In this case, this basically unstructured IV&V is sometimes called "system verification" [6] and has essentially the same characteristics as requirements verification. Therefore, this book treats them as one and the same for simplicity sake. Conversely, when a prototype CD system is built, it is possible to have a phased (albeit abbreviated) IV&V effort. But, in either case, the occurrence of an IV&V contract this early in development is rather unlikely. There are many reasons for this reluctance on behalf of the customer, including lack of formalism in development, barely adequate non-MIL-STD documentation, small budgets, multiple awards making IV&V difficult, compressed schedules, and less formal reviews. The list could get very long. The most notable exception would most likely be when the procuring organization has an organic asset that could perform a reduced scope version of IV&V. The term "organic" means that within various commands and agencies there are assets already in place that regularly perform IV&V and product assurance on developing systems. This form of IV&V is always extremely useful in helping to ensure that program objectives are being met and that the emerging system definition is as complete as possible.

As mentioned in the previous chapter (in Section 2.3), a primary goal of the CD phase is to define the system well enough to generate an adequate system specification which, when approved, becomes the functional baseline. Thus, IV&V in this phase concentrates on verifying the requirements. These come from many sources and are influenced strongly by the state of the practice in technology, national and international issues, needs of the military, industry, and science, and the like. For example, people want adequate defense until the Army wants to put the launcher in their backyard and then they protest very loudly, so system designers must react to the sometimes difficult realities of political pressure. System requirements are very often affected by a number of outside influences and interfaces to other systems that already have defined operational constraints. In DOD, a formal mission need statement (MNS) is written to begin the acquisition process. Once funding is approved, an engineering process is begun that examines the technology, materials, mission, threat, and other influences. The ultimate goal of this process is to evolve a theoretical system that satisfies the defined mission and operational needs. Trade studies and analyses then examine the life cycle costs, system effectiveness, development risks, logistics, personnel requirements, and compatibility with other systems to produce a preferred configuration. This is the most logical entry point for IV&V. This is especially important if breadboard models or computer simulations of the system are built or used in support of the analysis. Remember that competing CD contractors may each be developing their own prototypes for evaluation.

Upon determination of the best candidate concept, it is customary to write a system concept paper, integrated program summary and its supporting appendices, several plans and reports (as listed in Table 2-3 in the previous chapter), and the system specification. IV&V will figure heavily in the analysis and evaluation of the candidate systems and the review of these documents. In fact, IV&V will most likely run independent simulations of all or at least of the preferred candidate systems to assist in their evaluation. After a series of iterations, these documents are approved and the system specification is baselined. This act, designated the "functional baseline," means that the document is placed under configuration control so that changes cannot be made without a formal approval cycle involving the government program manager and others in authority and control of the program. These documents are necessary to support the transition of the system to the next phase. On major systems, the review process can go as high as the Defense Acquisition Board (DAB) and are often directly reviewed by the U.S. Secretary of Defense. The first review is called the "program decision" in that it determines whether to approve the system for the next phase, return the concept for additional study, or kill the program. Programs of lesser significance are transitioned to the next phase with a review by the component head or acquisition executive. Additional analysis help from IV&V in this phase can ensure a much more complete and realistic system specification as well as contribute to the successful passage of the milestone.

An additional role for IV&V can occur when the developing agency is without development contractors and is faced with completing and approving the system specification and sometimes subsystem performance criteria as well. IV&V may well be the only organization with the capabilities to perform an in-depth analysis of the system-level requirements and help interpret and merge the data from multiple CD efforts into the system specification. Many large programs have transitioned to the next phase handicapped by an inadequate system specification. The inevitable results are: cost and schedule overruns, less than optimal system performance, and dissatisfied users. IV&V is a cost effective remedy for this situation.

3.1.3 Independent Verification and Validation During Demonstration and Validation

IV&V is more common in this phase, but is still not as frequent as during full-scale engineering development (FSED). Many government agencies and program offices have systems engineering and technical assistance (SETA) contractors that can perform part of the role that an IV&V contractor would normally perform. Although they may not have all the assets, tools, orientation, or contractual charter to duplicate the roll of IV&V, they definitely compete for the available funds and often prevent IV&V from occurring during this phase. As described for CD, organic IV&V assets may now participate, or the effort may be contracted outside the parent organization. In any case, IV&V for Dem/Val programs is usually characterized as a "mini" version of what one would expect for the full-scale engineering development (FSED) effort. The reasons include limited funding; effort usually spread over two or more developers; less-than-robust documentation; the fact that final hardware is not available, making for compromises in software; situations where some software functionality is knowingly missing or kludged to work; and the fact that emphasis is not on finding everything wrong with these systems, since they are being built and tested primarily for "proof of principle." Instead, IV&V emphasis for this phase should be on verifying that the system and software requirement specifications are as complete, consistent, and comprehensive as possible; that the designs are similarly well-defined and documented; that the testing effort really demonstrates the user's needs, mission goals and performance capabilities of the system; and that shortcomings of the prototypes can be adequately explained and placed high on the priority for early solution. Thus, IV&V for Dem/Val concentrates on the core issues and problems and not so much on strict adherence to every standard, practice, and procedure that is required in the next phase to build production quality software and hardware.

The preferred entry point for IV&V is at the beginning of the Dem/Val program. This enables maximum benefit to be derived from early detection of inconsistencies, weaknesses, and errors in the requirements specifications. Regardless of the entry point, one of the primary IV&V efforts throughout this phase is to review and evaluate the software (and hardware to a lesser degree) requirements specifications that will move forward into the FSED program and keep them in sync with the system specification, which may require some modification as well. When these software (and hardware) requirements specifications are finally approved, they serve as the "allocated baseline" for the system.

IV&V will probably have to worry about competing prototypes, so much of the analysis and verification activity is done twice. Therefore, the tools selected should be as general purpose as possible and not biased toward either competing system. If a simulation is used, it should be able to model and represent both systems with the same fidelity and depth. The use of computer-aided software engineering (CASE) tools by either or both developers is considered a definite plus. IV&V would very likely want to use the same CASE tool for additional verification studies and keep the addition of other tools to a minimum to control costs. The data and artifacts produced by a good CASE tool can easily transition into FSED and support the idea of growing and maturing of the prototype in the next phase as well as supplying reusable designs, algorithms, and even some of the code if it is adequately developed and documented. Until the recent past, Dem/Val systems were aimed primarily at solving the high-risk, long-lead technology issues and tended to ignore those facets of the system design believed to be well within the state of the art. Therefore, quite often the design of the software was far less than optimal, documentation was weak, and controls were sporadic. In other words, things were a mess. However, in the last few years, which coincide with the introduction and use of DOD-STD-2167A, things have improved. I believe that one reason for this improvement is that most Dem/Val contracts now insist on using this standard and allow tailoring to relax unnecessarily constraining parts.

Many Dem/Val programs have some form of "live" test program where both contractors demonstrate their prototypes against the performance standards in the contract and against each other. The competition between Dem/Val contractors is often called a "fly off" or "shoot out" with the winner usually ending up with the FSED contract. Two types of government testing, developmental (DT II) and operational (OT II) are common to the Dem/Val effort. IV&V usually witnesses and evaluates both test efforts and has very little opportunity to do any independent IV&V testing, which is hopefully not the case later in FSED.

Finally, IV&V support is essential when the time comes to synthesize all the results of testing and evaluation in the specifications and produce the documents for transitioning the program into FSED. In essence, IV&V validates the functional and allocated baselines. IV&V can also help in review and verification of the key documents used to transition the program through Milestone II.

3.1.4   Independent Verification and Validation During Full-Scale Engineering (and Manufacturing) Development

The FSED system benefits the most from a full, in-phase IV&V effort. It does not matter whether this support comes from organic resources or from an outside contractor as long as it starts as early as possible. In reality, the starting point is often less than ideal because IV&V usually does not begin before the development contract is awarded. Then there is another delay while the IV&V contract is initiated. If IV&V was in place at the end of Dem/Val, then this delayed start should not present a problem. We have pointed out several times already that the greatest cost–benefit ratio in IV&V comes from requirements verification, wherein defects in requirements can be caught before they begin to ripple forward. So even if the development effort is already into preliminary design when IV&V gets started, some retrospective requirements verification activity needs to occur. If this step is skipped, IV&V will never be sure that the baselines are really correct and adequate to support the design effort, unless it was already done at the end of Dem/Val by IV&V.

It may be somewhat trite, but IV&V for FSED needs to have a "no-holds-barred" attitude toward the software and hardware. The reason that hardware keeps popping up in a discussion that is oriented heavily to software is that hardware must be there to run the software. When systems are being developed on existing, well-perfected hardware platforms, most of the concerns are then shifted to software. However, when hardware is special-purpose and evolving along with the software, IV&V will have to suspect and examine both when problems so indicate. There is a natural tendency for software people to blame the hardware and vice versa. A large number of software problems occur from misuse of hardware and operating system features. The crux of this situation is that IV&V has to pay attention to hardware; how much attention is a function of the kind and maturity of the hardware and its ultimate use. A couple of examples illustrate the point. Large database-oriented systems that run on general-purpose DP hardware need to pay little attention to hardware. Guided missiles, where the software (and firmware) is very tightly coupled to the hardware, require a lot of hardware verification and eventual system-level validation, which includes the hardware.

As IV&V for the FSED effort gets underway, the selection of software analysis tools that are complementary to those being used by the developer is very important. This complies with Rule 4 discussed in Section 1.4. The goal in IV&V tool selection is not to tell the developer what he or she already knows, but something different. Here there is a fine point that must be reckoned with when the developer has made a large investment in a costly and comprehensive CASE tool that has produced architectural models, prototypes, databases, diagrams and charts, and other forms of special requirements and design documentation and information. The question frequently asked is, "What should IV&V do in this situation?" The answer can take several forms:

1. IV&V can install the same CASE tool, request and receive the artifacts, and continue analysis and verification using capabilities not exploited fully by the developer. This is very cost-effective, but may leave undetected problems deep inside the design.

2. IV&V can request, receive, and examine the artifacts and based on this analysis use its own automated tools to further investigate suspect technical areas. This is a popular approach and offers new perspectives on the completeness and consistency of the design.

3. IV&V can do a combination of 1 and 2 above, which is the most effective approach, but can also be rather costly if many new tools are introduced. This combination has the most advantages if administered correctly.

4. IV&V can use a comprehensive CASE tool independent of and different from that used by the developer, derive an independent set of requirements and design, and then compare the two. Although this sounds reasonable on the

surface, it is usually a bigger job than IV&V resources and schedule allow. The IV&V analyst can easily fall into an abyss of unmatched requirements and incompatible designs. I therefore tend to shy away from this approach.

Once coding starts IV&V shifts emphasis to a role of standards enforcement, code-to-design comparisons, and static analysis. Then, as larger and larger collections of code become available, IV&V attempts to split its resources and attention between monitoring the development contractor's testing effort and conceiving and running independent IV&V tests including dynamic analysis, simulations, and excursions of contractor tests to determine where the system breaks and how errors propagate. Independent testing requires a computer system (or testbed) which can mimic that of the development contractor. IV&V will play a significant role in government developmental testing (DT III) and operational testing (OT III).

There are numerous other tasks that IV&V will very likely be requested to perform. All too often the status reporting on large software efforts is at a level that conceals the true state of the evolving product. This can happen for any number of reasons, but IV&V should be in a very good position to provide independent assessments including the application and administration of management indicators and software quality indicators called *metrics* (explained in Section 12.2). IV&V will also be called upon to review and comment on key plans and other documentation such as user manuals, test plans and procedures, installation manuals, etc. When systems enter production, they are customarily accompanied by a technical data package, which contains all the essential information that would enable a second source contractor to produce the product. IV&V should review at least the software portion of this package.

It should be obvious that IV&V for FSED is a very comprehensive effort, limited only by funding, which in turn limits the manpower and tools that can be applied, and by the curiosity and investigative skills of the analysts and engineers assigned to the effort. This description was intended to only provide an overview of the IV&V activities as they relate to the three phases of the acquisition cycle. The details of each phase of verification and validation are the subject of the next section.

3.2   LOOKING AT INDEPENDENT VERIFICATION AND VALIDATION BY PHASE

This book has made the point several times that IV&V mimics the development cycle; therefore, to provide a more in-depth understanding, it is necessary to examine each phase separately. Remember that the development model being used is from DOD-STD-2167A [24] which means that the discussion that follows uses the DOD names for specifications, software components, tests and the like. To convert these descriptions to the generic commercial model is a pretty simple mental process if you have studied and absorbed the contents of Chapter 2, so it will not be repeated here. In Section 3.3, we discuss IV&V for a typical in-house development process, in what can be characterized as a worst-case scenario, in order to amplify the difficulty of performing IV&V if some of the development elements are inadequate or are even missing.

Before beginning the phase-by-phase discussions, the reader is reminded that the IV&V phases align approximately with the development phases and require that the customer or developing agency serve as interface and buffer between the two, as shown in Figure 3-2. This figure illustrates the basic IV&V concept that each verification phase performs its phase-specific processes introspectively, then feeds forward to the next phase. This occurs until the validation phase is reached, when the process reverses. Here IV&V "validates" the software performance back against the software requirements specifications and the system performance against the system specification. Figure 3-3 shows the IV&V process flow diagram which illustrates the forward- and backward-looking philosophy of a comprehensive IV&V approach. I once used the Roman deity *Janus* to illustrate this ability to look in both directions and so named an IV&V methodology (circa 1977). This is why it is so important to continuously track changes and additions to the specifications maintaining the baselines without compromise as the development proceeds. Otherwise, no one would know for certain if the software and system are being tested to the right set of requirements. Lest this sound like idle speculation, please note that

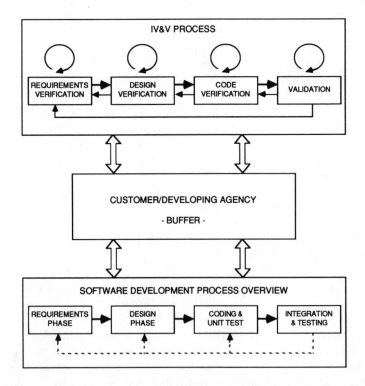

Figure 3-2   The relationship between software development and independent verification and validation.

many complex systems have been built to the wrong requirements and have required very substantial amounts of labor, hardware, and years to correct. Documented cases show that some systems have exceeded their original contract price by a factor of 4 or 5. IV&V must be dedicated to keeping this from happening.

3.2.1   Requirements Verification

The greatest concern of IV&V in this phase is to ensure that all the originating requirements are expressed correctly and fully in the system specification and that they are consistently decomposed and allocated to subordinate hardware and software requirements specifications. This decomposition must not only account for all these requirements in the next level documents to ensure completeness, but it has to make sure that the meaning did not get corrupted and, in fact, that it got further refined when necessary. This refinement process, sometimes called "fleshing out," means that the system engineers, analysts, and specification writers add subordinate details called derived requirements. DOD-STD-2167A [20] requires that a requirements tracing table be included in the software requirement specifications (SRSs) to ensure that they are all accounted for. Just a few year ago, IV&V had to develop separate requirements-tracing databases to do this function, which is usually still the case in the commercial world. This traceability is essential to the orderly generation and subsequent verification of the documents, so if it is supplied, IV&V will verify it completely; if not, IV&V will build one. Once all these requirements (or "capabilities," as they are also called) are accounted for, IV&V starts the engineering evaluation and verification activities to examine their correctness, internal and interrelational consistency, and their testability. Virtually all capabilities can be tested in some manner, but it is not simple in many cases; therefore, a strategy for checking each one has to be evolved. The development contractor takes a turn first determining how to do it; then IV&V verifies these approaches. Sometimes capabilities have to be confirmed by observing the behavior of the system or from indirect effects, which becomes a somewhat intuitive and less-than-ideal approach. Simulation and modeling are very useful tools available to the IV&V analyst to confirm behavior and/or performance.

While the verification of the functional parts of the system is taking place at both system and configuration-item level, IV&V verifies all the interfaces as documented in the interface requirements specification. This document is sort of the roadmap of the system. Without it, you cannot get there from here. IV&V is forced to look at other views of the system in addition to those used by the developer. This means that if the developer stresses data flow, then IV&V needs to verify the data flow diagrams for correctness and completeness, but also should add a complementary technique to examine the software structure. More details of this IV&V strategy are given in Chapter 5, but this should give the reader the concept. IV&V always goes for added perspectives in an attempt to discover something the developer did not see or fully understand.

There are two very promising techniques in requirements engineering that need to be mentioned: one is rapid prototyping and the other is formal specification

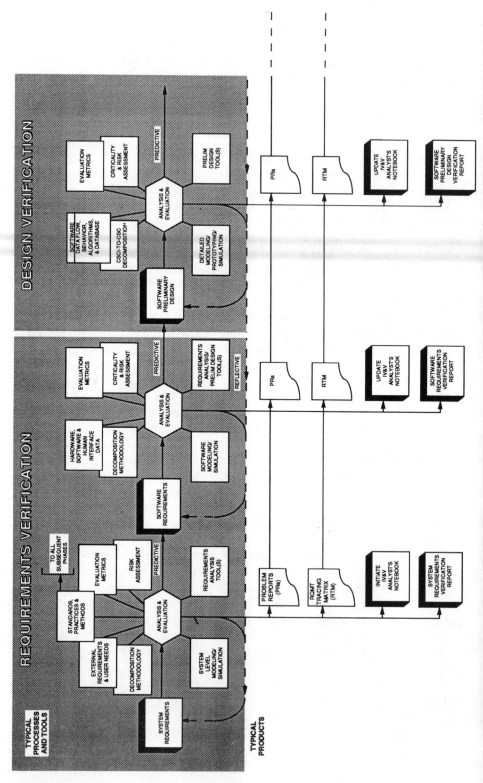

72

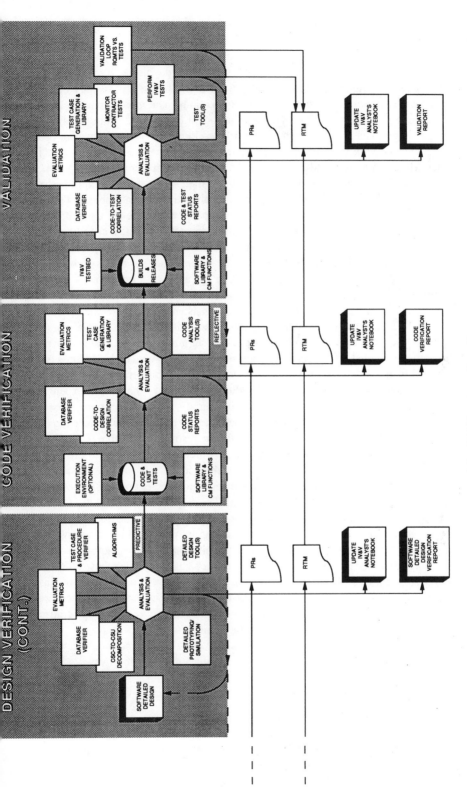

Figure 3-3 IV&V process flow diagram.

73

languages (not to be confused with programming languages). They both have costs associated with them, but they both have significant paybacks. Rapid prototyping tools allow the analyst or engineer to begin defining the system, usually on a CRT screen with a series of symbols and interconnections. The more sophisticated tools allow the user to define icons (symbols that look a little like the thing it is portraying). As the model grows, it can have attributes like behavior and physical properties associated with the icons and can be made to execute the model in a specified order. More and more detail can be added until the system architecture is pretty well laid out and confirmed to be reasonable. IV&V then works with the rapid prototype to determine its completeness and how well it solves the system problem. The major shortcoming with the current tools of this type is that none of them produce a traditional specification, so someone has to interpret the graphical specification and then write the system and software specifications based on this prototype, and things can get corrupted in the process. The other technique uses special requirements or specification languages. They can be used at least two ways: one, a traditional system specification can be written (in English) according to the standard and converted into the special language for consistency and correctness checking. Two, the developer can begin defining the system directly in the special language. In both cases, the tool can eventually produce an automated equivalent (or nearly so) to the traditional documents. Why has not the whole world embraced this type of tool? Well, they are gaining ground but have fairly high learning curves, are relatively complex, require knowledge of additional languages, have been expensive to acquire and use, and have not been multiuser. For IV&V to attempt to use a language-based CASE tool on its own, where the developer has not chosen to do so, may prove to be too large an undertaking for the resources available. Case Study D in Part IV of this book recites an example in which I attempted to do this. A great deal more detail on these tools is given in Chapter 4.

In addition to the specifications, the software development plan (SDP) is the next most important document for verification. The SDP is a consolidation of many programmatic requirements that once were expressed in separate documents (or not expressed at all). The contents of this document are presented in summary form in Table 3-1. The parts of the plan that have significant effects on software development are identified and evaluated for internal consistency, adequacy, correctness, and completeness. In addition, IV&V verifies that the actual procedures, processes, organization, and facilities discussed in the plan are in place and operating as specified. The planning for and installation of the software tools and the configuration management system are of utmost importance to IV&V.

Now that the book has presented the major activities of requirements verification, it might be desirable to put them in summary form as follows:

- Acquire necessary software analysis and CASE tools
- Perform verification using:
    Software analysis and CASE tools provided by IV&V
    Copies of selected contractor tools
    Simulations and modeling

TABLE 3-1. Software Development Plan Contents

1. Scope
   Identification
   System overview
   Document overview
   Relationship to other plans
2. Referenced documents
3. Software development management
   Project organization & resources
      Contractor facilities
      GFE
      Organizational structure
      Personnel
   Schedule & milestones
      Activities
      Activity network
      Source identification
   Risk management
   Security
   Interface with assoc. contractors
   Interface with software IV&V agent
   Subcontractor management
   Formal reviews
   Software library
   Corrective action process
   Problem/change report
4. Software engineering
   Organization & resources
      Organizational structure
      Personnel
      Software eng. environment
   Software standards & Procedures
      Software development tech. & method
      Software development files
      Design standards
      Coding standards
   Non-developmental software
      Reused software
      Commercial off the shelf (COTS)

5. Formal qualification testing
   Organization & resources
      Organization structure
      Personnel
   Test approach/philosophy
   Test planning assump. &
      constraints
6. Software product evaluations
   Organization & Resources
      Organization structure
      Personnel
   Software prod. eval. proc. & tools
      procedures
      Tools
   Subcontractor products
   Software prod. eval. records
   Activity-dependent prod. eval.
      Software prod. eval.
7. Software configuration mgmt.
   Organization & resources
      Organizational structure
      Personnel
   Configuration identification
      Developmental config. ID.
      Identification methods
   Configuration control
      Flow of config. cont.
      Reporting documentation
      Review procedures
      Storage, handling & delivery
      Additional control
   Configuration status accounting
   Configuration audits
      Prep. for spec. authentication
      CM major milestones
8. Other software devel. functions
   Appendices (as rqd.)

- Verify the system specification
- Verify the software requirements specifications
- Verify the interface requirements specification
- Verify the hardware prime item specifications if required
- Verify the software development plan and its implementation
- Verify requirements tracing between documents (perform it if not done)

- Perform criticality and risk assessment of requirements
- Review user interface needs
- Review input and output data requirements
- Review the trade studies for the system
- Review test requirements, planning, and strategy
- Participate in all reviews and meetings that affect the system
- Produce problem reports (PRs) as required.

What has just been described is the comprehensive version of requirements verification typical of the kinds of IV&V activities found in a full, in-phase IV&V effort for an FSED program. Suggestions on tailoring an IV&V effort to fit resource and schedule constraints is found in Chapter 11. It should also be mentioned that requirements verification does not have to make a sharp cutoff when preliminary design of the system begins. In fact, there is usually an overlap, so that any unresolved requirements issues continue to get appropriate attention until finally settled. On some very large jobs in the past, there have been open items against requirements until the very end, requiring IV&V to continue tracking and reminding the customer of them on at least a monthly basis. This kind of open-item tracking and reporting is fundamental to IV&V. In any case, IV&V's primary goal in this phase is to provide the customer with very high confidence that the system (especially the software) is well enough defined to enter preliminary design. The customer should be willing to delay that start if IV&V analysis indicates that the documentation and other development artifacts are not adequate. This kind of decision should be based on a series of metrics being applied to the program, as discussed in Section 12.2.

3.2.2 Design Verification

Design verification is considered a two-step process since virtually all commercial and DOD development models are divided into preliminary and detailed design subphases. Perhaps the easiest way to boost the understanding at this point is with an example, as shown in Figure 3-4. Take a process-control problem where the computer software configuration item (CSCI) is the XYZ Control System. It consists of many first-level (high-level) computer software components (CSCs), one of which is the alarm process, which determines if the system being controlled can continue to operate and notifies operators when abnormal conditions occur, etc. The CSC alarm process has two subordinate CSCs, one for digital points and the other for analog points. There are then four different types of digital point processors, and that part of the control system is completely decomposed to the unit level. The preliminary design serves to acknowledge all the CSC-to-CSCI and CSC-to-CSC interfaces and the data and control flow among them, states and modes, memory and timing needs, etc. On large systems having multiple CSCIs, design verification goes back to the system/segment design document (SSDD) and verifies the CSCI-to-CSCI (and hardware configuration item) interfaces and high-level data flow

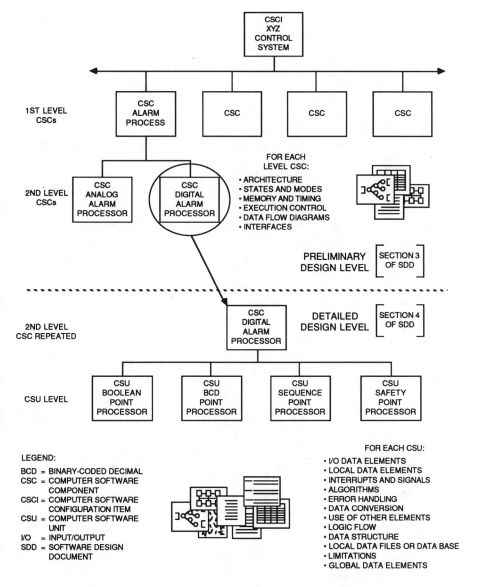

Figure 3-4   Simplified view of preliminary vs. detailed design.

among them. In either case, IV&V verifies all the requirements cross-referencing between the software requirements specification (SRS) and the software design document (SDD). If modeling and even simulation seems appropriate at this point, it is performed. The principal document that must be compared to the independently derived verification results is the SDD, but only Section 3 of that document at this time. The key is knowing where to stop the preliminary design verification process.

Many software authorities call this the "symbolic" semantic level. The details are missing but the structure and behavior of the CSCs can be characterized quite adequately. If rapid prototyping or simulation tools are used, they can provide an executable model of the software that will be fairly representative of the final version, at least in terms of its operational sequences and data flow. This information can be used to help balance the software processes across the available timing windows and hardware resources, especially when multiple or parallel processing is involved. This is as far as preliminary design verification should go.

Meanwhile, the development contractor is preparing for the preliminary design review (PDR) wherein all the artifacts (data flows, control flows, timing data, study results, benchmarks, I/O data, user interfaces, etc.) and documentation (especially Section 3 of the SDD) will be presented to the customer. In addition, the software test plan and preliminary interface design document (IDD) are both produced at this time and are subject to design verification. The development contractor hopes to prove that the design is mature and complete enough to move ahead to detailed design. The results derived from the IV&V team's independent analysis and verification have a lot to do with this decision.

For the moment, assume that the PDR went well and the development contractor begins the next subphase. Detailed design, as depicted in Figure 3-3, now goes to the "logical" semantic level, which is characterized by data files and records, indices, program logic (diagrams, pseudocode, program design language, etc.), algorithms ready for coding, etc. IV&V now drops down to the unit level with the developer. In the example, the digital alarm processor CSC is now "exploded" to show the detailed design for its four computer software units (CSUs). These are documented in Section 4 of the same SDD discussed above. It is very important that the customer specify in the development contract that IV&V is to receive incremental releases of this detailed design documentation. These releases should begin as soon as CSC module writeups (of individual subsections) found in Section 4 of the SDD are generated. Even though this information will be piecemeal, it allows IV&V to get started and can give the customer and developer early feedback on the adequacy of the design. As shown in Figure 3-3, the level of detail is much greater at the detailed design level than in the previous subphase. While the SDD is being generated, the development contractor produces the software test descriptions (STDs) and the IDD. Although the IDD can be verified along with the SDD, the test descriptions cannot. Chances are too that the test descriptions will not be made available much in advance of the critical design review (CDR), so there will not be much time to devote to them during this phase. To simplify the discussion, both the test plan and test descriptions will be discussed in Section 3.2.4 on validation.

Now that the reader has a basic understanding of design verification, it should be beneficial to summarize the process:

- Acquire necessary software analysis and CASE tools
- Perform verification using:
  Software analysis tools

Simulation or rapid prototyping

Copies of selected contractor tools

- Verify software design document (SDD)
- Verify interface design document (IDD)
- Verify software test plan (STP) during this time period
- Verify requirements tracing into the SDD from SRS
- Verify user interface needs (screens, menus, controls, templates . . .)
- Verify input and output data requirements at detailed level
- Verify selected algorithms, beginning with most critical first
- Perform design risk assessment
- Review timing, sizing, and memory allocations (especially for real-time systems)
- Review how well developer is following software development plan
- Participate in all reviews and meetings that affect the system
- Produce problem reports (PRs) as required.

Emphasis on the design phase and consequently on design verification has increased dramatically since structured design methodologies became popular. As late as the early 1970s, most of the attention was on (1) coding and (2) integration and testing. If you think about it for a moment, the reasons are obvious. A lot of coding began without any real design and the result was that it could not be integrated without Herculean efforts, so the distribution of resources was weighted strongly toward that end of the development cycle. Especially now that CASE tools are becoming commonplace, the idea of spending about half of the program resources before coding starts is probably about right. If automatic code generators are used, design can take an even greater share. IV&V has to be able to adjust to whatever distribution is deemed appropriate by the customer. More on this in Chapter 11.

3.2.3 Code Verification

Code verification is that activity that includes evaluation of the code itself, consistency and correctness between the code and the SDD, and how well the code follows the standards and practices set forth in the DOD/MIL-STDs and the software development plan. When the code itself is involved, it is examined for errors and inadequacies in such things as the specification portion, logic, sequencing, data structures, execution paths, mathematical correctness of algorithms, error handling, and interfaces. The code is also verified against the detailed design in the SDD so that inconsistencies between it and the implementation are caught and rectified quickly. Suggested changes to this document will go before the contractor's internal configuration control board (CCB) for consideration. Some form of inspection is appropriate to ensure that the agreed-to standards are being followed. As code reuse becomes more common, standards become even more important since the developer will never know where his or her code may end up. IV&V will probably find it most effective to pass the code through an automated tool to inspect it for possible standards violations. When static analyzers are used by IV&V, standards enforcement is usually a feature of such tools. Incidentally, these are language-specific tools. Static analyzers do much more than just standards enforcement, checking such things as logic errors, unreachable statements, symbol usage, uninitialized variables, structural integrity, syntax, and set/use statistics.

Because unit testing is considered by virtually all developers to be part of coding, IV&V will want to get a copy of each unit as soon as it passes the contractor unit test(s). This means a lot of code will be available piecemeal, but that does not matter. IV&V will process this code through the several verification steps mentioned and send the results back to the developer via the customer as quickly as possible, usually in a day or two, to minimize impact.

Remember that during this phase, IV&V does not "execute" the code; that is part of validation. The three primary motives in code verification are to catch a large portion of the construction errors before the code is passed from the programmer's environment to the test environment, ensure that good design and coding practices are being followed, and ensure that the software design is accurately represented in the code. The code verification phase can be summarized as follows:

- Verify consistency between the code and SDD
- Verify that approved standards and practices are being followed
- Verify logical structure and syntax
- Verify terms in data dictionary
- Verify input data (names, types, classes, formats, etc.)
- Verify output data (names, types, classes, formats, etc.)
- Verify that algorithms are complete and have correct scaling, notation, conversion, number system, error handling, etc.
- Verify versions of compiler, operating system, and utilities
- Review software library and release/version control for adequacy
- Participate in all reviews and meetings that affect the system
- Produce problem reports (PRs) as required.

In Chapter 2 in the discussions on coding, it was mentioned that top-down design and implementation could possibly cause the development effort to have multiple critical design reviews (CDRs). The only real consequence to IV&V if this is the case will be that the major program phases will be overlapped more than usual, with design and code verification as well as validation occurring simultaneously. It is even more common to find coding of parts of the system going on long after other parts have entered validation and they may even be designated as incremental releases (builds). The reason this is mentioned here is to alert the reader that IV&V does not necessarily have cleanly separated phases and generally follows development's lead, although it may lag a little behind.

3.2.4 Validation

Validation is that IV&V activity that ensures that every requirement is qualified in an appropriate manner through demonstration, analysis, or inspection. Further, validation ensures that every performance requirement is adequately tested, and that testing is not being performed needlessly. To accomplish this as efficiently as possible, software validation compares the CSCI level test results to the requirements found in its software requirements specification (SRS). System validation compares the higher level test results to the requirements found in the system specification. In short, validation helps to bound and fill in the total test program, assuring the customer and the ultimate users of the system that the software product is adequate and reliable. There are three basic and essential activities that take place more or less together during validation:

- *Monitoring Contractor's Testing.* Analyzing the actual tests performed by the contractor is a very cost-effective way to learn more about specific problems in the code as they occur, as well as how it performs in general. Often IV&V will repeat some of these tests to take a more detailed look at a specific area, function, or group of tasks or processes. Duplication of the exact test conditions is very important, else the results could be totally useless.
- *Independent IV&V Tests.* These enable concentration on the areas of known problems and weaknesses, alternatives, response to stress and loading, and otherwise provide a variety of data inputs and outputs, test conditions, scenarios, and system loading.
- *Independent Analysis.* This activity enables IV&V to identify and exhaustively test high-risk or highly sophisticated portions of the code (like complex algorithms or global aspects like system calibration or error control and propagation) using testbeds or high-fidelity simulations, as available.

As problems are uncovered during validation, IV&V must have the support of the customer to funnel reports back to the developer as rapidly as possible. Normally, IV&V will not concern itself with every test performed by the contractor, but rather will select the most meaningful tests from the overall plan and concentrate efforts upon these. This selection process designates these tests as "key-event tests" and are typically chosen by examining the integration plan and selecting the most important mid- and end-point tests as candidates. IV&V then examines its resources and makes the final selection based on the amount of test data expected from each one, conflicts with other tests, and how many people are required, and how long the test is expected to run. Remember that IV&V has a much smaller resource pool than the developer, so care must be taken to select the tests with the highest potential payoff. Also there is a planning guideline that recommends that IV&V divide the validation resources in half between monitoring development contractor tests and performing independent testing and analysis. This division can be changed depending on individual circumstances and availability of hardware to support independent testing and analysis.

Since the subject of testbeds and simulations has already been mentioned, it is important to realize that IV&V should be able to supply the necessary computer hardware, support software (operating system, compiler, utilities, etc.), and analysis and CASE tools to mimic what the development contractor is using. In so many words, this means that IV&V should be able to run the developer's code, stimulate it, and get the same results. When real-time systems are involved, IV&V may not be able to duplicate the run times, but must be able to interpret and handle the differences in clock time to derive meaningful information from the test. This may require instruction-level emulation of the target hardware. Other IV&V test configurations include limited hardware in the loop (HWIL), in which some, usually critical, pieces of the final target system are hooked up to operate in the testbed with the computer providing realistic stimuli and responses. The IV&V testbed is usually built around general-purpose computers or high-performance workstations and should be capable of supporting runtime instrumentation, compilers to match the developer's, analysis and CASE tools, data recording and reduction, simulation and, if necessary, limited HWIL devices. When the target system is being hosted on MIL-Spec hardware such as 1750A processors, IV&V may use a hardware test set especially designed for that architecture. The not-so-hidden message in all of this is that IV&V needs to have a broad spectrum of hardware and software tools, capabilities, and experienced personnel.

While on the subject of tools, one of the most effective tools that IV&V can use on most software projects is a dynamic analyzer. This family of tools is language-specific so they are built for Ada, Jovial, Fortran, C, COBOL, CMS-2, etc. The dynamic analyzer allows IV&V to take small manageable "chunks" of code and execute them on the tool independent of the target system. A chunk could be a single CSU, multiple CSUs, one or more CSCs, etc. perhaps up to a few thousand lines of code. The idea is to test groups of functionality independent of each other and debug them before they are integrated with other chunks. When this is done in concert with the static analyzer discussed in Section 3.2.3 on Code Verification, IV&V can catch 75–95% [8] of the errors that would otherwise be integrated into the system. These analyzers are well worth the investment and have proven to be some of IV&V's most effective validation tools.

Although the software test plan (STP) is produced during preliminary design and the software test description (STD) is produced during detailed design, their review and evaluation is more a validation activity than design activity. Verification of the actual test cases and procedures (scripts) can best be done by witnessing the test and determining if the information was accurate. Some degree of flexibility and tolerance is needed early in testing while the procedures are being scrubbed, but later during formal qualification testing (FQT), it is not acceptable for the development contractor to try to use flawed or red-lined test descriptions. IV&V should use the contractor's test documents as a basis or independent validation tests whenever possible.

The following are typical validation activities:

- Review and evaluate software test plan (STP) for each CSCI
- Select key-event tests for monitoring and data collection

- Validate mapping of software requirements specification (SRS) "testable" requirements into the STD to ensure complete test coverage
- Validate each software test description (STD) against an actual test
- Validate that each testable requirement was tested per STD
- Develop and run independent tests based on problem occurrences and also to gain added insight on software performance boundaries and limits, error handling and propagation, data loss, abnormal operation, etc.
- Run dynamic analysis tools on code to find defects and weaknesses
- Participate in the test readiness review (TRR) to confirm that code is ready for formal CSCI-level testing
- Perform interface evaluation (especially with hardware in the loop)
- Run simulations on critical algorithms and compare actual performance to simulation results
- Validate that SDD is ready to transition to software product specification at the end of testing and is included in the product baseline
- Validate user's and operator's manuals
- Track CCB actions/open item status
- Participate in reviews, audits, and meetings that affect the system
- Produce problem reports (PRs) as required.

The reader should once again be reminded of the definition of validation given in Chapter 1: *Validation is the process of executing the software to exercise the hardware and comparing the test results to the required performance.* By this time, the readers should have a much deeper understanding of the implications of this statement and especially of how many seemingly minor activities had to be performed leading up to this point. By verifying the specifications (and all that they include) and then the code, IV&V can say with very high confidence that validation can accomplish its goal as stated above.

3.3 A BRIEF GLIMPSE AT INDEPENDENT VERIFICATION AND VALIDATION FOR IN-HOUSE DEVELOPMENT

Because in-house software (and system) does not usually involve outside contractors unless they are hired to work with and supplement existing staff, the standards, practices, techniques, and documentation are largely left to the discretion of the lead technical personnel in the data-processing (DP) department (or its equivalent). Therefore, it is very difficult to characterize a "typical" in-house commercial development effort. The software products vary from almost totally unstructured and undocumented to those that resemble a MIL-STD effort. To illustrate the point, a friend of mine recently assumed managership of a large DP center for a commercial business. The story he tells is grim. All of the operational programs were undocumented and existed several places (mostly in desk drawers) on disk and tape without an adequate numbering or identification scheme. User documentation was largely notes and marked up listings. There was no configuration control and the directories and would-be software library were a mess. When programs failed, a lot of finger-pointing occurred and it was often because someone tried to use the wrong software version, invalid input data, or specified the options incorrectly. He found that management elsewhere in the company was very dissatisfied with the DP depart-ment, yet they were a significant contributor to the problem. For years they had pressured the DP organization to "have me a working program for so and so in a few weeks," so the programmers were forced to develop some stopgap code without documentation and struggle to get it debugged and working. This temporary code became the only artifact of the process and no one ever had time go back and "do it right." This happened over and over until the whole operation was threatened, DP personnel morale was terrible, and the situation affected the profitability of the company because of mistakes and delays.

Several years ago, I was on a team that evaluated a very large DP organization that developed all their software in house. Upon surveying the operation, we found as many as 16 separately purchased copies of the same software tool residing on the development system, no configuration or change control in place, and many thou-sands of stored tapes that were unlabeled and of unknown origin that were therefore useless. Most of the software was in assembly language and had many layers of uncontrolled patches.

The question in both cases is "Can you apply IV&V to the development process under these circumstances?" The answer is "yes," but is has some conditions attached. First, I would recommend an audit-level IV&V activity to go in, survey the conditions, and make recommendations on how to fix the major problems. What you would like to see happen is for the in-house developers to suddenly begin to follow the development process described in Section 2.1. Will it happen? Not without some continuous management pressure, training, and motivation aimed at improving the DP group's self-esteem and working conditions. Thus, the audit-level IV&V team needs to revitalize the organization by: (1) developing a life cycle model which describes what should be occurring, (2) recommending a suitable development methodology with the necessary software tools, (3) helping arrange for (and possibly perform some) training and orientation, (4) evaluating current hard-ware for possible upgrades, and (5) urging the company to begin a pilot develop-ment program that includes IV&V so that corrective feedback can occur to keep the new approach on track. Also during this time both organizations can collaborate on the writing of a software development plan similar to the one outlined in Section 2.1.1. This document should then become the definitive guide to all future develop-ment and sustaining software efforts and, therefore, should be examined peri-odically (semi-annually or yearly) to keep it current with the state of the practice and whatever changes occur in the DP organization, facilities, or equipment.

Once the pilot program gets underway, the IV&V should revert to a full, in-phase effort much like that described in Section 3.2, except that it will be of smaller scale and tailored to the commercial model specific to this particular customer. Because embracing new methods and tools always is done with reluctance from some of the old-line staff, IV&V should be prepared to contribute more to correct deficiencies than normal and should be more tolerant of personal attitudes. It is my firm belief that without IV&V to perform the "watchdog" role to keep the new approach on track, some of the software people would quickly revert to the old habits and need to be encouraged: "Try it the right way, you'll love it once you get the hang of it!"

Do not think that this is a general indictment, since most in-house operations do most of the development-oriented activities well enough to get by. What it does say is that software development practices vary all over the spectrum and that there is a sort of minimum acceptable level below which software cannot be developed or maintained efficiently or effectively. IV&V can make a significant contribution regardless of the software it supports, it is just a matter of knowing how to tailor the approach to optimize the results. If you are interested in a self-evaluation of your software development process, I encourage you to read and follow the method described in Chapter 15.

3.4 CHAPTER SUMMARY

- In terms of the DOD acquisition cycle, very few concept development (CD) programs have ever had IV&V. Occasionally, the agency has an organic IV&V organization that performs it in the CD phase.
- During demonstration and validation (Dem/Val), IV&V is more likely to occur but will probably be scaled down to a mini version where emphasis is on evaluation of the competing prototypes and not so much on the exact letter of the MIL-STDs.
- IV&V is very useful during Dem/Val, since by the end of this phase, the second baseline will have been established and the system will be ready to go directly into preliminary design as soon as the FSED contract is awarded. Thus, most of the requirements verification work can be done before FSED if an IV&V contract is in place.
- Traditionally, most IV&V efforts occur when programs are in full-scale engineering development. Then, the earlier the IV&V effort starts, generally the more cost-effective it is.
- IV&V for commercial contracted or in-house development can be extremely effective regardless of how well or poorly the developer is performing. The secret here is concentrating the IV&V resources where they have the most impact on the system being developed and on the development environment in place.
- Tailoring IV&V to program specifics is a highly individual judgment call and can be aided by studying lessons learned on past programs. This is a major reason for including the case studies at the end of this book.

3.5 WHAT COMES NEXT

Now that the reader has a fundamental knowledge of the activities and subprocesses of each IV&V phase, Part II goes inside each of these steps to explain how it is accomplished and especially how to select appropriate tools, techniques, processes, and procedures to maximize the benefits to the software project.

PART II

AN ANTHOLOGY OF INDEPENDENT VERIFICATION AND VALIDATION DISCIPLINES: THE DETAILED HOW-TO-DO-IT GUIDE

4

COMPUTER-AIDED SOFTWARE ENGINEERING TOOLS FOR SOFTWARE DEVELOPMENT AND INDEPENDENT VERIFICATION AND VALIDATION

It seems appropriate to discuss computer-aided software engineering (CASE) tools before getting into the phase-specific details, since many of the more comprehensive tools are used in more than one phase. Thus, the purpose of this chapter is to present an overview of the entire CASE subject and a survey of a number of the better-known CASE tools. The individual detailed IV&V chapters (5, 6, 7, and 8) will refer to this material as needed to aid in selecting and matching tools to particular applications.

4.1 EXPANDING THE DEFINITION OF COMPUTER-AIDED SOFTWARE ENGINEERING

In the late 1980s, CASE tools had progressed far enough that simply to call them by that identifier was not quite definitive enough, so several new terms were introduced in an attempt to classify them better than before. CASE tools used in systems analysis, requirements engineering, preliminary design, and program and configuration management are known as *upper-CASE tools;* whereas, those used for detailed process design, simulation, code development and testing are called *lower-CASE tools.* Then, if the CASE tools were worked into a shell or environment where they could run on a single platform and share a common database, user interface, etc., they became known as *integrated* or *I-CASE tools,* and are even sometimes called *computer-integrated software engineering (CISE) tools.* Groups of tools are also called *toolkits* especially when they cover more than one phase or do several functions. But things did not stop there; they went on to the development of frameworks and software engineering environments (SEEs) that typically do two things: First, the SEE has a basic set of CASE tools, which are tightly coupled (integrated into a common user interface and database) such that the user can navigate from one tool to another by menu selection or poking on icons or graphic objects. Second, the SEE enables its host platform to accept other tools from outside, which can be added either as tightly or loosely coupled adjuncts to the basic set of tools.

Imagine the flexibility? In fact, there may even be a risk from all this flexibility. What if Joe Programmer adds tools that Sally Koder does not have on her workstation? How does one configuration control the possible proliferation of tools? The possibilities for things to get out of control are nearly endless. The reader should be aware that I-CASE and especially large-scale SEEs bring with them renewed concern for the effective management and control of the development and engineering environments. IV&V now must evaluate the effectiveness and adequacy of the SEE and its tools before selecting its particular IV&V tools for each task area. As mentioned several times earlier, IV&V hopes to share as much of the developer's tool base as possible and then add only what is needed to "round out" the coverage. It should also be noted that the typical SEE is a very large software package that requires significant computer resources and user training. They are all very costly to procure, install and operate, so decisions that involve acquisition and use of a SEE will have far-reaching consequences on your organization.

4.2   HOW FAR AHEAD CAN WE *SEE?*

In DOD especially, there is a trend toward government-owned SEEs. Two of the most notable are the Software Life Cycle Support Environment (SLCSE), sponsored by the U.S. Air Force out of Rome (Air Development Center) Lab in New York, which is a full-blown SEE, and the Strategic Defense Development System (SDDS), sponsored by the U.S. Army Strategic Defense Command at Huntsville, Alabama, which is an evolving platform upon which upper- and lower-CASE tools can be hosted. Both of these are now or will be in the future government-furnished products and available free of charge for use on selected government contracts. They also are representative of the kinds of tools that are available in the marketplace. The Europeans have developed significant tools and environments, including the Integrated Project Support Environment (IPSE) by Imperial Software Technology. The Japanese are working on theirs. The DARPA STARS program and the Software Engineering Institute (SEI) at Carnegie-Mellon University have several initiatives aimed at advancing the utility and comprehensiveness of current tool technology. There is even a strong possibility that certain of the government-sponsored tool programs will allow and encourage commercialization; that is, allow contractors to invest in and co-own the tools. It is difficult to understand how the legal aspects of such an arrangement could possibly work; however, if they can be resolved, then it might help produce a de facto standard SEE and CASE tool library for every contractor who does government contracts. Proposals would no longer have to convince the government that one contractor's toolset was superior to the others; they would all be using the same set of engineering and development software. Sort of scary, is it not? Actually, that would be a great day!

Most of the large aerospace companies have either begun or are planning to build their own development environments around existing hardware, since many have a very large investment which simply cannot be discarded. This makes portable tools a very attractive and cost-effective solution.

Numerous software tool vendors have excellent toolkits that cover part of the life cycle, and new ones are in development that eventually hope to cover the entire development spectrum. The flip side of this situation is that virtually all major computer manufacturers are involved in tools to some extent, even if these are supplied by third-party vendors. The makers of high-performance workstations especially are all struggling to beat each other to the market with full life cycle I-CASE toolsets, which will pretty well qualify as complete software engineering environments except that they will only run on one kind of machine. Software tool vendors usually try to make their tools as portable as possible; whereas, hardware makers want to sell only their platforms and will not go out of their way to accommodate portable software. It is an interesting dilemma. As this book was being written that there is no single I-CASE product that does it all. That is something we have to look forward to in the decade of the 1990s; we are at the threshold of some very exciting things in the I-CASE arena. The first question is who will win the race, second is how much will it cost, and third is how fast will it be copied?

4.3 TOOL SELECTION

With the preliminaries out of the way, I want to remind the reader that I do not want to endorse one tool vendor over another; rather, what I will attempt to do is identify particular capabilities needed for given IV&V applications. Then, if a tools happens to provide those features, it will be named as a candidate. Other tool brands, including those that I have not named or included in my survey, can be freely interchanged with those mentioned as long as you match the capabilities. There are now hundreds (perhaps thousands) of good, useful tools in the marketplace and I could not possibly include them all, so I chose those that appear to offer the most features and coverage or that provide a unique capability. Please do not feel slighted if I forgot your favorite tool.

Since IV&V rides piggyback on the development effort, the first part of the survey deals with tools for software development and then matches these with IV&V needs. In some situations, IV&V can use a copy of the development tool or perhaps just the output. If that is not sufficient, IV&V will supplement the developer's tool with a carefully made choice for independent analysis. These are difficult decisions and depend a great deal on ongoing assessments of how well the developer is doing and how comprehensively he is using the tools that were initially chosen. For example, if the developer uses the Distributed Computing Design System (DCDS) tool (refer to Section 4.5) with its formal requirements and design languages, it is very likely that IV&V will share this tool. It is free, it is comprehensive, it is locks the developer into predefined methods and procedures, and it even produces DOD-STD documentation. IV&V, in cases like this, verifies how well the developer uses the tool and follows the methodologies and then invests in another verification technique like expanded simulation and alternate expressions of concurrency and tasking, wherein the basic assumptions that feed the developer's tool can be challenged. IV&V must always develop a strategy that capitalizes on both the strengths and weaknesses of the developer's approach; otherwise, there can be a lot of wasted effort and very little knowledge gained.

4.4   THE TOOL CONTINUUM

There is a software tool continuum that runs from editors, utilities, debuggers, pretty printers, spreadsheets, etc. at the low end to the full life cycle I-CASE tools, hardware testbeds, SEEs, test environments, etc. at the high end. The low-end tools can cost as little as $50 and the high-end $25 million or more. The latter is the estimated development cost of a large scale SEE, so copies would be a lot less, but far from cheap, especially when you factor in the hardware and other licenses required. This wide cost range makes the task of selecting tools very difficult. It also makes the idea of government-furnished and public domain tools very appealing. But then you must make the tradeoffs between cost and user efficiency and proficiency. Sometimes it may turn out to be cheaper in the long run to buy the tools, training, and hardware you need. Figures I have heard through unofficial channels range up to $25,000 per person per year for each developer's workstation (used in the generic sense) hardware and software. Software developers face these kinds of decisions daily. Fortunately, this book does not have to make those kinds of basic choices; rather, it gives advice on IV&V tool selection after the developer's choice is made. Remember that IV&V attempts to use whatever tools it can from the developer, looks for alternatives that provide different perspectives, and attempts to fill any voids that exist.

4.5   TOOL SURVEYS

Tables 4-1 and 4-2 contain the survey of 50 CASE tools that fall into two major categories, those that are used on real-time mission-critical computer resources (MCCR) and non-real-time management information and business systems. The first noticeable distinction between the two is that virtually all of the real-time paradigms include control flow in some form, whereas the MIS type generally do not; and second, real-time tools target on Ada, C, Fortran, LISP, and Pascal, whereas MIS targets COBOL, SQL and other fourth-generation languages (4GLs). Real time worries a great deal about processor load balancing and utilization, timing, tasking, scheduling, priorities, and deadlines, while MIS concerns focus on database efficiency, schema, queries, data integrity, recovery, etc. Therefore, it seems appropriate to divide the tools into these two broad categories. Incidentally, the real-time tools will work for MIS problems a lot better than vice versa. Early examples of CASE tools that used data flow diagrams without control flow or logic sequence notation did not work very well on real-time problems, although they did very well for MIS software design.

In this survey, I have attempted to classify the scope of each tool and the development phases that it covers. Then I wanted to know several important features of each tools, its paradigm, whether it has a formal language, if it supports prototyping, simulation, reverse engineering, automated code generation, etc. I was a little surprised to find that so many tools concentrate only on design and coding. This tells me something very interesting, that requirements and testing are still being ignored by a lot of tool vendors. In fact, most tools that do rapid prototyping begin by defining bubbles and arcs, assign behavior to the bubbles, and try very hard to ignore the textual aspects (i.e., the specification of the problem for which a solution is being attempted). The theory of these tools must be that if you exercise the prototype enough you can figure out all the things that are missing. Life in the software fast lane just does not work that way.

I also surveyed a few of the major computer hardware makers who are in the process of supplying their own I-CASE tools, as recorded in Table 4-3. Several of those listed have supported third-party tools for a number of years, but I am most interested in those that the vendors have packaged to sell as their own products even if they use the support of a software house to provide this capability. One observation I find true in most cases is that tightly bound tools tend to be more efficient than the more portable universal tools, simply because they take more advantage of hardware features. This is one good reason to pick a hardware platform and use it exclusively. There are times, however, when you will not have that luxury, as is the case when the customer dictates the hardware and perhaps even the development environment. These are things you must consider when thinking about acquiring software tools for development or IV&V. CASE tools represent a very large investment and can greatly affect your corporate culture. Thoroughly evaluate your needs and type of software involved before rushing out to acquire the latest and greatest I-CASE toolset. If you are naive in the tool area, perhaps you should bring in a consultant to help you decide which tools are best suited to your company's products and development practices. The other approach is to invite several vendors to brief and demonstrate their products and perform an evaluation of the type suggested in Section 11.2.1 of this book. Chapters 5 through 8 will refer to a few candidate tools by name or type to satisfy the needs of that phase. The survey material in this chapter should help identify alternative tools with similar capabilities.

TABLE 4-1. CASE Tool Survey for Real-Time Software

Tool Name (These Names Are All Registered TM & Copyrighted)	Type				Phases Covered					Principal Paradigm
	UC	LC	I-CASE	SEE	R	PD	DD	C	I&T	
AdaQuest & Other Automated Test Systems By GRC		√	√					√	√	
Ada-Z by TASC		√				√	√	√		
AISLE and ADADL Family of Tools by Software Systems Design Inc.	•	√	√		•	√	√	√	√	Booch/Buhr
Atherton Backplane	√	√	√	√	√	√	√	√	√	Various, Open Architecture
AutoCode By Integrated Systems		√				√	√	√	√	
Byron By Intemetrics		√				√	√	•		
CADRE Teamwork	√	√	√		√	√	√	√	•	Yourdon-Demarco & Others
CARDtools		√	√			√	√	√	•	Yourdon-Demarco, Ward-Mellor
Cradle By Yourdon	•	√	√		•	√	√	√	•	Yourdon
Distributed Computing Design System (DCDS)	√	√	√		√	√	√	√	•	Loosely Based on Michael Jackson
EPOS By Software Products & Services	•	√	√		•	√	√	√	•	Yourdon-Demarco & Hatley-Pirbhai
Excelerator/RTS By Index Technology		√	√		•	√	√	√	•	Chen, Y-D, G-S, Hatley, W-M, etc.
ISTAR	√	√	√	√	√	√	√	√	√	Various

TABLE 4.1. (*Continued*)

Formal Spec. Lang.	Primary Diagrams	Proto-typing	Simu-lation	Code Gen.	Test Supt.	DOD-STD Doc. Gen.	PDL	Remarks	Good Stand-Alone IV&V Tool
					√			Ada, FORTRAN, COBOL, JOVIAL	√
	Structure Charts	√		Ada			√	Compatible With VAXSET	√
	DFD	√		•	√	√	Ada	Includes OOD	√
	Various	•	•	•	•		•	Partial Implementation	√
Graphic	Block Diagrams	√	√	Ada & FORTRAN	√	•	√		
				•	•	√	Ada	Coding & Testing Tool	√
Graphic	D&CFD	√	√	Ada	√	√	Ada	Modular Tools	√
Graphic	D&CFD	√			√	√	√	Ada & C	√
Graphic	D&CFD	√		•	√	•	√	Ada, C, & Pascal	√
SSL, RSL, DDL, MDL, TSL	F_NETS R_NETS	√	√	Ada	•	√	Ada	Primarily Specification and Design Tool	
√	D&CFD	√		Ada, Pascal, FORTRAN, COBOL, PL1	•	•	√		√
	D&CFD	√			•	•	√	Basic, C, COBOL, PL1	•
PSL/ PSA		•	•	•	•		•	Partial Implementation	

(continued)

TABLE 4-1. CASE Tool Survey for Real-Time Software

Tool Name (These Names Are All Registered TM & Copyrighted)	Type				Phases Covered					Principal Paradigm
	UC	LC	I-CASE	SEE	R	PD	DD	C	I&T	
McCabe Instrumentation Tool, McCabe Assoc.		✓				✓	✓	✓		
PAMS by Myrias Computer Corporation		✓				•	✓	✓		
Power Tools by Iconix	•	✓	✓		•	✓	✓	✓	•	Yourdon-Demarco Ward-Mellor and Hatley
Prokit by McDonnell Douglas		✓	✓		✓	✓	✓	✓	✓	Various
ProMod	✓	✓	✓		✓	✓	✓	✓	✓	Yourdon-Demarco Hatley-Pirbhai
Refine by Reasoning Systems	✓	✓	✓	✓	✓	✓	✓	✓	✓	Knowledge-Based
Requirements Driven Development (RDD) by Ascent Logic	✓		•		✓	✓	•			RDD-Unique
Software Life Cycle Support Environment (SLCSE)	✓	✓	✓	✓	✓	✓	✓	✓	✓	Open Architecture
Software Through Pictures by IDE	✓	✓	✓		•	✓	✓	✓	•	All popular paradigms
Statemate by i-Logix		✓				✓	✓	✓		Statemate-unique
Strategic Defense Development System (SDDS)		✓	✓	✓		✓	✓	✓	✓	Loosely Based on Hatley-Pirbhai
Technology for the Automated Generation of Systems (TAGS) by Teledyne Brown Eng.	•	✓	✓	✓	•	✓	✓	✓	•	TAGS-unique

√ Comprehensive; bullet (•) Partial; DFD = Data flow diagram; D&CFD = Data and control flow diagrams; Y-D = Yourdon-Damarco; G-S = Gane-Sarson; W-M = Ward-Mellor; UC, upperCASE; LC, lower CASE; I-CASE, integrated computer-aided software engineering; SEE, software engineering environment; R, requirements; PD, preliminary design; DD, detailed design; C, coding; IORL, input/output requirements language; I&T, integration

TABLE 4.1. (*Continued*)

Formal Spec. Lang.	Primary Diagrams	Proto-typing	Simu-lation	Code Gen.	Test Supt.	DOD-STD Doc. Gen.	PDL	Remarks	Good Stand-Alone IV&V Tool
					✓			Focuses on Code and Testing	✓
		✓		FORTRAN & C	•			Parallel Processing Tool	✓
	D&CFD, Buhr	✓			•		PDL	Includes SOOD	✓
	D&CFD	✓	✓	•	✓	•	✓		✓
	D&CFD	✓		Ada, C & Pascal	✓	•	✓		✓
✓	D&CFD	✓	✓	LISP & Ada	✓	•	✓		
SSL	D&CFD	✓	•				•	Based on DCDS	
	D&CFD	✓	•	•	✓	✓	•	Partial Implementation	
Graphic	D&CFD	✓	•	Ada, C, Pascal, FORTRAN	•	✓	✓		✓
Graphic	State Charts	✓	✓	✓	•	•	✓		✓
Graphic & SDDL	D&CFD	✓	•	Ada	•	✓	✓	Partial Implementation	
ORL	D&CFD	✓	✓	Ada/ VHDL	•	✓	Ada/ VHDL		

and testing; CODE GEN., Code generator; DOD-STD. DOC GEN., document generation; PDL, program design language; SDDL, specification design definition language; SSL, system specification language; RSL, requirements specification language; DDL, distributed design language; MDL, Module development language; TSL; Test support language; SOOD, Structured object-oriented design; VHDL, Very high density (design) language

TABLE 4-2. CASE Tool Survey for Non-Real-Time Software

Tool Name (These Names Are All Registered TM & Copyrighted)	Type				Phases Covered					Principal Paradigm
	UC	LC	I-CASE	SEE	R	PD	DD	C	I&T	
ANATOOL by Advanced Logical Software	•	✓				✓	✓	✓		Yourdon-Damarco
APS by SAGE Software		✓	✓			✓	✓	✓	•	Customized
Auto-mate Plus by Learmonth & Burchett Management Systems	•	✓	✓		•	✓	✓	✓	•	LBMS
CASE* Designer by Oracle	✓	✓	✓		✓	✓	✓	✓	•	Independent
Chen CASE Tools	•	✓	✓		•	✓	✓	✓	•	Chen, Martin
COBOL Generator by Digital Equipment	•	✓	✓		•	✓	✓	✓	✓	Yourdon-Demarco
CorVision by CORTEX	•	✓	✓		•	✓	✓	✓	✓	Various
DesignAid by NASTEC		✓	✓			✓	✓	✓	•	Yourdon-Orr, W-M Chen, G-S
Designer by Visual Software		✓				✓	✓	✓		Independent
EMPRESS Toolset	✓	✓	✓		✓	✓	✓	✓	✓	Independent
Excelerator by Index Technology	•	✓	✓		•	✓	✓	✓	•	Bachman, Chen Y-D, G-S, Jackson, Merise
Foresight by Athena Systems		✓	✓			✓	✓	✓	•	Hatley—Pirbhai Ward-Mellor
FOUNDATION by Arthur Anderson	✓	✓	✓		✓	✓	✓	✓	✓	Proprietary
Information Engineering Workbench by Knowledgeware	✓	✓	✓		✓	✓	✓	✓	•	James Martin
INGRES Toolset	✓	✓	✓		✓	✓	✓	✓	✓	Independent

Formal Spec. Lang.	Primary Diagrams	Proto-typing	Code Gen.	Test Supt.	Auto-Doc. Gen.	SQL	Remarks	Good Stand-Alone IV&V Tool
	DFD	√		•				√
	Screens	√	•	√	•		COBOL	√
	DFD	√	•	√	√		COBOL	√
L, SQL, percard, percard	Screens	√	√	√	√	√	Comprehensive DBMS Toolset	
	Various	√	√	√	•		PC-based	√
	DFD	√	√	√	√		COBOL	√
	DFD	√	√	√	√		VAX-based	√
	DFD	√		•	•		Can be used in Realtime Applications	√
	DFD	√		•	•		PC-based	√
L & L	Screens	√	√	√	√	√	Comprehensive DBMS toolset	
	DFD & Others	√	•	√	•		Basic, C, COBOL, PL1 (Also available in Realtime version)	√
	D&CFD	√	•	√	•		SUN-based; can be used in Real-time Applications	√
	DFD	√	•	√	•		COBOL	
	Various	√	COBOL	√	√		Very Large 3rd Party Interfaces	√
L & L	Screens	√	√	√	√	√	Comprehensive DBMS Toolset	

(*continued*)

TABLE 4-2. CASE Tool Survey for Non-Real-Time Software

Tool Name (These Names Are All Registered TM & Copyrighted)	Type				Phases Covered					Principal Paradigm
	UC	LC	I-CASE	SEE	R	PD	DD	C	I&T	
Jackson System Development (JSD)	✓	✓	✓		✓	✓	✓	✓	•	Michael Jackson
Life Cycle Productivity Systems (LPS) by American Management Systems		✓	✓			✓	✓	✓	•	Yourdon-Demarco, Jackson, etc.
Maestro by Softlab	•	✓	✓		•	✓	✓	✓	•	Customized
META Systems	✓	✓				✓	✓			Yourdon-Demarco
MULTI/CAM by AGS Management Systems, Inc		✓					✓	✓		Yourdon-Demarco
PACBASE by CGI Systems		✓	✓			✓	✓	✓	✓	Merise & Yourdon
Recoder by Language Technology	•	✓	✓		•	✓	✓	✓	•	Yourdon-Demarco
SYBASE SQL Server & Toolset	✓	✓	✓		✓	✓	✓	✓	✓	Independent
SYLVA Tools by CADWARE	✓	✓	✓		✓	✓	✓	✓	✓	Constantine, Demarco, Gane-Sarson, Ward-Mellor
THE DEVELOPER by ASYST Technologies	✓	✓			✓	✓	✓	✓		Yourdon-Demarco

√ comprehensive; bullet (•) partial; DBMS = database management system; DFD = data flow diagram; D&CFD = data and control flow diagrams; Y-D = Yourdon-Demarco; G-S = Gane-Sarson; W-M = Ward-Mellor; CODE GEN., code generator; AUTO. DOC. GEN., automated document generation; SQL, standard query

TABLE 4-2. (*Continued*)

Formal Spec. Lang.	Primary Diagrams	Proto-typing	Code Gen.	Test Supt.	Auto-Doc. Gen.	SQL	Remarks	Good Stand-Alone IV&V Tool
	Jackson Diagrams	√	COBOL	√	√		OOD; targets several HOLs	√
	DFDs & Others	√	•	√	•		COBOL	
	Various	√	•	√	•		C, COBOL, FORTRAN and PL1	√
PSL/ PSA	DFD	√		•			Also Has Reverse Engineering Tools	√
	DFD	√		•				
	DFD	√	•	√	√		COBOL	√
	DFD	√	•	√	•		COBOL	√
4GL & SQL	Screens	√	√	√		√	Comprehensive DBMS Toolset	
	DFD & Others	√	•	√	√		C and COBOL	√
	DFD	√		•			Features Import/ Export Features	√

language; 4GL, Fourth-generation language; PSL/PSA problem statement language/problem statement analyzer; OOD, object-oriented design; HOL, higher-order language.

101

TABLE 4-3. Examples of Hardware Vendor Integrated Computer-Aided Software Engineering (I-CASE) Tools

Vendor	Principal CASE Product	Methodologies	Type	Life Cycle Phases[a]						Sources
				R	PD	DD	C	I&T	O&M	
Alliant	3rd Party Suppliers		Software Engineering							3rd party CASE tools
Concurrent Computer Corp.	CASEE Tools	Yourdon-Demarco, etc.	Software Engineering	✓	✓	✓	✓	•	✓	CASEE plus 3rd party CASE tools
Digital Equipment Corp.	VAXset, CDD/Plus, Etc.	All popular paradigms	Information & Software Engineering	•	✓	✓	✓	✓	✓	DEC tools plus very large assortment of 3rd party CASE tools
Hewlett-Packard Co.	SoftBench		Software Engineering			•	✓			SoftBench plus large number of 3rd party CASE tools
Macintosh	Apple ETO	All popular paradigms	Information & Software Engineering		•	✓	✓	•		Apple ETO plus very large assortment of 3rd party CASE tools
Silicon Graphics	CASEVision		Software Engineering			•	✓	✓	•	CASEVision plus many 3rd party CASE tools
Sun Microsystems	3rd Party Suppliers		Information & Software Engineering							Very large assortment of 3rd party CASE tools
Tektronix	TekCASE		Information & Software Engineering		•	✓	✓	✓	✓	Interfaces with DEC VAXset; good number of 3rd party CASE tools
Texas Instruments Inc.	Information Engineering Facility (IEF)	James Martin	Information Engineering	•	✓	✓	✓	✓	✓	IEF plus 3rd party CASE tools

[a] All phases can be covered by appropriate selection of 3rd party CASE tools; however, efficiency is often better when tools are integrated to run on a particular

4.6 HOW DEVELOPMENT TOOLS INTERACT WITH INDEPENDENT VERIFICATION AND VALIDATION TOOLS

Figure 4-1 shows the interaction between the developer and IV&V regarding software tools. In this example, I have chosen a typical lower-CASE toolset for the developer, which concentrates heavily on design. The letter "P" denotes the developer as the primary user of this toolset and the letter "S" identifies IV&V as the secondary user. IV&V has two choices at this point: Obtain a copy of the developer's tool and request input and output data, which is the preferred approach, or simply request output from the tools for analysis. In the first case, IV&V can perform in a much more independent manner and at greater technical depth than in the second case. If the CASE tool is not available to IV&V, then it is likely that IV&V will introduce another tool for verification that offers a slightly different perspective than the developer's tool. In the Figure 4-1 example, the customer or developing agency should serve as the information funnel between the two parties. Notice also that IV&V introduces a requirements engineering tool and sends results back to the developer. Then, once coding gets underway, IV&V introduces addi-

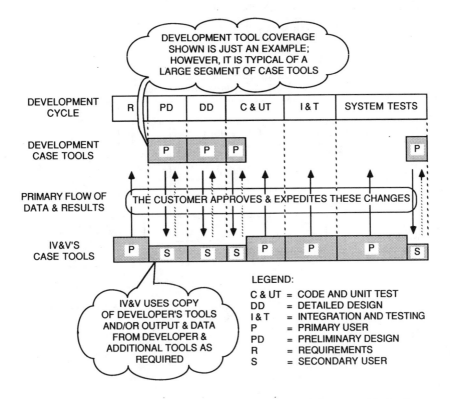

Figure 4-1 How independent verification and validation tools interact with development tools.

tional tools where the developer has none and, therefore, is the primary user. As a general rule, phases covered by the developer's tools provide a corresponding reduction in IV&V tool requirements. The tools survey can be used to identify the general characteristics of the developer's CASE tools and to help select IV&V tools that cover the gaps and that offer different analysis perspectives. Figure 4-2 shows an example with actual CASE tools by name to further clarify the interaction between IV&V and development. I chose the DCDS I-CASE tool for the developer. This is a very comprehensive tool with five formal languages, simulation capabilities, automated production of DOD-STD-2167A documentation, etc. In this situation, IV&V can acquire copies of DCDS without difficulty and would do so. Thus, IV&V will share output and results with the developer and perform independent investigations and analysis as deemed necessary. In the precode period, IV&V will concentrate on completeness and internal consistency of the specifications,

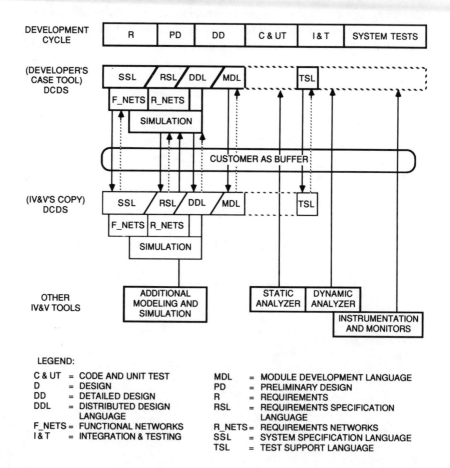

Figure 4-2 An example of applying actual computer-aided software engineering (CASE) tools.

algorithm analysis, designs for error handling, load balancing, task scheduling, data and control flow, etc. In addition to the DCDS simulation, IV&V may find it necessary to do independent modeling and simulation of high-risk parts of the software, especially complex algorithms. It may also be necessary to introduce other minor tools for specific analysis tasks.

Once code is available, IV&V would like to be in a position to pass all software through a static analyzer for standards enforcement, structure checking, and extended syntax checking. This process gives the developer quick turnaround and comprehensive reports on the "goodness" of the code. This step is considered part of code verification because it applies to unit testing. In the next phase, IV&V recommends a dynamic analysis tool, which can execute the code for path analysis, run-time behavior, assertion checking, etc. These two tools used correctly can detect 75–95% of the construction faults in a typical software program. This frees the developer to concentrate on the more difficult problems. During integration and testing, IV&V will also examine error propagation, performance boundaries, and the effects of test cases that stress the system to determine how gracefully it handles these situations. In some test configurations, instrumentation and monitors will have to be provided to collect the necessary information. On some types of systems, IV&V will perform hardware proofing to confirm all physical resources and interfaces as well as temporal mapping of the software to the hardware.

This example should promote a better understanding of how the CASE tool matching process occurs between IV&V and development. Additional CASE tool examples for each phase will be given in their individual sections, which follow.

4.7 CHAPTER SUMMARY

- CASE tools have become so diversified and multifaceted that it is necessary to identify those as upper-CASE that deal with requirements, preliminary design, and programmatic issues and as lower-CASE those that deal with detailed design, code and test.
- When CASE tools are combined so that they can share data, user interfaces, and common features, they are called *integrated-CASE* or *I-CASE* for short.
- When a framework or shell is developed to further integrate CASE tools and other user and management software, this is called a *software engineering environment* (*SEE*) or some similar acronym, like software support environment (SSE). This book prefers to use the term SEE.
- International standards for CASE tools and SEEs are making tools more portable and easier to integrate into other environments.
- CASE tools can be broken down into two main classes—those for real-time software development and those for non-real-time software.
- The software tool costs run from less than $100 for simple and popular ones to well into the millions of dollars for elaborate SEEs for large development organizations.

- Many computer hardware vendors are developing their own SEEs to better integrate the basic tools to gain efficiency and trustworthiness and to reduce cost.
- Most CASE tools work equally well for development and IV&V. The two users often have different motives for using the tool and hence can derive different information and perspectives from the same tool.
- Software tools are a very cost-effective way of performing IV&V.

4.8   WHAT COMES NEXT

The next four chapters discuss the details of each IV&V phase. Chapter 5 begins with conceptualization of the system and moves through the formal process of requirements generation and verification detailing each step in a "how to do it" presentation.

5
REQUIREMENTS
VERIFICATION

Requirements verification is a two-part process which, at completion, ensures that the software is ready to proceed into design with a high degree of confidence. The first part centers around the adequacy of the system specification and the second part similarly addresses the software requirements specifications and sometimes the hardware requirements found in prime- and critical-item specifications. This book focuses on software and therefore does little more than acknowledge the hardware when necessary to promote understanding and to completely describe a concept.

In addition to the specifications mentioned, there are other documents that have very strong relationships with them that have to be verified to complete the process. These are the interface requirements specification (IRS) and the system/segment design document (SSDD), which in a sense is also an interface document as well, and, lest we ignore it, the software development plan (SDP), which orchestrates much of the support activity and facilities—development practices and standards, quality assurance, configuration management, computer hardware, support environment, support software, etc. The relationship among the key documents in this phase is shown in Figure 5-1. IV&V tries diligently to make sure that all these factors and processes are in sync and harmony.

5.1 ACQUIRING THE NECESSARY SOFTWARE ANALYSIS AND COMPUTER-AIDED SOFTWARE ENGINEERING TOOLS

There is a definite shortage of good, comprehensive requirement engineering tools, and some that are supposed to be are really no more than specification analysis tools, which assume that the requirements already exist and are written down someplace else. Fortunately, however, there are enough good ones that IV&V can always find one to complement the developer's tool; or IV&V may chose to get a

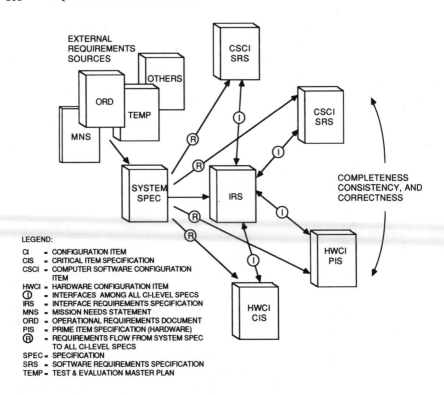

Figure 5-1 Key relationship among first two levels of specifications.

copy of the latter, which is only viable when the developer has invested great amounts of effort in preparing input data for the tool, as with the government-sponsored Distributed Computing Design System (DCDS) and the Requirements Driven Development (RDD) by Ascent Logic, both of which use formal system specification languages. Once the initial investment has been made, the tools perform consistency and completeness checking, establish valid interfaces and relationships, and offer graphical representations of the resulting networks. When used correctly, both these tools specify requirements very thoroughly, making verification focus on the sources and how accurately the input data was prepared.

Cadre Teamwork, Design Aid by Nastec, the Jackson System Development, and the Information Engineering Workbench by Knowledgeware all use a combination of text and graphics to perform the systems analysis and engineering that leads to the identification and definition of the requirements. Cadre Teamwork offers computer-aided production of DOD-STD-2167A specifications.

Once the development tool has been selected, IV&V should do a profile of its capabilities to determine if it is comprehensive enough for IV&V use as well, or if another tool needs to be acquired and used for IV&V. If the developer is using one of the tools just mentioned, it is probably quite acceptable for IV&V to obtain its own copy of that tool and use as much developer-supplied data as possible. On the other hand, if one of the less-comprehensive tools, or perhaps no tool at all is specified for this phase, then IV&V should select one with good rapid prototyping and graphic capabilities (like R-Trace, ProMod, or SA from Cadre Teamwork) but should not try to do the developer's job, which in so many words says: Do not select a big language-driven tool like DCDS as a stand-alone IV&V tool. These are primarily development tools and not IV&V tools, and they require far too many resources for the average IV&V contract. That is why I strongly recommend that IV&V share them with the developer, but definitely not try to go it alone. The IV&V tool selection process depends heavily on what is available, budget constraints, the type of system being built, and the developer's tools. Try not to overkill the tool issue, especially in this phase. What is essential is a tool that can provide:

- A requirements database that can be linked to successor specifications by explicit references. About the most elaborate you ever need to get here is perhaps a dBASE database or a multipurpose package like Reflex or Enable.
- The ability to associate functional properties to physical architecture, both for software and hardware
- The ability to associate behavioral and performance requirements with design statements and tests
- A measure of completeness of the resulting specifications produced in this phase.

Regardless of the tools selected, there is still a lot of good old-fashioned engineering analysis and human judgment in requirements verification. Tools help the analyst work more efficiently and in a more structured way, but tools do not think (yet!) so caveat emptor when it comes to selecting and acquiring tools.

5.2 USING SOFTWARE TOOLS

I have used DCDS as an example because it represents a complex and comprehensive approach to requirements specification and analysis. It is well suited for large and very large systems (1 to 10 million lines of code) but not very cost-effective on small systems, although it will work just fine. As mentioned in the previous paragraph, however, it assumes that the developer is the primary user and that IV&V acquires the necessary copies of the tool in order to operate efficiently. IV&V needs to be on the receiving end of the System Specification Language (SSL) database prepared using the System Requirements Engineering Methodology (SYSREM). The syntax, schema, and form of SSL lends itself nicely to object-oriented design concepts. From that point onward, IV&V can produce F_Nets, evaluate the organization and allocation of functions, assess the stimuli-response chains, examine the relationships and interfaces, and generally do a very thorough job of verifying the requirements and exploring alternatives. The system specification is produced automatically from the database and consistency, completeness, and correctness checking is likewise automated. Thus, IV&V is simplified when this tool is used. The IV&V analysts are able to concentrate on tuning and proofing the requirements, not on their initial definition and allocation. Theoretically, this should result in a much better system specification than we usually see.

The simulation capabilities of DCDS allow the user to execute the model that results from the SSL database. In this way, connectivity, completeness, organization, and rough order of execution of the system can be evaluated and changed to provide a more optimum configuration. It is an excellent practice to attempt to balance the intelligence of the system across as much of the functionality as possible. This is especially beneficial if the software is to be divided up onto multiple or parallel processors. It helps to balance the development effort and the processing load. The level of simulation provided by the DCDS tool is not intended to evaluate detailed software designs and will have to be supplemented by other forms of modeling and simulation to evaluate complex algorithms and system performance.

When it is time to verify the software requirements specification (SRS), IV&V uses the Requirements Specification Language (RSL) database prepared using the Software Requirements Engineering Methodology (SREM). SREM is the oldest part of DCDS and defines input, process, and output chains and produces diagrams called R_Nets, which are roughly equivalent to functional flow diagrams with control notation. They provide a good, usable graphical description of the software. This part of the tool produces an automated version of the SRS. Again, consistency and completeness checking is supported by automated functions. As was the case with the system specification, IV&V still has a significant effort in verifying the interfaces, input data, process definitions, output data, behavioral considerations, and physical constraints (sizing, memory, etc.). Specifications prepared using SREM tend to be more complete and consistent and of generally higher quality than those prepared without the use of a formal language. These methodologies come with a relatively high investment in support systems, training, and user effort. This is why DCDS is generally suited to large software development, where the initial costs are absorbed by easier response to changes, better quality computer-aided documentation, and a much more robust set of requirements.

5.3 ANATOMY OF A REQUIREMENT

Before a requirement specification can be verified, you have to know something about how to recognize, classify, and dissect (parse) requirements. In fact, you really need to know how to generate requirements from scratch so that you can bring that level of understanding to bear on the analysis process. In its simplest form, the process can begin by writing down the operational goals of the system you want to build, what its inputs and outputs will be, how it should process and transform the input, how often and in what form the outputs are needed, etc. As you continue to describe the characteristic and attributes you want the system to have, they begin to accumulate in categories—physical properties, functions, displays, controls, forms, features, external interfaces that may require cooperation with other systems, internal interfaces that link all the pieces together, and the list goes on and on. In object-oriented design, the pieces are called *objects,* which are in turn categorized into *classes.* Object-oriented happens to be an excellent way of defining systems because it allows multiple levels of abstraction, which are intuitively easy to understand. Objects can be any size and get real-world names, not some contrived nomenclature. DOD-STD-2167A [24] and others provide an outline and format for the specifications that define the categories (or classes) of requirements by their primary characteristics, helping to ensure that the resulting specification covers all the necessary topics. The next act is to attempt to make the specification complete and correct. To do this, you have to parse the sentence.

The following advice can be used both when developing and evaluating requirements. The object of this activity is to evolve a set of unambiguous and internally consistent requirements.

1. Read the specification looking for noun phrases. Each of these is evaluated to determine if it infers one of the following:

- Physical property or attribute
- Functional characteristic
- Performance or behavior
- Process
- Structure
- Interface or interaction
- Input or output
- Support function
- Feature.

If so, the phrase is likely a requirement; if not, it can be disregarded or at least ignored for the time being. The seemingly useless phrases sometimes clarify or elaborate on a genuine requirement, so do not be too hasty to cast them out without a revisit or two.

2. When the noun phrases (in paragraph 1 above) identify physical or processing entities, these become *objects* or *process nodes* and appear in the overall architecture. Actions stated by the verbs—"generates, produces, triggers, drives, converts, processes"—infer *behavior.* So you can now identify the two primitives necessary to define systems—nodes (objects) and behavior. Data then flows through the nodes, becomes transformed by the behavior of the node, and repeats the process until it eventually becomes an output.

3. Sometimes requirements are loaded with ambiguity, which has to be repaired before proceeding. Typical problems include:

- Different words for the same thing
- The same words for different things

- Excessive use of adjectives without specific meaning such as "large, many, several, rapid, slow," etc.
- Lack of quantifiers when needed
- Implied or masked subjects
- Non sequiturs
- Indefinite or nonspecific interfaces
- Jargon

4. There is a test that the analyst can often use to help define architectural entities (objects) whenever a process is defined: Is it the name of a function, feature, physical thing, or task (like those shown in Figure 3-4, for example) that is required for the system to operate correctly? Such objects very often become processing nodes and invariably have behavior associated with them. This kind of requirement directly imposes design with little or no translation required. It may require amplification or elaboration, but the requirement node is the same as the design node. Systems evolve very gracefully and with little difficulty if this convention is practiced.

5. Another way to examine requirements that aids in determining if a test should be associated with them is to divide them into two domains as follows:

- Form. These requirements include: interfaces, both internal and external; prerequisite states and conditions; design constraints imposed by hardware, environment, phenomena, technology, and physical properties that the system must satisfy; and architecture. These form requirements just mentioned can be observed as the system becomes defined; attempts to test them are inappropriate.
- Function. These requirements include: behavior, processing, data- and message-passing, control schema, sequencing and ordering, and interfaces that exist logically. These can usually be considered performance requirements and are generally testable—if not directly, at least by inference.

Once the analyst can differentiate between testable and nontestable requirements, it is much easier to assess the adequacy of the test plan. It should be noted also that global performance requirements often affect many functions simultaneously. This can be determined by diagramming techniques like data flow diagrams, which show connectivity and process interaction. Thus, test coverage can only be determined with certainty by examining all the paths or functional threads that are influenced by each requirement.

Hopefully, you will no longer merely accept the written word in a specification as gospel. Challenge the construction and context, trying to determine if the writer really meant what was said or if the requirement is flawed. There is overwhelming evidence collected over the past 30 years that requirements documents are the weakest link in the software chain. And the worst part is that many times the developer does not know just how bad it is until far too late in the process to correct it without major impact to the program. IV&V is aimed squarely at this target.

5.4   VERIFYING THE SYSTEM SPECIFICATION

So far the discussion has centered on several requirement tools and how to recognize a requirement from just another statement in the document. Now the focus falls specifically on the system specification, where its requirements come from, and how they are analyzed and verified. The verification process is shown in Figure 5-2, which includes typical evaluation factors for three common types of systems—a DOD weapon system, a commercial management information system, and an industrial process control system. Notice that the rest of the verification process is generic; that is, it works on all kinds of system specifications. As you can see also, the process does not rely primarily on tools, but rather on the analyst, who may elect to use tools wherever it makes sense. For example, benchmarking, simulation, rapid prototyping and similar performance-oriented evaluations invariably require a computer and some form of software tools that the analyst acquires or in some cases develops for those purposes. A word of caution: when performing early throughput studies and benchmarking, use a mix of algorithms and database transactions that closely approximates those expected in the final system, not some standard test cases provided by the hardware vendors. These are always optimized and are difficult to equal in real-world applications.

When you examine the evaluation factors for a weapon system or even for a process-control system, you should be struck by the breadth of the knowledge base that is required of the IV&V organization. Very small businesses (those having fewer than 50 employees) may have a difficult staffing problem finding analysts with the requisite skills to perform large IV&V efforts effectively. The level of sophisticated analysis required, the computer resources, the tool repertoire, and the pool of experienced people present a challenge to all companies regardless of size who want to perform comprehensive IV&V. Returning to Figure 5-2, this verification process is designed to progress from the simple to the complex. Step 1 examines the specification for adherence to standards, which can include what is euphemistically called "best commercial practices." Figure 5-3, derived from DOD-STD-2167A, serves as a checklist for the contents of a typical system specification. Step 2 (Figure 5-2) evaluates how well the requirements are stated and can be based in part on advice given in our Section 5.3. When CASE tools are used in the development of the requirements, there is usually a database and artifacts like diagrams, special languages, and the computer-generated specification. IV&V will review all of this material for adequacy and correctness as a part of Step 2 to ensure that the tool is being used correctly. CASE-produced specifications vary from computer-aided support using templates, which requires significant editing and additional input, to virtually automatic generation of the document. Evaluate the tool selected to determine how much of the process is really automatic. Step 3 (Figure 5-2) assesses how complete the document appears to be prior to an in-depth analysis. This is usually the level of analysis that most software quality-assurance programs cover. Very few have the resources or tools to delve further into the technical content of the specification. Up to this point the document is examined on its own merit; however, beginning with Step 4 of Figure 5-2, external factors are

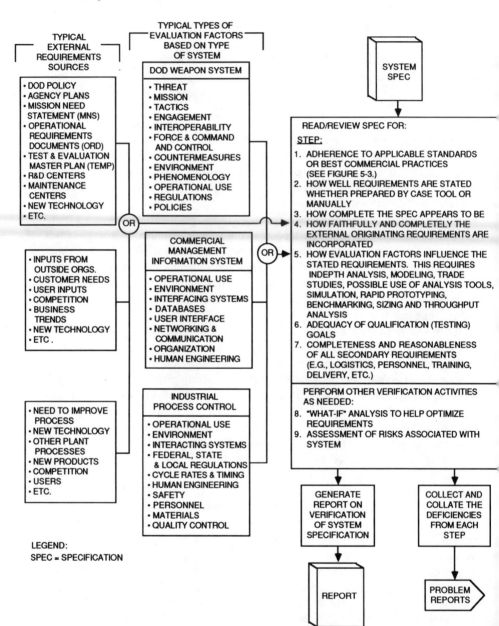

Figure 5-2 Verification of the system specification.

CONTENTS	VERIFIED	REMARKS
1. NOT APPLICABLE FOR IV&V		
2. NOT APPLICABLE FOR IV&V		
3. SYSTEM REQUIREMENTS		

DESCRIPTION
CHARACTERISTICS
  PERFORMANCE CHARACTERISTICS
  SYSTEM CAPABILITIES
  PHYSICAL CHARACTERISTICS
  SYSTEM QUALITY FACTORS
  ENVIRONMENTAL CONDITIONS
  TRANSPORTABILITY
  FLEXIBILITY & EXPANSION
  PORTABILITY		

DESIGN & CONSTRUCTION
  MATERIALS
  ELECTROMAGNETIC RADIATION
  NAMEPLATES & MARKING
  WORKMANSHIP
  INTERCHANGEABILITY
  SAFETY
  HUMAN ENGINEERING
  NUCLEAR CONTROL
  SYSTEM SECURITY
  GFP USAGE
  RESERVE CAPACITY		

DOCUMENTATION
LOGISTICS
PERSONNEL & TRAINING
  PERSONNEL
  TRAINING
CHARACTERISTICS OF
  SUBORDINATE ELEMENTS
  PRECEDENCE
  QUALIFICATION
  STANDARD SAMPLE
  PREPRODUCTION SAMPLE		

4. QA PROVISIONS		
5. PREPARATION FOR DELIVERY		

INTENDED USE
  MISSION
  THREAT		

Figure 5-3   System specification checklist.

introduced to ensure that the system fits correctly within its global or company context and that all external originating requirements are adequately incorporated or otherwise accommodated. Step 5 gets to the core analytical challenges. Here is where all the requirements have to be considered in reference to the evaluation factors. Remember that those evaluation factors shown in Figure 5-2 are typical and some engineering judgment needs to be used in evolving the final tailored list for each system. It is in Step 5 that IV&V proves as far as possible that each requirement is valid or invalid, vague or adequate, correct or ambiguous. It is important to have access to the developer's trade studies, benchmarks, sizing and timing studies, preliminary algorithms, models, etc. IV&V then reexamines these artifacts, using independently derived evaluation criteria, and compares the results. When a significant mismatch is found, more analysis occurs until a conclusion is reached and recommendations are made. IV&V will use whatever tool and support system that seems appropriate and cost-effective for a given application, including independent modeling, simulation, rapid prototyping, and diagramming. Step 6 examines the testability of the requirements and then compares the independently derived assessment to that given in the specification. Step 7 evaluates what I call the secondary requirements, those that are peripheral to and in support of the system's main technical objectives. These secondary objectives include such things as logistic support, personnel and training, precedence, definitions of samples, and delivery requirements. It is not that these are less important, but rather that many of them do not translate directly into design.

Step 8 addresses "what-if" studies that attempt to optimize portions of the system in ways different from the path selected by the developer. This step can be considered optional since there will be cases where this type of study makes sense and cases where it is unnecessary. Analysis of this type is especially effective early in a program when the system definition is still evolving and architecture is uncertain. Studies of this type have changed the number and allocation of CSCIs, operating philosophy, database management systems, number of processors, amount of memory, repair philosophy, software modularity, and other items too numerous to name. Thus, "what-if" studies are too important to leave out of an IV&V methodology but will not always be employed.

Step 9 deals with risk. There are so many types of risks that to address the subject comprehensively would take its own book; however, those that I refer to here are the ones that surface as a consequence of performing Steps 4 through 8. Many of these risks result from a borderline or optimistic requirement. An example I recall was that any user console on a certain nameless system "shall respond to the user within 2 seconds after a request." Initially, both the developer and the customer thought this was a reasonable requirement. Once the system was developed and being integrated, it was discovered that response time was a function of how many users were logged on and what tasks were running, so that requirement could not be met under most real operational conditions and never if the system was being stressed. That was a high-risk requirement and should have been mitigated by a different design or changed early when it was not impacting delivery and sell-off of the system. Anyway, as the IV&V analyst performs the verification of the system specification, there should be a place where high-risk items are collected, prioritized, and reported to the customer. I recommend using the IV&V analyst's notebook discussed in Section 5.5 to collect this information. Another time I was asked to evaluate a design for a transportation system. The thing that struck me immediately was that there was only one computer to control the entire movement of trains. So I said, "Where is the redundancy, the backup computer?" They mumbled something about it not failing. . . . A while later I read about hundreds of people being stranded in a tunnel when the computer failed. I'll bet they got a backup computer shortly after that. The point in this discussion is that all systems have some form of risk; it may be loss of input data, loss of output, inconvenient shutdown, degraded performance when you need it the most, or inaccurate results.

Whatever the risk is, be alert to it, record it when you discover it, and analyze and report it to the customer as soon as possible.

The final activities in this verification process are to collect and collate the deficiencies discovered from all verification steps, write an appropriate set of problem reports against the specification, and generate a written report on the verification of the system specification. IV&V reports should all be as factual and informative as possible with little or no fluff. Keep them as short and unambiguous as possible. A briefing that parallels each report is a common practice, but depends on customer preference.

5.5 VERIFYING THE SOFTWARE REQUIREMENTS SPECIFICATIONS

At the onset, it should be remembered that there is a software requirements specification (SRS) for each computer software configuration item (CSCI) in the system. Smallish systems will probably only have a single CSCI; whereas, large systems can have several or even many, if they are very large. Not only is there a separate SRS, but there is also an entire family of design and interface specifications, user and operator manuals, test plans and specifications, etc., for each CSCI. Thus, the first problem is to know where the requirements coming from the system specification ended up. For example, if there are three CSCIs, then the software requirements get allocated to three places. There can also be global requirements that apply to all three CSCIs, so the allocation is seldom ever mutually exclusive. It is only reasonable that one of the first steps in SRS verification is to ascertain what should be included in a particular SRS. Even though DOD-STD-2167A [24] requires explicit cross-referencing between these documents, IV&V will verify that process to ensure that nothing got left out.

Thus, one of the primary goals of this verification activity is to ensure that the SRS is complete, correct, and consistent within itself and with any other SRSs in the system, and further that each SRS is traceable back to the originating requirements in the system specification.

The verification of an SRS is very similar procedurally to that used for a system specification. This is done deliberately because it puts the analyst in a familiar, structured approach that moves from simple to complex analysis. After a few projects the order of verification becomes second nature. Figure 5-4 illustrates this verification process. Notice that there are now four evaluation data sources. These represent originating requirements from the system specification and then a collection of information from various sources that the analyst will collect and catalog as the job proceeds. I use what I call an IV&V analyst's notebook set up with dividers for this purpose. You could use your personal computer or terminal also, but I find retaining a hard copy of miscellaneous data and informal notes more useful, portable, and accessible than computer files. Incidentally, this notebook grows throughout the project and forms a valuable source of information for reports and briefings

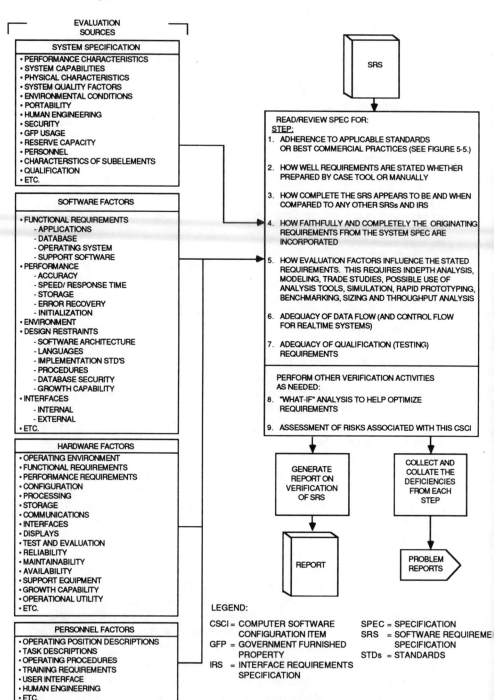

Figure 5-4   Verification of software requirements specifications.

as well as serving its primary purpose as an analysis aid. The tables of evaluation factors shown in Figure 5-4 can serve as a table of contents and checklist for the analyst as he or she builds the notebook. Some information trickles down from the verification of the system specification, but most will be generated and obtained through performing these procedures, especially Step 5 in Figure 5-4.

Step 1 (Figure 5-4) examines the SRS for adherence to standards, which includes best commercial practices. Figure 5-5, derived from DOD-STD-2167A, serves as a

CONTENTS	VERIFIED	REMARKS
1. NOT APPLICABLE FOR IV&V		
2. NOT APPLICABLE FOR IV&V		
3. ENGINEERING REQUIREMENTS		

CSCI EXTERNAL INTERFACE REQUIREMENTS
  CSCI CAPABILITY REQUIREMENTS
 	
    CAPABILITY & PROJECT-UNIQUE ID
      •
      •
      •
  CSCI INTERNAL INTERFACES
    DATA AND CONTROL FLOW TO CSC LEVEL		

CSCI DATA ELEMENTS
    INTERNALS
    PROJECT-UNIQUE ID
    DESCRIPTION
    UNITS OF MEASURE
    LIMIT/RANGE OF VALUES
    ACCURACY
    PRECISION
    INTERNAL INTERFACES
      •
      •
      •
    EXTERNAL
    PROJECT-UNIQUE ID
    INTERFACE
    SOURCE/DESTINATION
    REFERENCE IN IRS		

ADAPTATION REQUIREMENTS
 	
    INSTALLATION-DEPENDENT DATA
    OPERATIONAL PARAMETERS
  SIZING AND TIMING REQUIREMENTS
  SAFETY REQUIREMENTS
  SECURITY REQUIREMENTS
  DESIGN CONSTRAINTS
  SOFTWARE QUALITY FACTORS
  HUMAN ENGINEERING
  REQUIREMENTS TRACEABILITY		

4. QUALIFICATION REQUIREMENTS		
QUALIFICATION METHODS SPECIAL QUALIFICATION REQUIREMENTS		
5. PREPARATION FOR DELIVERY		

LEGEND:

CSC   = COMPUTER SOFTWARE COMPONENTY
CSCI = COMPUTER SOFTWARE CONFIGURATION ITEM
IRS   = INTERFACE REQUIREMENTS SPECIFICATION

Figure 5-5 Software requirements specifications checklist.

checklist for the contents of a typical SRS. Step 2 (Figure 5-4) evaluates how well the requirements are stated, and it is based on advice given in Section 5.3. As was the situation with the system specification when CASE tools were used in the development of the requirements, there is usually a database and artifacts like data flow diagrams, sometimes special software requirements languages, and perhaps a computer-generated SRS. IV&V will review all of this material for adequacy and correctness as a part of Step 2 to ensure that the tool is being used correctly. CASE-produced software requirements specifications vary from computer-aided support that uses templates, which require significant editing and additional input, to virtually automatic generation of the document. Evaluate the tool selected to determine how much of the process is really automatic. Step 3 (Figure 5-4) assesses how complete the document appears to be prior to an in-depth analysis. When more than one SRS is involved in the verification process, completeness checking involves verifying every requirement referenced in all SRSs. This will uncover missing, overlapping, global, and misassigned requirements. Then, within each SRS, checks are made on the derived requirements that were spawned from within the document itself. There are evaluation indicators (metrics) that can be applied to these documents, which help determine percent complete as well as several other quality criteria. The application of metrics is discussed in Section 12.2.

Up to this point each SRS is examined on its own merit; however, beginning with Step 4 (Figure 5-4), external factors are introduced to ensure that the software fits correctly within its global or system context and that all external originating requirements are adequately incorporated or otherwise accommodated. Step 5 (Figure 5-4) gets to the core analytical challenges. Here is where software requirements have to be considered in reference to the evaluation factors. Remember that those shown on Figure 5-4 are typical and some engineering judgment needs to be used in evolving the final list for each CSCI. It is in this step that IV&V proves as far as possible that each software requirement is valid or invalid, vague or adequate, correct or ambiguous, and consistent or inconsistent with its companions. It is important to have access to the developer's trade studies, benchmarks, sizing and timing studies, preliminary algorithms, models, etc. IV&V then reexamines these artifacts using independently derived evaluation criteria and compares the results. When a significant mismatch is found, more analysis occurs until a conclusion is reached and recommendations are made. IV&V will use whatever tool and support system seems appropriate and cost-effective for a given application, including independent modeling, simulation, rapid prototyping, and additional diagramming. Step 6 (Figure 5-4) evaluates the adequacy of the data flow (and control flow if required) diagrams to completely graphically describe the software. Step 7 (Figure 5-4) examines the qualification (test) requirements and then compares the independently derived assessment to those found in the specification. Step 8 performs "what-if" analysis that attempt to optimize critical portions of the software in ways different from that selected by the developer. This step is optional since there will be cases where this type of study makes sense and cases where it is unnecessary. Studies of this type have changed the allocation of requirements and capabilities to particular CSCIs, altered operating rules, changed database schema and file structure, reassigned software processes to different processors, changed algorithms and logic, altered memory allocation, improved software modularity, and resulted in other changes too numerous to name. "What-if" studies are a very important part of an IV&V methodology. And finally, Step 9 deals with risk. As the IV&V analyst performs the verification of the SRS, high-risk items are recorded, prioritized, and reported to the customer. All systems have some form of risk; it may be loss of input data, loss of or corruption of output data, degraded performance when you need it the most, or calculation errors that propagate through the system with catastrophic results. Whatever the risk is, be alert to it and record it when you discover it and consider how to mitigate it whenever time allows.

The two final activities in this verification process are to collect and collate the deficiencies discovered from all verification steps, write an appropriate set of problem reports against the SRS, and generate a written report on the verification of the SRS.

The other significant verification activities, discussed briefly in Sections 5.4 and 5.5, are described in more detail in the remainder of this chapter. This material presents detailed "how-to-do-it" advice as well as tools, techniques, and methods that can be used to perform a comprehensive requirements verification activity.

5.6 VERIFYING THE INTERFACE REQUIREMENTS SPECIFICATION

The interface requirements specification (IRS) defines all the interfaces among all of the configuration item (CI) specifications. Figure 5-6 shows how this document serves to bind the system together. It should be noted that the IRS only concerns itself with interfaces external to the CIs. Those of you who are familiar with

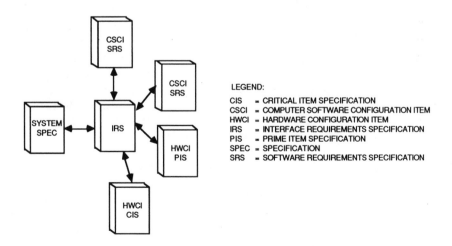

Figure 5-6 The interface requirements specification (IRS) binds the system together.

hardware systems can equate the IRS to a wire run list where the origin and destination of all interconnections are listed, together with a description of what is on each particular wire. Remember this is only an analogy and the IRS in reality may deal with such things as the various messages that flow between two points on a common interface.

In this case, IV&V will concern itself with the quality and completeness of the interface diagrams and then the tabular data associated with each. IV&V will check to determine whether the CIs execute concurrently or sequentially. If concurrent, the method of synchronization will be evaluated. Next, the communication protocol and priority level will be verified. Then, the detailed data requirements will be verified according to the following information:

- A project-unique identifier for each data element
- A brief description of the data element
- The CI that is the source of the data element
- The CI that uses the data element
- The units of measure (meters, hertz, seconds, etc.)
- The limit/range of values
- The accuracy required of the data element
- The precision or resolution required of the data element.

IV&V will be very watchful that the interfaces match the corresponding information found in the SRSs and other CI-level specifications. Any deficiencies will become candidates for problem reports and IV&V will report on this verification activity as a topic in the final report on requirements verification.

5.7 VERIFYING THE HARDWARE PRIME-ITEM SPECIFICATIONS IF REQUIRED

This book is oriented strongly toward software; however, there may be occasions when it is necessary to verify part or even all of the hardware-related prime-item specification (PIS) or critical-item specification (CIS). Instead of this book telling expressly how to perform this function, I will tell you how to go about it. Between the evaluation factors listed for verification of the system specification (Figure 5-2) and SRS (Figure 5-4), the IV&V analyst can construct a comprehensive list of hardware factors for the system in question. If a MIL-STD like 490 [22] is cited in the contract, there will be a data item directive (DID) referenced that will contain an detailed outline of the PIS or CIS that can serve as a checklist. These sources should be sufficient to coordinate an effective review and verification of the hardware documents.

There are CASE-like tools for hardware called computer-aided design (CAD), Computer-aided engineering (CAE), and computer-aided manufacturing (CAM) tools. Some CASE tools have been based on CAD tools and a few can produce very high density (design) language (VHDL), which is somewhat analogous to software pseudocode. The most notable of the I-CASE tools that fall into this category is the TAGS tool by Teledyne Brown Engineering (see the tool survey, Table 4-1.) Therefore, it behooves the IV&V analyst to determine if any kind of automated tools were used to produce the hardware and/or its specifications before going very far into the verification process. If so, collect the tool artifacts and evaluate them along with the specification.

Most of the time, IV&V is interested in specific items or functions described in the hardware specifications and not in the total document. It is very appropriate to verify all the interfaces as well as review the hardware features that control or affect the behavior of the software such as clocks, interrupts, device drivers, analog-to-digital converters, storage devices, controllers, and the like. Thus, IV&V gains as much knowledge about the hardware as necessary to understand and anticipate the behavior of the software.

5.8 VERIFYING THE SOFTWARE DEVELOPMENT PLAN AND ITS IMPLEMENTATION

Table 3-1 presented the contents of the software development plan (SDP). Although the following thought is not original on my part, it emphasizes the first point I want to make. Pay careful attention! Imagine that you have no plan, so you do not quite know where you are; in fact, you probably are not sure where you have been, so you cannot possibly know where you are going and even if you accidentally get to where you want to be, you will not know it. Believe it or not, a lot of software has been written in this manner and a lot of unhappy customers have said a lot of ugly things to a lot of well-meaning software developers. The SDP attempts to remedy this situation.

The second point I want to make sure that you appreciate is that the best plan in the world will not work if it is ignored. Very often, the plan is treated as an early deliverable and collects dust on everyone's bookshelves after a few months. Believe me, the SDP should be out on the desks, coffee-stained and dog-eared; it is a living document that should be used frequently. IV&V acknowledges this and performs an initial review of the document, which serves several purposes, one of which is to assist in selection of IV&V tools and methods to complement those of the developer. Remember that IV&V is locked into a great deal of what the developer does, so what better way to anticipate where you are going than to follow the plan? Monthly, at least, IV&V will compare what it knows about the project to the plan and will report to the customer on how well the two track. If it appears that the developer is drifting away from the plan, IV&V will make an appropriate noise. If everyone agrees that the plan needs to be changed, that is acceptable as long as the customer approves it and it is properly coordinated. IV&V cannot afford to let the SDP gather dust. Some customers require IV&V to write its own plan. In these cases, the IV&V plan is very closely linked to the SDP, and if one changes, the other probably will too. Generation of an IV&V plan is discussed in Section 11.2.

Specific IV&V tasks associated with the review and enforcement of the SDP are presented in Section 9.2.1 and therefore are not introduced here.

5.9 VERIFYING REQUIREMENTS TRACING BETWEEN DOCUMENTS

The reason that this subject is singled out in this manner is that unless the software development effort is prepared under a standard like DOD-STD-2167A [24], it is not likely to have a requirements tracing matrix (RTM) imposed. Earlier attempts to provide this kind of traceability were usually inadequate and once done were never updated, so they were essentially useless. IV&V has a better idea. The first RTM I am familiar with was built by the IV&V contractor around 1973 for the Safeguard Anti-Ballistic Missile System and served to trace all levels of requirements to and from all of the specifications. Before we built it, nobody knew what requirement went where or who belonged to whom, etc. You get the general idea. Anyway, the idea of the RTM caught on and we incorporated it into all our IV&V programs and advertised the advantages of it to all of the military services. Later on (whether we influenced it or not, I do not know) RTMs began to appear in the standards. In the 1980s, we successfully introduced the concept to the nuclear power industry. As time went by, we continued to improve the presentation, so that the one I discuss here does the following: It links the originating requirements in the system specification to their destination in the software and hardware requirements specifications (SRS, PIS, and CIS). It then links the SRS to Section 3 of the software design document (SDD). It then links Section 3 to Section 4 and on to the CSC and ultimately the CSU that incorporates the requirement. The last step is to reference one or more tests to each "testable" requirement. If no such test can be identified, the RTM has just become useful in showing a hole in the test coverage. By reversing the sort and listing tests first, the number of requirements validated per test can be observed. What else can I find out from the RTM? I know what requirements are embodied in what code so that if I want to change a requirement, I can quickly ascertain the amount of code that is impacted. Conversely, if I want to change the design or code, I can determine what requirements are affected. RTMs have been shown to be very effective in reducing the time and uncertainty in evaluating engineering change proposals (ECPs). In fact, once the developers discover how useful the RTM is, they invariably want copies. It is one of the most useful databases that can be built for a software project.

In any case, whether the standard imposes the tracing function within the specifications (as in DOD-STD-2167A) or a separate RTM is developed, IV&V has a fundamental responsibility to the project to ensure that all requirements are correctly traced to all appropriate levels of specifications and that the references are reverified whenever a change occurs. This not only helps keep the functional and allocated baselines intact, but greatly facilitates the audits at the end of the development period, as discussed in Chapter 9.

5.10 CRITICALITY AND RISK ASSESSMENT OF REQUIREMENTS

Very often, criticality and risk go hand in hand. In these situations, the most critical functions many times represent the greatest development risk. On several large systems that I have been associated with, the most critical functions were implemented very late in the development cycle and consequently were poorly designed and tested. This software then produced a disproportional number of bugs and required extraordinary effort to refine it to the point where it was usable. This is precisely what you do not want to have happen, so the goal of this step is to recognize and do something to mitigate the risks as early as possible. As mentioned in Sections 5.4 and 5.5, the IV&V analyst should record high-risk items and critical functions as the specifications are being verified. But this initial discovery process is probably not focused enough to do a complete assessment, so there should be a separate review directed first at determining the high-risk items and, second, at assessing their criticality.

There are numerous ways to classify risks, such as the following categories:

- *Management.* The challenge of directing, coordinating, and controlling the project efficiently and effectively
- *Organization.* The risks associated with assembling the correct staff and structure to effectively run the program for the duration of the effort
- *Facilities.* the ability to acquire or build the facility to properly match the needs of the system. Many times the facility has an important relationship with the software system (e.g., a wind tunnel, a radar site, a power plant, or a factory)
- *Hardware development/availability.* The risks associated with concurrent development of special hardware to work in conjunction with the software (e.g., a missile, an automated plant process, or a toll collection system) and with the availability of sufficient prototype or production hardware to support software development and testing
- *Software development.* The numerous risks associated with software development—compilers, operating systems, tools, reusable components, algorithms, methodologies, environments, etc.
- *Technology.* Especially the risks associated with new technology, wherein the products or processes are being used for the first time, including high-energy lasers, neutral particle beam generators, new types of computer chips, space power systems, etc.
- *Schedule.* The risks associated with overly optimistic or erroneous scheduling, which can be impacted by virtually any other type of risk
- Other risks peculiar to the type of system being considered.

Table 5-1 addresses two of the risk areas just identified—schedule and technology—and gives some typical examples in each category.

5.11 REVIEWING USER INTERFACE NEEDS

Most software systems today are interactive to some degree, allowing the user to interact with the hardware and software through display terminals of some type.

TABLE 5-1. Examples of Risk Factors and Their Control

Risk Factors	Mitigation (or Abatement) Approach
Schedule	
• Ambitious schedule	• Use high productivity CASE tools • Reuse large amounts of software • Conduct parallel development efforts • Adjust development order to shorten schedule
• Inadequate documentation for vendor products	• Where choices are available, carefully select vendors with proven records of timely deliveries, accurate documentation, and excellent maintenance practices
• Late delivery of products	• Where possible, insist on late delivery penalties and on firm maintenance agreements
• Changing requirements that impact schedule	• Many CASE tools reduce the impact of changes by positive tracking and accurate assessment processes • Attempt generic designs that are more flexible and less susceptible to minor change impacts • Invest greater percent of project funds in pre-code stages • Invest in comprehensive user survey to improve validity of requirements. Use an RTM • Use IV&V to help in change impact evaluation
• Too many meetings with various agencies and other contractors that impact schedule	• Assign specific managers to focus on each interface. Insulate the PM from trivial meetings when possible. Combine meetings when possible
Technology	
• Incomplete definition of hardware	• Employ all available simulations & emulations • Extrapolate designs from older systems • Stay in close touch with hardware vendors • Build hardware prototypes of critical components
• Real-time performance demands may exceed hardware capabilities	• Perform tradeoff analysis between hardware and performance needs • Determine if software can compensate for hardware shortcomings via improved algorithms • Use modular hardware that can accept incremental upgrades
• Ability to create a realistic test environment	• Improve fidelity of testbed or simulation • Use national testing ranges/assets • Use automated testing tools
• Hardware devices are required but are immature	• Adapt maintenance plans to facilitate swapout or frequent maintenance • Work with hardware vendor to improve manufacturing processes • Ask for parallel testing reports
• New exotic hardware is required	• Designate as long lead item • Begin multisource prototype procurement early • Incentivize early delivery • Run comparison test among competitors • Seek IR&D investment by competitors

Cathode ray tube (CRT) displays are the most common, with plasma panels and liquid crystal displays (LCDs) gaining ground because they are flat and require less power drain. Very often, systems that are built around commercial off-the-shelf (COTS) hardware use CRT displays and keyboards more or less as is. The developer may designate part of the keyboard for special functions, which allows a degree of tailoring to occur, or he or she may even have special keys or the entire keyboard customized. In some cases, input devices are added to aid in input and control—a mouse, trackball, joystick, touch panel, etc. In any case, displays, keyboards, and adjunct devices serve as the most common system interfaces today. There are also exotic devices that recognize and respond to speech, movement, sound, etc., and offer exciting adaptation for numerous applications.

There is a great deal of human engineering required to optimize all the factors associated with specifying and designing user interfaces. IV&V's involvement should roughly match the sophistication and novelty of the user interface. This means that for displays using a standard terminal, keyboard and perhaps a mouse, IV&V can rely largely on the human engineering provided by the manufacturer and concentrate mostly on what the displays look like, how they are controlled, and how well engineered they are. Incidentally, this is no small job on complex systems. Nuclear power plants are a good example of complex displays using graphical mimics in color of the reactor core, mimics of other plant subsystems, meteorological plots of air currents near the plant, etc. These displays are controlled in several ways—by cursor, special function keys, menu selection, and some even initiate automatically when alarm conditions occur. Weapon systems typically use displays to show the coordinates of targets and threatening objects, their location and tracks, and the intercepts by the countermeasures. Management information systems (MIS) show selected data in the form and format most useful to the user. Process control systems may have very simple displays and/or screens and controls designed for unfriendly environments like pot rooms and machine shops. In all of these cases, IV&V has to decide how much is enough and where to put its limited resources. Because IV&V is in the enviable position of being the first outside user of the system, there will be numerous opportunities to evaluate the user interface as the system evolves. Modern developers who use rapid prototyping during the early phases will usually begin by developing the basic user interface so that it becomes stable and serves as a foundation for all of the remaining design work. Remember that it is in the requirements phase that the basic layout and functionality for the user interface is decided. The cost of changes to the user interface escalates quickly in subsequent development phases.

5.12 REVIEWING INPUT AND OUTPUT DATA REQUIREMENTS

This type of analysis should start by verifying the outputs. This may seem backward when you first think about it, but it really is the correct logical order. If you know exactly the form, format, and contents of the output, you can then determine what inputs are needed to derive that output. The other way, there is a lot of second guessing and there may be inputs and transformations (processes) defined that are not needed. Yes, this actually happens! There is a complication to this approach, which says that if ad hoc queries and user-defined functions are allowed in the system, then all outputs cannot be defined in advance so you verify only those that can be defined and do not worry so much about restricting the inputs.

Wise developers survey the users early in the program to aid in defining the outputs. IV&V should try to obtain a copy of this material for use in verification, or IV&V may elect to survey the users and operators independently. This effort is supported by the data flow diagrams (or equivalent) produced for the SRSs and the interface descriptions in the IRS. Once the outputs are verified, attention can be focused on the inputs. The IV&V analyst will also have the opportunity to perform a preliminary assessment of the processes and transformations required to produce the outputs from the specified inputs.

5.13   REVIEWING THE TRADE STUDIES FOR THE SYSTEM

IV&V should request the results of trade studies performed by the developer when the requirements were being developed. These usually include such things as evaluating several hardware configurations and options. This can include computers, display terminals, I/O devices, data acquisition front-ends, communication options such as fiber optics vs. wire, multiprocessing vs. parallel processing, development system vs. final target hardware, computer peripherals, networking, and the like. Very often, selecting lower-cost hardware places more of a burden on the software, so tradeoffs are usually parametric in nature, with direct and inverse relationships influencing the final outcome. In fact, sometimes the decision points are the intersection of a set of curves where hardware and software capabilities or costs or features are optimum. The customer and IV&V as well should not simply take the developer's word that trade studies were performed that resulted in the hardware and software being proposed. Ask to see the data and draw your own conclusions. If IV&V doubts that part of the study was sufficient to produce the conclusions reached, do some independent analysis, and if things still come up looking suspicious, request through the customer that the developer rework or elaborate on part of the trade study. It is a lot cheaper to fix things early than it is to find out later that the processor cannot run the software or that the memory will not hold the database or application program load module. These things happen in the real world. One project I know of had to do a major computer upgrade in the middle of development just to get a system that would handle the load and throughput. The initial benchmarks were very optimistic and inadequate, and the sizing estimates were low by 30–40%. That spells *overrun*.

As mentioned a couple of paragraphs earlier, new or emerging technology very often has an optimistic performance specification. I could mention several examples, but I do not want to offend anyone or get sued, so just take my word for it—this really happens. That is why some RFPs insist that the bidder propose only components with at least one year of operational use in the field. This helps a great deal to provide realism to the inputs for the trade studies. You can even query some of the users and get an additional opinion. IV&V has to be inquisitive if not suspicious at times of the data used to formulate the system, and especially to prove the advantage of one hardware item over another.

So far, most of this discussion has centered on reviewing and verifying the developer's trade studies. Now it is time to turn our attention to independent trade studies that are performed by IV&V to provide additional information on issues and items that represent considerable doubt or risk to the system. I recommend that an analysis tool like GRC's DSIGNR* be used to perform this effort. The tool helps the analyst organize the input and format the output in a useful manner for parametric analysis. It handles both hardware and software tradeoff issues and is especially useful in sizing and throughput analysis. Other IV&V options include independent modeling and simulation, but I would urge you to not attempt to elaborate a simulation unless you already have most of it built from another similar project. Rapid prototyping tools can also be used in place of simulations to assess system architecture (see the tool survey in Section 4.1 for assistance in tool selection). Even then I recommend that the effort be focused on critical parts of the system and not the whole thing. These efforts take a significant investment in computer resources, manpower, and time. Another alternative is to build an elaborate benchmark program that is representative of the types of processing that the new system will be expected to perform and have the manufacturers run it while you witness it. This is a popular approach and at least gives a good idea of relative performance differences among the candidate processors and devices.

5.14 REVIEWING TEST REQUIREMENTS, PLANNING, AND STRATEGY

Some systems have a test and evaluation master plan (TEMP) generated by the customer with inputs from all of the organizations that will interact or interface with the system. This document plans the developmental testing (DT) and evaluation and operational testing (OT) and evaluation (also known as DT&E and OT&E). Systems developed for the DOD especially require long-range test planning so that test ranges and facilities can be scheduled and prepared with instrumentation, targets, and even mock threats and countermeasures. Thus, when IV&V is initiated, one of the first documents looked for is the TEMP. It is an oversight document that all individual test plans for each program phase must fit within. If there is no TEMP, IV&V will need to interview the customer to ascertain the overall test and evaluation strategy, installation, and phaseover plan. This kind of information is essential to the review of the qualification test requirements and test plans. The MIL-STDs require that qualification methods for each requirement be stated according to one of three categories—demonstration (testing), analysis, or inspection. (You may want

*A product of General Research Corporation, Huntsville, Alabama.

to reread Section 5.3 of this book, which discusses why some requirements are testable and some are not.) In any event, the testable ones are of greatest interest to IV&V, because they end up in the software test plan and eventually in the software test descriptions.

IV&V will verify the qualification sections of both the system specification and the SRSs to ensure that all requirements are treated appropriately. It is also prudent to review the overall test strategy and plans to ensure that facilities and outside resources will be available when needed.

5.15   PARTICIPATING IN ALL REVIEWS AND MEETINGS THAT AFFECT THE SYSTEM

IV&V needs to be included in all meetings between the customer and the developer except those that discuss private contract issues like award fee, staffing, management, or contract performance assessment. Chapter 9 discusses IV&V participation in all the key reviews and audits for the system. During the requirements phase, it is customary to expect to attend the system requirements review (SRR), system design review (SDR), and the software specification review (SSR), unless one or more of these events have already occurred by the time IV&V is initiated. If this is the case, IV&V will review the minutes, and if a significant number of open items resulted, IV&V should track them until closure. If a large number of such items exist, IV&V should generate an open/action item tracking list and maintain it for the customer throughout the development period.

It is usual that the customer and developer get together at least monthly to discuss status, problems, issues, schedule, and performance. IV&V should attend and participate in these meetings. IV&V will also meet with the customer on an as-required basis both in preparation for meetings and in debriefings after the meetings with the developer. When IV&V discovers something that needs to be discussed with the customer, developer, or both, there should be a mechanism to call meetings with the appropriate technical and management people present. IV&V's major responsibility is to notify the customer, who then decides what to do and when to do it. IV&V must have the capability to put briefings together quickly and effectively.

5.16   PRODUCING PROBLEM REPORTS

IV&V will use the developer's problem report (PR) system and forms, whether electronic or hard-copy. Handling of IV&V-initiated PRs should be no different than handling those prepared by any other source. IV&V will have read-only access to the PR database and will retain sufficient old copies to conduct periodic audits to ensure that no unapproved or unauthorized changes occur. There is additional discussion on this subject in Chapter 10, which deals with configuration management.

5.17   INDEPENDENT VERIFICATION AND VALIDATION PRODUCTS OF THE REQUIREMENTS VERIFICATION PHASE

The following is a list of anticipated IV&V products for this phase:

1. System specification verification report
2. Software requirements specification verification report(s)
3. Requirements verification report
   - Summary of document reviews
   - Summary of criticality and risk assessment
   - Review of user interface
   - Review of I/O data requirements
   - Review of trade studies
   - Review of test planning
   - Summary of meetings and formal reviews attended
   - List of PRs produced
   - Open/action item list
4. IV&V analyst's notebook
   - Evaluation factors
   - Independent verification studies and results
   - Software tools used
   - Miscellaneous information worth saving.

5.18   CHAPTER SUMMARY

- The requirements verification phase offers the biggest potential saving to software development efforts since it can uncover and correct many deficiencies that otherwise can go undetected until late in the development cycle, where correction is much more expensive and problems ripple throughout all of the other phases.
- Good specifications require significant investment in time and resources. IV&V should be prepared to do whatever is appropriate to ensure completeness, consistency, and correctness of the key specifications.
- Traceability of requirements from the originating sources and into design, code, and testing is one of the essential procedures initiated in this phase.
- CASE tools can very often be shared between the developer and IV&V; however, IV&V should not normally take on the exclusive use of highly complex development tools like DCDS because the input effort is so labor-intensive.
- The requirements phase has the least number of CASE tools, and most of these

are characterized more as specification analysis tools than requirements engineering tools. The latter is where the greatest need is and where IV&V has one of its greatest challenges.

- One of the fundamental problems in this phase is being able to parse a requirement into its basic elements and then use this information effectively to define nodes and objects, behavior, and interfaces.
- Requirements verification checks the key specifications for adherence to standards, completeness, incorporation of originating requirements, adequacy of derived requirements, numerous evaluation factors, qualification criteria, risks, and other necessary factors to ensure that they completely satisfy the needs of that phase.

5.19 WHAT COMES NEXT

Chapter 6 deals with design verification, the second major IV&V phase. It is divided into two parts—preliminary and detailed design. Chapter 6 continues in the same theme as this chapter, except that the level of detail increases.

6
DESIGN VERIFICATION

Design verification is a two-part process that, at completion, ensures that the software is ready to proceed into coding with a high degree of confidence. The first part is called *preliminary design* and the second is *detailed design*. This entire chapter deals exclusively with the design of software, and the only time hardware is mentioned is in support of software discussions.

This chapter is based for the most part on the current DOD-STD model, which produces a two-part software design specification (SDD). This SDD is completed through Section 3 as part one during preliminary design and from Section 4 forward to capture the detailed design. Several older standards also called for a two-part software development specification that did exactly the same thing. When the basic DOD-STD-2167 [24] came out in June of 1985, it called for a software top-level design document (STLDD), followed by a lower level software detailed design document (SDDD) and a separate database design document (DBDD). When DOD-STD-2167A was adopted [24], it improved things immensely by creating the two-part SDD, which meshes very nicely with the design phase itself and is simpler than most other design document approaches. In fact, it is about as simple as it can be and still support a two-part design process.

The preliminary design review (PDR) marks the transition from preliminary to detailed design and the critical design review (CDR) effectively ends the design phase. (These reviews are described in Chapter 9.) I used the word "effectively" because there is always some design rework required during coding, so the design phase does not usually cut off completely for some time. Earlier, Chapter 3 mentioned variations in the development cycle that can result in incremental PDRs and CDRs, but for sake of simplification, the discussion of design verification in this section considers these reviews as single events.

6.1 ACQUIRING THE NECESSARY SOFTWARE ANALYSIS AND COMPUTER-AIDED SOFTWARE ENGINEERING TOOLS

There is an abundance of computer-aided software engineering (CASE) tools for software design; in fact, most CASE tools have been built for this purpose. The reader is urged to consult the tool survey in Chapter 4 to better appreciate this observation. The idea of automated software tools has its genesis in the design phase, where tools started as diagramming aids and gradually evolved to more comprehensive and sophisticated concepts and paradigms. I remember the tools of the mid-1960s; you had to use a big flatbed plotter to draw charts because high-resolution graphics and companion printers did not exist. It took hours to prepare and print a big chart that can now roll of a laser printer in just seconds, and today million-pixel colorgraphic displays and color copiers are commonplace. By the 1970s, the technology graduated to terminals, and attempts were made to put graphics on VT-100 type (text) screens. Diagonal lines looked like lightning bolts and boxes were made of asterisks or dashes. It was pretty awful! The point in all this nostalgia is that hardware technology now supports the tool market very adequately in most situations; however, there are still a few shortcomings in screen-based systems that may always be there: you cannot jump around as easily as you can in a book, users or operators experience greater fatigue and stress, you cannot read a J-size drawing (at least 3 ft. high by 4 to 5 ft. long) on a 19-inch screen, and even laptops are not really as portable as books. Regardless of the opinions of the advocates of a paperless society, hard copy is still going to be with us for a good while longer. Probably the greatest shortcoming of most tools today is that the displays are still too small. But all these things aside, tools remove a great deal of the drudgery and time-consuming checking that humans used to have to do. They are a great productivity- and quality-enhancer, they do not get tired, they do not make mistakes on their own, and they give repeatable results.

As mentioned a couple of times earlier in the book, real-time systems need to be concerned about process and task control, sequencing, scheduling, and timing. Non-real-time systems, like information systems, do not. Therefore, the design paradigms are different. Non-real-time systems are typically designed using data flow diagrams or some equivalent. The most popular methodologies have come from work by Yourdon, Constantine, and Demarco; Michael Jackson; James Martin; and Warnier and Orr. The last two are more textual and tabular than truly graphical, but they all accomplish about the same thing. On the other hand, real-time software requires a form of notation that enables behavior, or what is commonly referred to as "control flow," to be included. There were real-time extensions to several of the above methods and then a couple of newer paradigms entered the scene—Ward and Mellor, which combine control and data flow; and Hatley and Pirbhai, which show the two separately. Because this is a somewhat dynamic area, there are some others on the horizon as well that show promise, but most tools available today use one of the conventions just mentioned. I thought it was important for the reader to know the methodology embedded in the tools, so I included this information when available in the tool survey given in Chapter 4. The software methodologists referred to in this section are both widely published and frequently referenced in numerous publications on software engineering. To gain an appreciation of the paradigms of the first group who deal mostly with non-real-time systems I recommend *Diagramming Techniques for Analysts and Programmers* by James Martin and Carma McClure, Prentice-Hall, 1985. To better understand the real-time methodologies, please refer to *Computer-Aided Software Design* by Max Schindler, John Wiley and Sons, 1990.

The next section discusses the main types of tools that are needed in the design phase. IV&V will use methodology information in performing its evaluation of the developer's tools in order to determine what tools IV&V should select to complement and augment them.

6.2 USING SOFTWARE TOOLS

IV&V has a primary interest in four major technical areas in design—data flow, behavior, algorithms, and database—that also become strong candidates for CASE tools. Some tools try to cover all four areas, but the majority concentrate on data flow, creation of a data dictionary, and to a far lesser degree on algorithm analysis and details of behavior. This should become clearer upon examining some of the specific attributes of CASE tools as well as some of the popular brand-name products.

Because many CASE tools are now packaged as toolkits, you must decide what parts of the toolkit apply to design and what parts you need for IV&V. A few examples should illustrate the point: Texas Instruments Information Engineering Facility, TRW-developed DCDS, Cadre's Teamwork, Excelerator from Index Technology, Software Through Pictures by IDE, and Statemate from i-Logix are just a few of the comprehensive toolkits that span more than just the design phase. Now if the toolkit was already being used in the previous phase, stick with it for continuity. If this is the situation, then the analysis tools already will have been put to the test and some tool databases will exist that transition nicely in this phase. If not, then the job is a little more difficult. In either case, you will now be concentrating on the tools that support data flow (and control flow for real time), logical data modeling, state transitions, screen and report definitions, database elements and file structure, prototyping down to an executable program design language (PDL), specification analysis and consistency checking, and some method of algorithm evaluation. Many times the last item simply is not part of the toolkit. One effective technique is to implement (build a rapid prototype) complex algorithms on a different computer, for example on a personal computer (PC), workstation, or even a programmable calculator and test it for all input extremes. Spreadsheet programs are also a very effective way of doing parametric analysis of the variables in an algorithm. It may also be quite appropriate to suggest alternative solutions and test them at the same time.

In real-time software when the behavior or so-called control flow is analyzed, the designer has to have a very good idea of how much time each package, subroutine, I/O transaction, etc., requires. He or she then lays out timing templates in an effort to minimize contention; balance processing across any synchronous frames; and allow time for asynchronous tasks, interrupt handling, and error detection and handling.

The last major tool area that strongly concerns IV&V deals with databases and brings an interesting division with it. The first part deals with what one could call the *run-time database,* which is used by the applications code in both real-time and non-real-time systems. This is sometimes mapped into fixed memory locations, especially in embedded mission-critical computer resource (MCCR) systems or it can use virtual memory dynamically allocated by the system as needed. Here the designer of the software typically designs this database as he or she requires it and puts the file and element definitions in the data dictionary. This is typically called *local and global memory.* The other part of the database concern to IV&V deals with what we generally call *database management systems* (DBMSs). These began in the 1970s as report-generation tools and grew within the next decade to include elaborate query capabilities, many user support features, and supported the evolution of what we call fourth-generation languages (4GLs). There are then two classes of these 4GLs and their accompanying development tools—end user and professional programmer. Examples of end-user 4GLs and tools include FOCUS, NOMAD, RAMIS-II, QMF, and QBE. Examples of professional-programmer 4GLs and tools include SQL, IDEAL, ADS/ONLINE, and NATURAL. [9] Those that are suitable for end-user applications enable report-writer, screen-builder, and query capabilities with nonprocedural code. The other category, for the professional programmers, allows both procedural and nonprocedural code. They also allow incorporation of a DBMS into a real-time system, although there is always an overhead burden when this is done, which can become very restrictive. An alternative is to use a DBMS off line for generation of the run-time database; you thus can have the best of both worlds. In either case, the use of a 4GL provides many shortcuts and advantages. Carma McClure [9] points out many of the advantage and disadvantages of 4GLs and their tools, as shown in Table 6-1. The procedural code included in the process is considered difficult to maintain and debug, whereas the nonprocedural code is handled internally to the DBMS and is usually quite robust. In any case, 4GLs offer an alternative to traditional development and IV&V as well.

6.3   VERIFYING SOFTWARE DESIGN DOCUMENT

Figure 6-1 shows the relationships and interfaces among the various design tasks and refers the reader to detailed discussions found in subsequent sections (6.7 through 6.14). IV&V has major concerns with virtually all of these tasks since they all contribute to the contents of the software design document (SDD). Remember that the SDD is prepared at two separate times. The first three sections of the SDD cover preliminary design, which encompasses the computer software configuration item (CSCI) and its primary and subordinate computer software components (CSCs). The remainder of the SDD covers detailed design, which spans from the CSCs to the computer software units (CSUs). Except for the level of detail, the two design processes are very similar and are tightly coupled by internal referencing within the SDD.

As was the case in requirements verification, the design verification process is generic and highly adaptive. That is to say, it will work on any kind of software

TABLE 6-1. Fourth-Generation Languages: Pluses and Minuses

Advantages

- Application development is faster
- Testing is easier because generated code is highly reliable
- Fourth-generation languages are user friendly
- Fourth-generation programs are easy to understand because ill-structured constructs are not allowed
- Many fourth-generation languages are linked to DBMS with built-in dictionaries to help avoid data-related errors
- Many fourth-generation languages are self-documenting
- End users can write and maintain entire fourth-generation application systems

Disadvantages

- Many fourth-generation tools are DBMS specific and operating system specific limiting their portability
- Many fourth-generation tools do not provide a concurrent data update capability
- Many fourth-generation tools do not have an automatic recovery/restart capability
- Most fourth-generation applications are unable to efficiently handle high-volume transaction processing and hence do not work well in real time
- Many fourth-generation programs are incompatible with existing systems written in second- and third-generation languages
- Fourth-generation languages are not standardized
- Fourth-generation tools produce less efficient code than that of earlier generation languages
- Fourth-generation programs use an excessive amount of computer resources

project and with a wide assortment of design and analytical tools. I even know of a few software shops that still do not use CASE tools and somehow manage to produce acceptable products. These are also still a lot of companies that provide programmer work areas as opposed to giving each member of the staff his or her own terminal, computer, or workstation.

Like all of the verification processes described in this book, verification of the SDD progresses from the simple to the complex, in accordance with Figure 6-2. Step 1 examines the SDD for adherence to standards, which once again includes best commercial practices. Since the review of the SDD takes place twice, once for preliminary and again for detailed design, there is a two-part checklist, Figure 6-3, which is based on DOD-STD-2167A [24]. Step 2 (Figure 6-2) evaluates how well the design is stated in the document. When a formal design language is used, the tool will normally perform a number of consistency and completeness checks on the database created for the language. Several of the graphic-oriented data flow diagramming tools also have consistency checking. In any event, IV&V will verify the completeness and internal consistency of the data flow presentation and assess the logical organization and resulting architecture. Step 3 (Figure 6-2) assesses how complete the document appears to be prior to an in-depth analysis. When multiple

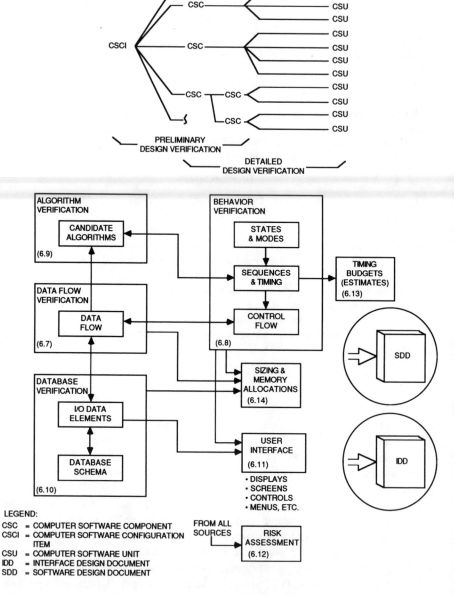

Figure 6-1 Design verification. Relationships and interfaces among various design tasks. (Numbers in parens, e.g. (6.9), refer to section numbers in Chapter 6 that supply further detail on subject.)

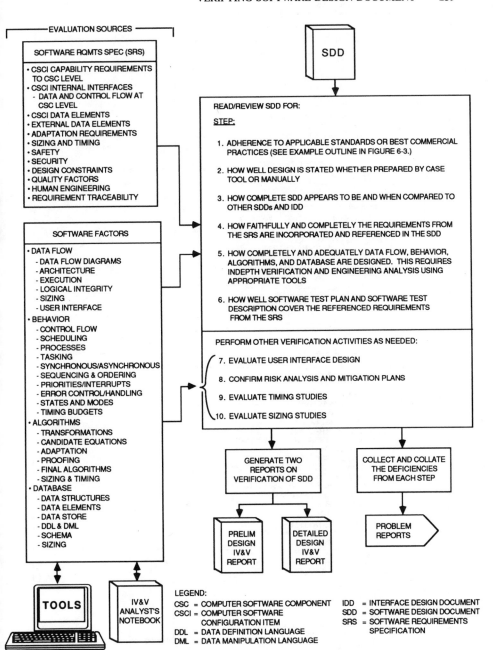

Figure 6-2 Verification of the software design document.

CONTENTS	VERIFIED	REMARKS
1. NOT APPLICABLE FOR IV&V		
2. NOT APPLICABLE FOR IV&V		
3. PRELIMINARY DESIGN		

CSCI OVERVIEW
  CSCI ARCHITECTURE
  SYSTEM STATES & MODES
  MEMORY AND PROCESSING TIME ALLOCATION
CSCI DESIGN DESCRIPTION
  CSC NAME AND PROJECT-UNIQUE ID
    REQUIREMENTS ALLOCATED TO THE CSC
    CSC PRELIM DESIGN - CONTROL & DATA FLOW
    INTERNAL INTERFACES
    DERIVED REQUIREMENTS FOR THE CSC
      SUBORDINATE CSCs
        REPEAT FOR EACH CSC		

4. DETAILED DESIGN		

CSC NAME AND PROJECT-UNIQUE ID
  EXECUTION CONTROL & DATA FLOW
  EXTERNAL INTERFACES TO CSC
    CSU NAME AND PROJECT-UNIQUE ID
      DESIGN REQUIREMENTS (ALLOCATED TO CSC)
      DESIGN OF CSU
        DIAGRAMS, CHARTS, PDL, TOOLS, ETC.
          I/O DATA ELEMENTS
          LOCAL DATA ELEMENTS
          INTERRUPTS AND SIGNALS
          ALGORITHMS
          ERROR HANDLING
          DATA CONVERSION
          USE OF OTHER ELEMENTS
          LOGIC FLOW
          DATA STRUCTURES
          LOCAL DATA FILES OR DATABASE
          LIMITATIONS		

5. CSCI DATA ELEMENTS		

GLOBAL DATA ELEMENTS
  INTERNAL TO CSCI
    NAME OF DATA ELEMENT
    A BRIEF DESCRIPTION
    UNIT OF MEASURE
    LIMIT/RANGE OF VALUES
    ACCURACY REQUIRED
    PRECISION/RESOLUTION (SIGNIFICANT DIGITS)
    REFRESH RATE
    LEGALITY CHECKS
    DATA TYPE (INTEGER, ASCII, FIXED, REAL)
    DATA REPRESENTATION/FORMAT
    CSU WHERE ELEMENT IS SET/CALCULATED
    CSU WHERE ELEMENT IS USED
    DATA SOURCE
  EXTERNAL TO CSCI
    IDENTIFY DATA ELEMENT
    IDENTIFY INTERFACE BY NAME & PROJECT-UNIQUE ID
    REFERENCE IDD		

6. CSCI DATA FILES		

DATA FILE TO CSC/CSU CROSS REFERENCE
DATA FILE NAME & PROJECT-UNIQUE ID THAT IS SHARED BY
MORE THAN ONE CSU
  PURPOSE
  SIZE
  ACCESS METHOD (RANDOM OR SEQUENTIAL)
  DESCRIBE STRUCTURE AND SIZE OF RECORDS
  DESCRIBE DATA IN FILE (AS IN 5 ABOVE)		

7. REQUIREMENTS TRACEABILITY (BEGINS IN PRELIM DESIGN)		
CSU TRACING TO SRS		

Row labels on left margin: PRELIMINARY DESIGN (sections 3); DETAILED DESIGN (sections 5)

LEGEND:

CSC = COMPUTER SOFTWARE COMPONENT
CSCI = COMPUTER SOFTWARE CONFIGURATION ITEM
CSU = COMPUTER SOFTWARE UNIT

IDD = INTERFACE DESIGN DOCUMENT
I/O = INPUT/OUTPUT
PDL = PROGRAM DESIGN LANGUAGE
SRS = SOFTWARE REQUIREMENTS SPECIFICATION

Figure 6-3   Software design document checklist.

SDDs are involved, completeness checking involves verifying that all requirements are properly allocated to at least one SDD. This should uncover any missing or incorrect references. Once the detailed design appears in the SDD, this check also involves verifying the tracing between Sections 3 and 4 of the SDD. There are evaluation indicators (metrics) that can be applied to these documents that help determine percent complete as well as several other quality factors. The application of IV&V metrics is discussed in Section 12.2.

Just as with the requirements documents, each SDD has been examined on its own merit up to this point, but beginning with Step 4 (Figure 6-2) external factors are introduced to aid in verification of the software design. Step 4 carefully cross-checks all the requirements in the SRS with those in the SDD to make certain that all capabilities are faithfully accommodated. Then, when Section 4 is generated, IV&V cross-checks that the capabilities are covered by detailed design. Step 5 performs the in-depth verification of data flow, behavior, algorithms, and database. The interface design document (IDD) is used to verify external interfaces to the CSCI in question. This is actually a two-way verification between the two books—SDD to IDD and vice versa—and supports both data flow and database verification. Real-time systems require several extra verification activities in this step, which include behavioral analysis and algorithm evaluation and verification. Behavior of a system include such things as control flow, task scheduling and timing, sequencing, priorities, and states and modes. Algorithm efficiency is more important to real-time systems than to those in which absolute timing does not matter, but algorithm verification is important to both types of systems. Sometimes algorithms are based on equations found in a math book or technical paper that usually require some type of adaptation for use in the system in question. Then it must be verified as producing accurate calculation results and offer at least a somewhat optimum mathematical and logical solution. Algorithm proofing is very often performed by coding a prototype version that is run on a computer and verified with a calculator or spreadsheet program. Very elaborate ones can be coded and run on a testbed or in a simulation environment for proofing and fine tuning. Once the designer has high confidence in the algorithm that has evolved, it can be offered for use. Finally, the database area is verified. Here IV&V looks at the data elements, structures and stores and can develop good independent sizing estimates for the database. The data definition language (DDL) and data manipulation language (DML) are also evaluated when appropriate. Step 6 (Figure 6-2) is in a sense partially outside the SDD in that it verifies that the software test plan and software test descriptions are adequate to test and demonstrate the design that is defined in the SDD. Step 7 verifies that the user interface design covers the needs of the user in terms of input and output capabilities. This is likely a two-step process since preliminary screens, controls, and displays are usually required by the preliminary design review (PDR) and the detailed versions are needed before the critical design review (CDR). The user interface is one of the most critical parts of any system and deserves considerable attention by IV&V. Step 8 revisits the earlier risk analysis that has been performed on the software to ensure that all design risks have been addressed and hopefully eliminated. Steps 9 and 10 evaluate the developer's timing and sizing studies by comparing them to independently derived results from the verification effort. Detailed discussions of each of these verification activities are given later on in this section, starting with Section 6.7.

6.4 VERIFYING THE INTERFACE DESIGN DOCUMENT

The interface design document (IDD) is the logical extension of the interface requirements specification (IRS). Thus, like the IRS, it is a system-level document containing all the interface design data for all of the software and hardware configuration items (CSCIs and HWCIs) in the system. The IDD goes up to the edge of each configuration item, not inside.

IV&V concerns itself with the consistency and completeness of the interface diagrams and the descriptive information associated with each discrete interface. The interfaces in the IDD and each design document must match exactly. As I pointed out in the previous section, the IDD is very much like a hardware wire run list that completely describes each circuit external to the configuration items. The primary items that IV&V examines are listed as follows:

1. Interface diagrams
2. Purpose of each interface
3. Complete description of each data element:
   - Project-unique ID for each element
   - Brief description
   - The configuration item that is the source of the data element
   - The configuration item that is the user of the data element
   - The units of measure
   - The limit/range
   - The accuracy required
   - The precision or resolution required
   - The refresh frequency
   - Legality checks
   - Data type (integer, ASCII, real . . .)
   - Data format
   - Priority
4. Message descriptions
   - Interface priority
   - Communications protocol
5. Design details of the protocol
6. Any other details considered necessary (fiber optic transmission, special cabling or routing, security, etc.).

IV&V will be very careful to make sure that the elements match between the IDD and the details in the SDD. Any deficiencies will become problem reports and IV&V will be prepared to report on this verification activity as a topic for each formal design review (PDR and CDR) and again in the final report on design verification.

6.5   VERIFYING SOFTWARE TEST PLAN AND THE SOFTWARE TEST DESCRIPTION DURING THE DESIGN VERIFICATION TIME PERIOD

IV&V will verify the software test plans during the preliminary design phase and the software test descriptions during the detailed design period. The details of these verification activities are given in Chapter 8, "Validation," to consolidate all of the discussions about testing in one place. The reader is reminded, however, to make available the necessary staffing and other resources for this activity during the design period.

6.6   VERIFYING REQUIREMENTS TRACING INTO THE SOFTWARE DESIGN DOCUMENT FROM THE SOFTWARE REQUIREMENTS SPECIFICATION

DOD-STD-2167A requires explicit references of all capability requirements found in the software requirements specification (SRS) to specific capabilities in Section 3 of the software design document (SDD). And, because the system specification and the SRS were completely verified in the earlier verification activities, it can be assumed that the SDD will have its correct set of requirements allocated to it. IV&V verifies all of the references. In cases where the DOD-STD is not used, the requirements tracing matrix (RTM) described in Section 5.9 in Chapter 5 should be utilized by IV&V to perform the tracing function. In this situation, the SDD references will be linked to the SRS capabilities to ensure a 100% cross-connection. The first-level references in the SDD are to the computer software component (CSC) level. Once inside this document, each CSC expands into its associated computer software units (CSUs) and the referencing is completed by identifying the software name of the unit of code in which the capability will be implemented when coding occurs. Later on, tests are linked to the CSUs and the complete path is established up and down the requirements-to-test ladder. As mentioned previously, the RTM is a very valuable aid in evaluating the impact of proposed changes, maintaining baselines, and in finding which software elements are affected by particular tests. The database for the RTM can be developed and maintained using simple database software on a PC-level machine.

6.7   VERIFYING DATA FLOW

The first point that must be made is that data flow does not have to be defined graphically by a series of diagrams, although that happens to be a very popular way of doing it. Data flow diagrams came along in the early to mid-1970s as a way of formally designing systems in what was often called the "structured" approach. Most of the early work came out of a handful of authors associated with Ed Yourdon—Larry Constantine, Tom Demarco, Chris Gane, Glen Myers, Trish Sarson, and Wayne Stevens. Together, they wrote several books and numerous papers on structured analysis and design.* The basic data flow diagram uses four special symbols to convey information on: (1) environmental elements with which the system interfaces, (2) the processes, (3) the data flows, and (4) the storage elements. The environmental elements are also called *terminators* and are usually a square or rectangle. Processes are usually rectangles with rounded corners because the circles that were first used waste too much space when used for text. Data flows are curved or straight lines with directional arrows that name the data being passed. And finally, the data store is usually indicated by a three sided rectangle (one side left open). Data flow diagrams (DFDs) are very effective in translating requirements into intermediate levels of design, but they do not convey enough detail to do the entire job. DFDs do not express control, who does the work, what techniques are used in processing, or exactly what data elements are involved. Yourdon and associates recognized these weaknesses and evolved a lower level series of diagrams called *structure charts;* other techniques have evolved as well to fill the gaps in detail. The data dictionaries provide most of the detail needed for each database element. There are other types of diagrams that do virtually the same thing as data flow diagrams, but the latter are the most popular. The types of things that IV&V looks for in DFD verification are:

- Completeness and consistency of coverage
- Mixed symbology is not allowed
- Each data flow has a unique label (name) and appears in the data dictionary
- Each process label is unique and as descriptive as possible
- Outside interaction appears in a terminator symbol
- Differentiation between environment and outside users
- Reads and writes should not be included
- Read-only processes should be avoided
- Write-only processes should be carefully justified
- Overloading a single diagram should be avoided
- Simplifying of each DFD and reducing crossovers to a minimum.

---

*Carma McClure's book *CASE is Software Automation* [9] devotes much of Chapter 3 to discussing the methods and techniques of these pioneers in software engineering and structured analysis.

There are also textual equivalents to DFDs, which have been popularized by Warnier and Orr and by James Martin. These typically use braces and brackets and special symbols to collect and organize functional elements and enable the decomposition of processes to the lowest level. The Warnier-Orr technique focuses on three structured programming constructs—sequence, selection, and repetition. The left-to-right pattern forces a structured top-down approach and it is very simple to convert the diagrams into programming-language constructs. The types of things that IV&V looks for with this type of design documentation includes the following:

- Sequence and repetition constructs require a verb and object when describing processing
- Selection construct simply states the conditions
- Arrange sequential processes in a vertical format
- Use a series of nested Warnier-Orr diagrams for large systems
- Use explicit cross-referencing between diagrams to connect them
- Do not mix constructs within a bracket.

IV&V may find it necessary to use a technique like Warnier–Orr diagrams as a verification tool. They are easy and inexpensive to use and offer a good return on investment.

Regardless of the development method or tool used to describe the data flow for the software, IV&V will evaluate the primary source for correctness, completeness, and consistency and may find it necessary to use an additional mechanism to prove a weakness or inconsistency in the developer's data flow.

6.8   VERIFYING BEHAVIORAL FACTORS, ESPECIALLY IN REAL-TIME SYSTEMS

I have emphasized several times before and will state again that behavior is much more of an issue in real-time systems than non-real-time ones. This is true mostly because if a real-time system misses a processing deadline, everything stands a good chance of collapsing. If the designer is smart enough to allow for a few missed deadlines, we call the system "fault tolerant" or "fail-soft" or use some other descriptor to indicate that the software can accept some processing abnormalities. Most non-real-time systems do not impose strict deadlines on their processing and simply allow a process to take whatever time it needs to finish execution. The book addresses the real-time problem because it plagues so many systems today.

The biggest single addition to structure analysis and design technology in the decade of the 1980s was the addition of control flow. Many of us wrestled with what to call it for years before, because it was perceived that it was necessary. Two pairs of individuals are given credit for perfecting the technique and it has been widely incorporated in the latest CASE tools. The team of Derek Hatley and Imtiaz Pirbhai developed their approach, which closely follows DFDs for the data flow and provides separate diagrams for control flow. Paul Ward and Stephen Mellor, on the other hand, combined control and data flow on a single graph. Max Schindler discusses both paradigms in some detail [10]. Both methods recognize both continuous and discrete time elements. There are a number of difficult decisions that have to be made when designing complex software that include the states and modes of operation and whether on not to show each as a separate set of diagrams. The answer really depends on the specific system. Do the least that works. The next set of issues interact in that they are affected by the algorithms selected for the system. Complex and sophisticated algorithms generally take longer to run than simple ones, as you probably already knew. Let me remind you, though, that the execution time has a profound effect on the system design. Many processes will not wait, so the software has to run in a finite amount of time. IV&V examines the algorithms and timing budgets to ensure that all the tasks that have to can run when they are scheduled. This is a very tedious part of design, that of balancing the available computing resources against what the system must do. A missile attempting to intercept a maneuvering target may have to cycle virtually all of its software at a 100 Hz rate. That is what is meant by real-time processing.

6.9   VERIFYING SELECTED ALGORITHMS, BEGINNING WITH THE MOST CRITICAL FIRST

Chances are IV&V will not have the resources to perform an in-depth study of every last algorithm in the system, so typically a quick examination is made to determine those that have the highest criticality to system operation, and those are then verified in priority order. In preliminary design, candidate mathematical solutions (equations and formula) are sought that have a high likelihood of solving the problem in the time allotted. Tradeoffs are made between accuracy and speed, fidelity and size, sophistication and cost, and other parametric relationships. In the detailed design phase, the number of candidate algorithms will have been reduced to a minimum, but there still may be room for improvement or refinement. There are cases where the IV&V contractor may have expertise and in-depth knowledge of specific processes that are better than those of the developer. On one specific large system I recall, the IV&V contractor had much better nuclear modeling expertise than the developer and was able to offer much improved models and algorithms for system use than the developer had specified and designed. On that same system, through a series of independent simulations, IV&V was able to greatly improve some of the tracking algorithms as well.

6.10   VERIFYING THE DATABASE STRUCTURE AND ELEMENTS

There are many aspects to the database that require verification. One view of database architecture is as follows:

- Highest level: data flow and data store definitions from DFDs
- Intermediate level: data structures
- Detailed level: data elements.

This allows the generation of separate data dictionaries at each level or the creation of a single one that evolves to increasing levels of detail. I prefer the latter. The types of information that IV&V looks for in the data element description includes the following:

- A unique ID for each element
- An adequate description
- The origin of the data element
- The destination of the data element
- The units of measure
- The limit/range
- The accuracy required
- The precision or resolution required
- The refresh frequency (or update rate)
- Legality checks
- Data type (integer, ASCII, real . . .)
- Data format
- Priority.

Other aspects of the database include input preparation and verification, user interaction, error detection, and output verification. The more interactive the system, the more likely that inputs and outputs can be viewed on the screen, so IV&V will also verify the displays and controls used for those purposes.

6.11   VERIFYING USER INTERFACE (SCREENS, MENUS, CONTROLS, TEMPLATES ETC.)

Many systems today are built around standard windowing software like X-windows and its derivatives, which supply many of the tools to build and control screens for almost any purpose. In these cases, IV&V concentrates on the content of the screens and not so much on the background software used to build them, unless it happens to be a new product. Occasionally, even the veteran vendors hit the market with a software product that is not quite ready, and if you attempt to use it, the risk goes up sharply. I have served as an unintentional beta test site for more than one hardware vendor who struggled for a year or more to bring the true performance capabilities of a user interface device or workstation up to the level being advertised initially. (Vendors usually call their own internal test facilities "alpha" test sites and refer to the first friendly users as "beta" sites. The assumption is that beta users do not expect a perfect product; they, in fact, serve to help the vendor find hidden problems in the product.) It sometimes happens that they just do not ever attain the performance listed on their spec sheet. What do you do in these situations? You usually help them fix their problems and your program gets incredibly impacted and your boss does not like you anymore. That is what really happens. IV&V needs to be alert to and suspicious of untried and unproven technology; when you identify an item like the one I have just described, add it to the list of risks and think about what might be done to help reduce it. Ask for one to use for a while and check it out thoroughly before you buy. If the vendor will not loan you one, you probably don't want to do business with him or her anyway.

The things that IV&V should consider when evaluating the user interface include:

- Convenient placement of controls where hand–eye coordination seems natural and intuitive
- Operation requiring minimal movement that is scaled to the motion gradients needed to perform the action, where sensitivity is matched to the required movement
- Amount of data being displayed, its organization and fonts used
- Screens that have a dialog box conveniently and consistently placed screen after screen, requiring minimum cursor movement
- Manageable amount of clutter and number of multiple windows in view
- Angle, color, intensity and glare on the screen
- Comfortable seating and arm positions
- The speed with which the operator or user is required to respond to the system and the system response time to the user
- The arrangement and organization of menus and other access controls
- The simplicity/complexity of input required for operation
- Consistency of conventions used among the various displays; were they tightly controlled or was each designer free to express individual whims? This gets very important when colors begin to have meaning to the operator (e.g., red = warning, yellow = caution, green = normal) or when icons and mimics mean specific things
- The ability to bulletproof the keyboard so that if someone backs up and sits on it, the system will not crash. Think about that one!
- And finally, the contents of each screen. Is it what the user needs and wants? Did the developer survey the user community first? Is there some versatility and flexibility? How difficult is the system to use? Can the software drop the user in limbo?

As you can tell from the various examples, it is very difficult to make up a checklist of what IV&V should look for when verifying the user interface design.

Use the suggestions given above, tempered by the particular type of system and the criticality of the user interface. If the display is key to the outcome of a weapon engagement, give it a lot more attention than if it merely displays lists of data. Use common sense.

6.12   REVIEWING DESIGN RISKS

Design risk assessment is a two-sided problem. One facet is to evaluate the risks that were identified and are being managed by the developer. The other category is the group of risks that IV&V identifies during its verification activities. In the first case, IV&V monitors how well the developer controls and manages those risks that were identified early on in the project. In the second case, IV&V argues to get a reasonable priority assigned to those risks that it identifies. The process is essentially the same in either case and generally follows the form given below:

- Risk identification
- Categorization of the risk
- Analysis of potential impact
- Assignment of corrective action
- Monitoring the results of abatement plans until final closure.

The identification process can take many forms and come from many sources. Risk factor collection comes from such things as use of metrics, program reviews, cost reports, schedule analysis, status reports, specification reviews, working groups, historical data, individual experience, and judgment. Once identified, a database should be set up by the developer for tracking purposes. The customer should have the final approval on the prioritization of the list. Categorization divides risks up by appropriate classes and enables quantification based on such factors as technological maturity and complexity, dependency on other technology, consequences of failure, schedule impacts, performance impact, and cost impacts. Risk-reduction plans will be generated and monitored by the developer, customer, and IV&V to ensure effective management and abatement.

6.13   REVIEWING TIMING BUDGETS, ESPECIALLY IN REAL-TIME SYSTEMS

IV&V reviews the developer's timing budgets for realism based on algorithm, calling sequence, and data flow analyses with limited use of simulation and prototyping to confirm its conclusions on selected parts of the software. Comparisons to other similar systems can also provide rough approximations for timing analysis. It may even be wise to code certain key algorithms in advance, so that actual execution times can be measured and designs optimized if need be. The amount and type of I/O performed by parts of the system can have a great effect on run times and may require better memory management than was being planned. In any case, IV&V will be alert to any timing ambiguities and discrepancies among the various parts of the software.

Another timing consideration occurs on systems that accept data from external sources and/or that can be interrupted from another system or interface. The design of the system should be such that these outside influences cannot violate the critical synchronous processing loops, because if they are allowed to do so, unpredictable system behavior will result. It is much better to use a mailbox approach or wait for the right place in the processing frame before allowing the interrupt to activate. This sort of thing affects timing budgets, since these types of contingencies must always be included.

6.14 REVIEWING SIZING AND MEMORY ALLOCATIONS, ESPECIALLY IN REAL-TIME SYSTEMS

Sizing and memory-allocation estimates come from several sources—data stores, retained database, runtime database, algorithms, amount and cycle times for I/O, archiving, logging, number of processes active, user demands, and the like. Many systems idle much of the time but have to have sufficient capacity to handle peak loads without degrading performance. There is a real problem in sizing the hardware: you have wasted resources if you go beyond the margin specified in the contract and you are deficient if you undersize the system. Therefore, the underlying ideas that specify exactly how the spare capacity of the system will be measured must be written down and negotiated before the contract is signed.

Memory allocation is much more critical in embedded computer systems, such as those found in weapons systems than in a software system that resides on a big mainframe. In either case, however, IV&V looks for poorly allocated resources by verifying the memory mapping performed by the developer. If the candidate system has a 16-bit architecture, then extreme care must be taken in assigning the main memory, since the address word length is definitely a limiting factor. On the majority of big systems for the decade of the 1990s and beyond, however, memory limits will no longer be the problem they once were.

IV&V will perform whatever independent assessments seem necessary to establish valid sizing figures and memory allocations for the software, based on the characteristics of the system and the criticality that these factors bear on its final acceptance.

6.15 REVIEWING HOW WELL THE DEVELOPER IS FOLLOWING THE SOFTWARE DEVELOPMENT PLAN

The review of the software development plan (SDP) is discussed later in the book in Section 9.2.1. However, it is during design that it is extremely important that the developer follow the plan to the letter or, if valid reasons occur, change the plan quickly and alter the development process accordingly. Changes of this type might occur if there is a technology breakthrough or a sudden redirection in the program. IV&V will monitor the developer's adherence to the SDP and report monthly in writing on the status. If an unauthorized departure from the plan occurs, IV&V will notify the customer immediately and initiate a work-around if necessary to avoid any impact until the situation is remedied.

6.16 PARTICIPATING IN ALL REVIEWS AND MEETINGS THAT AFFECT THE SYSTEM

As mentioned previously in Section 5.15, IV&V needs to be included in all meetings between the customer and the developer except those that discuss private contract issues. During the design phase, it is customary to expect to attend the preliminary design review (PDR) and the critical design review (CDR) as discussed in detail in Sections 9.1.4 and 9.1.5. IV&V should also attend and participate in all meetings between the customer and developer that discuss status, problems, technical issues, schedule, and performance. IV&V will also meet with the customer on an as-required basis both in preparation for meetings and in debriefings after the meetings with the developer. When IV&V discovers something that needs to be discussed, there should be a mechanism to call meetings with the appropriate technical and management people present. IV&V's major responsibility is to notify the customer, who then decides what to do and when to do it.

6.17 PRODUCING PROBLEM REPORTS

IV&V will use the developer's problem report (PR) system and forms, whether electronic or hard-copy. Handling of IV&V-initiated PRs should be no different than handling those prepared by any other source. IV&V will have read-only access to the PR database and will retain sufficient old copies to conduct periodic audits to ensure that no unapproved or unauthorized changes occur. There is additional discussion on this subject in Chapter 10, which deals with configuration management.

6.18 INDEPENDENT VERIFICATION AND VALIDATION PRODUCTS FROM THE DESIGN VERIFICATION PHASE

The following is a list of anticipated IV&V products for this phase:

1. Preliminary and detailed design IV&V reports, each containing:
   - Summary of document reviews
   - Verification of requirements tracing into the design
   - Verification of interfaces
   - Verification of data flow

- Verification of behavior (control flow)
- Verification of algorithms
- Verification of database
- Review of user interface
- Review of design risks
- Review of timing, sizing, and memory allocation
- Review of software development plan conformance
- Summary of meetings and formal reviews attended
- List of PRs produced
- Open/action item list

2. IV&V analyst's notebook

- Evaluation factors
- Independent verification studies and results
- Software tools used
- Miscellaneous information worth saving.

6.19   CHAPTER SUMMARY

- The DOD development cycle divides design into two parts—preliminary and detailed design. The first deals with the overall CSCI and its CSCs, while the second provides the details from the CSCs down to the program design language (PDL) or pseudocode level for the CSUs.
- Although there are numerous tasks in this phase, the four major areas focus on algorithm, data flow, database, and behavior analysis and verification.
- Algorithm efficiency is generally more important to real-time systems than to non-real-time ones. Dynamic execution is the best way to test their efficiency.
- Data flow can be verified using the developer's diagrams or independently generated IV&V data flows. Independent ones are sometimes difficult to verify and represent a rather large investment in time and resources.
- If the database uses a mature DBMS, then most of the verification tools accompany the software package. If not, IV&V will either have to perform a lot of manual checking and/or generate automated check programs based on the structure, element descriptions, formats, and file organization rules of the system in question.
- Behavior analysis is focused on the control flows, task scheduling, and interrupt handlers that the developer should have produced and whatever timing templates and studies are available. IV&V then verifies these and augments them with whatever independent timing analysis seems appropriate for that software.
- Design verification also examines the design risks and determines if they are being reduced to a minimum during this phase.

- The critical design review (CDR) marks the last time that the customer can cost-effectively stop the project if obvious deficiencies exist in the design.
- Up to 50% of the IV&V resources can be consumed by the end of the design phase.

6.20 WHAT COMES NEXT

This chapter marks the end of what is called the precode period. Chapter 7 deals with code. From the code stage on actual software should be produced instead of just specifications. Part of code verification will be to compare the emerging software product to the documentation produced during design. Thus, the two phases are not only tightly coupled, but tend to overlap, since many developers build code incrementally while some design is still going on. In that case, more than one CDR can be expected.

7
CODE VERIFICATION

Code verification consists of several tasks that confirm that the developer is follow-ing the software development plan (SDP), that the code matches the design as closely as possible, and that the database and software application and support libraries are adequately configured and maintained. In addition, it ensures that IV&V gets access to code as soon as it is released, even when it is piecemeal, for inspection and static analysis via an appropriate CASE tool. This process is shown in Figure 7-1, which also provides references to detailed "how-to-do-it" discussions that complete this chapter.

IV&V should not attempt to cross swords with the developer's software quality assurance organization and, therefore, has no reason to ask to see the developer's unit development folders (UDFs) or to request access to prerelease versions of the software, as this would only waste valuable resources. The biggest payoff that IV&V offers the project during this phase is to serve as the first outside evaluator of the code. By using a static analysis tool that matches the software language being used, IV&V can check and return the code to the developer in a matter of a few days (how many depends on how urgent the need) with a profile of its deficiencies and overall quality. I have worked both the development and IV&V sides of this prac-tice, and I like the results in either case. Static analysis tools find numerous things that the developer did not know were hidden there or that are missing. These tools are very cost-effective and available for virtually all of the higher-order languages including Ada, C, Fortran, Pascal, COBOL, CMS-2, JOVIAL, and others.

IV&V depends upon the developer's library system to provide frequent software releases so that IV&V can maintain its own software library. In this way, there will be a minimum of interference between the two organizations and IV&V is free to do anything it deems necessary with the code. Thus, the customer needs to make arrangements for these code transfers when the basic contracts are negotiated.

154

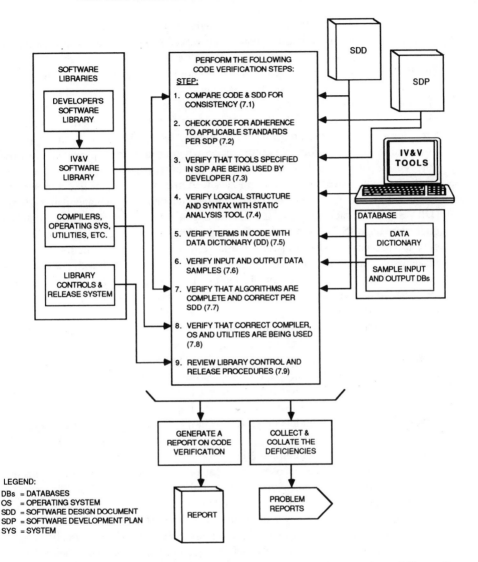

Figure 7-1 The code verification process. (Numbers in parens refer to sections of Chapter 7 that supply more detailed information.)

7.1 VERIFYING CONSISTENCY BETWEEN THE CODE AND THE SOFTWARE DESIGN DOCUMENT

The software design document (SDD) will have been fully verified by the end of the design phase and, therefore, it can be assumed that it represents the definitive description of how the software should behave and be built. In fact, at this point the

SDD is known as the "code-to" document, which literally means that the coder can implement that design verbatim. There is, however, a considerable effort required to convert the program design language (PDL) or pseudocode produced during design into the programming language of choice. There are CASE tools that perform this function that are called *automated code generators,* but most invoke a high amount of labor in converting the design data into a complete enough form for the generator to process. The big catch with all current code generators is that they do not produce very elegant code. In fact, most of the code is not acceptable for real-time applications and requires considerable optimization when used in those applications. I do not want to paint a totally negative picture, however, because these tools are constantly being improved and work extremely well in certain domains like transaction-oriented business systems. The large commercial database management systems (DBMSs) like Oracle, Ingres, and Empress generate applications using standard query language (SQL), which is a fourth-generation language (4GL) that is very easy to use. These DBMSs also have a large assortment of construction tools that make display and I/O generation and formatting much easier than with conventional systems. These systems are not cheap, but they bring a sort of "spreadsheet" mentality to database-oriented systems. The tool survey in Chapter 4 covers a wide range of these tools.

The point in discussing all of these alternatives is to remind the reader that there is not a single way to turn the detailed design into code. There are many variations. Real-time software is traditionally the most difficult and presents the biggest challenge to IV&V; therefore, it is the model chosen for this section.

This verification task, referred to in Step 1 in Figure 7-1, compares the SDD to the code. Because most real-time systems are implemented in Ada, C, Fortran, or JOVIAL, the PDL or pseudocode produced in the detailed design phase frequently strongly resembles the target language. Ada is very often used as a PDL, which means that the analyst can compare the SDD to the code quite easily, allowing for the growth of detail in the code. The goal of this task is to find discrepancies between the two. Deficiencies may occur on either or both sides. IV&V attempts to isolate the cause and assesses the magnitude of the problem. Eventually, the developer will have to address each deficiency for the customer with IV&V present.

The best technique I know in performing this activity is to browse the listings on a screen or hardcopy with the SDD alongside and compare the two. Then mark up book or printout as appropriate when deficiencies are detected. If you browse the screen, print out what is needed to have an identifiable record of the problem.

7.2   VERIFYING THAT SPECIFIED STANDARDS AND PRACTICES ARE BEING FOLLOWED

Step 2 (Figure 7-1) in the code verification task is based upon the standards and practices specified in the software development plan (SDP) written early in the development cycle. It is possible that these standards and practices have been superseded by improved ones in the meantime or that the developer has other good reasons for deviation. In either of these cases, IV&V will need to adjust its approach accordingly. However, if the developer simply decides not to follow what was determined to be adequate in the beginning, IV&V alerts the customer. Usually, there are one or two programmers that for any number of reasons decide not to follow the rest of the team, so this activity really needs to follow two paths—a global one that looks at the project in its totality and specific reviews that look at individual software units as they become available. Individual offenders can be identified and corrective steps taken by the developer to remedy the situation. The issues can include such things as:

- Does everyone follow consistent naming conventions?
- Does everyone use the same versions of system and support software?
- Does everyone use tools consistently?
- Does everyone retain the proper unit test information?
- Does everyone use the same basis for unit testing (valid and coordinated drivers, models, etc.)?
- Does each programmer have his or her own development directories and follow a consistent process when moving software over to the system directories?
- Are software builds, major compilations, and system backups scheduled often and on a noninterference basis?
- Is there a database administrator to manage all data artifacts?
- Does everyone use the same approved coding practices?
- Does the code prepared by various programmers look similar or does it display individual personality?

IV&V needs to select those items and issues relating to standards and practices that have the biggest impact on the quality and future maintainability of the software for its coding checklist. Section 7.4 discusses static analysis tools that can also contribute heavily to standards enforcement. Thus, between observing the types of violations that occur and studying the tool output, IV&V can get an accurate profile of how well the developer is following the standards and practices without ever having to come face to face with and bothering the programmers. That is something you should avoid in most contract situations, unless the developer specifically requests a direct interface at that level. The customer must approve this type of interaction and may find it advantageous to monitor any meetings between the developer and IV&V. There are a few contracts that I am familiar with where this was encouraged, but it is rather rare.

7.3 VERIFYING THAT THE DEVELOPER IS USING SPECIFIED CODING TOOLS

Step 3 (Figure 7-1) can be characterized as an audit-level activity. Most tools have information fields that tell the user the time and date and the version of the tool software being used. Therefore, it is a simple matter to perform periodic checks to ensure that the correct copy of the tool is available. Typical *development tools* used in this phase include but are not limited to the following types:

- Diagramming tools carried over from design
- Procedural outliner/diagrammer
- Code generation software (compiler, linker, loader, etc.)
- Symbolic debugger (very important)
- Editor, pretty printer, etc.
- Unit development file (UDF) program
- Code analyzer
- File/data manipulator
- Test drivers and input data generator
- Test coverage analyzer
- Static analyzer (see Section 7.4)
- Performance monitor.

IV&V would most likely only use the last six tools on this list if analysis of the code is the focus of its effort. However, if IV&V wants to experiment with coding alternatives, all of the tools listed would be useful in developing, compiling, and debugging the code.

7.4   VERIFYING LOGICAL STRUCTURE AND SYNTAX WITH STATIC ANALYSIS

Static analysis tools began life in the early 1970s and were aimed at finding the types of problems that could be detected by scanning the source code, but not executing it. Dr. Ed Miller* and a couple of his cohorts including Michael Paige were notable pioneers in this form of automated testing. Even their early tools were comprehensive, but they produced masses of output that required a learned user to interpret. But things have gotten a lot better and the results have been simplified and bundled for convenience. Several of these tools produce what we call *software metrics,* which are quantifiable measures that describe how well each facet meets its predefined criteria. Some tools just produce raw metric data, while others process and structure it through statistical programs to determine such things as complexity, coupling, and quality factors. Most of these tools have a companion dynamic analyzer, which is used during integration and testing, as discussed in Section 8.5.1.

A series of excellent modern tools of this type are offered by GRC in Santa Barbara, California, for most of the popular high-order languages. GRC's Ada tool,

---

*E. F. Miller, Jr., *Methodology for Comprehensive Software Testing.* Griffiss Air Force Base, New York: Rome Air Development Center, 1975.

first identified as the Ada Test and Verification System (ATVS) and later as Ada-Quest, offers the following capabilities in the static mode:

- Compilation unit structure analysis
- Control flow (branch) analysis
- Standards analysis (user selectable checking options)
- Global entity cross-reference: representation clause, entity cross-reference, type/object cross-reference, type dependency, exception cross-reference, generic instantiation
- Object use analysis
- Exception propagation analysis
- Task/object location analysis
- Call dependency analysis: invocation cross-reference, invocation bands, compilation unit dependency, library unit dependency, compilation order
- Source code data collection.

As you can tell, there is a significant amount of output data from such tools to digest, in some cases to summarize, and to supply to the developer. No analyst can possibly match the tool for thoroughness, speed, or consistency so I encourage IV&V to use these types of tools whenever possible.

7.5 VERIFYING TERMS BETWEEN DATA DICTIONARY AND CODE

As the code is analyzed with respect to the SDD, there is a companion IV&V activity, Step 5 (Figure 7-1), that compares the entries in the data dictionary to the element names appearing both in the code and in the interface, global, and local data definitions in the SDD. This activity ensures consistency among the three items that share the data definitions. Missing or conflicting information will be supplied back to the developer for resolution.

7.6 VERIFYING SAMPLE INPUT AND OUTPUT DATA

During development, it is customary for the developer to generate sample input data that are totally representative of the actual input data. Coincidentally, the system generates output data that have a correlation to these particular inputs. It is necessary to retain and track these corresponding sets of I/O data during testing. IV&V checks to make sure that the developer is adequately identifying and archiving these artifacts and that the correct input data are specified for particular tests. This is especially important when the system has multiple operating modes or more than one test driver.

7.7   VERIFYING ALGORITHMS PER THE SOFTWARE DESIGN DOCUMENT

As the code is analyzed with respect to the SDD, there is a companion IV&V activity, Step 7 (Figure 7-1), that compares the algorithms appearing in the code to those in the SDD. This activity ensures consistency between the two and enables the IV&V analyst to consult earlier assessments, models, simulations, prototypes, etc. of the algorithms to determine if they are accurately and completely implemented. Something as simple as a typographically mistake or a missing or incorrect sign can make the code behave very strangely. This type of code reading and interpretation requires a skilled programmer/analyst to verify the implementation to the design.

7.8   VERIFYING VERSIONS OF THE COMPILER, OPERATING SYSTEM, AND UTILITIES

This can be characterized as an audit-level activity. Most systems have information fields that tell the user the time, date, OS version, compiler version, etc. used to create the software. IV&V looks for any inconsistencies in this data and stays coordinated with the developer's configuration management organization to track the current versions, and updates to the system and support software. When an upgrade is planned by the developer, it should be coordinated with all project personnel including IV&V and should be approved by the customer beforehand. This should minimize the impact, but be prepared for a lot of temporary instability in the system wherever an operating system or compiler is updated.

7.9   REVIEWING SOFTWARE LIBRARY AND RELEASE/VERSION CONTROL

Since IV&V operates its own software library as a recipient from the developer's library, it can continuously monitor the developer's control and release procedures, adherence to scheduled events, completeness of the product, and consistency with which the releases occur. The IV&V software library needs to have sufficient on-line storage to archive several versions of the software, not just the latest one. The reason for this requirement is that IV&V may still be analyzing and studying an earlier implementation and will almost always need to compare the latest release to the previous one to see what changed and figure out why.

7.10   PARTICIPATING IN ALL REVIEWS AND MEETINGS THAT AFFECT THE SYSTEM

There are no major design reviews scheduled during the code phase. It is still customary that the customer and developer get together at least monthly to discuss status, problems, issues, schedule, and performance. IV&V should attend and participate in these meetings and may be asked to present an independent assessment of software status at the request of the customer. IV&V will also meet with the customer on an as-required basis both in preparation for and in debriefing after the meetings with the developer. IV&V should have a mechanism to call meetings with the appropriate technical and management people present to discuss time-critical issues. IV&V's major responsibility is to notify the customer, who then decides what to do and when to do it. IV&V must have the capability to put briefings together quickly and effectively.

There should be a very efficient procedure worked out to get software moved between development and IV&V libraries and to get code verification results from IV&V back to the developer.

7.11 PRODUCING PROBLEM REPORTS

IV&V will use the developer's problem report (PR) system and forms, whether electronic or hard copy. Handling of IV&V-initiated PRs should be no different than handling those prepared by any other source. IV&V will have read-only access to the PR database and will retain sufficient old copies to conduct periodic audits to ensure that no unapproved or unauthorized changes occur.

There is additional discussion on this subject in Chapter 10, which deals with configuration management.

7.12 INDEPENDENT VERIFICATION AND VALIDATION PRODUCTS FROM THE CODE VERIFICATION PHASE

The following is a list of the anticipated IV&V products for this phase:

1. Results from the code to software design document (SDD) comparison
   - Deficiencies and discrepancies
   - Verification of the data dictionary
   - Verification of algorithms between code and SDD
   - Open/action item list
2. Review of conformance to software development plan
3. Results of static analysis and standards checking
4. Results of auditing developer's software library, database archives, and system and support software maintenance and update practices
5. IV&V analyst's notebook
   - code to SDD comparison data
   - Results of audits

- Independent code verification studies and results (including metrics)
- Software tools used
6. Listing of all PRs produced.

7.13 CHAPTER SUMMARY

- Code verification relies heavily on the software design document and the software development plan.
- Efficient code verification depends on having a similar but smaller code management capability to that of the developer. This means that IV&V must have a software library and a computer system to host it. It also means that IV&V has to be able to read, manipulate, and, many times, execute the code. In some cases, IV&V may require a development environment to explore implementation alternatives.
- Because unit testing is considered by most software authorities to be part of the coding phase, IV&V offers a complementary activity called *static analysis,* which examines the code for standards violations, variable set-use data, syntax errors, calling order, etc. This is a very effective way to catch a large number of construction faults before they reach the integration and testing phase.
- Static analyzers are available for just about all of the popular higher-order languages (HOLs) and for several assemblers. They are very popular and highly cost-effective verification tools.
- IV&V requires the data dictionary (or its equivalent), sample input and output data, and a complete description of the data elements, files, etc.
- Code verification continues the algorithm analysis begun in design, but now compares the actual code to the specification.
- Many of the code development tools can also be used by IV&V to aid in the verification process.
- IV&V normally does not examine the developer's unit development files.
- When earlier criticality or risk assessment points to a critical software component, it may be necessary to more thoroughly analyze that code. Sometimes an executable model, spread sheet, or other means of plotting the parametric relationships of the key variables gives the IV&V analyst a much better perspective on how it should work.
- Some of the latest paradigms use automated code generators, which produce acceptable code for non-real-time transaction-oriented business systems; however, the jury is still out for mission-critical computer resource (MCCR) real-time systems, where code optimization is invariably required. To date, these code generators do not produce very elegant or efficient software, and those that attempt to do so have extremely large input data preparation requirements such as additional languages, etc.

- Normally any tool that *executes* the code is considered *"testing"* and is included as part of validation, discussed in the next chapter.

7.14   WHAT COMES NEXT

Chapter 8 presents the details on how to perform validation, which corresponds to the integration and testing phase of software development. Validation normally consists of riding the coattails of the developer's testing effort and performing independent IV&V testing and analysis using some form of testbed and automated testing tools.

8
VALIDATION

Back in Chapter 1, validation was defined as "the process of executing the software to exercise the hardware and comparing the test results to the required performance." Said another way, validation tests the software requirements against what was said in the software requirements specification (SRS) and at a more global level it may test the entire system against what was said in the system specification. IV&V makes sure that all of the requirements are covered by sufficiently adequate testing to be able to say without equivocation that the system meets the stated performance goals and the users' needs as long as it passes all of these tests. It sounds pretty simple put like that, does it not?

Some validation prerequisite work goes on before the integration and testing (I&T) phase begins, as shown in Figure 8-1. Yet, it is all described in this section so that the complete process can be defined and described in one place. Early activities begin in the requirements phase when the qualification methods are being evaluated and rationalized during the verification of the specifications. The next event occurs during preliminary design when the software test plans (STPs) are produced by the developer and reviewed by IV&V. It continues during detailed design, when the software test descriptions (STDs) are released and reviewed. Then finally, validation begins in earnest as the software enters I&T. At this point, I recommend allocation of one part of the validation resources to monitor the developer's test program and committing the other part to independent testing and investigations directed at problems detected during testing and any special analysis (such as timing, loading, error propagation, etc.) that seems necessary. This philosophy allows a flexible approach, which goes where the development effort leads it without running out of resources. Validation must be tailored to fit the system and type of software, matched to available resources, and adapted to the testing environment.

Figure 8-2 is an overview of the validation process and includes book section references to detailed discussions of each significant activity. Several of these activities actually occur in parallel: deciding which of the developer's tests to monitor, developing the IV&V test strategy, and configuring the IV&V testbed. Then, both

DEVELOPMENT CYCLE

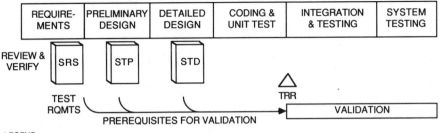

LEGEND:

RQMTS = REQUIREMENTS
SRS   = SOFTWARE REQUIREMENTS SPECIFICATION
STD   = SOFTWARE TEST DESCRIPTION
STP   = SOFTWARE TEST PLAN
TRR   = TEST READINESS REVIEW

Figure 8-1   Validation across the development cycle.

developer's and IV&V's tests are run followed by validation of test results, review of several documents, and production of a final report. The paralleling and chaining of the validation process steps will look something like Figure 8-3.

You have already been reminded that Step 1, which reviews the developer's software test plans and descriptions, occurs earlier in the program and is discussed here for sake of continuity. Step 2 requires a close study of the developer's test build and release plan to determine which tests to designate as key event tests. Stated simply, IV&V needs to know which tests are the most important. These are usually the critical mid- and end-point tests, top-level computer software component (CSC) tests, and certainly almost all of the computer software configuration item (CSCI) level tests. The selection does, however, depend heavily on the way the system is being implemented—top-down, middle-out, or bottom-up (refer to Section 2.1.3 for a refresher if needed) and the number of incremental builds. Step 3 then monitors the developer's tests that were designated in Step 2. Monitoring means that a test package will be prepared for IV&V to evaluate, but does not mean that all such tests will actually be witnessed by IV&V. This determination can be made as the customer and IV&V see fit, based on how testing is progressing. Step 4 is one of the more complicated activities. It determines where IV&V testing should be focused—partly on preplanned tests and partly on ad hoc tests spawned by problems uncovered in developer's tests. Step 5 defines, configures, installs, and operates the IV&V testbed. This testbed can take on many forms from a few software analysis tools on a general purpose host to elaborate hardware-in-the-loop facilities, high-fidelity simulations, instrumentation, analog and digital drivers, etc. that can even match the developer's test facilities. Step 6 covers the running of the IV&V tests and, when appropriate, the comparison of results with those from the developer. Step 7 does whatever is necessary to confirm that the actual tests run validate the requirements traced to them. All of the testing effort comes together in this step. Steps 8 and 9 validate the software product specification (SPS) and the software

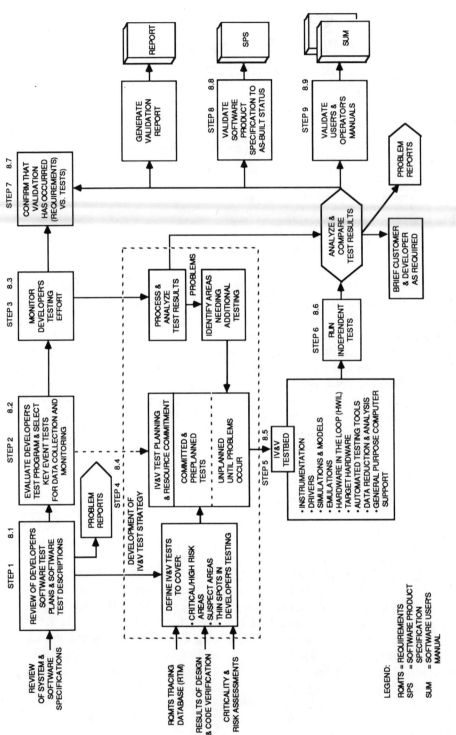

Figure 8-2 Validation process overview. (Numbers and steps refer to more detailed sections in Chapter 8.)

166

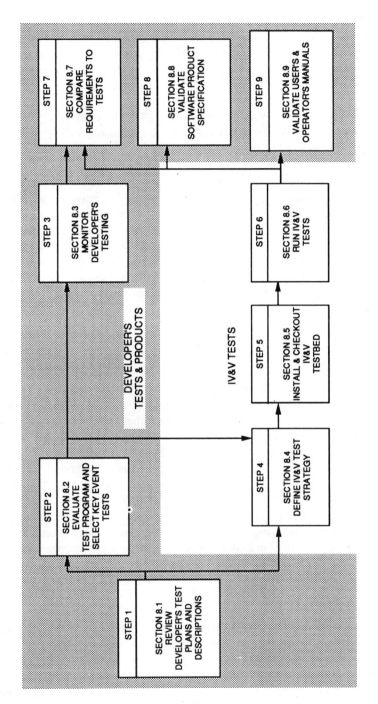

Figure 8-3 Serial and parallel steps in validation.

user's and computer system operator's manuals. IV&V also participates in the audits at the end of testing that are described in Chapter 9.

Now that you have a better idea of the overall processes and activities included in validation, let us turn our attention to the detailed "how-to-do-it" discussions that comprise this chapter.

8.1 REVIEWING AND EVALUATING THE SOFTWARE TEST PLAN AND SOFTWARE TEST DESCRIPTION FOR EACH COMPUTER SOFTWARE CONFIGURATION ITEM

IV&V will review and evaluate the software test plan (STP) during the preliminary design phase to ensure that it includes all of the testable requirements described in Section 3 and qualified in Section 4 of the software requirements specification (SRS). IV&V will then perform a similar review and evaluation of the software test description (STD) during detailed design, except for the detailed procedures and formal test preparations, which are reviewed and evaluated in CSC-level integration and test when they are made available. Both of these actions are comprehensive reviews and are based on the DOD-STD-2167A [24] model that is used throughout this chapter.

8.1.1 The Software Test Plan

The STP actually defines the formal qualification tests (FQT) for the CSCI-based on the requirements in the SRS. To do this comprehensively, however, requires that the software functions and performance capabilities at the CSC level be very well-understood and tested during integration. Otherwise, the tester might be tempted to try to go from unit testing directly to CSCI-level testing, which of course will not work. Because the standard allows the developer to write the STP down to the CSC level, I totally encourage this depth as the only acceptable means of defining a comprehensive FQT program for complex real-time systems. Figure 8-4 is an IV&V checklist for the review and evaluation of the STP. IV&V will check the document for compliance to the applicable standard, consistency between it and the SRS, and correctness of the various elements of the plan. The interface requirements specification (IRS) will also be used in evaluating interface tests, especially when multiple CSCIs or significant external interfaces are involved.

8.1.2 The Software Test Description

The software test description (STD) defines the details of the formal qualification tests (FQT) for the CSCI, based on the requirements in the SRS. As is the case in the software test plan, the STD also is better carried to the CSC level to ensure a comprehensive FQT. Figure 8-5 is an IV&V checklist for the review and evaluation of the STD. IV&V will check the document for compliance to the standard, consistency between it and the STP, and correctness of the various elements of the plan.

CONTENTS	VERIFIED	REMARKS
1. NOT APPLICABLE FOR IV&V		
2. NOT APPLICABLE FOR IV&V		
3. SOFTWARE TEST ENVIRONMENT		

SOFTWARE ITEMS
    HARDWARE AND FIRMWARE ITEMS
    PROPRIETARY NATURE/GOVERNMENT RIGHTS
    INSTALLATION, TESTING, AND CONTROL		

4. FORMAL QUALIFICATION TEST IDENTIFICATION		

CSCI NAME
        GENERAL TEST REQUIREMENTS
            SIZE & EXECUTION TIME
            INPUT DATA
            ERROR CONTROL
        TEST CLASSES
        TEST LEVELS
            CSCI
            CSC
            CSC
            •
            •
            •
            CSCI TO CSCI
            CSCI TO HWCI		

TEST DEFINITIONS
        TEST OBJECTIVE
        SPECIAL REQUIREMENTS
        TEST LEVEL
        TEST TYPE OR CLASS
        QUALIFICATION METHOD
        CROSS-REFERENCE TO RQMTS IN SRS
        CROSS-REFERENCE TO RQMTS IN IRS
        TYPE OF DATA TO BE RECORDED
        ASSUMPTIONS AND CONSTRAINTS
        TEST SCHEDULE		

5. DATA RECORDING, REDUCTION, AND ANALYSIS		

LEGEND:

CSC	= COMPUTER SOFTWARE COMPONENT
CSCI	= COMPUTER SOFTWARE CONFIGURATION ITEM
HWCI	= HARDWARE CONFIGURATION ITEM
IRS	= INTERFACE REQUIREMENTS SPECIFICATION
RQMTS	= REQUIREMENTS
SRS	= SOFWARE REQUIREMENTS SPECIFICATION

Figure 8-4 Software test plan checklist.

8.2 EVALUATE DEVELOPER'S TEST PROGRAM AND SELECT KEY-EVENT TESTS FOR DATA COLLECTION AND MONITORING

It is very important that IV&V be involved in testing as early as possible, literally from the time that software is first released from the programmers to the integration and testing organization. This release sometimes occurs via a formal review called the test readiness review (TRR). Developers typically plan two types of testing—preliminary and formal qualification tests (PQT and FQT)—whether the whole industry calls them by those names or not. PQTs are the low-level CSU-to-CSC integration and buildup tests that, according to the standards, do not require formal test plans or procedures. Most conscientious developers go ahead anyway preparing an internal plan and test network chart for how the software will be integrated and

CONTENTS	VERIFIED	REMARKS
1. NOT APPLICABLE FOR IV&V		
2. NOT APPLICABLE FOR IV&V		
3. FORMAL QUALIFICATION TEST PREPARATIONS		

TEST NAME
  TEST SCHEDULE
  PRE-TEST PROCEDURES
    HARDWARE PREPARATION
    SOFTWARE PREPARATION
      STORAGE MEDIUM OF CSCI
      STORAGE MEDIUM OF ANY SUPPORT SOFTWARE
      WHEN SUPPORT SOFTWARE IS TO BE LOADED
      INITIALIZATION OF COMMON SOFTWARE
    OTHER PRE-TEST PREPARATIONS		

4. FORMAL QUALIFICATION TEST DESCRIPTIONS		

TEST NAME
  TEST CASE
    REQUIREMENTS TRACEABILITY
    INITIALIZATION
      HW & SW CONFIGURATION
      INITIAL SETTINGS
      PRESET HARDWARE CONDITIONS
      INITIAL CONDITIONS USED IN MEASUREMENTS
      CONDITIONS OF SIMULATED ENVIRONMENT
      SPECIAL INSTRUCTIONS
    TEST INPUTS
      NAME, PURPOSE, AND DESCRIPTION
      SOURCE OF TEST INPUT/SELECTION
      WHETHER TEST INPUT IS REAL OR SIMULATED
      TIME OR EVENT SEQUENCE		

EXPECTED TEST RESULTS
    CRITERIA FOR EVALUATING RESULTS
      ACCURACY REQUIREMENTS
      UPPER AND LOWER BOUNDS
      MAX AND MIN DURATION OF TEST
      PASS/FAIL STATUS
      SEVERITY OF PROCESSING ERRORS ASSOCIATED
      WITH RESULT ADDITIONAL CRITERIA
    TEST PROCEDURES
      TEST ACTIONS AND EQUIPMENT OPERATION
      REQUIRED FOR EACH STEP
      EXPECTED RESULT FOR EACH STEP
      EVALUATION CRITERIA FOR EACH STEP AS
      APPROPRIATE
    ASSUMPTIONS AND CONSTRAINTS		

LEGEND:

CSCI = COMPUTER SOFTWARE CONFIGURATION ITEM
HW   = HARDWARE
SW   = SOFTWARE

Figure 8-5 Software test description checklist.

initially tested. These early tests help to build confidence in the software and verify the FQT test descriptions (and test procedures). The FQT is planned and carried out in accordance with the STP and STD discussed in the previous paragraph. When the two types of testing are considered together, there are typically a lot of tests. It is not likely or even necessary that IV&V would attempt to monitor every test; rather, it is a much better strategy to select the more important mid- and end-point tests for monitoring and data collection. Mid-point tests, as the name implies, are those that occur about halfway through the I&T of a function or process. When critical path charts are used in test planning, these points can be readily identified as can the end-point tests which often bring together several functions or capabilities into a single combined test. These are essential monitoring points for IV&V. This way, the limited IV&V resources can be concentrated where the greatest return can be expected. These are called *key-event tests* to denote their relative importance. A rule of thumb that I advocate is to limit the number of key-event tests that IV&V witnesses and analyzes in detail to 4 or 5 per month. It is better to do a thorough evaluation on fewer tests than to attempt too many and not be able to perform well. Once these tests are selected, the information is (1) sent to the customer, who will notify the developer what to expect and (2) fed to Step 4, where it is used to help plan independent testing.

8.3   MONITORING THE DEVELOPER'S TESTING

Monitoring the developer's tests does not necessarily mean eye-witnessing the tests. Monitoring and test data collection can be performed by the developer's software quality assurance and sent overnight to IV&V when it is inconvenient or otherwise not possible for IV&V to be there in person. This is more acceptable in early testing than toward the end, when all of the features and functions are being demonstrated. Then it is vital that IV&V be there in person to witness the tests. There is just too much going on in CSCI-level tests to leave to others and, equally important, IV&V often gets to serve as a user or operator, man a console or workstation, collect data, etc.

8.4   DEVELOPMENT OF THE INDEPENDENT VERIFICATION AND VALIDATION TEST STRATEGY

The IV&V test strategy, shown in Figure 8-2 depends upon several factors, some of which are known in advance and some of which occur during testing. Those that are known come from the following sources:

- Requirements tracing matrix (RTM) or function
- Results of design and code verification
- Results of criticality and risk assessments
- Perceived gaps or weaknesses in the developer's test planning
- Selection of the key-event tests for IV&V monitoring
- Any other appropriate source, such as persistent problems that the developer has with a certain aspect of the system.

The unknown, ad hoc factors basically come from the developer's testing as it is being performed. However, this does not assume that IV&V will look in depth at all the problems that occur or that tests that ran to completion will be ignored. Sometimes something will occur in a test that triggers IV&V to act on a piece of data that may not even be a primary part of the test in question. This can happen because developers sometimes jury rig or alter a test to pass the acceptance criteria, yet the program still has obvious problems that are dismissed with the wave of a hand. If this looks like a bigger problem brewing ahead, IV&V evaluates and tests it to see if this is true. At times, IV&V has to follow instincts and good engineering judgment based on experience on other systems or domain knowledge that the developer may not have.

In a recent example of this, IV&V noticed that a particular development computer system began to behave oddly every morning (during the summer) about the time everyone logged on. The developer blamed the problem on the operating system or sudden load changes, especially multiple simultaneous compiles, and yelled at the vendor's system engineers. An IV&V engineer came in early for a couple of days and watched the system crash. He thought he had a clue, so the third day he brought in a line voltage monitor and showed that every morning all the building air conditioning was turned on at the same time and the voltage dropped well below 100 VAC for 10 to 20 seconds. The system just could not take it especially during daily startup. Further investigation into the wiring in the building found a lot of overheated "green" copper wire with the insulation cooked off of it. The utility department added a new transformer, the building got a lot of new wiring, and the computer got healthy again.

Another completely different kind of problem happened a few years earlier; IV&V noticed an excessive, yet completely random range error in a tracking system. This value was not even being looked at in the particular tests being run, but IV&V decided to investigate the cause anyway. In a week or so, the cause was determined and a fix coded and run on the IV&V testbed. Meanwhile the developer got to the set of tests that looked at how accurately the tracker was performing and was dismayed to find the random range error. IV&V was immediately able to brief the problem and the proposed fix winning the respect of both the developer and customer. These are the kinds of things that make the difference between a very effective and a mediocre effort.

The seeming stochastic nature of some types of software faults can lead the IV&V analyst down many blind alleys and false assumptions. Very often these types of random errors result from one process doing something to another at the wrong time. Therefore, the analyst invariably has to execute the code with some form of traps or other means of collecting the data in such a way that none of the timing aspects are disturbed at all. Sometimes these types of problems are so complex and difficult to set up and recreate that IV&V should work with the developer. This is invariably the situation when the developer owns the only actual target hardware and the IV&V testbed cannot economically replicate it. Thus, one of the strategies must cover what to do when IV&V testing resources are insufficient to isolate the problem without excessive cost and effort. This is one time that we strongly recommend that the developer and IV&V work closely together.

8.5 DEFINING AND CONFIGURING THE INDEPENDENT VERIFICATION AND VALIDATION TESTBED

This book refers to the independent test facilities as the "IV&V testbed," whether it is small and uncomplicated or very large and elaborate. Because the testbed is very important, the book first addresses the test environment and then the configuration and provisioning of the testbed.

8.5.1 Defining the Test Environment

The definition and selection of the IV&V hardware facilities, software, and tools depend upon a large number of variables, which make a standard or generalized characterization very difficult. These variables stem from the following types of considerations:

- How is the system implemented, integrated, and tested?
- What percentage of the testing effort will be spent fine-tuning the system?
- Will system tests involve real targets, flights, intercepts, online users, and inputs from other active interfaces, etc.?
- Can the actual operational environment be accurately simulated?
- Does the system push the state of the art or practice?
- Are mission, operation, fielding, or threat dynamics likely to cause frequent changes to the software?
- What automated test tools does the developer have and use?
- How much will simulations be used to assess the system performance?
- When will target hardware be available? What can be used in the interim for software development? Will a cross-compiler be needed?
- What operating system will be used?
- What higher-order language and compiler will be used?
- How will human engineering, including displays and controls, be evaluated?
- How much of the system's behavior depends on the human in the loop?
- Is the system real time, near real time, or non-real time?
- How much money and scheduled time are available for validation?
- Is software development separated geographically from the hardware development?
- If many systems are to be produced, are all exactly alike or will each have unique features?

This list of questions is by no means all-inclusive, but rather is representative of the kinds of issues and characteristics that dictate and influence testing. I will elaborate on several of the more important ones in the remainder of this discussion.

1. The first assumption that will be made is that IV&V will have its own facilities. There are rare cases in which IV&V is asked to share the developer's facilities, which usually makes for an unhealthy environment. IV&V would no doubt rank low in priority for time on the system, take late night or early morning shifts, and run the risk of being bumped off the system completely if the developer's test program gets behind schedule, which almost always happens. In addition to causing possible scheduling problems for the developer, making him or her nervous by the constant presence of IV&V people, and complicating accounting problems, the two parties will probably each have some amount of proprietary software that they want to protect. This is probably enough reason in itself to require separate facilities. Before discounting the possibility of a joint facility, I will admit that it has worked on rare occasions, but requires extraordinary management dedication, tact, and cooperation from both parties. Also it helps a great deal if the customer (or government) owns the development facilities.

2. The next assumption is that IV&V will obtain a computer system on which to host its software tools, copies of the developer's CASE tools, configuration status accounting system, software libraries, documentation library, simulations, and any other support software-related items. This system may or may not be able to directly support testing. If not, then a computer dedicated solely to that purpose should also be obtained and will serve as operational host for various software tools, the compiler, test drivers, test data, databases, user interface, and possibly the applications software library. To give a simple explanation for this situation, if the target system is a VAX, then a VAX of almost any size can serve as the IV&V testbed host. Conversely, if a special-purpose processor without a real operating system is the target hardware, it would not be suitable as a support software host and something like a VAX just might be chosen for that purpose. In some cases, the support computer can also serve as the driver for testing software on the target computer. You do what you can afford and what makes sense.

3. There will have to be dedicated space for a physical library for software archives and system backups, databases, documentation, test data and results, manuals, vendor software, etc. Big jobs require big libraries. One IV&V job I worked on stored well over 2000 tapes and about as many documents, numerous disks, and several offices full of printouts. Also you may need to worry about classified artifacts in the library, which of course will divide it into two parts and force a precise accounting and tracking of all of the classified contents in accordance with security regulations.

4. IV&V would always like to provide a totally realistic environment in which the code can be executed. Timing is an especially critical parameter in all real-time systems and must be considered when designing or selecting the test tools, since many that instrument the code add some amount of overhead, which slows down the execution of the software corrupting the timing. Other considerations include the methods chosen to drive, stimulate, or exercise the software. These aids can include scenario and threat generation that create realistic sensor and threat environments, portray variable traffic levels for the communications network, and generate various system stimuli and various forms of inputs and outputs in support of testing. Not only is test realism a major concern, but the instrumentation needed to record and reduce the data is also very important.

5. There is also the other class of test tools, which does not require the target computer or a realistic test environment. These accept executable collections of code and examine them on a support computer for logical and functional integrity. Dynamic analyzers are typical of this class of tools.

The basic concept that must be kept in mind in the selection and provisioning of the testbed is to complement individual software tools that the developer has as well as acquiring a copy of his or her major CASE tools, simulators, drivers, and other big-investment items being used. Just how far you are able to follow through with this concept will have a large effect on your effectiveness in performing IV&V. Remember that independently developed models, simulations, and emulations will give slightly different results than those of the developer and consequently may not be very effective in detailed timing and performance analysis. It should also be noted that system and support software—compilers, operating systems, linkers, etc.—must be the same between the developer and IV&V to ensure consistent results. Instead of trying to identify all the individual support software items needed, just be sure that IV&V has the essential items to change source code, compile it, and execute it for independent assessment.

8.5.2 Configuring and Provisioning the Testbed

Figure 8-6 illustrates the tool and test support continuum. At the low end, you can expect to find a PC or general-purpose computer with a few analysis tools. Then at the high end, you typically find the inclusion of special-purpose hardware that either emulates the target system or is an actual copy of the target system. For IV&V to get its hands on the target hardware was once very rare; however, since many systems today are hosted on standard processors, it is now much more common. There are special purpose workstations that emulate many of the common chip sets, including MIL-STD-1750A processors with a combination of hardware and software. There are also cross-compiler and testing systems like the Rational that converts software developed on a general-purpose host computer to the target processors. Although these are essentially development systems, they can also play an occasional role in IV&V.

Notice that about halfway across the continuum that software tools give way to a more hardware-oriented approach. This confirms that IV&V CASE tools can normally be hosted on a mainframe or high-performance workstation and do not require special-purpose hardware. This aspect of CASE tools provides a great deal of flexibility and allows an organization or company to build up a comprehensive IV&V tool capability usable on a wide range of applications, especially if the number of higher order languages is few. This conclusion is based on the fact that so

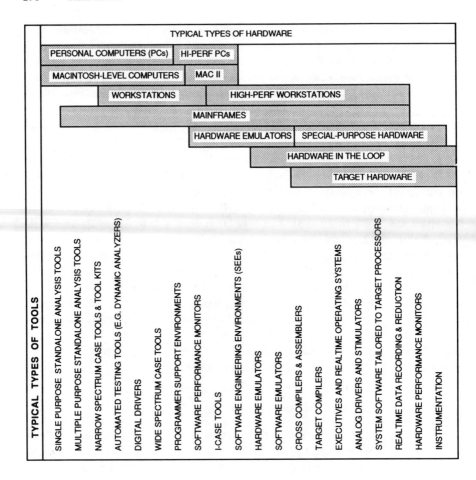

Figure 8-6 Independent verification and validation testbed continuum of tools.

many tools are language-specific. For example, if you develop and equip a testbed for Ada, it will not be of much use on C or Fortran code.

The next facet of the IV&V testbed that needs to be addressed is how to tailor and adapt it to the needs of a specific project. This does not mean that you simply acquire everything up to a certain level. In fact, it is usually just the opposite; you typically pick a few low-end tools, some out of the middle, and a few from the top to provide a well-balanced approach. A few examples should help explain this concept:

- *Example 1: IV&V on a Small JOVIAL-Based High-Performance Missile System*. I would begin by selecting the least number of tools that provide the greatest coverage and return on investment (ROI): From the low end, the requirements-tracing matrix (RTM) tool; at the intermediate level, a JOVIAL code analyzer (static and dynamic); and at the high end, a six-degree-of-freedom (6DOF) hi-fi simulation and as much hardware in the loop (HWIL) as the project can afford.
- *Example 2: IV&V on a Medium-Sized COBOL-Based Business System*. Once again I would select the least number of tools that provides the greatest coverage and ROI. From the low end, the RTM tool; at the intermediate level, a copy of the data flow/data dictionary tool used by the developer, so that I could do parallel analysis, and a COBOL code analyzer (static and dynamic); and at the high end, a hardware system like the developer's. This last item can be the cheapest model of that vendor's product line that duplicates the way the target system will run and that supports the same compiler and operating system versions, or you may simply buy time on a comparable machine.
- *Example 3: IV&V on a Medium-Sized Fortran-Based Real-Time System*. Again I go for the least number of tools that offer the biggest payback. From the low end I might need an editor, debugger, and a requirements analysis tool; at the intermediate level, a copy of the developer's CASE tools and digital drivers, a Fortran code analyzer, and something to help measure execution times and to instrument the hardware, like a comprehensive performance monitor; and finally at the top end, I will require a hardware system that is either the cheapest model of that vendor's product line that duplicates the way the target system will run and that supports the same compiler and operating system versions or a copy of the target hardware.

I think that three examples are enough to give you the feel for tool and support hardware selection. It should also be noted that IV&V is a very flexible and adaptive process that will vary from contractor to contractor and from group to group; also, the tools and hardware facilities already in place will definitely affect the approach. If you already own three tools and know how to use them, you will be reluctant (and probably foolish as well) to rush out and buy two new ones that duplicate the existing capabilities. Thus, expect some variations in both the selection of specific tools and in the IV&V approach to validation.

Figure 8-7 shows a typical comprehensive IV&V testbed suitable for a real-time weapon system. Remember that the exact configuration will vary depending upon the developer's tools and system particulars and the IV&V resources and objectives.

8.6   RUNNING INDEPENDENT VALIDATION TESTS

IV&V should always base its tests on the developer's tests wherever possible to save generating them from scratch. This provides a good basis and structure for the independent tests and greatly reduces the preparation time. Many of the validation

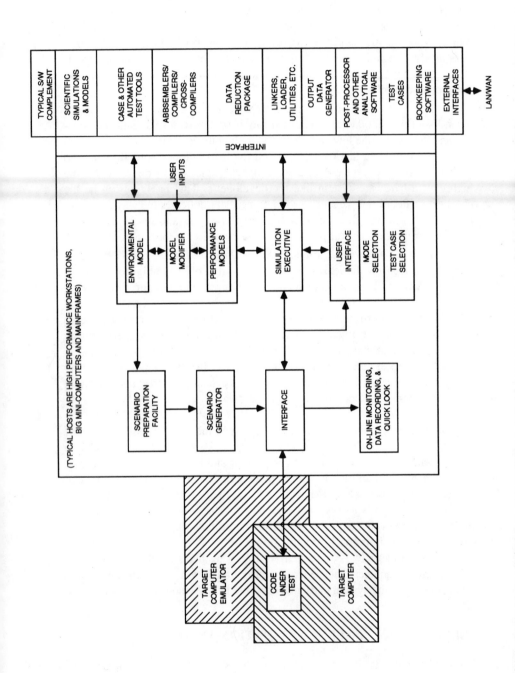

178

tests are run to help analyze problems discovered during developer testing. In this case, the results will be compared. If IV&V thinks it has isolated the problem, problem reports will be written and briefing materials will be generated, if needed. The key distinction between developer and IV&V testing is in their different perspectives. The developer is concerned with "meeting the spec," but IV&V wants to determine such things as the system failure points, performance boundaries, and error propagation. Since few systems are ever completely tested, IV&V's efforts contribute to the overall quality in at least two ways: (1) by the discovery of errors and faults left undetected or unsolved by the developer, and (2) by supplying a different set of test conditions, parameters, environment, and human operators. By becoming the first user, IV&V can contribute significantly to the eventual reliable and consistent operation of the software and system.

8.7   CONFIRMING VALIDATION OF REQUIREMENTS TO TESTS

This step is the culmination of all the previous steps in that it enables IV&V to gain sufficiently high confidence that all of the testable requirements are validated through collection of actual test results. It also performs a two-way check that (1) ensures that all testable requirements have one or more tests linked to them and (2) ensures that all tests have one or more requirements that justify them.

8.8   VALIDATION OF THE SOFTWARE PRODUCT SPECIFICATION

The primary source document for the software product specification (SPS) is the software design document (SDD). The goal of this step is to confirm that the SPS faithfully represents the "as-built" status of the software. Since IV&V tries very hard to keep up with all of the changes in the design and code as they occur, this is not considered a "do-it-all-at-the-end" type of job, but rather is an ongoing exercise. In effect, this activity validates the SPS against the software using listings or browsing the code to confirm the implementation. The main parts of the SPS are as follows:

- The SDD, updated to as-built status
- Source code listings (sometimes only on electronic medium)
- Compiler or assembler version and revision level used to create the software
- Measured resource utilization
- Notes of general interest
- Appendices as required.

8.9   VALIDATING SOFTWARE USERS' AND SYSTEM OPERATORS' MANUALS

The software user's manual (SUM) is very similar in content to the detailed test procedures portion of the software test description (STD). Therefore, the SUM can be validated as IV&V witnesses the developer's tests. Similarly, there are operating procedures required in many systems that can also be validated during the same tests. If there are any features or functions that are not demonstrated sufficiently to completely validate these manuals, a deficiency in the test program has just been discovered and a problem report should be generated to correct the situation. IV&V should always be ready to brief both the customer and the developer concerning any deficiencies that it discovers.

8.10   TRACKING CONFIGURATION CONTROL BOARD ACTIONS AND OPEN-ITEM STATUS

It is very important that IV&V monitor the actions of the configuration control board (CCB) very closely, especially during formal qualification testing (FQT). It is very easy to treat too lightly or ignore small problems when facing major performance-related issues, so IV&V spreads its attention across the spectrum in an attempt to balance the analysis given all problems. Minor symptoms sometimes lead to discovery of much bigger problems lying just below the surface, a sort of "iceberg effect," so IV&V should deliberately concentrate on problems that the developer tends to put off. IV&V will attend all CCB meetings with the customer and serve on the customer's behalf. The developer should be using an action/open item tracking list, but if not, IV&V can develop and maintain one for the customer. More details on the CCB and the configuration status accounting system (CSAS) are found in Section 10.2.2.

8.11   PARTICIPATING IN ALL REVIEWS, AUDITS, AND MEETINGS THAT AFFECT THE SYSTEM

The test readiness review (TRR) is the formal review that marks the handover of code from the programmers to the integration and testing (I&T) activity and, hence, the beginning of validation. IV&V will participate in this review mainly to find out what code is being transferred at that time. When incremental builds are planned, there will be multiple TRRs, which correspond to the major deliveries.

It is customary that the customer and developer get together at least monthly during I&T to discuss status, action/open items, problems, issues, schedule, and performance. IV&V should attend and participate in these meetings. IV&V will also meet with the customer on an as-required basis both in preparation for and in debriefing after the meetings with the developer. When IV&V discovers something that needs to be discussed with the customer, developer, or both, there should be a mechanism to call meetings with the appropriate technical and management people present. IV&V's major responsibility is to notify the customer, who then decides what to do and when to do it. IV&V must have the capability to put briefings together quickly and effectively.

There should be a very efficient procedure worked out to get software moved between the developer's and IV&V's libraries and to get dynamic analysis and other validation test results from IV&V back to the developer.

IV&V will also participate on behalf of the customer in the functional configuration audit (FCA) and the physical configuration audit (PCA) and the formal qualification review (FQR) held at or very near the end of FQT. Details on this participation are given in Sections 9.1.7 through 9.1.9 (Chapter 9).

8.12 PRODUCING PROBLEM REPORTS

Problem reports (PRs) are handled the same way in each IV&V phase. IV&V will use the developer's problem report (PR) system and forms, whether electronic or hard copy. Handling of IV&V-initiated PRs should be no different than those prepared by any other source. IV&V will have read-only access to the PR database and will retain sufficient old copies to conduct periodic audits to ensure that no unapproved or unauthorized changes occur.

There is additional discussion on this subject in Chapter 10, which deals with configuration management.

8.13 PORTRAYAL OF A TESTING SCENARIO FROM AN INDEPENDENT VERIFICATION AND VALIDATION PERSPECTIVE

This section walks the reader through a typical test sequence. It defines the types of documentation that normally accompany a test and then goes through a step-by-step analysis of the test itself to promote a better understanding of the process.

8.13.1 Defining the Test Artifacts

Test Documentation. This includes the test plans, descriptions, procedures, scripts, test cases, scenarios, etc., which describe what and how the test was to be run. Some of this material can be used as backup to determine if the test was run as planned.

Test Reports. The tester should document the results of the test, including acceptance criteria, any deviations from the test documentation, problems encountered, deficiencies identified, and open items.

Test Logs. These are manually produced records of the test events in chronological order as they occurred during the test. Test logs may come from software quality assurance (SQA), the test director, and/or subsystem test monitors. They should contain all actions not recorded by the standard data reduction (e.g., system terminal hard copy), switch settings, indicator lights, display boards, hardware configuration and status, etc.

Test Observer Reports. Government and IV&V observers at the test should document their observations. This information will augment the test logs.

Test Inputs. Test inputs include all manual actions recorded on the test logs, simulated or real scenario data (targets, intercomputer messages, etc.), initial data file contents, hardware states and configurations, and other data used to drive the test.

Hard Copy Output. Test data is recorded during and after the test in the form of printer, teletype (TTY), terminal, plotter, etc. output. The printer data may include memory and register dumps, traces, selectable data-recording dumps by the tester, quick-look data, etc. The TTY or terminal output will be a hard copy of the dialogue conducted at each of these devices.

Recorded Data Output. Data recorded on disc or tape during the test must be available for examination. The most common form of these data are key variables, memory locations, registers, I/O status, interrupt status, etc. that occurred during the test. IV&V can perform its own data reduction and/or interpretation to examine problems and draw independent conclusions.

Problem Reports/Deficiency Reports. Problems and deficiencies that the tester uncovered and/or solved will be recorded as part of the configuration management (CM) procedures. IV&V will use these reports as starting points to examine the test data in order to determine the cause and extent of the problems or deficiencies.

Software and Database. The source and/or assembled code listings, including data files, etc. will be used in isolating errors and determining their causes and extent.

8.13.2 Test Assessment

The typical steps and procedures that are normally followed by IV&V are described below. The exact test-assessment approach will of course be a function of the available data and system attributes, so this should only be considered an example.

Deciding What to Collect

Step 1. Before the actual assessment and examination process begins, all the available inputs to the task should be collected.

Step 2. IV&V will first examine the test logs to determine if the test was run according to the test plan, description, procedure, and script. It is the experience of the industry that approximately 20% of all test "errors" turn out to be errors in the test procedure and operator actions. The wrong input scenario or program version can easily go unnoticed during test setup. Even if there were no problems encountered in the test, a minor change in the test procedure or script must be assessed in terms of the validity of the results and collected test data. A baseline of what actually was tested must be established before the test evaluation can proceed.

Step 3. IV&V will revalidate the test acceptance criteria using the tester-produced test data. If this independent assessment results in problems or deficiencies, the test evaluation will continue as described below. Each problem or deficiency reported by the tester or independently by IV&V will be examined in detail in order to determine the cause and extent, followed by a PR.

Step 4. The test inputs will be assessed first. This involves (a) examining the input scenario (real or simulated) by reviewing dumps of input messages, sequences, target data, converted analog data, etc.; (b) examining memory contents at time zero; (c) reviewing the hardware configuration and initial state of the hardware at time zero; and (d) verifying that the correct software version was loaded.

Step 5. Data recorded and reduced by the tester will be examined before IV&V attempts to independently reduce any other data. If the data are not sufficient to isolate the problem, then other recorded data will be reduced.

Step 6. Memory and register dumps and traces will usually not be utilized in the event that the recorded data is not adequate (e.g., the system crashed and the recorded data are lost). Analyzing memory and register dumps and traces is very time-consuming and requires system programmers skilled in the computer and operating system being used in testing.

Analyzing What Happened

Step 7. Once the proper test data have been assessed, the cause of the problem or deficiency can usually be determined. Potential causes of problems or deficiencies include:

- Error in the test plan, description, procedure, or script
- Operator error
- Data recording failure
- Hardware failure
- Software bugs (coding errors)
- Design error, which produces a coding error
- Requirements error (in the SRS), which produces a design error, etc.
- System requirements problem (in the system spec), which misdefines a software function
- Errors that cannot be isolated or repeated. It is important that data be archived on these "transient" errors for future evaluation when test data is collected from other tests in hopes that there will be a clue to their cause.

Step 8. Code reading may be required to isolate specific software problems. If the inputs and outputs to routines have been recorded and a discrepancy exists, then manually examining the code will possibly determine the answer to the problem.

Step 9. It may be necessary to run a test independently to collect additional data to isolate the problem. Often the appropriate timeframe or type of data needed to isolate the problem will not have been recorded. IV&V will usually recommend that the same test or a new test that concentrates on the problem area be run.

Step 10. After the cause of the problem or deficiency is determined, IV&V will determine the extent of the situation. This may involve proposing solutions for minor problems (e.g., ones related to code, design, test procedures), recommending design or test plan revisions, recommending engineering change proposals (ECPs), or recommending further analysis into a requirements change. A test report will be written that documents the test analysis performed and the IV&V results. Problem reports (PRs) will also be written on all errors uncovered.

Keeping the Records Straight

Step 11. The configuration status accounting system (CSAS) files will be updated. In this way, history data can be maintained to generate:

* A periodic report of PRs over a defined period (usually monthly)
* A summary-level description of the PRs
* A plan for the resolution of outstanding PRs
* A generalized trend analysis which allows SQA and IV&V to plot the PR data
* A trend analysis depicting the significance of PRs in terms of complexity.

Step 12. A determination of the validity of the tester-generated problem reports will be made. Each PR will be related back to the environment in which it occurred. The test script, procedure, and operator log will be examined. In cases where the PR reflects a genuine specification deficiency, the paragraph number and description shall be entered into the record.

Step 13. Determination of which problem reports require conversion to a change recommendation and eventual ECP will be made. This judgment is based upon the technical analysis of the problem report and may result in modifications to the specifications (and other system documentation such as operator handbooks and maintenance manuals) or a modification to the software proper. This determination will also be provided to the SQA organization.

Step 14. If an ECP results from the problem report, IV&V will recommend a priority for the change based on its system impact and also suggest its categorization as a "test only" change or a formal modification to the software under test. Most changes discovered during testing are treated as "test-only" changes initially—due to the schedule urgency of most test programs—and later after retest, are formalized into ECPs if required. Test-only changes are quick (and sometimes dirty) fixes, which may ignore coding elegance and are not accompanied by the sometimes lengthy specification errata that goes with a final ECP. Care must be taken to ensure preservation of version integrity during such fix procedures. Code that contains one or more "test-only" fixes is usually reserved for "friendly users" and should not be used in runs for the record, unless there is no other choice.

Step 15. IV&V will use both tester-generated and IV&V results to update the tracking database. Tracing of requirements through the design, code, and test plans and finally to the test results is an important IV&V recordkeeping function. IV&V may also update acceptance criteria to actual test results if there is a significant difference. This will enable IV&V to report ongoing validation results to the developer in a quantitative manner. IV&V should also compile a list of testing "open items" as a result of this test analysis. The list will contain all problems and deficiencies that have not been resolved, either by the contractor, tester, or IV&V.

8.14 INDEPENDENT VERIFICATION AND VALIDATION PRODUCTS FROM THE VALIDATION PHASE

The following is a list of the anticipated IV&V products for this phase:

1. Results from the review of the developer's software test plans and descriptions (STPs and STDs)
2. Listing or network of key-event tests selected for monitoring by IV&V
3. Generation of the formal validation report, including such things as;
   - Results from monitoring the developer's testing
   - Results from running the IV&V test tool(s) on the code
   - Summary of preplanned IV&V tests
   - Summary of the ad hoc IV&V tests that were run in response to problems that occurred during testing and investigations initiated by IV&V
   - Description of the IV&V testbed and its complement of tools
   - IV&V test results (data and analysis can be referenced)
   - List of any briefings given the customer and developer on validation activities
   - Validation summary comparing the requirements and tests
   - Validation of the software product specification, user's and operator's manuals
   - Summary of functional configuration audit, formal qualification review, and physical configuration audit
   - Final conclusions and recommendations for the operational or production period.

4. IV&V analyst's notebook
   - Requirements-to-test comparison data
   - Results of audits and reviews
   - Independent validation studies and results
   - Software tools used
5. Listing of all PRs produced and their status at the end of formal qualification tests (FQT).

8.15 CHAPTER SUMMARY

- Validation is the culmination of the four-part IV&V methodology. Its primary purpose is to ensure that the requirements found in the specifications are properly tested and meet the specified performance.
- Validation evaluates the developer's test planning and monitors the tests, determines where IV&V resources can best be spent, and then performs independent testing and analysis.
- Validation attempts to strike a balance between analyzing the developer's testing and performing independent testing. If budget constraints preclude both, trade off more of the independent tests and concentrate on finding the problems in the developer's tests.
- Validation requires some form of testbed. In the simplest case this could be a big PC or Macintosh; in the most complex case, perhaps a network of high performance workstations, a big mini computer, or even a main frame. What we are is saying is that there is no limit or cutoff to the hardware at the upper end. Try to get what you need without overdoing it. It has to host and run your IV&V tools, the software library, and execute the code at a minimum.
- IV&V people should be allowed to participate "hands on" in the developmental and operational testing of the system. Both contracts and later the software development plan should state how the relationship is expected to work. Thus, IV&V becomes the first outside user of the system.
- There are usually too many developer tests to monitor them all, so IV&V has evolved an approach of monitoring only key-event tests. These are key mid-point and end-point tests that offer significant data and that are in the critical path. These are tests with meaning and importance that offer IV&V fertile ground for evaluation.
- Validation not only confirms the test-to-requirement relationship, but also ensures that the software product specifications and user/operator documents are error-free and represent the actual system "as built."
- Validation should last at least until successful selloff or acceptance of the software and passage of the necessary audits to ensure that all artifacts are as represented.

8.16 WHAT COMES NEXT

The next chapter describes the technical reviews and audits that are necessary to ensure good management visibility and coordination among the customer, the developer, and IV&V. The chapter also covers the key planning documents that help control the project throughout its development and that IV&V relies upon heavily for its detailed planning.

9
KEY PLANS, REVIEWS, AND AUDITS

Government procurements especially are marked by a highly structured and formalized set of planning documents and a series of periodic reviews and audits collectively designed to aid in the planning, definition, monitoring, control, and coordination of the development process. Most of the requirements for the early planning documents have grown from the necessity to define in advance how something should be developed, supported, managed, and evaluated so that resources and logistic support can be committed when needed. Much of the commercial and industrial sectors also take advantage of this framework for the plans, specifications, and reviews in order to strengthen and better structure their software development efforts.

Because each military service has a slightly different set of planning and management documents and defined times for when they are needed in the acquisition life cycle, it is not practical to develop a single generic list that will serve every situation. Therefore, this chapter will only address these documents in general terms. The book divides these documents into those routinely prepared by the development contractor and those prepared by the government. The government documents are based on the DOD 5000 directives and instructions, revised in February 1991 [14, 16, 17].

Technical reviews and audits are the checks and balances between the developing agency and its software contractor (and subordinate contractors, as the case may be). Since the IV&V organization normally assists and takes the side of the customer agency, a mild adversary relationship may develop between IV&V and the other contractors, whose primary concerns are with producing the software. This relationship is considered normal, but a word of caution: It is essential that conduct of the IV&V organization at technical reviews and meetings be above reproach since it is easy to become arrogant and overly critical. IV&V's position should be one of friendly persuasion, not confrontation.

9.1   KEY REVIEWS AND AUDITS

Key technical reviews are strategically placed at or near the natural transition points of the development process. By establishing the formal requirement to review the program status in this periodic fashion, the customer and IV&V can greatly enhance their control and influence over the final product. The reviews and audits described here are based on MIL-STD-1521 [13], which is the definitive guide within DOD. Remember that the activities and actions described in this section are those that IV&V will perform and not what the developer does; although they sound a lot alike, the orientation is different.

Most of the commercial world follows this general approach to reviews, but does not observe them all, as will be explained later in this section. Figure 9-1 shows the reviews and audits where they are most likely to occur for the DOD and commercial models. The key technical reviews of interest to IV&V are as follows:

1. *System Requirements Review (SRR).* The SRR occurs to evaluate the adequacy of the preliminary system specification and initial allocation of requirements to hardware configuration items (HWCIs) and software configuration items (CSCIs). There can be multiple SRRs, if required. In the classical three-step acquisition cycle, the SRRs occur in the CD phase and as late as the demonstration and validation (Dem/Val) phase. If IV&V is not active at the time of these reviews, the briefing materials and minutes will be reviewed once IV&V begins.

2. *System Design Review (SDR).* The SDR occurs when system requirements are firm and the system specification is ready to become identified as the "functional" baseline of the system. This review examines the preliminary operational concept, hardware, software, and interface specifications. SDR can occur as early as the end of the concept definition (CD) period (the preferred point in time), during Dem/Val, or as late as the beginning of full-scale engineering development (FSED), if there was trouble getting approval on the system specification. Many DOD programs repeat the SDR after a phase transition to ensure the system specification is as complete and correct as possible. If IV&V is not active at the time of this review, the briefing materials and minutes will be reviewed once IV&V begins.

3. *Software Specification Review (SSR).* The SSR occurs when the hardware, software, and interface requirements specifications are ready for approval and identification as the "allocated" baseline. In the classic three-step acquisition, this review can occur at the end of Dem/Val (the preferred point in time) or early in FSED, but always after the SDR. If IV&V is not active at the time of this review, the briefing materials and minutes will be reviewed once IV&V begins. When planning an IV&V effort, the customer should try to have IV&V on-board before this review.

4. *Preliminary Design Review (PDR).* The PDR occurs when the system is well enough defined to support the generation of the preliminary design as described

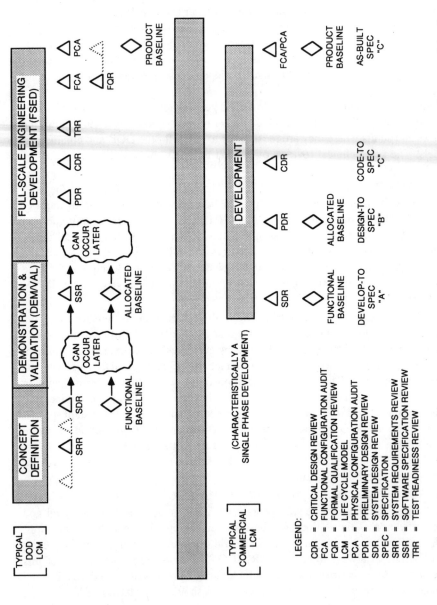

Figure 9-1 When the key reviews are likely to occur in the life cycle model (LCM), comparison of commercial and Department of Defense LCM.

in Section 3 of the software design documents (SDD) and the system is ready to transition to the detailed design subphase. The PDR can be a single event or can be spaced out to cover each configuration item separately or in convenient groupings. In the commercial world, the SSR and PDR are usually combined and simply called the PDR, and the equivalent to the allocated baseline occurs then.

5. *Critical Design Review (CDR).* The CDR occurs when the detailed design described in Section 4 of the SDD and other related documents is ready for review. A successful CDR approves the software design so that formal coding can begin. When rapid prototyping is used earlier in the program and produces functioning code, it is considered "preliminary" and not subject to the "no code gets written before CDR" rule, even if it is reused later. The CDR can be conducted incrementally when reasonable to do so. The whole software world recognizes the importance of a CDR-like review and most developers regardless of customer (DOD, government, or commercial) call it by this name.

These five reviews cover roughly the first half of typical development efforts. Of the five, the commercial world generally recognizes the SDR, PDR, and CDR as essential to adequate development practices. This works well for them since invariably their developments are single-phase efforts and do not require reviews spread over a concept definition or demonstration and validation.

About the middle of the integration and testing (I & T) phase, after CSC-level testing has confirmed that the code is "robust" enough to begin CSCI-level testing, the contractor holds a test readiness review (TRR). When several chunks of code are transitioned at different times, there will be corresponding TRRs for each aggregation. TRR can also mark the handover of code from the programmers to the testers, which is especially important if the contractor has an independent test organization. Toward the end of the testing phase, it is common to hold reviews and audits to determine how well the "as-built" system meets the previously defined requirements and design and if the formal documentation (including specifications, manuals, drawings, and data) is sufficient even to the point of supporting a second-source selection for production. (Second sourcing is a hardware carry-over and generally applies only to maintenance of software since "production" of software is mostly just a copying procedure.) This means briefly that enough information on how the system was built has been collected to hand it over to another qualified contractor so that duplicates can be built or so that this other party could maintain it in the future. This information is called the *technical data package* (TDP) by most government agencies. IV&V serves as part of the auditing staff to look not only for omissions and errors in the TDP but also to examine it for things that should not be there. In software, it is easy to slip in a few "goodies" like a compiler, multiple versions of code, or special maintenance, debug, and utility software that are not part of the baseline, which could jeopardize the integrity of the entire software system of a tactical or strategic weapon or communication system. These are just a few of the things that IV&V looks for; they are considered very important to the future health and maintainability of the system. The audits and reviews most important to IV&V are described below:

- *Test Readiness Review (TRR)*. The TRR occurs when software is ready for formal CSCI-level testing to begin. TRR can mark the handover of code to the I & T organization and usually occurs at about the midpoint of this phase.
- *Functional Configuration Audit (FCA)*. The FCA occurs prior to software acceptance testing to validate that each CSCI's actual performance complies with its software (and hardware, as required) and interface requirements specifications. Thus, the test results are verified against the performance criteria as stated in the requirements specifications and as described in appropriate user's, operator's, and diagnostic manuals. FCAs can be conducted on a progressive basis.
- *Physical Configuration Audit (PCA)*. The PCA occurs to examine the "as-built" version of a configuration item (CSCI or HWCI) against its design documentation in order to establish the product baseline. Thus, it examines documents, drawings, data, listings, records, and test results to ensure validated configuration identification of each configuration item (CI). PCA also looks for things that are there that should not be and sees that they are removed.
- *Formal Qualification Review (FQR); also known by other names*. The FQR occurs as a series of tests, inspections, or analytical processes by which each end item (HWCI or CSCI) is certified as having met its specification (and hence the letter of the contract) and is at the required performance level. If possible, the FQR should be combined with the FCA; however, uncertainty in testing results may shift the FQR as late as post-PCA during system testing whenever the necessary tests have been successfully run to enable "certification" of the CIs.

With this overview of the reviews and audits accomplished, it is only appropriate to discuss each one in detail as it relates to IV&V.

9.1.1 System Requirements Review

The purpose of the system requirements review (SRR) is to ascertain the adequacy of the contractor's efforts in defining system requirements. To accomplish this, the available output of the contractor's systems engineering activity is reviewed and verified by IV&V for responsiveness to the statement of work, externally generated originating requirements, known interfaces, and constraints imposed by regulations, other agencies, and the contract.

As stated in the introduction to this section, IV&V is usually not in force when this review occurs and it will often therefore be performed in retrospect. In any case, the IV&V analysts examine how well the functional analysis has defined the preliminary hardware and software entities, which eventually become configuration items. Other factors such as facilities, physical limitations, manufacturing capabilities, human factors engineering, logistics, cost, and schedule all influence the formation and definition of the system. IV&V brings to this early evaluation of the system and its preliminary system specification an identification of risks and critical factors, a measure of adequacy of the initial synthesis of hardware and software, and a list of deficiencies, omissions, and inconsistencies.

If IV&V happens to be in effect when this review occurs, a verification of external requirements from all available sources will be included much like that described in the next section on the System Design Review (SDR). The steps outlined below are typical of the actions taken by IV&V for the SRR.

- Verify the preliminary system synthesis and its functional allocation
- Verify the sources of the externally generated originating requirements into the preliminary system specification
- Give special attention to the user, mission, and operational requirements from all sources to verify if they are covered in the preliminary system specification
- Assess the life cycle and related cost analysis data for realism
- Verify the draft system interface and interoperability requirements
- Verify that the program risks are recognized and prioritized
- Verify that the test requirements and test strategy are identified
- Verify that all required system engineering management activities are addressed at least in draft form
- Perform discrete adequacy and completeness checks in accordance with MIL-STD-1521B [13] guidelines, Section 10, Appendix A. These are imposed on the development contractor, and IV&V will verify that they are performed in the spirit of the standard.

9.1.2   System Design Review

The goal of the system design review (SDR) is verification of the system (A-level) specification. To accomplish this, the IV&V analyst must (1) have access to and knowledge of the various source documents that generated any of the requirements from outside the engineering process and (2) share in the engineering analysis, trade studies, early prototyping, and so on that created and defined the system as documented in the system specification.

In the commercial world, the requirements that drive the generation of a new or improved system usually come from within the company or institution, but often from outside the data-processing (DP) organization. These requirements are sometimes informally stated, but invariably must involve the ultimate user so that the DP group can get firsthand information on what the system must do, when and how fast it has to do it, and a myriad of other details. Looking at the other extreme—defense systems—we find the externally generated requirements coming from a wide range of documents including such things as the mission need statement (MNS), operational requirements document (ORD), acquisition program baseline (APB), test and evaluation master plan (TEMP), and even documentation from predecessor systems, when appropriate. This list is not intended to be exhaustive, only representative, and varies a great deal depending on the military service branch and the type of system being considered. IV&V should check and verify whatever source documents may exist that provide valid originating requirements and attempt to resolve any that appear to be conflicting or ambiguous, but IV&V will more than likely never be involved with producing these documents. If the system is extremely large like the Strategic Defense System or the Space Station, it is good practice for IV&V to generate a database of originating requirements so that this tracing and verifying activity can be performed only once to confirm these sources. Do not be disappointed when you find that there are some serious disconnects when you try to go back too far, especially across interagency boundaries. Document whatever you find even if it has gaps. IV&V cannot always find every missing link, but the customer deserves to know the real situation.

While the sources of the externally generated requirements are being determined and traced, IV&V examines all of the internally generated trade studies, simulation results, engineering analysis, and prototypes as are available. IV&V draws its own engineering conclusions from this material and compares them to the contractor's conclusions. In areas of significant disagreement, IV&V will use whatever methods seem appropriate to gain additional insight—independent modeling, sensitivity analysis, parametric comparisons, simulation, analysis tools, etc. In systems engineering, this process is called *synthesis* wherein the combination of many technical factors are brought together to form the complete system. This is an iterative process, which may cycle numerous times before such parameters as cost, size, power consumption, performance, communication interfaces, human factors, cycle time, etc. are balanced well enough to form the desired system solution. Each engineering discipline has its turn at challenging and refining its part of the system and, consequently, the system specification. IV&V follows a half-step behind, questioning all the decisions that seem important. It is a job for an inquisitive and experienced systems analyst. I have said several times before and will say it again, "IV&V needs experienced people. How else would they know where to look and how to evaluate the correctness and completeness of the system at this early stage of its evolution?" Thus, the SDR is a very important review and the results from IV&V are greatly affected by the choice of people and tools available. The steps outlined below are typical of the actions taken by IV&V for the SDR.

- Verify the sources and tracing of the externally generated originating requirements into the system specification
- Verify the system synthesis and its ensuing functional allocation as documented in preliminary HWCI and CSCI requirements specifications. Data flow diagrams are a typical method used to depict the functional allocation and decomposition of the system
- Give special attention to the user, mission, and operational requirements from all sources to thoroughly verify how well the system specification handles them
- Assess the life cycle and related cost-analysis data for realism
- Verify the interface and interoperability requirements of the system

- Verify that the program risks are thoroughly understood, ranked, and reduced as far as possible
- Perform independent verification as described in Chapter 5 of this book
- Verify that hardware proofing is complete, when appropriate
- Verify that the test requirements, Section 4, of the specification are as complete, rational, and adequate as possible
- Verify that all required system engineering management activities are addressed
- Perform discrete quality and adequacy checks in accordance with MIL-STD-1521B guidelines [13], Section 20, Appendix B. These are imposed on the development contractor; IV&V will verify that they are performed in the spirit of the standard. When the system specification is approved as a consequence of this review, it becomes the functional baseline.

9.1.3 Software Specification Review

The software specification review (SSR) is strictly a software review that examines the CSCI-level software requirements specifications (SRSs) for completeness, consistency, correctness, adequacy, and adherence to the standards. When approved, the SRSs and their companion interface requirements specification combine to define the allocated baseline.

One of the very important IV&V checks at this time is to confirm that all requirements in the system specification have a destination in one or more of the HWCI or CSCI requirements specifications. Even though the contractor is required to completely reference the requirements in this manner, IV&V verifies this tracing. IV&V is also very concerned with the external interfaces to each CSCI and then, within the CSCI, linkages to the capability networks that form as the inputs and outputs are defined. It is common to use either a CASE tool or manual technique to depict data and control flow between functions that form the CSCI. This usually results in defining at least the first-level computer software components (CSCs), which serve as collection points (or nodes) for related capabilities. The data elements, operational parameters, human engineering, and design constraints are also verified at this time. As mentioned previously, most commercial developers merge this review into the PDR, discussed next. The steps outlined below are typical of the actions taken by IV&V for the SSR.

- Verify tracing of requirements from the system specification to the SRS
- Verify the input, processing, and output of each function via data and control flow supplied by the contractor. Alternative software configurations may be produced by IV&V when contractor solutions seem at odds with good engineering practices
- Verify the overall CSCI performance requirements, including timing, storage, and similar constraints

- Verify external interfaces. This can be a very significant effort on large systems with a large number of CSCIs
- Verify that the qualification methods seem reasonable and valid for each requirement
- Perform independent verification as described in Chapter 5 of this book
- Give special attention to the user, mission, and operational capabilities
- Perform discrete quality and adequacy checks in accordance with MIL-STD-1521B guidelines [13], Section 30, Appendix C. These are imposed on the development contractor and IV&V will verify that they are performed in the spirit of the standard. When the software requirements specifications are approved as a consequence of this review, they define the allocated baseline.

9.1.4 Preliminary Design Review

The preliminary design review (PDR) is a formal review of the basic design of the software (and actually the behavior of that part of the system) on a CSCI basis. It should be mentioned that there will probably be a hardware PDR, especially if new hardware is developed for the system. If a general-purpose host computer is used, it may be appropriate to combine any hardware-related discussions into the software PDR. In any case, the government guide, MIL-STD-1521B [13] has a section on hardware aimed at close scrutiny of the prime item and/or critical item (hardware) specifications. This examination checks such things as functional and physical layout, electromagnetic compatibility, mechanical engineering, packaging, safety, interface requirements, mock-ups, drawings, etc. It also covers firmware. As most of you know, firmware is "software on a chip." The reason it is covered under hardware at the PDR is that a lot of hardware is required to program the chips and verify the programs and their installations. Then the erasable permanent read-only memory (EPROM) chip that contains the software is handled like a hardware part, except that the revision level of the software is sealed onto the outside of the chip for positive identification.

Turning our attention back to software, IV&V is very concerned with the adequacy of the software design document (SDD) up through Section 3 of the SDD. Once again traceability of capabilities from the SRS is very important to ensure that the functionality being designed will meet the specified requirements. This process defines computer software components (CSCs), which satisfy sets of related capabilities. Data and control flows produced either manually or by a CASE tool depict the layout and behavior of these CSCs. IV&V will verify these flows for all states and modes. Also IV&V will examine the allocation of memory and timing for each CSC.

IV&V will also assess the development tools with at least two thoughts in mind: First, how comprehensive and appropriate is each tool for the design effort and how can IV&V share in its use and/or output and, second, what IV&V tools should be selected to complement the developer's tools. Software support environments and facilities are reviewed with similar thoughts in mind. The steps outlined below are typical of the actions taken by IV&V for the PDR.

- Verify CSCI-level structure and interfaces
- Verify tracing of requirements from SRS to the SDD (found in Section 3 of the SDD)
- Verify the input, processing, and output of each CSC via data and control flow supplied by the contractor (CASE-produced or other)
- Verify the CSC performance requirements, including timing, storage, and similar constraints
- Perform independent design verification as described in Chapter 6 of this book
- Identify any special security considerations
- Verify the facilities including support and system software, development tools, utilities, libraries, databases, etc.
- Identify all related documentation
- Review user's, operator's, maintenance, and diagnostic manuals
- Perform discrete quality and adequacy checks in accordance with MIL-STD-1521B guidelines [13], Section 40, Appendix D. These are imposed on the development contractor; IV&V will verify that they are performed in the spirit of the standard.

9.1.5 Critical Design Review

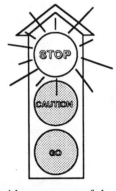

The critical design review (CDR) is the last place you can economically stop the software train if you think it is on the wrong track. Theoretically at least, there should be no formal (final) code written until after this review blesses the design and turns on the green light. I stated earlier that rapid prototyping produces code very early in development, but the official position should be that this is not part of the final code. If it appears both possible and appropriate to reuse some of the prototype code, then all well and good and hurrah for the developer, but remember no one is bound to it contractually. If the customer and/or IV&V is not satisfied with some part of the software design and can prove it inadequate to a reasonable extent, do not allow the developer to go into the next phase. Stop everything and fix the design deficiencies first. If you do not, every repair later on will cost you up to 10 times [8] as much as it will to fix it here. CDR should be viewed as a safety net for the customer and a stop light for the development contractor. Life has a lot of red lights; why should a big expensive software project be allowed to "run the red light" just because it has a lot of inertia? The best analogy I can think of is the joke in which the two dumb hunters have shot their first deer and are dragging it back to their car, hind-feet first when another hunter passes them and says "it is a lot easier to pick up the head and drag it that way." So they take his advice and after an hour of dragging the deer, one says to the other, "that guy sure was right, this is a lot easier, but we are getting farther from the car all the time." A lot of software projects get separated and lost from the requirements and go merrily along making great progress, only in the wrong direction. Use the CDR to put everyone on the right course. Get this message loud and clear: Do not hesitate to stop and reorient the project and especially make it a practice to go back and fix things found at CDR before allowing the project to start the coding phase.

The major IV&V emphasis at CDR is to ensure that the software design is correct, consistent, and complete enough for development to proceed into coding. These verifications occur against the software design document (SDD) and the interface design document (IDD) for each CSCI and against the other artifacts that the design process and IV&V jointly produce. Even though the SDD is a very comprehensive document, there is invariably much design information that does not find its way into the book, so IV&V attempts to gather as much of that material as possible for analysis. Then, using independent methods, IV&V either further exploits the supplied data or uses its own tools and methods to gain other technical perspectives. This IV&V process, which deals with the verification of algorithms, program logic, task timing and scheduling, software architecture, and data structure, is described in detail in Chapter 6. If firmware is used anywhere in the system, it will be evaluated along with the software. Because it is not possible to isolate the software from the hardware, IV&V will examine those hardware constraints and characteristics that affect the software. The steps outlined below are typical of the actions taken by IV&V for the CDR.

- Verify CSC- and CSU-level structure and interfaces
- Verify consistency and traceability between Sections 3 and 4 of the SDD
- Verify each SDD and IDD in its entirety
- Verify the input, processing, and output of each CSU via data and control flow supplied by the contractor (CASE-produced or other)
- Verify the CSU performance requirements, including timing, storage, and similar constraints
- Perform independent design verification as described in Chapter 6 of this book
- Address any special security requirements
- Verify the facilities including support and system software, compiler(s), coding and test tools, utilities, libraries, databases, etc.
- Verify all related documentation (e.g., user's, operator's, maintenance, and diagnostic manuals)
- Perform discrete quality and adequacy checks in accordance with MIL-STD-1521B guidelines [13], Section 50, Appendix E. These are imposed on the development contractor; IV&V will verify that they are performed in the spirit of the standard.

9.1.6 Test Readiness Review

By this point in the program, the focus of IV&V is on assessing the adequacy of the code to enter full-blown CSCI-level testing. In support of this activity, test plans and test descriptions, user documentation (user's, operator's, and diagnostic's manuals), and status of pending changes to both software and documentation will be reviewed and evaluated. This review usually occurs toward the end of the preliminary qualification tests (PQT) after the CSC integration is complete and the contractor has had success running initial CSCI-level tests. This stabilizing period allows the software test descriptions and user documentation to be corrected and made consistent where necessary. It is very important for the user procedures to match the test procedures since they are often one and the same.

The TRR sometimes marks the handover of software from the programming group to the test organization, especially when the two are independent of each other. The steps outlined below are typical of the actions taken by IV&V for the TRR.

- Verify adequacy and completeness of the CSC-level integration
- Verify completeness of the software test plans and descriptions
- Verify consistency between test descriptions and user's manual(s)
- Verify other user-level documents (e.g., operator and diagnostic manuals)
- Verify the status of all pending changes to both the code and documents
- Verify the test environment and support facilities including drivers, compilers, libraries, controls, and security
- Verify the methods used for retaining and archiving test data and reporting the results of tests
- Perform discrete checks in accordance with MIL-STD-1521B guidelines [13], Section 60, Appendix F.

9.1.7 Functional Configuration Audit

It is quite acceptable for the IV&V organization to be integrated into the customer's auditing team. This way the developing agency can focus the IV&V efforts where there appears to be the greatest need. But regardless of the way in which the team is organized, the goal is to verify that the configurations item's actual performance complies precisely (or exceeds) with what is stated in the requirements specifications. This can be viewed as a process wherein the test data is compared to the test descriptions which had previously been compared to the specifications and the other user-level documents to ensure a good match among them.

Even though this book focuses on software, the hardware also receives similar treatment and includes such things as verification of drawings, provisioning lists, quality assurance testing results, etc. Returning to software, the developing contractor is required to brief the auditing team on the test results for each CSCI. The contractor should present a plan for addressing any requirements that were not met.

Part of the audit carefully compares the test results to the plans/descriptions/procedures and documents any deficiencies. This is also an opportunity for IV&V to review the minutes of the PDR and CDR to make sure that all pertinent action items have been closed and that the configuration status accounting records do not show any pending changes that could affect the baselining of the software or system. The steps outlined below are typical of the actions taken by IV&V for the functional configuration audit (FCA).

- Audit completeness of the software test plans and descriptions for complete coverage of the requirements in the SRSs that require formal testing
- Audit actual test results against the test documents, and report any deficiencies
- Verify consistency between test descriptions and user's manual(s) or other user-level documents (e.g., operator and diagnostic manuals)
- Audit the status of all pending changes to both the code and documents via status accounting records
- Audit all updated previously delivered documents
- Review PDR and CDR minutes to ensure closure of all action items
- Review all databases and any allocation-sensitive data
- Perform checks in accordance with MIL-STD-1521B guidelines [13], Section 70, Appendix G.

9.1.8 Formal Qualification Review

Even though MIL-STD-1521B discusses the formal qualification review (FQR) after the PCA, I think it is more appropriate to discuss them in the order presented here since the FQR more than likely is combined with the FCA or occurs shortly thereafter. This is true as long as the software testing at the CSCI level is sufficient to "certify" performance. Conversely, if such certification requires thorough integration of the total system, FQR is likely to be postponed until after the PCA. The conditions for and characteristics of the FQR are summarized as follows:

- In cases where the FCA and FQR can be combined, certification will be an act of the FQR portion
- When the agency responsible for qualifying configuration items judges that the system is not ready for the FQR, it will be delayed to as late as the end of system testing, if necessary.
- When the separate FQR event is scheduled, it will strongly resemble an FCA and duplication of effort will be avoided wherever possible. The FCA records will be audited and the new/additional data will be added to the records to extend the FCA.
- The contractor will record the date of certification and the test records as part of the configuration item's permanent data record

- IV&V performs its part of the FQR in accordance with MIL-STD-1521B guidelines [13], Section 90, Appendix I, as directed by the customer.

9.1.9 Physical Configuration Audit

The physical configuration audit (PCA), as the name implies, takes a very hard look at all of the software artifacts that establish the "product" baseline for each CSCI. These are primarily the as-built software product specification, software listings (or magnetically stored equivalent), version description document, and user and maintenance documents. For hardware, the PCA is usually directed at the first production article, but in software there is not so obvious a distinction, so the PCA is usually against the version that passed the final acceptance tests. In performing the PCA, IV&V not only checks that the required items are all there and properly identified, but looks very carefully to ensure that no software that should not be part of the delivery has been left in the officially released version. After a successful PCA, all subsequent changes to the system (or its software) will be processed as official engineering change actions. The steps outlines below are typical of the actions taken by IV&V for the software portion of the PCA.

- Audit the completeness, correctness, and consistency of the software product specification (audit the code-to to as-built transition)
- Review the minutes of the FCA/FQR for discrepancies and actions taken
- Verify the design descriptions for proper entries, symbols, labels, tags, references, and data descriptions
- Confirm requirements tracing from the SRS to Section 3 of the SDD
- Confirm that Section 4 of the SDD matches the code
- Review the software user's, operator's, diagnostic, firmware, and programmer's manuals for consistency and completeness
- Audit the actual CSCI media "to be delivered" for any inconsistencies
- Perform discrete checks in accordance with MIL-STD-1521B guidelines [13], Section 80, Appendix H.

9.2 KEY CONTRACTOR-DEVELOPED PLANNING DOCUMENTS

Planning documents can generally be divided into two major categories: those produced by the customer, sponsoring agency, or developing organization (the government, for example) and those written and developed by the development contractor. Usually by the time the IV&V contract is awarded, most of the government-developed plans (as discussed in Section 2.3 of Chapter 2) are already well-established and have often been revised several times. Many agencies have their own guidebooks and technical directives, which are usually well-maintained and contain the particular standards and practices that contractors are required by the contract to follow. Therefore, this book deliberately excludes these documents from direct IV&V actions, but advocates that IV&V use them to track the contractor's compliance when development issues are affected by these plans—for example, determining how well the contractor's test program matches the government-produced test and evaluation master plan (TEMP).

There may be infrequent cases when IV&V will be called upon to review and evaluate a government-prepared plan. In these cases, a search of the standards will invariably uncover a standard or regulation and usually its data item directive (DID), which contains a detailed outline and instructions for the preparation of the document, which IV&V then follows to aid in the review process. It should be remembered that the government does not want blind compliance to a standard that poorly or only partially fits the particular program to which it is applied. That is why the government has encouraged tailoring since the advent of DOD-STD-2167 [24], so that the contractors can adjust and optimize the deliverables to the program. This is also true of IV&V deliverables; they should be adjusted to meet the needs of each program.

One of the most important "good" things that DOD-STD-2167A [24] did was reduce the number of plans that the contractor has to produce to a minimum. A decade before there was a separate plan for every discipline and subdiscipline. It was not unusual for a DOD software procurement to have separate configuration management plan, quality assurance plan, standards and practices, software development plan, human factors management plan, risk management plan, operational concept document, coordinated test plan, program management plan, system engineering management plan, etc. . . the list made your head swim. A lot of this information was valuable, but a lot was overlapping and consequently could give conflicting direction, so the forgers of DOD-STD-2167A decided that both the government and the contractor should each produce one consolidated document containing as much of the pertinent development information as possible. The government produces a computer resource life-cycle management plan (CRLCMP) based on the older computer resource management plan (CRMP). The purpose of this document is to help the contractors prepare compliant bids wherein they can match their proposals to the facilities and software environment already in place or being planned within the developing agency's organization and/or its maintenance organization. As more and more systems are maintained in government-run post-deployment software support (PDSS) centers, it is incumbent upon the government to minimize hardware and software proliferation. The CRLCMP (pronounced *cril'comp*) accomplishes this information transfer to the proposing contractors. How well they, in turn, match their proposal to the government capabilities may mean the difference between winning or losing the contract, as it should.

9.2.1 Software Development Plan

The contractor's key plan under DOD-STD-2167A [24] is the software development plan (SDP), which as we mentioned is a consolidation of many disciplines that were previously documented in separate books. It covers software development management, software engineering, formal qualification testing, product evaluation, configuration management, and other functions, as appropriate. IV&V will review and evaluate the SDP (1) in accordance with the appropriate data-item directive (DID) to determine its compliance with the standard and (2) in reference to the CRLCMP to assess how well it meshes with the government's facilities, capabilities, and plans. IV&V of the SDP is discussed in the following listings. Once the customer is satisfied that the SDP reflects what should be done by the contractor throughout the development, IV&V can be called upon periodically to audit and verify how well the contractor is following the document. The following steps are typical of IV&V's review of the SDP:

Software Development Management

- Evaluate contractor's facilities to ensure adequate data processing (DP) facilities and software development environment
- Review all government-furnished equipment (GFE) required by the contract effort and the schedule of when it is needed
- Review contractor's organization, resources, and personnel for adequacy in performing these tasks
- Verify the schedule and program milestones
- Review the activity networks for conflicts, omissions, critical paths, and reserves
- Review plans for obtaining hardware, firmware, and software resources
- Verify and prioritize risk areas and evaluate contractor's mitigation scheme
- Verify that security procedures are adequate
- Review planned interfaces to other contractors
- Review planned interface with IV&V
- Review subcontract management scheme
- Review plans for conducting formal reviews
- Verify plans for the software library for adequacy
- Review corrective action procedures
- Review problem report and change report form formats for adequacy.

Software Engineering

- Review contractor's organization, resources, and personnel for adequacy in performing the tasks
- Verify software engineering environment for adequacy
- Verify all required software items needed, such as compilers, operating systems, tools, test drivers, utilities, etc.
- Verify all hardware and firmware items needed for the software engineering environment
- Review proprietary and government rights to the software

- Verify the contractor's plan for installing and testing the software engineering environment prior to use
- Verify adequacy of the software standards and procedures
- Verify adequacy of the development techniques and methodologies
- Review format of unit development files (UDFs)
- Review design standards for adequacy
- Review coding standards for adequacy
- Verify plans for using nondevelopment software including GFE, reusable, and commercial software

Formal Qualification Testing

- Review contractor's organization, resources, and personnel for adequacy in performing the tasks
- Verify contractor's testing approach and philosophy
- Verify that testing approach matches the test and evaluation master plan
- Review test planning assumptions and constraints

Software Product Evaluations

- Review contractor's organization, resources, and personnel for adequacy in performing the tasks
- Verify software product evaluation procedures and tools
- Review procedures for evaluating and qualifying subcontractor products
- Review contractor's plans for recording each product evaluation
- Review contractor's plans for recording activity-dependent product evaluations

Software Configuration Management

- Review contractor's organization, resources, and personnel for adequacy in performing the tasks
- Verify configuration identification scheme for the software
- Verify configuration control flow and reporting documentation used to control problem reports and changes
- Verify review procedures and formation of the configuration control board (CCB)
- Review procedures for storage, handling, and delivery of project media
- Verify configuration status accounting process and database
- Review plans for configuration audits
- Review plans for specification authentication
- Review all configuration management milestones

Other Software Development Functions (Optional)

- Review contractor's organization, resources, and personnel for adequacy in performing these tasks
- Verify methods and procedures as required.

9.2.2 Software Quality Program Plan

Besides the SDP, the other development contractor's plan that very much involves IV&V review is the software quality program plan (SQPP). Here are two very different organizations—software quality assurance inside the developer's organization and IV&V outside that organization—each oriented at helping to shape the quality of the product. Yes, the goals are similar, but the perspectives are very different. What is most important is that IV&V not duplicate what the developer's quality organization is doing (and vice versa to a lesser degree). Do not forget that IV&V will most likely adjust to what quality does, not the other way around. So once the SQPP is reviewed, IV&V will have a good understanding of the quality organization and its tools, methods, procedures and records. IV&V then has only to tailor its tools and methods to complement those of the quality assurance and development organizations. To illustrate the point, if quality uses an automated standards enforcer tool in its review of the code units, IV&V can (a) use a different tool in hopes of finding things that quality's tool did not or (b) not look for standards violations and expend those resources on a different verification task. The customer should make the decision after hearing the pros and cons of both approaches. I have said many times that IV&V needs to remain flexible and adaptive to the changing needs of the program. I think this example makes that point clearly.

Once the customer is satisfied that the SQPP reflects what should be done by the contractor throughout the development, IV&V can be called upon periodically to audit and verify how well the contractor is following the plan. Recent initiatives within DOD have increased the emphasis on total quality management (TQM), which can play a large part in enforcement of good quality practices at all levels of the organization. One should remember that TQM is as much an attitude as a process.

When IV&V reviews the SQPP, the basic outline for the document, found in DOD-STD-2168 [25], is used as a guide to ensure complete coverage. Some tailoring of the SQPP is allowed, which can affect the contents. The following verification review checklist of the SQPP is based on a comprehensive software quality program.

General Requirements

- Review the objectives of the quality program for both deliverable and non-deliverable software
- Review the organizational responsibility statements for adequacy

- Review the documentation and implementing instructions for adequacy
- Review the planning and availability of appropriate resources
- Review how quality will interact and interface with the development organization
- Review plans for quality recordkeeping for adequacy
- Review software corrective-action handling
- Review plans for product certification
- Review plans for management reviews of the entire software quality program
- Review access rights and methods for the customer (and IV&V)

Detailed Requirements

- Verify procedures for ongoing evaluations of the software
- Verify procedures for ongoing evaluations of the documentation
- Verify procedures for ongoing evaluations of the processes used in developing the software. Subparts of this verification step are very similar to the evaluation of the software development plan (SDP) presented in the previous section.
- Verify procedures for assessing the adequacy of the software development library
- Verify procedures for evaluations of nondevelopmental software
- Verify procedures for evaluations of nondeliverable software
- Verify procedures for evaluations of deliverable elements of the software engineering and test environments
- Verify procedures for evaluations of subcontractor management
- Verify procedures for evaluations of inspection acceptance and preparation for delivery
- Review plans for participation in formal reviews and audits.

By reviewing and verifying the SQPP, IV&V can (1) feed back any deficiencies to the customer for correction, and (2) optimize its IV&V program plan to share data and information coming out of the quality program, eliminate unwanted redundancy, and complement the evaluations planned by the SQP with its own independent verification actions wherever it is deemed necessary. This enables a good balance to be obtained between IV&V and software quality assurance.

9.2.3 Other Planning Documents

There are numerous planning documents that support the program from its very inception to well into its operational period. IV&V may be called upon at any time to review any of these for adequacy and correctness, but there is another role for these documents as well. Very often IV&V can take advantage of the information found therein to clarify vague requirements, improve a process or procedure, avoid redundant effort, and help coordinate and manage numerous activities. Therefore,

IV&V should become familiar with these documents, but not necessarily review or use them extensively. Just how much of this sort of verification effort is found in a typical IV&V program is very difficult to estimate. There is a rule of thumb that I have practiced that may help: If the mainline specifications are for the most part adequate, traceable, and consistent and the development is approximately on schedule, there is probably little need to dredge up old volumes of "forgotten lore": however, if things start getting mushy and vague, especially in the requirements area, then suspect everything and go back and open these books and trace the genesis of every originating requirement possible, especially within the area of concern. It can be a big effort, but it can save the software from calamity downstream. As I have said before, there is nothing worse than building correct software that solves the wrong problem.

To summarize, I advocate spending IV&V resources where they will do the most good and that is usually not wasting time reviewing all of the old plans. They have their place in a reference library and there they can be very useful when needed, but that need is occasional at best.

9.3 CHAPTER SUMMARY

- DOD procurements identify a process of formal reviews, which help to assure an orderly development process.
- DOD defines nine different kinds of reviews and audits, which generally fall at natural transition points in the program, and hence are often considered to be milestones.
- Most of the commercial and other government software developers use the main ones—SDR, PDR, and CDR.
- These formal reviews start with requirements reviews, transition to design reviews, and conclude with audits of the testing and documents to ensure that the customer gets what was planned and contracted for in the first place.
- IV&V concentrates on two key contractor planning documents—the software development plan (SDP) and the software quality program plan (SQPP).
- We suggest that other planning documents be reviewed and used on an as-needed basis and not routinely considered for IV&V unless specially requested by the customer or conditions warrant.

9.4 WHAT COMES NEXT

So far the book has talked some about configuration management (CM) and has introduced the reader to several terms that pertain to configuration items for software and hardware. Chapter 10 goes further and explains in detail the various parts of CM, why they are important to development and IV&V, and how changes to the system are controlled to protect both the developer and the customer.

10
CONFIGURATION MANAGEMENT

What if an auto parts store had to guess which of its tens of thousands of parts fit your make and model car, or if you were told "buy a new washing machine" because the repairman could not identify the right replacement part? Of if you bought a computer-controlled system and one day it quit and no one could figure out what exact software configuration was running on it, so you had to buy a new system. These three examples are not as ridiculous as you might think at first glance. It has taken most of this century to develop methods of marking, identifying, and standardizing hardware so that it could be ordered, manufactured, distributed, inventoried, and replaced efficiently. Manufacturer's codes, serial numbers, part numbers, modification codes, Federal stock numbers . . . the list goes on and on, but it works very efficiently. Software has struggled through the same sort of growing pains and still faces numerous problems, mostly brought about because of lack of standard approaches. The various software constituents—commercial, industrial, governmental, etc.—use different conventions to identify, mark, label, and manage the identification, version control, and release of software. And there is the matter of vocabulary; configuration management (CM) has its own unique names for things that have specific meaning, but the commercial world has been slow to accept the government/defense industry nomenclature unless a company happens to work in both markets. We hope this book will help sway some of the commercial software practitioners to accept the DOD way of viewing configuration management of software. There are many reasons that I think that this is the right direction, including a well-thought-out and well-developed CM model that integrates smoothly into the system life cycle model, well-defined divisions and disciplines, appropriate names for the artifacts, and mature processes for control, management, coordination, and direction. The first step for the uninitiated is to learn the definitions, and the next step is to study the four main parts with an eye cast on how IV&V is affected by and interacts with a typical project's configuration management system.

10.1 DEFINITIONS

1. Configuration management (CM) can be defined as a four-part discipline of applying technical and administrative direction, control, and surveillance to:
- Identify and document the functional and physical characteristics of a hardware or software configuration item, which is called *configuration identification*
- Control changes to those characteristics, which is called *configuration and change control*
- Record and report change processing and implementation status, which is called *configuration status accounting*
- Audit the process and its records, which is called *configuration audit.*

2. A configuration item (CI) is defined as an aggregation of hardware or software which satisfies an end-use function and is designated as an entity for configuration management. In order to differentiate groups of these CIs in software and hardware, two terms are generally in use:
- Hardware configuration item (HWCI), for example, can be a computer, missile, launcher, radar, air conditioner. Big, complex systems usually have several HWCIs that correspond to separate groups of functions. Each HWCI is documented with a separate set of specifications, drawings, and manuals.
- Computer software configuration item (CSCI) is an aggregation of software suitable in size to have a corresponding family of specifications to define it. Most moderately sized software systems have one or at most a few CSCIs. Remember that each CSCI has its own requirements and design specifications, user manual, test plan and descriptions, etc. and is managed and controlled as an entity. When systems have very many CSCIs, think of all the different documents and tests and interfaces that have to be considered. Then software people in their infinite wisdom invented a subordinate part to the CSCI called the "computer software component," which is about as vague as the CSCI definition.
- Computer software components (CSCs) are the building blocks that make up a CSCI. The really fascinating thing is that when the powers that be realized that software functionality can be nested at more than three levels, they suddenly found themselves with CSCs inside CSCs that could even be inside other CSCs, so these components can be almost anything and any size you want them to be. I will give an example very soon that will help you to understand this concept.
- Computer software units (CSUs). These "units" are little things that cannot be further decomposed. CSUs are basic software elements, CSCs are like compounds, and CSCIs are like a beaker full of compounds. All of this vagueness is highly annoying to everyone who ever tries to understand how software is configured.

Before defining anything else, I feel it is incumbent on me to attempt to better define the CI building blocks. I have used the following example many times in my classes and it seems to help. Please refer to Figure 10-1 for the visual flow of the example. The overall system is a power plant, the system segment (which we will talk about a little later) is the safety monitoring and control facility, the CSCI is the data acquisition subsystem, which is made up of many first-level CSCs, one of which is the "alarm process." The alarm process subsystem is required to process both digital and analog type points, so the alarm process CSC is further divided into two second-level CSCs—the analog alarm processor and the digital alarm processor. To process all types of digital alarms requires four "subroutine"-level CSUs—Boolean, binary-coded decimal (BCD), sequence-of-events (SOE), and safety point processors. In developing complex layers of software like interactive user interfaces, it is not unusual to have up to five nested levels of CSCs. There does

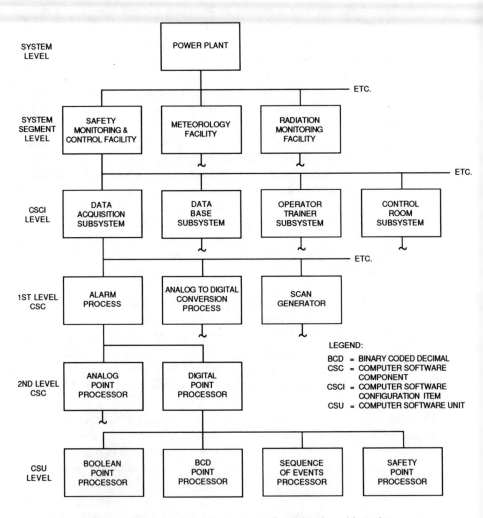

Figure 10-1 An example of the configuration item hierarchy.

not seem to be a better name for these nebulous little creatures, so CM, which tries to be so specific in every other way, is stuck with the most ambiguous thing in software, that of trying to define a CSCI and a CSC in concrete terms that everyone can immediately understand.

If you will pardon another somewhat perverse observation, you know that your CSCI is too big when you cannot document it in one physical volume (maximum of 500–600 pages) of each type of specification (requirements, design, etc.). Conversely, the CSCI is too small when you end up with a great big pile of skinny little books. It has a lot to do with how much software can be successfully managed and developed by a dedicated team. My experience indicates that 30 is about the maximum number of people that can work closely together on a tightly coupled software effort [7], that is, ergo, the practical limit for a CSCI development team. This team of 30 should be able to design, develop, integrate, and test up to 250,000 lines of moderately complex code over a 30 to 36-month period, if they have adequate tools. Software that gets much bigger than this really should be broken into more than one CSCI. Now what if the team were given tools aimed at significant productivity enhancement? That race is still being run as I write this, and the results seem to vary all over the tote board. Once we can factor out the "Hawthorne Effect" [4] and learning curves; collect statistics from real programs and not only pilot studies; and once the number of samples becomes large enough to smooth the figures, we will be able to measure the real increases. The reason that some of the claims are suspect is that one guru-level programmer I know produced in three months what three fairly senior programmers failed to produce in one year. That is a factor of better than 12:1, and it was done completely without CASE tools, with only a symbolic debugger and screen editor. (By the way, that particular code never failed or had a latent defect discovered in it in several years of operational use.) Thus, when you estimate the size of the CSCI and the schedule for its development and factor in the productivity rates for your organization for that particular kind of code and the language being used, you can get a good idea of the size staff that is needed for the effort. If you are not familiar with this process, you may want to refer to Dr. Barry Boehm's excellent book on the COCOMO Model [1]. If the estimate goes well beyond the 30-person limit, your CSCI is probably too big. If it goes below 10, the CSCI could encompass more functionality if, and only if, it is natural to do so. Do not force arbitrary divisions or combining of CSCIs; they are usually pretty well self-defining by the way common functions migrate together and interfaces evolve. Sizing and estimating remains one of the most difficult aspects of software planning.

Baselining is the next configuration management term that requires a definition. Webster's defines a baseline in this context as a *foundation or basis*. Systems evolve through a couple of levels of abstraction before they become the final physical thing that we hope functions the way we want it to. The first level is the formal requirements—they are like an architect's rendering of a building sitting ideally on its property together with a narrative about all the things you can do in and with the building. This is analogous to the system (or A-level) specification and a model of the system (the architect's rendering). When you approve the drawings and the specification sheet, work can go forward with confidence that the overall approach is what you want. This approved plan becomes the *functional baseline,* and it cannot be changed unless both parties agree to negotiate on possible cost, schedule, and technical impacts of doing so. In software-intensive systems, changes go before a configuration control board (CCB) for resolution. Now back to the analogy: the architect (or designer) then lays out all the rooms, hallways, HVAC, lighting, plumbing, windows, etc. This process "allocates" functions to different subsystems and physically places them in the building. When complete and approved, you now have a much more detailed set of requirements at the subsystem level, which we call the *allocated baseline.* In the systems that we deal with in this book, these requirements are allocated to the HWCI and CSCI (B-level) requirements specifications. There are sometimes additional baselines defined by the developer to aid in the control of the design process, but officially these two are the really vital ones that keep things on track during development. Then finally, the last official baseline occurs when everything is finished and ready for delivery and title transfer. It is called the *product baseline,* because it certifies that all the documentation concerning that which was produced is accurate and complete. In software-intensive systems, this point is reached when all the design detail is converted to "as-built" status. In essence, this baselining occurs when the design specifications are converted to product specifications, listings are available in some useful form, and the necessary records are compiled and audited. Thus, there are three critical baselines in most software systems that occur in unison with the approval of the system (A), CSCI (B), and product (C) specifications.

10.2   OVERVIEW OF INDEPENDENT VERIFICATION AND VALIDATION'S ROLE IN CONFIGURATION MANAGEMENT

Probably the easiest way to visualize how IV&V fits into the CM scheme is to discuss responsibilities and typical exchanges between the developing agency or customer and the development contractor. Figure 10-2 is provided to assist in this discussion. The contractor has primary responsibility for configuration identification, control, and status accounting. The customer has secondary responsibility as well as approval/disapproval authority. What this means in so many words is that the contractor originates the scheme for marking and identifying the documents, code, etc., establishes mechanisms for positive control, and produces the configuration status accounting records against which the government or any outside organization can audit.

IV&V evaluates the configuration identification scheme (as described in the software development plan) that the contractor proposes to use and then periodically verifies that it is being followed and that it remains adequate. The configuration identification function (1) identifies and specifies the technical documentation, especially the specifications, (2) defines the baselines and exactly what goes into each, (3) defines item numbering, typing, and identification, and (4) determines what should constitute acceptance and delivery of the system.

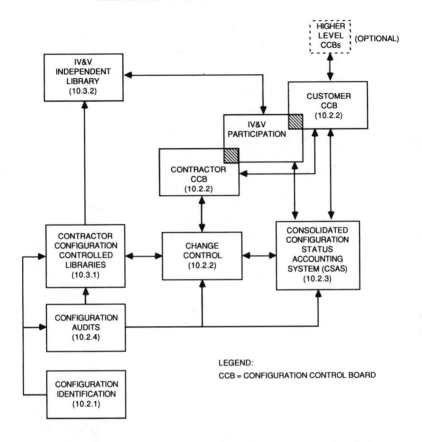

Figure 10-2 A visual index to configuration management functions.

The purpose of configuration and change control is basically to maintain project artifacts in a protected environment and to prevent unnecessary or marginal changes while expediting the approval and implementation of the worthwhile ones. Thus, configuration control can be viewed as the software, document, and data libraries that allow controlled access and updating so that these artifacts do not get lost, corrupted, and accidentally destroyed. Change control includes the change decision-making process and the equally important functions of setting change priorities and of assuring that the necessary instructions and funding authorizations are issued promptly for approved changes. One of the chief mechanisms to accomplish this control is the configuration control board (CCB). In my naive days, I envisioned the CCB as a group of managers and technical people in a meeting who listen to all sides of each case, after which everyone votes, with the majority count determining the winning side. Let me assure you that, although the CCB listens to both sides, there is only one vote and that is cast by the chairperson; it is completely autocratic, not democratic. Now to further complicate things, there can be CCBs at various levels in the organization. NASA has up to four CCB levels, but it is more common to find two—one inside the contractor's organization and the other, higher-level board that is centered about the customer. If the spending authority of the normal government board is exceeded, the program may be forced to convene a board higher up the ladder. In any case IV&V attends and contributes, as requested by the customer, to the technical evaluations of engineering change proposals (ECPs) and other proposed changes. Change control and the system that tracks all the actions are inexorably linked, which brings us to the third part of CM.

The status of activities (reported problems and change status) against any particular artifact—for example, a specification or software package—appears as part of a historical configuration accounting record. Because large programs frequently have hundreds of active "accounting" records at any one time, an automated configuration status accounting system (CSAS) is recommended for their management and disposition. Because of the availability of netted computer systems even at the PC level, it is now quite feasible for all parties to have access to and use of a single CSAS, which is usually under direct control of the contractor with oversight protection from the customer. This saves a great deal of duplicated effort and expense. In cases where this is not practical, separate CSAS systems can be operated autonomously, but all parties must have access to each other's files, which usually produces a complicated arrangement (a mess). IV&V will also share the CSAS and will periodically audit the database to make sure that records have not been lost or changed. It should be noted that the CSAS contains *permanent records* wherein open items like problem reports and change actions can be "closed" when complete, but the record of the transactions is never purged. Years later, it may be necessary to go back to these records to check on the disposition of a change or problem to resolve a contractual or warranty issue. If the records were deleted upon closure, this could not be accomplished. The reason that the customer has oversight authority is to require that the contractor restore any lost or altered records if this were ever to occur.

The principal entries into the CSAS are the numerous problem reports (PRs) that are eventually resolved and closed as part of the development experience by: (1) incorporation or (2) dropped as unsound or unnecessary. When PRs result in accepted changes, several things can occur, as follows:

- If the change does not affect a baselined document and is not considered out of scope, the contractor makes the change and closes the PR. These are the most common types of changes and are categorized as Class II, which implies no impact to the program.
- If the change affects a baselined document but is still not considered out of scope, the contractor makes the change and issues a specification change notice (SCN) to handle the document revision. These are usually Class II but under certain circumstances can be considered Class I.
- If the change appears to be out of scope, it becomes a candidate for an engineering change proposal (ECP). If the ECP is approved, an engineering

change order (ECO) is written and the contract is effectively modified by this action. If documents are affected, SCNs are also issued. All changes that affect schedule, performance, cost, form, fit, function, and that otherwise modify the system are considered Class I changes. There is a more detailed discussion on Class I and II changes in Section 10.2.2.

The last CM function, configuration audit, does two things. It performs unscheduled in-process audits of how well CM is following its own internal rules and processes, and it participates in the two formal program audits—the functional and physical configuration audit (described in Section 9.1)—at the end of the program to add assurance that the system is ready for delivery. IV&V participates in these audits on the customer's behalf.

To summarize, IV&V evaluates and verifies the configuration identification activities, attends and participates in the CCB, evaluates problem reports and ECPs, tracks ECOs, uses and audits the CSAS database, and participates in the CM audits of the system. A more detailed look at these activities follow.

10.2.1 Configuration Identification

IV&V's interest in configuration identification is twofold. The first aspect is primarily one of ensuring that the customer's CM requirements levied on the contractor are sufficient to fully identify, baseline, document, and establish appropriate standards for development of the software product. A significant number of these requirements come from specific sections of the request for proposal (RFP), the contract data requirements list (CDRL), and the standards and regulations cited in the RFP. The second part involves how well the developer implements these requirements through the definition of appropriate baselines, generation of compliant specifications, use of proper naming conventions, and enforcing the appropriate standards for all of the software products. Configuration identification is a progressive process that names the three baselines (defined in Section 10.1) as follows:

- *Functional baseline,* also called the *functional configuration identification (FCI),* which is based upon the approved system specification
- *Allocated baseline,* also called the *allocated configuration identification (ACI),* which is based upon the approved software requirements specification(s)
- *Product baseline,* also called the *product configuration identification (PCI),* which is based upon the approved software product specification(s).

The commercial world does about the same thing but may refer to the baselines by different names. They typically follow the progressive baselining of the A, B, and C level specifications.

Turning our attention back to the DOD practices, MIL-S-83490 [18] and MIL-STD-490A [22] are two standards that define names, types, format, and content of both hardware and software specifications. Then, additional standards like DOD-

STD-2167A [24] include specific data item directives (DIDs), which give very exact outlines of the content of the software specifications. Additional numbering and manufacturing code information is taken from the *Cataloging Handbook, H-4-1, Federal Supply Code for Manufacturers* (FSCM).* When firmware is involved, software version/release practices are used on the computer program and hardware type/model/series identification is used on the physical medium, which is usually a programmable read-only memory (PROM). IV&V will review the identification scheme to ensure that it is adequate for the system in question. When naming software entities, the number of characters (length) and whether internal spaces are allowed varies with the language and compiler, so IV&V will review those practices for compliance and aptness. Names should be as readable and mnemonic as possible to aid in future maintenance and possible reuse.

There are three standard ways of defining the form in which a specification may be procured:

- Form 1: Specifications that comply to the MIL-STDs
- Form 2: Specifications prepared to commercial practices with supplementary military requirements
- Form 3: Specifications prepared to commercial practices.

IV&V will review the contract particulars to ensure that the correct form is specified and used. If it turns out that a particular form of document was specified and later found to be deficient, IV&V will make appropriate recommendations to the customer to remedy the situation.

10.2.2 Configuration and Change Control

Configuration control invariably includes change control. In fact, the two terms are often used interchangeably. The underlying purpose in configuration control is (1) to safeguard the baselines as they are defined and approved and (2) to prevent unnecessary or marginal changes while expediting the approval and implementation of the worthwhile ones. This assumes that only necessary and beneficial changes will be made. To do this efficiently, the developer, with customer concurrence, must decide on a priority and classification scheme as well as mechanisms to tightly control the change process.

The primary control mechanism is baselining. It figuratively, if not literally, places the baselined specifications under lock and key or at least surveillance so that unauthorized changes cannot occur, and it establishes the engineering change proposal (ECP) as the only official way to initiate a change. Further, once an ECP is generated, it goes before a configuration control board (CCB) to determine the

---

*This handbook can be obtained from the DOD Single Stock Point, Commanding Officer, U.S. Naval Publications and Forms Center (Attn: NPFC 1032), 5801 Tabor Avenue, Philadelphia, Pennsylvania, 19120.

impact of the proposed change, prioritize it, classify it, and decide on its fate. If the CCB decides to fund the ECP, the contract is thus amended and eventually the engineering change order (ECO) is issued to complete the transaction. If documentation is affected, a specification change notice (SCN) is produced with changes attached to amend the affected document(s). MIL-STD-480 [19] is the oversight document for generating ECPs. There are a progressive set of forms required for generating ECPs that thoroughly cover the requirements for the change. Those kinds of changes are called Class I changes and invariably affect one or more of the following:

- Any current baseline—FCI, ACI, or PCI
- Contractual provisions for fee, incentives, cost, schedule or performance, and guarantees, warranties, or deliveries
- Interface characteristics
- Reliability or maintainability
- Interchangeability
- Repair parts
- Technical manuals
- Configuration, form, fit, or function
- Performance
- Any computer software or firmware
- Safety

There is another type of change, designated Class II. These are essentially editorial in nature, do not affect any of the subjects discussed above, and are mostly performed against the documentation and nonfunctional parts of the code. The developer is free to make Class II changes unless doing so could somehow otherwise impact the project. The cost of Class II changes should be absorbed by the developer.

If a requirement cannot be satisfied by the current contract, the developer can request one of two actions—a deviation or a waiver. A deviation is usually a temporary request to depart from the specification for any number of reasons and has a specified time period associated with it. A waiver typically occurs toward the end of a program when it is discovered that some part of the system does not meet the specification and that all reasonable attempts to remedy the situation have been exhausted. A waiver is a permanent dispensation.

Now back to ECPs. If the originator lacks some of the vital information to perform a full assessment of the proposed change, he or she can initiate a preliminary ECP, which surfaces the problem and focuses attention on it. If the ECP has merit, a formal ECP is then generated. When the CM organization receives the ECP, it can be given a preliminary priority, which is confirmed by the CCB, or the CCB can unilaterally assign priority based on the following scheme, which is pretty much universally followed:

1. Emergency (these usually have a deadline of 24 hours):
   - If not accomplished without delay, it may seriously compromise national security, or
   - To correct a hazardous condition that could result in injury to personnel or damage or destruction of equipment.
2. Urgent (these usually have a deadline of 14 days):
   - If not accomplished expeditiously, it may seriously compromise the mission effectiveness of fielded systems, or
   - To correct a potentially hazardous condition, which may result in injury or damage to equipment, or
   - It is necessary to meet significant contract requirements
   - It affects an interface change to avoid schedule impact or increased cost
   - It affects value engineering or other cost savings above a certain ceiling.
3. Routine (these usually have a deadline of 45 days or whatever seems reasonable):
   - Covers all others not designated emergency or urgent
   - Routine ECPs are often scheduled to help balance staff work loads.

It should be noted, as stated earlier, that the CCB is not a democratic group; the chairperson is the ultimate autocrat and gets the lone vote. This is not to imply that his or her decision cannot be influenced or swayed by a convincing argument. In fact, the chairperson typically listens to both sides of each issue and then makes a determination much like a judge. There may also be interplay among the various factions, so IV&V will get an opportunity its express its opinion when requested. Attending the CCB gives IV&V a great deal of insight that otherwise would be lost, so its participation in all of the CCBs is imperative.

10.2.3 Configuration Status Accounting System

IV&V needs to be in a position to share the developer's configuration status accounting system (CSAS). This way, only one database and one user software package need to be developed and maintained. Not too many years ago, status accounting was done with hard-copy forms and file cabinets full of data. Today, almost everyone uses database-driven systems with electronic forms, but even these systems may still use hard-copy forms that the preparer fills out initially, which are then converted to the electronic medium. In any case, the types of data that need to be tracked in the CSAS are as follows:

- Problem reports, their status, and their corresponding correction reports
- ECPs, ECOs, and SCNs with their status
- Baseline status of the appropriate specifications

To do this according to MIL-STD-482 [21] requires a three-part approach. The first section is an explanation of the data elements; the second is a compilation of the data elements, use identifiers, etc.; and the third contains the databases. Specific parts of the third section include:

- A baseline index
- Configuration item identification and related data summary
- ECP index
- Modification status index
- Status report of the ECPs in process.

Portions of the data are used to define the engineering release records (ERRs) and verify that there are no outstanding ECP actions in process that have not been completed. IV&V will use the database just like any other user and will contribute problem reports whenever deficiencies are discovered. Because these records contain a permanent change history of the project, they cannot be deleted or altered in any way. IV&V will perform periodic audits to ensure that the database remains complete and correct. If the developer does not plot problem reports monthly against project phase, IV&V will do so to give the customer insight into how the software product is maturing. I have done this several times on large projects, and the results are very revealing. In addition, the CSAS is a vital source of status information for the configuration audits at the end of the project, as discussed in the following paragraph.

There are statistical approaches that attempt to use CSAS data to estimate when the system is mature enough for delivery. It has been my experience that these techniques can give a false indication that the system is better than it really is. I prefer the approach that uses tests run by IV&V aimed at trying to crash the system or stress it to the design limits to uncover otherwise hidden deficiencies. Availability tests wherein the system is expected to run for several hundred hours without any disruptions while users are playing with it or training on it offer a very good indication of system maturity.

10.2.4 Configuration Audits

As mentioned in the overview of this section, configuration audits are of two types—unscheduled audits conducted to see how well CM is following its own rules and procedures, and the functional (FCA) and physical configuration audits (PCA) near the end of the project. IV&V participates in both types on behalf of the customer and performs an additional monthly audit of the CSAS database to ensure that items do not disappear or change month to month. A complete description of the procedures followed by IV&V in participating in the FCA and PCA are found in Chapter 9 (Sections 9.1.7 and 9.1.9, respectively). The FCA is a means of validating that the configuration items have been completely tested and meet all the requirements and the PCA audits the documentation, software, database, and records to ensure that everything is complete and ready to deliver and that nothing extra is included in the delivered software.

10.3 LIBRARY SYSTEM

10.3.1 Developer's Library

Not very long ago, software people thought of libraries only as those set up for documentation and perhaps to store the physical media of the software. Perhaps it was when online development systems got sophisticated enough to have all kinds of directories and file managers that it became obvious that what we really had was a library, and the term became useful in describing all the support and applications software and documentation that resided on the computer. It is arguable whether the software library is truly a CM or a development asset, but regardless of your view, it all falls under control of CM, so I view it that way.

To complicate things a little more, there are code management systems, which in effect provide configuration and change control over all the code that is resident on that computer. These systems, like SCCS for multiuser UNIX-based systems, allow only authorized users to check out the unit for modification. The system keeps trace of changes, who made them, and when they were made. Because it operates on ASCII files, SCCS can just as well be applied to documentation, databases, and other nonprogram files. It stores the original file and then all the changes made to it. Each set of changes is given a version number. Then, to retrieve a particular version, the SCCS administrator applies the appropriate changes to the original file. SCCS is very effective and efficient for projects that require retention of multiple versions of the same basic software package. Other code management systems update the previous version with the latest changes, maintaining only the latest version. This keeps physical file space minimized, but makes restoration of older versions very difficult if not impossible except from backup archives. Still other code management systems allow multiple versions of the same basic software to be retained intact. The developer should select the system that best suits the dynamics and the particular needs of the project.

Documentation libraries are very often maintained in two forms—traditional hard copy and either as word-processing files or CASE tool files. The more sophisticated I-CASE and software engineering environments (SEEs) usually include online document generation and maintenance, so the library is automated in those instances.

The last division of the library that needs to be addressed is databases. This is a big problem in business systems. One non-DOD government job I once worked on had over a half-million reels of tape and somewhere along the way the cataloging and library system sort of broke down and no one knew why three-quarters of those tapes had been saved or what was on them. Of course not everyone has a problem of that magnitude, but every software developer and user faces some form of data storage and library problem. So our view of libraries is to include databases and other forms of miscellaneous data as long as they are pertinent to the project. Some organizations refer to this process as data resource management (DRM).

A few of the more important features that the library system should possess are as follows:

- A flexible, structured, large-capacity library with sufficient expansion capability. Storage capacity needs are always underestimated
- A well-documented, convenient mechanism for users to create, access, and modify the software and data stored in user-defined files in the library
- Controlled access so file owners can restrict modifications to their files as required, but allow availability to all legal users
- Deliveries from the development group to the configuration control group are automated via the library control and must contain status accounting information prior to completion of the delivery transaction
- Procedures and environment for the secure processing and storage of classified information, as required
- Adequate recovery measures so that lost or corrupted files can be recreated as required
- A management-reporting capability so that required status information and activity statistics from any file or collection of files can be accessed and reports provided for management at any desired level of detail.

10.3.2   Independent Verification and Validation Library

Although IV&V has no direct responsibility in the developer's library system, IV&V's influence can be very great. In addition, because IV&V needs significant amounts of data, documents, and code stored in the developer's library, it is essential that IV&V be able to access, retrieve, copy, and otherwise use whatever is required. This often requires that IV&V use the same library software or at least provide a similar capability.

When a IV&V contract is being considered during procurement, it is essential that sharing the library software be considered in the developer's contract to avoid duplication of effort and cost.

Most likely IV&V will only use a subset of the total library capabilities (i.e., enough to copy code for independent execution, collect and store necessary data and documentation, and track the testing effort). Those portions of the files that the developer wishes to keep as proprietary or private (which are not ready for outside users) should have restricted access. One important consideration is that IV&V should never be placed in a position where anything can be accessed that would jeopardize its position of trust with the developer. This is one reason why IV&V usually does not involve itself with unit testing, since the contractor is usually quite sensitive about unproven code being overly scrutinized.

10.4   HOW INDEPENDENT VERIFICATION AND VALIDATION EVALUATES A CONFIGURATION STATUS ACCOUNTING SYSTEM

There may be a case where the developer does not have an automated configuration status accounting system (CSAS) or is converting from a largely manual or poorly integrated CSAS to a comprehensive one that meets all the needs and capabilities described in Section 10.2.3. In either case, IV&V can be very helpful in ensuring that the customer and any other external user's needs are incorporated into the design of the new system.

The following considerations should be helpful to developers and IV&V alike since they describe a well-defined sequence of activities used to develop and evaluate a CSAS.

10.4.1 User Survey

A good automated system for tracking and evaluating software configuration and changes must be designed from the top down, starting with an appraisal of the various managers' and users' needs relative to software problem tracking and evaluation. For this reason, a good first step is a system user survey. This survey serves two purposes. The first is obvious—to solicit various users' needs and requirements and to gain better appreciation of their activities and how the accounting system will support their organizations. The second reason for the survey is more subtle, but no less important. This is to get eventual users involved early and aware of what is going on. Many automated computer-support systems fail not so much on their technical merits, per se, but rather on their overall lack of acceptance by the ultimate users. With this in mind, the survey would consist of two activities. The first is a formal notification of what is being developed and requests for each end user to specify what his or her particular requirements are. The second activity is to follow up these initial responses with discussions. Here such items as networking, output information and report formats, general user functions and participation in regard to problem reporting, ECPs, etc., are formulated.

10.4.2 Systems Analysis

The systems analysis task begins with a tabulation of the users against their various needs as a result of the system user survey. This is assessed and analyzed to determine what these users require in terms of quantities of data, access methods, system response times, input forms and support, etc. The output of this task is a delineation of all principal items that must go into the CSAS database, initial concept of the system operation in terms of what reports would routinely be generated in what timeframe, and last, performance requirements associated with such things as the response required from the system, maximum load that it can handle, anticipated load, etc.

10.4.3 Output Requirements

The purpose of this task is to determine the form and content of all required outputs of the automated system. Outputs here consist of two types. The first is hard-copy output reports. These could either be produced in one place, copied, and then distributed on a periodic basis, or users could access the database to generate their own reports. This discussion will consider that three reports are required. The first is the software problem report (PR). This report delineates the status of each software PR that has been reported and entered into the system. Normally, it will be indexed by computer software configuration item (CSCI) with subindexes on version numbers, if appropriate. The class of the PR will also be included. Typically in systems such as this, there are three or four priority classes of problem reports. The highest usually signifies an immediate operational need or the fact that the system cannot function until the problem is corrected. The lowest level problem reports are usually about routine improvements or minor software errors that have been uncovered that have no near-term effects on the system. The problem status should be included in this report: accepted/rejected, open/correction completed, ECP in preparation, etc.

Related and supportive to the problem report are two other required reports. The first is usually referred to as a *configuration item index*. Here, all computer software configuration items are identified and all documents associated with each item are denoted. Status reporting is usually assigned to the person responsible for that CSCI and/or document. The second related report is usually referred to as an *engineering change proposal (ECP) status log*. Here all ECPs and SCNs, their titles, and dates of initial submittal are delineated. These are correlated to the configuration item number that they are associated with and the problem report that initiated them. The status of the ECP is included and carries such items as whether the configuration control board (CCB) has acted on the ECP in terms of approval, disapproval, or if it is in review, etc. In some cases, cost for the change is associated with the ECP. As these output reports become defined, so does the file content. That is, each report item corresponds to a file/record item. Thus, the results of this task yield not only output report formats but file/record contents. It is here that the ultimate users should review the formats and types of reports expected.

The second aspect of the output requirements task is the initial definition and specification of the output display formats. These are prototypes of the actual displays that are planned for the CSAS and show the capabilities that can be expected from the accounting system. In general, most hard-copy report outputs are also available as displays, but there may also be displays that support ad hoc information queries and handle the responses and statistical results. These do not have to be predefined in the output requirements.

10.4.4   Input Design

The first input design task consists of developing appropriate problem report (PR) forms suitable for online data entry and hardcopy presentation, which can be used by individuals as a formal mechanism for getting problems into the system. The only criteria for developing the form is that it contain all data required by the accounting system and any other data required for the overall information process. The second activity under input design is the specification of the various input displays used to call up or activate various processes associated with the software tracking system or used to input actual data. The ECP, ECO, SCN, deviation, and waiver forms are all required as standard input forms and can be lifted directly from the appropriate MIL-STD, except that they too, like the PR form, should be converted to online data entry. The type of terminal in use greatly affects the appearance of the forms.

A key question at this time is whether multiple users have updating responsibilities. If there is a single updating organization or individual, the data contents tend to be less current than with multiple updating users, particularly if the organizations using the tracking system are physically separated. This is the point where the overall PR process must be completely defined, showing not only the automated tracking system functions, but their interrelationship to PR processing and various organizational responsibilities.

10.4.5 Database Management System Requirements Synthesis

The core of the CSAS is based on the functional capabilities of the selected database management system (DBMS). While the database management capabilities required for this type of system are not excessively complex or unique, the requirements for online ad hoc querying and updating of shared files, record selection, and report generation based on selectable subschema, and possibly subfile access limitations, all require care and foresight in this requirements synthesis. Areas outside of the database management system involving the host computer must also be considered—for example, basic recovery of data loss, any querying of information from remote terminals, and security. The output of this task is a tabulation of requirements to be levied upon the database management system. DBMSs like Oracle, Ingres, Sybase, and Empress provide all the capabilities that you would ever need to support a CSAS. The next part of this activity analyzes various types of file structure that would be best to support the storage, query, and retrieval needs of the CSAS.

10.4.6 Host Computer and Database Management System Selection

By this point in time, the developer should have a good estimate of the number of files, size, content, the types of reports required, and the types of access mechanisms and selection capabilities necessary. With these in hand, the selection of a host computer and DBMS is undertaken. This selection of the two is usually best combined, because you are looking for a total system capability and you must be sure that the DBMS runs efficiently on the computer you have in mind. External considerations such as cost, availability, and the system's possible use by the government on other projects will come into play also. This task can be iterated with DBMS requirements synthesis task to some extent, as the various alternative candidates are considered.

10.4.7 Summary of the Remaining Tasks

It is now up to the developer to implement the CSAS based on the requirements and design criteria that have been produced and verified in the earlier tasks. IV&V will have taken an active role in these earlier tasks to ensure that the CSAS addresses the user's needs through well-defined processes and interfaces in accordance with the appropriate standards.

One last suggestion would be to hold training seminars with all levels of the user community to not only explain the operation of the CSAS, but also the long-term benefits to the project of using and supporting this type of data collection. Historically, the failure of systems of this type can be traced not so much to faulty analysis of the requirements or to the actual design and development process, but more often to the lack of adequate instruction in the capabilities and usage of the implemented system. It has frequently been shown that in successful automated support system implementations, more time is required in "educating" and "informing" end users than was required to design the system, if it is built around a comprehensive DBMS. Remember that IV&V will assist in testing the new system as an early user and can critique the training material as well.

10.5 CHAPTER SUMMARY

- Although configuration management is primarily the responsibility of the developer, IV&V has a major role in ensuring that the developer plans for, implements, and then continues to follow good CM practices.
- IV&V evaluates the configuration identification scheme and then periodically audits the project to make sure that recommended practices are being followed.
- IV&V participates in the configuration control boards (CCBs).
- IV&V uses the configuration status accounting system (CSAS) like any other user, except that IV&V periodically audits the records (database) to make sure that nothing got changed that should not have been changed.
- During development, IV&V should be able to share or extract software from the developer's software library on a noninterference basis. IV&V needs are quite similar to the developer's, only somewhat reduced in scope.
- One of the primary maintenance goals of an IV&V library is to stay current with development.
- At the end of development, IV&V participates in the functional (FCA) and physical configuration audit (PCA) of the software, as described in Sections 9.1.7 and 9.1.9 of Chapter 9.

10.6 WHAT COMES NEXT

Part III of the book follows this chapter. It is a guide to planning and applying IV&V. The next chapter has a dual perspective in that it discusses IV&V program planning both from the customer's and the IV&V contractor's viewpoint.

PART III

A GUIDE TO PLANNING AND APPLYING INDEPENDENT VERIFICATION AND VALIDATION

11

EFFECTIVE PLANNING

This chapter assumes that IV&V will be a contracted effort. If an organic (agency- or company-internal) resource is used instead, the relationship between IV&V and the customer will be a little less complex since there will not have to be a contract, just some form of memorandum of agreement between the two organizations detailing whatever funding arrangements and work descriptions are required.

There are two major aspects of IV&V planning—that done by the customer prior to and for the procurement of IV&V services (Section 11.1) and that done by the IV&V contractor in response to the statement of work and during the performance of the contract (Section 11.2).

11.1 PROCUREMENT OF INDEPENDENT VERIFICATION AND VALIDATION SERVICES

The customer faces a number of decisions that are critical to the eventual success and cost-effectiveness of the IV&V effort. Typical questions to be answered are listed below; a short discussion of each is included in the remainder of this section.

1. How early should the IV&V contractor be brought on board and will the IV&V contract preclude or conflict with a system support contract?
2. How can the software development contract and IV&V contract requirements be coordinated in both procurements to minimize cost and duplication of effort and to maximize usefulness of data, support systems, CASE tools, and documentation?
3. Will geographic locations of the software development contractor and the IV&V contractor have an any effect on the procurement?
4. Can small-business contractors compete and perform effectively as IV&V contractors?

5. How large should the IV&V effort be in respect to total software development effort?

6. What will the IV&V contractor develop and supply as part of the effort and what can be government-furnished?

7. What sort of products can be expected from the IV&V effort?

8. Will there be any problem with data rights between the IV&V contractor and the software development contractor?

9. How can the IV&V contractor augment the customer's staff as an added resource? Should this be considered a good or bad practice?

10. How tightly locked in should the IV&V contractor's statement of work be? What percentage of IV&V's resources should be allocated against pre-defined tasks?

11. What criteria are needed to evaluate IV&V proposals to the maximum advantage of the procurer?

This list is intended to be representative of the types of issues that must be resolved prior to the IV&V contract procurement. The remainder of this section is devoted to answering these questions, although some interpretation may be required to adapt the recommendations to a particular situation.

11.1.1   How Early Can Independent Verification and Validation Begin and Will It Conflict with a System Support Contract?

My favorite answer to this question is that the IV&V contractor should be brought under contract in advance of the software development contract so that system and software requirements can be reviewed, analyzed, and scrubbed prior to issuance of the request for proposal (RFP) for the software effort. The IV&V contractor can then assist the customer in the technical review of the proposals and help ensure a better start to the main thrust. By having this advanced knowledge, the first design review after the development contract award can become a much more effective mechanism through which many of the real issues can be addressed instead of the usual "dog and pony show."* In these kinds of briefings, the important issues may remain buried and no one is quite sure where to challenge the development contractor's analysis and perspective on such things as allocation of functions, data flow, control flow, sizing and memory estimates, processor throughput and timing requirements, etc. Therefore, I would especially recommend the sort of contractual sequence wherein IV&V is brought on when the full-scale development effort is nearing procurement and there has not yet been any IV&V on the earlier efforts. This would allow time for IV&V to verify the system and software requirements

---

*A dog and pony show is a presentation full of dazzle and overconfidence, glossing over the hard to do things with a wave and promise that those items and issues will be high on the priority list, but never are. It typically tells the customer what he or she *wants to hear* with very little regard for hard facts.

specifications, review the minutes and other data from the design reviews that have already been held, evaluate the program risks and uncertainties, and perform whatever independent analysis seems appropriate. If you look at the role played by system engineering and technical assistance (SETA) contractors in DOD and architectural and engineering (A&E) firms in industry, you find that they traditionally are hired well before the development contract is awarded and perform as outlined above. If it can be done for them, why not do it for IV&V?

In cases where the IV&V contract cannot be awarded prior to award of the software development contract, every effort should be made to make the awards simultaneously or within a few days of each other. Even a delay of 30 days can put a real burden on the IV&V contractor that will take some time (often a couple of months) to overcome. The thing that has to be remembered is that the IV&V contractor has to learn as much about the system as the contractor and has many fewer human resources, so IV&V's task is difficult enough without being hampered by a late start.

The government experiences a long cycle time when bringing any contractor on board, so get everything worked out well in advance with the procurement organization. Have them recommend the best form for the contract and make sure the development contract acknowledges IV&V's needs for data, software, and documentation even though the customer will serve as the interface between the two contractors. In the nongovernment sector, a series of purchase orders to incrementally fund the IV&V effort can sometimes be used. These can usually be executed and approved in a week or two, minimizing startup delays.

The other half of Question 1 was "will an IV&V contract conflict with a system support contract?" There are several possible answers to this one. Yes, there will be a conflict unless the customer defines to both parties who does what. The best option I can think of if you want to keep them both involved is to let IV&V concentrate on the technical aspects and let the support contractor assist in management-related issues. Speaking to the customer, I would say that you do not want the burden of two contractors doing the same thing, so split up the work or eliminate one of the contractors, it is that simple. Then, why would you pick IV&V over the support contractor? IV&V is a true technical discipline, the other is not. IV&V has a methodology with tools and techniques already defined, the other does not. IV&V has a proven track record, the support contractor's is totally random. IV&V knows where to concentrate the resources in advance, the support contractor awaits direction from the customer. You get an excellent cost–benefit from IV&V, none from the other. The list goes on and on, but I think you get the message by now.

11.1.2 Coordinating the Needs of Software Development and Independent Verification and Validation Contractors

The most important thing to remember in coordinating the RFPs for software development and IV&V is "designed-in sharing." This way, the customer's total funds can go the farthest; the customer only has to pay once for each item, with minimal duplication of effort. The key to the success of this endeavor is in how carefully the contracts are written to protect the rights of both contractors while establishing the channels and mechanisms to make it possible for the IV&V contractor to have access to the following software developer's items:

- All specifications and other defining documentation
- All test documentation except for unit tests
- All technical reports and briefings to the customer (except financial)
- All code produced under contract
- Compilers and related software used in preparing and running code
- Data-reduction software
- Software library
- Configuration status accounting system (CSAS) user interface and database
- Emulators, simulations, and models produced under the software contract (unless designated as proprietary in advance)
- Any software CASE and analysis tools not considered proprietary that are used by the software contractor.

Certain software—for example, compilers, operating systems, and vendor tools—usually has to be licensed separately by both parties. In addition, the software developer should also be directed in the contract to allow monitoring of selected tests, to be agreed upon after the detailed test network and schedule are established. The number of key-event tests to be monitored and witnessed can only be determined after the particular system development effort is analyzed. This implies access to the software development contractor's facility and some measure of participation in the testing (e.g., manning consoles, measuring and recording data, etc.).

IV&V should have a seat on the configuration control board (CCB) and be allowed to submit problem reports (PRs) into the configuration status accounting system (CSAS) and should have unrestricted access to its database in a read-only mode.

11.1.3 Geographic Impacts

Geographic separation between the software development contractor and IV&V presents some minor problems associated with exchanging data, documentation, software, and analysis results. However, the advent of wide area networking, electronic mail, facsimile (fax) machines, and overnight express delivery service has reduced the problem to little more than an inconvenience. In my personal experience, it seems much more important for the IV&V to locate near the customer, rather than to be separated from the customer in order to be near the software development contractor. The main reason for this opinion is that IV&V personnel are normally aligned closely to the customer's organization and can therefore share the documentation and software library, CSAS, reports, briefings, etc. The IV&V

personnel are continuously advising the customer on technical issues, reviewing proposed changes, ECPs, etc., so there is a daily exchange of information, informal briefings, and impromptu conferences. If this interaction is lost, both the customer and IV&V efforts suffer. The only disadvantages in separating IV&V and software development efforts are the cost and delays in exchanging data and the per diem and transportation costs for technical meetings, design reviews, CCB meetings, conferences, etc. For these and other reasons I strongly advise against separating the customer and the IV&V group and really have no strong feelings on other geographic considerations.

11.1.4 The Role of Small Business in Independent Verification and Validation

There has been a long-term trend in DOD to funnel IV&V procurements exclusively to small businesses. Many of these "small-business set-aside" decisions are intended to satisfy a form of quota that says some percentage of the agency's business must go to small and disadvantaged small businesses, instead of being made solely on the basis of the ability of the companies in question to perform well on the contract. This quota situation can be remedied by having sufficient small business subcontracts buried in the prime contracts and allowing at least some IV&V contracts to go to unrestricted status. Anyway, it is a problem for medium-sized companies that satisfy all of the qualifications just to get an opportunity to compete and win IV&V contracts. These are the companies that probably have the best overall capabilities, tools, hardware resources, and depth of staff. My next choice is the small businesses that have a well-diversified contract base and a strong background in successful IV&V programs. To me, the least attractive choice for IV&V is the company regardless of size who will have to go out and hire the staff and buy the hardware and software just to perform the contract. These companies are very seldom really viable candidates for major IV&V efforts. Sometimes you may be pleasantly surprised to find an exceptional staff and sufficient concentration of all the right factors to make even a small "small business" a very viable IV&V contractor. The key factor here is that they concentrate on IV&V as a business area and make it one of their specialties.

In any case, the real evaluation issues are prior experience, current capabilities, methodology, and tools. If a small business concern or a disadvantaged or minority-owned small business (these are often referred to a *8a companies* as defined in the Federal Acquisition Regulations (FAR)) can demonstrate its adequacy in all four of these areas, then there is no reason not to allow them to bid on or receive the IV&V contract. Thus, size of the company is not nearly as important as dedication and commitment and a willingness to invest in the people and tools to make it work.

Because the real issue should be who is capable of doing the best job on an IV&V contract, the procurements should be open and unrestricted. Then if a small business desires to specialize in IV&V and acquires the skills and tools necessary to be competitive, they should have the same probability of winning as the larger company and vice versa.

11.1.5   How Large Should Independent Verification and Validation Be Compared to the Software Effort?

Because of the complexity of the answer to this question, I have devoted a significant portion of Chapter 13 to this subject. In my experience, it is possible to summarize the answer as a spread that runs from 3 to 26% of the cost of the software effort. However, these are definitely the extremes and do not represent typical IV&V programs in the least. The 3% effort was an endgame IV&V effort whose major concern was test monitoring and validation with only a few IV&V products, aside from independent reports on the testing. The 26% effort was full, in-phase IV&V program, which required the IV&V contractor to develop highly sophisticated simulations and analytical models, to perform a great deal of the actual testing, and to assist in the technical management of the effort. A significant cost in this latter effort also included computers and a sophisticated IV&V testbed with significant hardware in the loop for performance testing of the entire system. The software developer did not have to budget against these same kinds of hardware costs—they were given to him as part of the test environment. Thus, the 26% figure was a very unusual situation and I have never seen it repeated again.

From a larger sample of IV&V programs, it appears that the average IV&V cost is between 7.5% and 12%, depending upon whether the hardware and support software costs are included or not. Remember this is the percentage of IV&V costs in relation to the software development program. If the IV&V contractor is expected to provide or build a rather extensive testbed, the higher value (12%) could possibly be exceeded. Therefore, for very rough approximations, a figure of 10% is typical for initial estimates, to be followed by a more detailed study of what will be expected of the IV&V contractor, which can cause this number to vary a few percent either way. Effective planning in terms of coordinating both the software and IV&V contracts (Section 11.1.2) can reduce the overall cost to a minimum regardless of how it breaks down in the budget.

11.1.6   What Should the Independent Verification and Validation Effort Build and/or Supply?

Because there are certain core IV&V functions that are basic to any effort, the main concerns of this question are in the software testing tools, analytical simulations, emulations, testbeds, and project support software.

11.1.6.1   Software Tools. Fortunately, a very large number of software testing tools are making their way into the public domain and/or are available as packages, fully debugged and ready for installation and use. The IV&V testbed should be a collection of those deemed appropriate for a particular type of system, computer, and software language.

Some companies specializing in software testing are already building partially and fully integrated testing systems that perform many of the secondary roles, for example, easily constructed test drivers, machine-aided test case generation, path analysis, calling and execution sequence analysis, cross-compilation, software instrumentation, etc. These tools and their hardware platforms represent significant capital investment, which is usually amortized by billing the contract for their use or, if embedded in indirect cost, they contribute to higher overhead rates. The customer must have a good idea of how to pay for these "goodies" when the proposals are evaluated or he or she may be in for a shock downstream. It may be cheaper in the long run for the customer to buy the tools and hardware, let IV&V use them during development, and convert them over to maintenance support later on.

It is clear that the IV&V contractor must offer something in the way of unique CASE and analysis tools, since to duplicate the software contractor's efforts completely could be counterproductive. The best way to select these tools is to analyze what the software developer will most likely supply by analyzing the software development plan (SDP) and the proposal and ensure that the IV&V tools are complementary in that they perform "other checks and analysis" not already planned (see Section 11.2.1). If the developer makes a big investment in an I-CASE tool, IV&V can also use it, as long as different perspectives are sought.

11.1.6.2 *Analytical Simulations and Models.*

Many times, a major distinction between small and large business concerns is their existing repertoire of simulations and models. Thus, one key evaluation criterion in selecting the IV&V contractor should be the ready availability of these simulations and models for use on the proposed effort and/or the IV&V contractor's experience in building and modifying them successfully. If the IV&V contractor has to build such things from scratch during the contract, it is extremely difficult to validate them and have them accepted as accurate, especially if the schedule is tight.

Of course, not all such simulations can be off-the-shelf; some must be built during the contract. If they are to be shared, then the customer should consider having them built by the software development contractor, not the IV&V contractor. When they are to be stand-alone IV&V analysis aids, then a careful appraisal of how they are to be built (i.e., the formality of the design and development effort) must be made and appropriate requirements must be included in the RFP for IV&V. In DOD, the frequently asked question is: will the simulation need to be developed according to the military standards used for the development effort. In most cases the answer is "No, but it should have requirements, design, test, and user documentation defined and it should be generated in the logical order used to develop any other software." The most frequent exception to this rule occurs when the simulation is to be delivered along with the system to support maintenance or some peripheral activity like training or change verification.

11.1.6.3 *Emulations/Cross-Compilers.*

The emulation of concern to this discussion is that set of software that allows code development and testing to occur on a host computer prior to testing on the target computer. Many times a software developer will have to build such an emulator to take advantage of the throughput of a large general-purpose mainframe computer or because the target computer is not available early enough to prevent schedule problems. There are several vendor workstations and development systems that emulate the more popular chipsets including MIL-STD-1750A processors. This way even timing can be analyzed for deadlocks, hanging, overlaps, etc.

The cross-compiler does a similar function by allowing the code to be developed and tested on one machine and then compiled and/or assembled onto another computer. The portability of the Ada language is supposed to make this much easier. It is the usual practice for the software developer to build, procure, or supply these two types of software and to allow the IV&V contractor access, or to make copies available through the customer interface. Do not forget, the customer should always be active in or at least cognizant of all interactions between the software development contractor and IV&V.

11.1.6.4 Project Support Software. The significant forms of project support software include the configuration status accounting system (CSAS), software library, and any tracking systems that may be needed for requirements tracing, cost and performance monitoring and reporting, open/action item tracking, and general housekeeping functions. The first two items were discussed at length in Chapter 10 and should normally be specified in the software development contract as available for use by the IV&V contractor. The remaining systems are not expensive items and can usually be developed quickly using generic software packages on PC-level computers.

11.1.7 Typical Independent Verification and Validation Products

These, of course, vary widely depending upon the type of program, size of the effort, entry point in the development cycle, available resources, etc. Thus, it is difficult to define a given set of products. The products given in Table 11-1 are typical of the kinds of reports, data, and documents that could be produced by IV&V in each phase. In addition, the customer should expect to see a draft of the IV&V plan as part of each proposal.

It is quite effective for the IV&V contractor's progress report to present summary data and statistics on the software contractor's problem reports, specifications, code under test, test results, open items, and action items. This type of reporting will generally be developed from different sources (and/or perspective) than the development contractor's reports and forms a sound basis for second-opinion assessment of the overall software status. Long-term error trends and reliability data can be developed and analyzed by plotting problem reports, for example, on an inception-to-date basis.

11.1.8 Data Rights

A main concern of the procurer of IV&V services is to always clearly state in the contracts that all data, documents, and software produced under the contract(s) become the property of the customer. If any exception brought on by any claims of

TABLE 11-1. Typical IV&V Products, by Phase

Requirements Phase

- System specification verification report
- Software requirements specification verification report(s)
- Requirements verification report
  - Summary of document reviews
  - Summary of criticality and risk assessment
  - Review of user interface
  - Review of I/O data requirements
  - Review of trade studies
  - Review of test planning
  - List of meetings and formal reviews attended
  - List of PRs produced
  - Open/action item list
- IV&V analyst's notebook
  - Evaluation factors
  - Independent verification studies and results
  - Software tools used

Design Phase

- Preliminary and detailed design IV&V reports, each containing:
  - Summary of document reviews
  - Verification of requirements tracing
  - Verification of data flow
  - Verification of behavior
  - Verification of algorithms
  - Verification of database
  - Review of user interface
  - Review of design risks
  - Review of timing, sizing, and memory allocation
  - Review of software development plan conformance
  - List of meetings and formal reviews attended
  - List of PRs produced
  - Open/action item list
- IV&V analyst's notebook
  - Evaluation factors
  - Independent verification studies and results
  - Software tools used

Coding Phase

- Results from the code to SDD comparison
  - Deficiencies and discrepancies
  - Verification of the data dictionary
  - Verification of algorithms between code and SDD
  - List of PRs produced
  - Open/action item list

(continued)

TABLE 11-1. (*Continued*)

- Review of conformance to software development plan
- Results of static analysis tool and standards checking
- Results of auditing developer's software library, database archives, and system and support software maintenance practices
- IV&V analyst's notebook
  -Code to SDD comparison data
  -Results of audits
  -Independent code verification studies and results
  -Software tools used

Integration & Test Phase

- Results from the review of the developer's software test plans and descriptions (STPs and STDs)
- Listing or network of key event tests selected for monitoring by IV&V
- Generation of formal validation report including such things as
  -Results from monitoring the developer's testing
  -Results from running the IV&V test tool(s) on the code
  -Summary of pre-planned IV&V tests
  -Summary of the ad hoc IV&V tests that were run in response to problems that occurred during testing and investigations initiated by IV&V
  -Description of the IV&V testbed and its complement of tools
  -IV&V test results (data and analysis can be referenced)
  -List of any briefings given the customer and developer on validation activities
  -Validation summary comparing the requirements and tests
  -Validation of the software product specification, user's and operator's manuals
  -Summary of FCA, FQR, and PCA activities
  -Final conclusions and recommendations for the operational or production period
- IV&V analyst's notebook
  -Requirements-to-test comparison data
  -Results of audits and reviews
  -Independent validation studies and results
  -Software tools used
- Listing of all PRs produced and their status at the end of FQT

proprietary or other company private status is involved, the lawyers, contracting officers, and responsible procurement people must work out a reasonable solution. The main reason for mentioning this is that in the past a number of cases have occurred where a contractor developed or partially developed products under government contracts, and the products were later claimed as totally company-proprietary. Then later, when a new contract was proposed in the same technology area, the contractor, having the software in-house, had an unfair advantage over the competition and, in some cases, packaged and sold this or quite similar software as an off-the-shelf product to other customers.

Although some progress is being made in the copyright and patent arena, this still presents a significant problem. There is a great deal of theft of software, much of which is difficult to prosecute because so many techniques and algorithms are in the public domain. When in doubt, leave it to the lawyers to solve, but remain aware that there can be definite problems in this contract area, especially if they are ignored.

11.1.9 How Can Independent Verification and Validation Augment the Customer's Staff?

One very important aspect of IV&V is that it should be thought of as an added resource of the customer. IV&V should not, however, become totally "integrated" into the customer's organization since this would adversely affect the freedom, independence, and investigative curiosity of the IV&V group. A "close working relationship" is probably the best way to describe the necessary interaction. This can include daily contact, near-total exchange of technical information, frequent informal briefings, etc., but the two organizations must maintain themselves as separately managed entities. As mentioned previously, the customer should act as the go-between in the IV&V software and contractor relationship on all technical issues and serve as the funnel through which all data, documents, code and test materials change hands (in both directions). The customer can grant permission for direct exchanges, but should remain cognizant of all such activities. One way to accomplish this is to insist on cover letters on all transmittals that occur in both directions and to always send a copy to the customer.

11.1.10 Pointers on the Independent Verification and Validation Contract Statement of Work

The ten most significant items for the procurer of IV&V services to bear in mind are presented in summary form below:

1. Require a draft IV&V plan as part of the proposal.
2. Do not attempt to require an IV&V test plan until after the software developer's test plans are reviewed and analyzed.
3. Do not force the IV&V contractor to dedicate more than half his or her validation resources to predefined IV&V testing.
4. Specify the type of tools, simulations, models, support software, etc. that are to be expected from the software contractor to enable IV&V to reuse what makes sense and propose its own complementary tools and analysis aids, as needed.
5. If tools or analytical software are to be developed under the proposed contract, state the standards that will apply.
6. Ensure data rights on behalf of the procurer for all software items developed under the contract.
7. Ensure that test data are available from the software contractor immediately following designated key-event tests.

8. Ensure that the IV&V contractor can specify the extra data recording, etc. that is needed during software contractor tests that are to be monitored.

9. Ensure that the IV&V contractor will have the proper role in configuration management and CCB actions of both development contractor and customer.

10. Ensure that the IV&V contractor will have adequate interface with the software contractor's quality-assurance organization.

11.1.11 Evaluating Independent Verification and Validation Proposals

It is hoped that the procurer of IV&V services can avoid having cost as the significant factor in the selection and award process. Historically, when cost has been the primary driver, performance suffers. Therefore, the following evaluation weighting guidelines are recommended: 50–70%, technical factors; 20–30%, management factors; and 10–20%, cost.

This way cost can still be used as the final determinant among technically qualified responses, but cannot overwhelm the decision process. Hopefully, this will prevent buy-ins. Cost should also be evaluated from the basis of "realism," not simply the bottom-line number. This will also help a great deal in preventing mispricing.

A typical profile of IV&V evaluation factors is presented as follows:

1. *Methodology.* A sensible and cost-effective approach to:
   - Requirements analysis and tracing
   - Design analysis (including algorithms)
   - Code analysis and independent verification via tools
   - Validation using complementary testing and analysis aids to those used by the software contractor
2. *Tools and Analysis Aids*
   - Existing repertoire of models and simulations applicable to the system and technology involved
   - Cost-effective mix of manual and automated analysis aids
   - Well-presented development approach and rationale for any new tools or aids required
3. *Facilities*
   - Company-owned or priority access to appropriate computer facilities
   - Well-designed testbed with total capabilities (as discussed in chapters 7 and 8) to execute code and analyze results
   - Maximum and effective use of government-furnished facilities
4. *Staffing and Organization*
   - Staff experience on the type of system being developed
   - Ability to start immediately upon award of contract

- Organization that matches job and complements customer's organization
- Single-point interface (especially important if subcontractor is involved)
- Willing to support difficult geographic constraints

5. *Experience*
    - Staff experience in previous IV&V efforts
    - Staff experience in type of system, algorithms, computer language, etc.
    - Company experience in type of system involved, with proven track record of on-time, on-budget performance
    - Managerial and high-level corporate commitment.

11.1.12 50–50 Rule for Independent Verification and Validation Testing

The book has mentioned in several places that it is extremely beneficial to reserve a portion of the IV&V testing resource for unforeseen and uncommitted test analysis. This allows IV&V to investigate whatever problem symptoms appear during the developer's testing and to generate and run independent IV&V tests and/or analysis. Early in a development effort, before the developer's test descriptions and procedures are written, it is very difficult if not impossible for IV&V to completely define and develop its own independent test program. At best, IV&V will have a general idea, but not enough specific data to perform this task in full. Therefore, IV&V experience shows that it is a good rule of thumb to preplan and precommit the use of no more than 50% of the independent testing resources at the beginning of the program. Customers should be aware of this potential trap and should not expect a total preplan of the validation phase of IV&V.

11.2 THE INDEPENDENT VERIFICATION AND VALIDATION CONTRACTOR'S PLANNING EFFORT

Probably the most important consideration in IV&V planning revolves around the inherent flexibility of the methodology wherein optimization becomes the process of tailoring the approach to the unique constraints and attributes of:

- The system and its technology base
- The software development contractor and its maturity level (per Chapter 15)
- The customer and any outside organizations that may also be involved (e.g., an independent test and evaluation agency, regulatory agency or other contractors)
- The facilities available including GFE
- The budget and schedule
- The initial entry and end points of IV&V in the system acquisition life cycle.

Because these factors are impossible to predict in advance of an RFP and resulting proposal, this section presents the elements of a typical comprehensive IV&V

plan, which can be used as a checklist and guide for detailed planning. A high-level table of contents for a generic IV&V plan is given below; it serves as an index to the rest of this section.

IV&V Plan: Sample Table of Contents

1. Introduction and scope
2. Overview of methodology and approach
3. Requirements verification (for details, see Table 11-2)
4. Design verification (for details, see Table 11-3)
5. Code verification (for details, see Table 11-4)
6. Validation (for details, see Table 11-5)
7. Tools and analysis aids (refer to Section 11.2.1)
8. Support software (refer to Section 11.2.2)
9. Facilities (refer to Section 11.2.3)
10. Configuration management (refer to Section 11.2.4)
11. Interface with quality assurance (refer to Section 11.2.5)
12. Staff and organization (refer to Section 11.2.6)
    Appendices (as required).

When the software development contractor's test plans are approved, the IV&V contractor should produce an IV&V test plan, which delineates the contractor key-event tests that will be monitored and the independent IV&V tests that can be preplanned, as described in Chapter 8.

If IV&V is required to develop and/or deliver major software for this effort, an appendix should be written to the IV&V plan, which will in effect be a mini-software development plan (SDP), fully covering the development of each software deliverable. Significant items may require full military standard development if and only if they are needed after development of the system, in order to support it during its operational lifetime. Such cases are very rare, but you never know. Otherwise, the IV&V software products can usually be developed to commercial practices, which generally means much less rigorous documentation, reviews, and testing. The RFP must stipulate what is required.

Tables 11-2 through 11-5 provide the general outlines for the four major IV&V phases shown in the sample table of contents. Rough approximations of manpower for the IV&V bid can be developed by building a similar set of tables matched to the specific statement of work requirements in the IV&V RFP.

11.2.1 Tools and Analysis Aids

This section of the IV&V plan should contain the listing of the tools and analysis aids selected for the IV&V effort. The material should be presented as a critique of available or needed tools for each application by IV&V phase and should contain

TABLE 11-2. Typical Requirements Verification Activities

Typical Activity	Manpower Estimate
Verify the system specification (SS)	
Verify the software requirements specification (SRS)	
Verify the interface requirements specification (IRS)	
Verify the hardware prime item specification (PIS) if required	
Verify the software development plan (SDP) and its implementation	
Verify requirements tracing between documents	
Perform criticality and risk assessment of requirements	
Review user interface needs	
Review input and output data requirements	
Review trade studies for system	
Review test requirements, planning and strategy	
Participate in all reviews and meetings that affect the system	
Produce problem reports	

some limited tradeoff analysis discussing why the particular tools were chosen or why there is an identified need that can only be satisfied by a newly developed one. This method of presentation adds considerably to the credibility of the tools selected. It should also be noted in this section if there is an existing tool that requires modification; this should be accompanied by a rough approximation of the effort involved as well as the cost benefit of doing so.

11.2.1.1   Tool Selection and Evaluation. Tool selection involves numerous tangible, intangible, and uncertain factors that vary across the development cycle. As

TABLE 11-3. Typical Design Verification Activities

Typical Activity	Manpower Estimate
Verify the software design document (SDD)	
Verify the interface design document (IDD)	
Verify the requirements tracing into SDD for SRS	
Verify data flow	
Verify behavioral factors (especially real-time systems)	
Verify selected algorithms	
Verify database structures and elements	
Verify user interface	
Review design risks	
Review timing budgets (especially real-time systems)	
Review sizing and memory allocations (especially real-time systems)	
Review how well developer is following SDP	
Participate in all reviews and meetings that affect the system	
Produce problem reports	

TABLE 11-4. Typical Code Verification Activities

Typical Activity	Manpower Estimate
Verify consistency between code and SDD	
Verify that specified standards and practices are being followed	
Verify that developer is using specified coding tools	
Verify logical structure and syntax with static analysis	
Verify terms between data dictionary and code	
Verify sample input and output data	
Verify algorithms per SDD	
Verify versions of computer, operating systems and utilities	
Review software library and release/version control	
Participate in all reviews and meetings that affect the system	
Produce problem reports	

design choices, software tools, and programming methodologies are selected and put into use by the developer, the IV&V tool selection process can begin. The software engineer generally has little quantitative information on the relative performance of comparable tools or how cost-effective they are on an absolute scale. Direct experience on similar projects is a most valuable evaluation factor because the real costs of installation, training, use, and maintenance can then be determined. Such experience also separates the real from the promised benefits and reveals side effects or performance characteristics that can be unexpectedly beneficial or detrimental. Actual use takes in what is known as the "corporate culture," which has a very large influence on how the staff accepts and works with or against the tools and

TABLE 11-5. Typical Validation Activities

Typical Activity	Manpower Estimate
Review and evaluate software test plan (STP) and software test description (STD) for each CSCI	
Evaluate developer's test program and select key-event tests for data collection and monitoring	
Monitor developer's testing	
Develop IV&V test strategy	
Define and configure the IV&V testbed	
Run independent validation tests	
Confirm validation of requirements to tests	
Validate software product specification (SPS)	
Validate software user's and system operator's manuals	
Track CCB actions and open-item status	
Participate in all reviews, audits, and meetings that affect the system	
Produce problem reports	

methodologies. For example, take a company that has a good track record as a software developer. It suddenly finds itself failing to produce a satisfactory product on its first large Ada project. Everything seems to be going wrong despite the fact that management bought a new development system, new I-CASE tools, and a new database management system. Maybe they simply overwhelmed the staff with too much new material at one time, although sometimes this cannot be helped. It often produces casualties. Someone quits, and another, and perhaps another. If this occurs, do not panic! It is very difficult to teach people new ways of doing things. IV&V has to be aware that the developer may be learning new techniques and, if so, IV&V's job is going to be harder than it would be otherwise. If from all appearances this is the case, IV&V will have to bolster its analysis capabilities and tools and will probably find itself doing more original contributing than usual. To illustrate this idea, IV&V receives a draft specification. If the developer is really struggling to produce a barely adequate document, IV&V may have to write actual examples of how it should be done and give them back to the developer, rather than just be a technical critic. If a particular CASE tool or analytical simulation is needed to bolster the development effort, IV&V should be in a position to provide it. Therefore, some of the IV&V tool evaluation considerations need to be made as the program proceeds and information as to the general health of the development effort becomes known. Thus, the initial assessment may not always be enough. Be prepared to revisit this area several times during large projects.

Since many tools offer a similar complement of capabilities, other considerations can dominate the selection process. Cost factors include: development or acquisition investment and use factors, which include input data preparation time, computer time, analyst time, training, and maintenance. Direct hands-on experience with a particular tool is *the most satisfactory basis* for predicting costs on other projects. Life cycle cost and secondary evaluation criteria in areas such as maturity, versatility, familiarity, and user friendliness are additional factors in the selection process. The latter are more difficult to assess quantitatively so I have included additional information on those tool characteristics as follows:

- Maturity of a specific tool implementation considerably lowers the risk and costs of tool application, but may be difficult to quantify. When other factors are comparable, mature and proven tools should be selected. It is usually a big mistake to become a beta site for some tool vendor (as explained in Section 6.11).
- Versatility permits substitution or addition of elements or functions in order to tailor a tool for a specific task. This is sometimes accommodated by a series of user option "switches" that can be set for a particular application. Generally, versatility follows maturity in that additions and modifications are a natural consequence of a heavily used tool.
- Familiarity depends on many factors such as organization, available personnel, individual experience, company-sponsored training, and perhaps most of all, corporate commitment. While experience with a tool tends to smooth out user

problems, really useful tools are seldom overly elaborate, but rather are intuitive in their application. The advantage of familiar and predictable results in tool use can often outweigh a more powerful but poorly understood capability.

- "User friendly" was the most overused term in the computer world in 1990, so I made a promise to myself not to use it unless absolutely essential to the understanding of a concept. But it is important enough to discuss as a key attribute of tools since it describes the aspects of a tool that make you feel competent and comfortable about using it. The first user-friendly system I ever worked on was a Macintosh. In an hour or so, you could figure out the essentials. Since that time, many hundreds of software products have hit the market with that same touch and feel, and our world has changed for the better. You definitely need to look for tools that are as friendly as the Macintosh user interface.

Basically, one can conclude that there are two good methods for evaluating and selecting a set of IV&V tools and techniques—error coverage and cost benefits. The focus of the error coverage method is on absolute software and documentation correctness. For this method, the error set is delineated and correlated to IV&V tools and techniques coverage. The other method concerns cost benefits. Here the application of the automated tool or manual technique with its attendant benefits in cost savings or quality improvement is traded off against the development, operating, and maintenance costs of the tool or technique itself.

It is also important to remember that software tools and techniques become obsolete at an alarming rate, so perhaps both developers and IV&V organizations need to assess annually where they are and what new tools and techniques need to be phased in to keep their capabilities abreast of or ahead of their competitors. When you select some of the more comprehensive I-CASE toolsets, the vendor will be more than happy to keep you up to date. Even tool vendors may be trying to get a little extra mileage from an old design, so be alert to this problem. Thus, it is prudent to perform this assessment annually no matter whose tools you use.

11.2.1.2 Cost–Benefit Analysis in Tool Selection.

Cost-benefit analysis can be viewed as a series of steps, which are outlined as follows:

Step 1. Determine the percentage of total software budget by development phase. This will later yield value designated P_U, which represents percent of use for each tool, by phase.

Step 2. Determine the cost of acquiring or developing, maintaining, and operating each candidate tool. This value is designated T_C, which represents tool cost.

Step 3. Determine the effectiveness of each candidate tool in terms of error coverage, type of testing (e.g., static vs. dynamic), application, languages, portability, access methods, etc. These somewhat subjective assessments should be weighted and scaled from 0 to 1000 (best). These decimal values become the effectiveness coefficients, and are expressed as T_E.

Step 4. Calculate the effectiveness value, E_V, for each tool by the following equation:

$$P_U \times T_E = E_V \text{ for each tool}$$

Tools covering more than one development (or IV&V) phase therefore receive a greater effectiveness value than those used in a single phase only.

Step 5. Develop a matrix containing each tool by applicable phase. Then enter the effectiveness value, E_V, for each tool and divide by tool cost, T_C, to yield tool cost–benefit value, T_{CB}.

$$E_V \div T_C = T_{CB}$$

Step 6. Rank order the matrix by highest T_{CB} values and select those tools that are necessary and affordable under the terms of the contract.

11.2.2 Support Software

Generally, IV&V should plan to duplicate the exact versions of the support software being used by the software development contractor, plus whatever extra might be needed. Typical support software needed within the IV&V facility and/or testbed includes:

- Operating system
- Compiler(s)
- Cross-compiler, if needed
- Assembler
- Linker/loader
- Screen editor
- Software development contractor's data reduction software
- Debug packages
- Any special installation and test software
- Any maintenance and diagnostic software
- Selected utilities
- Special IV&V data reduction software
- Configuration management and library software
- Any CASE tools that need to be shared

- All of the analysis tools, simulations, and any other non-applications software that may be required to effectively perform the IV&V mission.

There is additional discussion on this subject in Chapter 8 that deals with the support software requirements for the IV&V testbed.

11.2.3 Facilities

A key factor in IV&V facility planning is the geographic separation among the customer, software developer, and IV&V. Isolation of the IV&V facility, especially from the customer, will likely result in greater expense in order to maintain an adequate software and document library, configuration status accounting system (CSAS), test documentation, and computer facilities. Close proximity (less than 25 miles) usually means that IV&V and the customer can share most of these items with little or no difficulty.

In any case, this section of the IV&V plan should contain a detailed description of planned facility, how government-furnished equipment and facilities will be used, and schedules and plans for any hardware and software acquisitions that have to be made to complete the facility. Detailed functional requirements for the facility are given in Chapter 8.

11.2.4 Configuration Management

The IV&V plan should delineate how IV&V intends to use the software development contractor's library system and configuration status accounting systems (CSAS) and how it plans to develop its own capabilities in both of these configuration management (CM) elements. Detailed suggestions are given in Chapter 10 relevant to both areas. If IV&V is faced with developing test tools and other software analysis aids, the plan must specify how IV&V intends to configuration-manage these products during their development as well as throughout their operational life. It should be acceptable to generally copy the software developer's CM scheme or use IV&V's own methods as long as the configuration identification, accounting and control procedures are in accordance with the applicable military standards, and the identification and status codes are compatible with the requirements of the customer's system. This will allow for adequate configuration control of the delivered software products after the contracts terminate and the customer assumes the responsibility for the software during the operation and support phase.

The IV&V plan should include details relating to CM interfaces, configuration control boards (CCBs), and operation of the library and CSAS.

11.2.5 Interface with Quality Assurance

There are two aspects to software quality assurance (SQA) that need to be addressed in the IV&V plan. First, the plan should describe the interface with the software developer's quality-assurance group. This will enable IV&V to share test results, results of reviews and audits, product evaluations, and other pertinent SQA actions.

The IV&V plan may also include a detailed description of how IV&V intends to review and critique the software development contractor's SQA planning and how recommendations will be made to correct deficiencies in the implementation and follow-through of SQA procedures and practices that are discovered by IV&V. Second, the plan should state how IV&V intends to perform SQA on any of its own products that become deliverables on the contract, to ensure adequate quality considerations.

11.2.6 Staff and Organization

Probably one of the simplest ways to profile the staff needs for IV&V is to analyze the system being developed by major functional area. A weapon system, for example, with a radar, a ground-based computer, a command and control system, and missiles self-defines at least five types of analysts: radar engineer, real-time software analysts, command and control analyst, and missile guidance and control analyst, and systems analysts to assess system integration and performance. The exact number of analysts and their role is usually a function of budget constraints and system particulars. Sometimes people may have to assume dual roles, but initially IV&V subgroups can be formed to match the major functional software divisions (CSCIs) in order to generally complement the software developer's organization. If IV&V software is to be produced, a mini-development group will be required. In addition, at least one IV&V software technologist should be assigned to define, adapt, and implement the best methodologies for the particular effort defined. He or she will lead the selection and specification process for tools, analysis aids and techniques, documentation, plans, and practices. IV&V support personnel should cover administration and coordination of the software library, configuration management, computer and facility operations, technical writing/editing, clerical support, and finance and accounting.

The management hierarchy should be as simple and straight-line as possible to ensure a short path to corporate management. This will help in obtaining the required senior staff commitment for successful performance, especially in dynamic programs. The selection of the manager should be based on prior experience, ability to understand and discuss (both informally and formally) the system technicalities, grasp of the IV&V technologies required, knowledge of tools and analysis techniques, and ability to work in a sometimes difficult political atmosphere. This role requires that the manager be able to tactfully inform the software developer of his/her deficiencies (usually via the customer or in his/her presence), keep the customer happy with the IV&V results, and coordinate and direct a dedicated staff. The several direct and indirect interfaces always present in IV&V efforts complicate the manager's job.

In summary, the IV&V organization will often strongly resemble the software development contractor's organization, only the scale is proportional to the difference in budgets. Thus, the simplest perspective on staffing is to ask the question, "If I had to build this system myself, who would I need?" Then divide by 10 and begin the selection process, adding or subtracting people, as resources allow.

11.3 CHAPTER SUMMARY

- This chapter has a dual perspective in that it discusses the planning and procurement of IV&V from both customer and IV&V viewpoints.
- Advice given a first-time customer is to start IV&V as early as possible, consider the data requirements in both contracts in advance, and be prepared to specify to IV&V just what you expect and when.
- Try to keep the procurement open and unrestricted, avoiding small-business set-asides.
- It is generally more important for IV&V to be local to the customer than to the developer. This could mean that you have to travel to witness tests.
- Do not attempt to allocate all the testing resources in advance as this will tie the hands of IV&V, preventing pursuit of problems that arise during the course of testing.
- IV&V evaluation should be focused on methodology, tools and analysis aids, facilities, staffing and organization, and experience.
- The IV&V contractor has to present its methodology in a coherent and realistic manner to satisfy the scope of work.
- The IV&V contractor has to perform a quantitative evaluation in order to select the best software tools for a particular project.
- The IV&V contractor has to interface gracefully with the developer's quality and configuration management organizations for uninhibited and responsive exchange of information.
- Whenever possible, the IV&V contractor should staff its organization to match that of the developer's, except at a much reduced scale.
- The IV&V contractor has to acquire and configure the testbed and support software needed to accomplish the program objectives.

11.4 WHAT COMES NEXT

The next chapter deals with optimizing the results of an IV&V program. It also deals with the application of metrics as a useful means of quantifying and measuring the quality of developer's key products. It then discusses how to perform a criticality assessment on the software. The chapter concludes with a summary of areas that offer significant promise in the future for better optimization of IV&V.

12

OPTIMIZING INDEPENDENT VERIFICATION AND VALIDATION RESULTS

This chapter is divided into three main sections, the first of which presents a series of pointers on how to optimize IV&V results (12.1). The second section (12.2) discusses software metrics which can be applied to both the requirements and design phases to help measure the quality of the specifications. The third section (12.3) covers an approach to assessing the criticality of software requirements.

12.1 PLANNING AND PERFORMING INDEPENDENT VERIFICATION AND VALIDATION

Many of the suggestions in this section appear in other parts of this book, but are so important to the success of the IV&V effort that it seems worthwhile to consolidate and reiterate them briefly.

1. Start as early as possible with an experienced core of IV&V experts and analysts who understand the technologies and type of system involved.
2. Use common sense and keep it as simple as possible no matter what it is. Elaborate tools that appear marvelous may be a user's nightmare.
3. Develop a responsive IV&V plan to match the job and the statement of work.
4. If system does not represent the leading edge of the state of the art, listen to experience and pay attention to the lessons learned from similar systems.
5. If system pushes the state of the art:
   - Look very hard at the unknown factors and perceived risks of the program and attempt to compare and correlate with known factors

- Rely on intuition of experienced personnel
- Study and examine the physical laws and properties encompassed by the system.

6. Recommend (or supply) higher fidelity models if the contractor's models do not faithfully reveal real-world conditions, phenomenology, environment, etc.

7. Measure your progress by the number of valid problem reports (PRs) written. It should at least equal the IV&V contract's budget percentage relative to the total software effort. If IV&V is 8% of the software budget, IV&V should write at least 8% of the PRs. I have seen several IV&V efforts where this number was exceeded by a factor of two. Caution: Do not turn the effort into a contest to see who can write the most PRs; that would be very counterproductive and will antagonize the developer.

8. Look out for overuse of nominal values in design and testing. What happens when the worst case really exists? That is when some systems absolutely have to work and typically when they tend to fail the most.

9. In real-time processes, check that interrupt times and levels do not become the controlling design feature instead of optimum implementation. In other words, always attempt to design processes to run well within their time slot, not just under the time limit.

10. Avoid overly serial logic sequences, which do not take advantage of multiprocessing and other concurrent processing capabilities. Design for as much parallel processing as the hardware allows.

11. Carefully select software contractor's tests for IV&V monitoring by examining test integration and build network mapping to examine only key mid- and end-point tests. Do not spread IV&V resources too thin by attempting to witness too many tests.

12. Do not overcommit preplanned IV&V tests to the denial of being able to search for problems as they occur. Set up contingency and backup tests to cover otherwise quiet periods to even out the IV&V analyst's workload. Strike a balance between contractor test monitoring and analysis and the independent IV&V testing. A 50–50 split is a good goal to shoot for in planning IV&V testing and support.

13. Where possible, participate in hands-on testing of the system. Man the consoles, verify documentation, record data, take pictures, do anything to get involved. Remember that IV&V needs the opportunity to become the first outside user of the system.

14. Attempt to spread IV&V resources to 50% pre-code analysis and 50% code analysis and testing. This is also a reasonable objective for modern development paradigms used by software developers. It is called the 50–50 rule, not to be confused with the division of validation resources discussed in 12 above.

15. Use tests as keys to specific areas:
    - If code is faulty, recommend a fix and possibly implement and test it.

- If design is faulty, exercise it on the testbed until you are sure of a better design, then recommend a fix.
- If a requirement is faulty, model and analyze alternatives, test the design on the testbed, then recommend a fix.

16. Whenever possible, participate in fixes and subsequent retesting of critical areas of the software.

17. Ensure an active near-daily interface with the customer, win his/her confidence early, make him/her dependent upon your advice on technical (and programmatic) matters.

18. Align the IV&V staff and organization to the functional divisions and structure of the software. If there are three CSCIs, name a lead analyst for each one (assuming resources allow).

19. Be careful not to offend the software development contractor; win his or her confidence and respect through quality work.

20. Select analysis tools and aids to complement those of the development contractor unless there has been a significant investment in major CASE tools. In this situation, it is considered quite prudent to get a copy of the developer's tools and use them in as many different ways as possible to gain additional perspectives on the software. Other IV&V tools can also augment the primary CASE tools. Just try not to duplicate what the developer is already doing.

21. Participate in the development contractor's and customer's configuration control and design review boards. This is a must to stay current and aware of everything that is going on with the development effort.

22. Quantify products of each phase of the development, report the status to the customer and developer, and maintain historical records of progress and problems. Use appropriate metrics to formally evaluate these products.

23. If anything (tool, analysis aid, documentation, drawing, test, etc.) is needed and it does not already exist, invent it, but keep it practical and not cute.

24. Tailor existing tools, simulations and models to suit each new job wherever possible. They will be much easier to validate than totally new designs.

25. Because IV&V is resource-limited, it pays to establish priorities and schedule work packages for each type of analysis; otherwise, important items may go unattended.

Although this list may seem somewhat long, it should be remembered that IV&V has a very complex set of interactive elements and none of these can really be treated too lightly.

12.2 USE OF METRICS IN INDEPENDENT VERIFICATION AND VALIDATION

Software development metrics are basically quantifiable measures of discrete quality attributes of documents, code, and tests. In IV&V, the most important use of metrics is in the evaluation of software requirements and design specifications, since the remainder of development is much more self-quantifying and the greatest positive impact on the program is derived from the early application of metrics. Before metrics came into use, the customer had to take the contractor's word or best-guess estimate (*guestimate*) on how complete the documents were, and this was often a hastily prepared monthly estimate with little foundation on fact. It might be as crude as counting pages written vs. original estimates or the number of pages or lines impacted by reviewers. Clearly, something had to be done to better quantify the assessment of key documentation. The metrics discussed here were especially created to enable IV&V to derive a good solid percent-complete figure on requirements and design documents. They have been thoroughly field tested and are about as simple as is possible without sacrificing any of the important attributes. Remember, you can measure and count lines of code, evaluate complexity by code inspection (manually or with automated tools), count errors, and measure test results (criteria that passed or failed), so these are not as important to IV&V as the specification metrics are. The collection of metrics by IV&V across all phases of development is acceptable but somewhat costly and tends to be the same as those that the developer collects and reports on, so try to avoid duplication of effort whenever possible. The important thing for IV&V is to give the customer an objective, independently derived set of performance and status indicators that provide a "second opinion" on the health of the project. Remember, it is in the precode period that completion estimates are notoriously suspect. Conversely, it is very hard to argue with actual counted lines of code or with tests that have been run, so measurement of these factors is generally much more accurate than the earlier ones.

The major need for metrics in analyzing specifications is that without some consistent form of value assessment, no one can say how valid or "complete" the document really is. The technique that is suggested here is simpler than most and, therefore, faster and cheaper to use. It does not depend on Halstead, McCabe, or Albrecht type of complexity measuring techniques. It has been used on several large IV&V programs and works satisfactorily. Another metric system can be substituted if desired, as long as it can provide a percentage of completion figure for the document being evaluated. Gene Walters [2] over a decade ago specified thresholds for the required rating of correctness of specifications at the key design reviews. His assumption was that if the specification falls below these values, the contractor should not be allowed to proceed until the document in question is improved to a point that it matches or exceeds the thresholds. I agree wholeheartedly with this idea. In the last few years I have seen numerical thresholds similar to these appear in government guidelines, which is a very encouraging sign.

After a great deal of analysis and thought, I have established what I believe to be a robust as well as somewhat conservative set of thresholds for the key specifications; below these thresholds, immediate remedial action is required to improve the documents to an acceptable level, to allow the program to proceed:

- At the system design review (SDR), the system specification should have a quality rating of 95%. I often go higher to perhaps 98% on the programs that have already gone through Dem/Val if the SDR in question is being conducted in FSED.

- At the preliminary design review (PDR), the system specification should meet or exceed 98%, and the software requirements specifications (SRSs) should be at least 95%.

- At the critical design review (CDR), the software requirements specifications (SRSs) should have a quality rating of at least 98%, and the preliminary software design documents (SDDs) should be at least 95%.

As a procurer of software, you can elect to reduce these thresholds a few points, but remember the multiplying effects of errors in downstream phases and use extreme caution. Dollars spent fixing requirements specifications early in the program are up to forty times more cost-effective than those spent in testing.

Historically, it is the unanswered, ill-defined parts of these specifications that invariably cause the greatest amount of rework during testing and integration. Thus, one of the primary goals of IV&V should be to elevate the quality (completeness, correctness, and consistency) of these specifications to a point that very little doubt remains as to what is to be implemented. Forgive a rhetorical question, but why should the development process proceed when no one is sure what to do, how to do it, and what the impact of the problem really means? Almost every major software program that ever got into budgetary and schedule trouble did so because the specifications were inadequate.

If metrics are to be used, it is helpful to specify the "acceptable" thresholds in the contract so that there should be no misunderstanding by any involved party. The basic set of evaluation criteria and scoring technique should also be stated.

12.2.1 Description of the Metrics System

Figure 12-1 is a flow diagram of the process of applying metrics to requirements and design specifications. Each requirement or design statement is evaluated on its own merit and its numerical score is placed on an evaluation matrix constructed for the purpose of totaling the score for the document being reviewed. This system of scoring takes deficiencies away from a perfect score as explained later.

12.2.1.1 System Specification. The system specification is reviewed and analyzed using available external requirement sources and evaluation factors, derived from studying the type of system as discussed in Chapter 5 (especially Figure 5-2). Major contributors to this evaluation include but are not limited to the following:

- Mission need statement (MNS)
- Operational requirements document (ORD)
- Test and evaluation master plan (TEMP)
- Review of earlier prototype of the system if there was one
- Any existing tradeoff studies

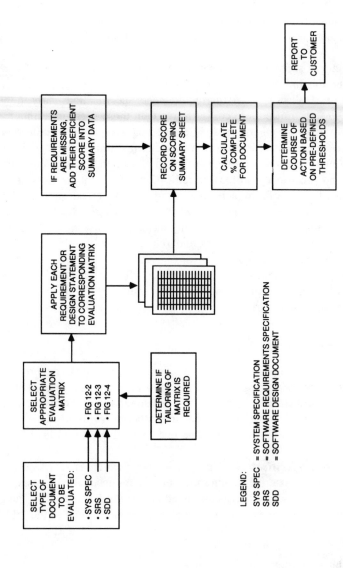

Figure 12-1 Applying metrics to specifications.

- Hardware descriptions and prototype designs
- System studies, analyses, evaluations, and reviews
- History of other similar systems
- Selected data from other sources, e.g., threat data, trend studies, technology assessments, etc.

In addition to assessing the requirements appearing in the system specification, the analyst also looks for requirements that should have been in the document and are not. The sum of the penalties tallied from the evaluation matrices and the missing requirements form the score which is, in effect, a percentage of completion figure.

12.2.1.2   Software Requirements Specification.   The software requirements specification (SRS) is reviewed and analyzed using appropriate requirement sources and evaluation factors derived from studying the type of system, as discussed in Chapter 5 (especially Figure 5-4). Major contributors to this evaluation include but are not limited to the following:

- The system specification (primary source)
- Selected portions of the sources used to assess the system specification
- Independent simulations and models
- Preliminary algorithms
- Data flow and interface diagrams (and control flow for real-time systems)
- Database architecture (schema) and file structure
- Test plans
- Hardware prototypes and preliminary configurations
- Interface documentation
- Software architecture
- Processing assumptions and constraints.

Requirements weighting by relative importance can be applied to the evaluation process by breaking down the software budget into its functional parts (aided by the work breakdown structure) and grouping the requirements by these divisions. For most applications, this is an unnecessary complication and does not add very much to the evaluation process.

12.2.1.3   Software Design Document.   The software design document (SDD) is reviewed and analyzed using appropriate requirement sources and evaluation factors derived from studying the type of system as discussed in Chapter 6 (especially Figure 6-2). Major contributors to this evaluation include but are not limited to the following:

- The software requirements specification (primary source)
- Algorithms and equations

- Database architecture
- Independent simulations and models
- Hardware including prototypes and development platforms
- Interfaces (both external and internal)
- Detailed data flow (and control flow for real-time systems)
- Database structures and elements
- Behavior (including tasking, scheduling, timing, etc.)
- Test descriptions and procedures

Weighting factors can also be used at this level of assessment, if desired, although they are less valuable for design analysis than for software requirements.

12.2.2 Description of the Evaluation Matrix

Almost any system of metrics for specifications can use the basic approach described in the previous paragraphs and pictured in Figure 12-1. Therefore, the difference between this system and many of the others is found in the evaluation matrix. This technique uses a subtractive form of scoring wherein each system requirement statement begins by having a perfect score of 13 assumed. The total number of requirements is then determined; for example, 254 requirements will yield a perfect score of $254 \times 13 = 3302$.

Deficiencies are then subtracted from the perfect score. If, for example, the total number of deficiencies noted provided a number of -263, then $3302 - 263 = 3039$, which is then divided by 3302; 3039 divided by $3302 = 92\%$, which is the percentage of completion for the document.

If two or more analysts perform independent reviews of the same specifications, their scores are averaged.

- Figure 12-2 shows the scoring criteria for system specification requirements and assumes a perfect score of 13 points.
- Figure 12-3 is similar but is used for software requirements specifications and assumes a perfect score of 16 points.
- Figure 12-4 is also similar but is used for software design documents and assumes a perfect score of 20 points.
- Figure 12-5 is an example of an actual requirements evaluation matrix used on a major IV&V program (Case Study No. D) described in Part IV of this book.

12.3   REQUIREMENTS CRITICALITY ASSESSMENT

Very large programs with many hundreds or even thousands of requirements often need some form of classification scheme to determine their relative importance in terms of such factors as performance, mission, safety, complexity, and cost risk.

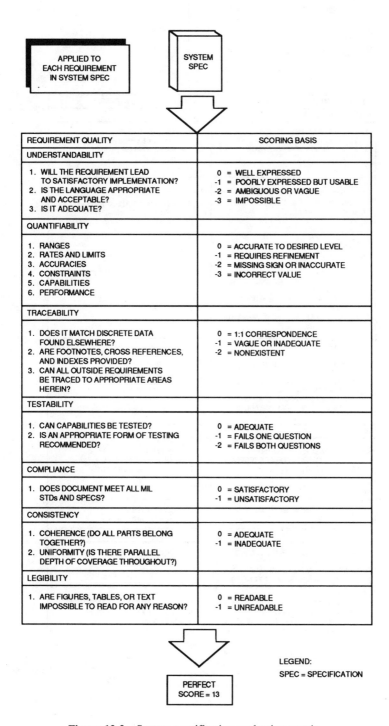

REQUIREMENT QUALITY	SCORING BASIS
UNDERSTANDABILITY	
1. WILL THE REQUIREMENT LEAD TO SATISFACTORY IMPLEMENTATION? 2. IS THE LANGUAGE APPROPRIATE AND ACCEPTABLE? 3. IS IT ADEQUATE?	0 = WELL EXPRESSED -1 = POORLY EXPRESSED BUT USABLE -2 = AMBIGUOUS OR VAGUE -3 = IMPOSSIBLE
QUANTIFIABILITY	
1. RANGES 2. RATES AND LIMITS 3. ACCURACIES 4. CONSTRAINTS 5. CAPABILITIES 6. PERFORMANCE	0 = ACCURATE TO DESIRED LEVEL -1 = REQUIRES REFINEMENT -2 = MISSING SIGN OR INACCURATE -3 = INCORRECT VALUE
TRACEABILITY	
1. DOES IT MATCH DISCRETE DATA FOUND ELSEWHERE? 2. ARE FOOTNOTES, CROSS REFERENCES, AND INDEXES PROVIDED? 3. CAN ALL OUTSIDE REQUIREMENTS BE TRACED TO APPROPRIATE AREAS HEREIN?	0 = 1:1 CORRESPONDENCE -1 = VAGUE OR INADEQUATE -2 = NONEXISTENT
TESTABILITY	
1. CAN CAPABILITIES BE TESTED? 2. IS AN APPROPRIATE FORM OF TESTING RECOMMENDED?	0 = ADEQUATE -1 = FAILS ONE QUESTION -2 = FAILS BOTH QUESTIONS
COMPLIANCE	
1. DOES DOCUMENT MEET ALL MIL STDs AND SPECS?	0 = SATISFACTORY -1 = UNSATISFACTORY
CONSISTENCY	
1. COHERENCE (DO ALL PARTS BELONG TOGETHER?) 2. UNIFORMITY (IS THERE PARALLEL DEPTH OF COVERAGE THROUGHOUT?)	0 = ADEQUATE -1 = INADEQUATE
LEGIBILITY	
1. ARE FIGURES, TABLES, OR TEXT IMPOSSIBLE TO READ FOR ANY REASON?	0 = READABLE -1 = UNREADABLE

APPLIED TO EACH REQUIREMENT IN SYSTEM SPEC

SYSTEM SPEC

PERFECT SCORE = 13

LEGEND:

SPEC = SPECIFICATION

Figure 12-2 System specification evaluation matrix.

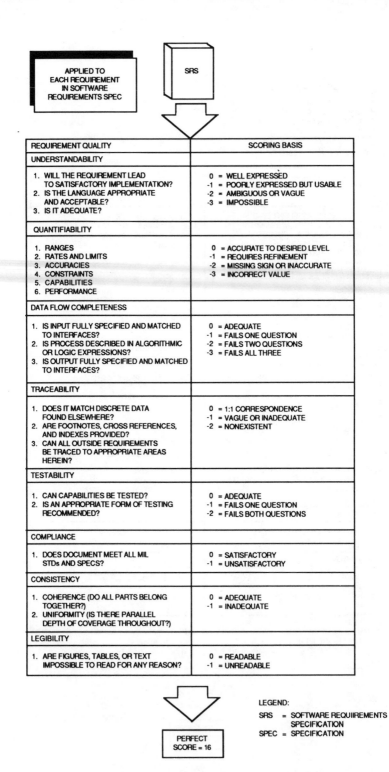

REQUIREMENT QUALITY	SCORING BASIS
UNDERSTANDABILITY	
1. WILL THE REQUIREMENT LEAD TO SATISFACTORY IMPLEMENTATION? 2. IS THE LANGUAGE APPROPRIATE AND ACCEPTABLE? 3. IS IT ADEQUATE?	0 = WELL EXPRESSED -1 = POORLY EXPRESSED BUT USABLE -2 = AMBIGUOUS OR VAGUE -3 = IMPOSSIBLE
QUANTIFIABILITY	
1. RANGES 2. RATES AND LIMITS 3. ACCURACIES 4. CONSTRAINTS 5. CAPABILITIES 6. PERFORMANCE	0 = ACCURATE TO DESIRED LEVEL -1 = REQUIRES REFINEMENT -2 = MISSING SIGN OR INACCURATE -3 = INCORRECT VALUE
DATA FLOW COMPLETENESS	
1. IS INPUT FULLY SPECIFIED AND MATCHED TO INTERFACES? 2. IS PROCESS DESCRIBED IN ALGORITHMIC OR LOGIC EXPRESSIONS? 3. IS OUTPUT FULLY SPECIFIED AND MATCHED TO INTERFACES?	0 = ADEQUATE -1 = FAILS ONE QUESTION -2 = FAILS TWO QUESTIONS -3 = FAILS ALL THREE
TRACEABILITY	
1. DOES IT MATCH DISCRETE DATA FOUND ELSEWHERE? 2. ARE FOOTNOTES, CROSS REFERENCES, AND INDEXES PROVIDED? 3. CAN ALL OUTSIDE REQUIREMENTS BE TRACED TO APPROPRIATE AREAS HEREIN?	0 = 1:1 CORRESPONDENCE -1 = VAGUE OR INADEQUATE -2 = NONEXISTENT
TESTABILITY	
1. CAN CAPABILITIES BE TESTED? 2. IS AN APPROPRIATE FORM OF TESTING RECOMMENDED?	0 = ADEQUATE -1 = FAILS ONE QUESTION -2 = FAILS BOTH QUESTIONS
COMPLIANCE	
1. DOES DOCUMENT MEET ALL MIL STDs AND SPECS?	0 = SATISFACTORY -1 = UNSATISFACTORY
CONSISTENCY	
1. COHERENCE (DO ALL PARTS BELONG TOGETHER?) 2. UNIFORMITY (IS THERE PARALLEL DEPTH OF COVERAGE THROUGHOUT?)	0 = ADEQUATE -1 = INADEQUATE
LEGIBILITY	
1. ARE FIGURES, TABLES, OR TEXT IMPOSSIBLE TO READ FOR ANY REASON?	0 = READABLE -1 = UNREADABLE

APPLIED TO EACH REQUIREMENT IN SOFTWARE REQUIREMENTS SPEC

SRS

PERFECT SCORE = 16

LEGEND:

SRS = SOFTWARE REQUIIREMENTS SPECIFICATION
SPEC = SPECIFICATION

Figure 12-3 Software requirement specification evaluation matrix.

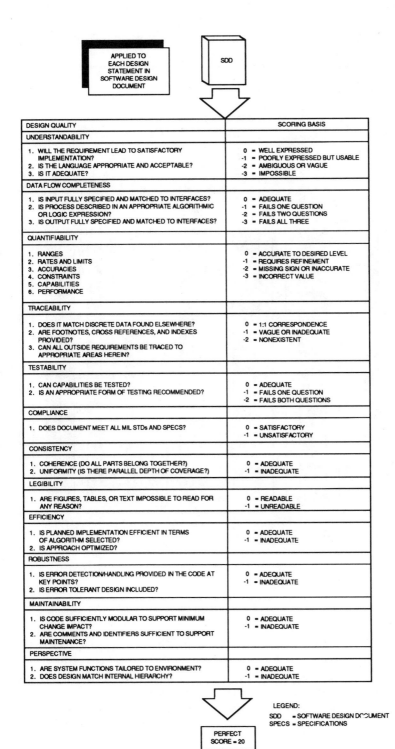

DESIGN QUALITY	SCORING BASIS
UNDERSTANDABILITY	
1. WILL THE REQUIREMENT LEAD TO SATISFACTORY IMPLEMENTATION? 2. IS THE LANGUAGE APPROPRIATE AND ACCEPTABLE? 3. IS IT ADEQUATE?	0 = WELL EXPRESSED -1 = POORLY EXPRESSED BUT USABLE -2 = AMBIGUOUS OR VAGUE -3 = IMPOSSIBLE
DATA FLOW COMPLETENESS	
1. IS INPUT FULLY SPECIFIED AND MATCHED TO INTERFACES? 2. IS PROCESS DESCRIBED IN AN APPROPRIATE ALGORITHMIC OR LOGIC EXPRESSION? 3. IS OUTPUT FULLY SPECIFIED AND MATCHED TO INTERFACES?	0 = ADEQUATE -1 = FAILS ONE QUESTION -2 = FAILS TWO QUESTIONS -3 = FAILS ALL THREE
QUANTIFIABILITY	
1. RANGES 2. RATES AND LIMITS 3. ACCURACIES 4. CONSTRAINTS 5. CAPABILITIES 6. PERFORMANCE	0 = ACCURATE TO DESIRED LEVEL -1 = REQUIRES REFINEMENT -2 = MISSING SIGN OR INACCURATE -3 = INCORRECT VALUE
TRACEABILITY	
1. DOES IT MATCH DISCRETE DATA FOUND ELSEWHERE? 2. ARE FOOTNOTES, CROSS REFERENCES, AND INDEXES PROVIDED? 3. CAN ALL OUTSIDE REQUIREMENTS BE TRACED TO APPROPRIATE AREAS HEREIN?	0 = 1:1 CORRESPONDENCE -1 = VAGUE OR INADEQUATE -2 = NONEXISTENT
TESTABILITY	
1. CAN CAPABILITIES BE TESTED? 2. IS AN APPROPRIATE FORM OF TESTING RECOMMENDED?	0 = ADEQUATE -1 = FAILS ONE QUESTION -2 = FAILS BOTH QUESTIONS
COMPLIANCE	
1. DOES DOCUMENT MEET ALL MIL STDs AND SPECS?	0 = SATISFACTORY -1 = UNSATISFACTORY
CONSISTENCY	
1. COHERENCE (DO ALL PARTS BELONG TOGETHER?) 2. UNIFORMITY (IS THERE PARALLEL DEPTH OF COVERAGE?)	0 = ADEQUATE -1 = INADEQUATE
LEGIBILITY	
1. ARE FIGURES, TABLES, OR TEXT IMPOSSIBLE TO READ FOR ANY REASON?	0 = READABLE -1 = UNREADABLE
EFFICIENCY	
1. IS PLANNED IMPLEMENTATION EFFICIENT IN TERMS OF ALGORITHM SELECTED? 2. IS APPROACH OPTIMIZED?	0 = ADEQUATE -1 = INADEQUATE
ROBUSTNESS	
1. IS ERROR DETECTION/HANDLING PROVIDED IN THE CODE AT KEY POINTS? 2. IS ERROR TOLERANT DESIGN INCLUDED?	0 = ADEQUATE -1 = INADEQUATE
MAINTAINABILITY	
1. IS CODE SUFFICIENTLY MODULAR TO SUPPORT MINIMUM CHANGE IMPACT? 2. ARE COMMENTS AND IDENTIFIERS SUFFICIENT TO SUPPORT MAINTENANCE?	0 = ADEQUATE -1 = INADEQUATE
PERSPECTIVE	
1. ARE SYSTEM FUNCTIONS TAILORED TO ENVIRONMENT? 2. DOES DESIGN MATCH INTERNAL HIERARCHY?	0 = ADEQUATE -1 = INADEQUATE

APPLIED TO EACH DESIGN STATEMENT IN SOFTWARE DESIGN DOCUMENT

SDD

LEGEND:
SDD = SOFTWARE DESIGN DOCUMENT
SPECS = SPECIFICATIONS

PERFECT SCORE = 20

Figure 12-4 Software design document evaluation matrix.

RQMTS NO.	UNDERSTANDABILITY	0 = WELL EXPRESSED	-1 = POOR, BUT USEABLE	-2 = AMBIGUOUS OR VAGUE	-3 = IMPOSSIBLE	QUANTIFIERS	0 = ACCURATE TO DESIRED LEVEL	-1 = REQUIRES REFINEMENT	-2 = MISSING SIGN, VALUE OR INACCURATE	-3 = INCORRECT VALUE	TRACEABILITY	0 = 1:1 CORRESPONDENCE	-1 = INADEQUATE	-2 = NONEXISTENT	TESTABILITY	0 = ADEQUATE	-1 = FAILS ONE QUESTION	-2 = FAILS BOTH QUESTIONS	COMPLIANCE	0 = ADEQUATE	-1 = UNSATISFACTORY	CONSISTENCY	0 = ADEQUATE	-1 = INADEQUATE	LEGIBILITY	0 = READABLE	-1 = UNREADABLE	SUBTOTAL OF MINUSES ONLY	A ADD 13 FOR EACH REQUIREMENT	B SUBTRACT MINUSES FROM PERFECT SCORE
11-12.001				X				X					X											X				-5	13	8
11-12.002			X					X					X											X				-4	13	9
11-15.002			X					X					X															-3	13	10
11-15.003			X						X				X											X				-5	13	8
11-15.004					X				X				X															-6	13	7
11-16.002			X					X					X															-3	13	10
11-16.003			X						X				X											X				-5	13	8
11-18.002			X					X					X															-3	13	10
11-21.001			X					X					X															-3	13	10
11-21.002			X						X				X															-4	13	9
11-21.003				X					X				X															-5	13	8
11-26.001			X					X					X															-3	13	10
11-26.002			X					X					X															-3	13	10
11-99.003			X						X				X				X				X							-6	13	7
14-15.002				X				X					X															-4	13	9
14-16.001				X				X					X											X				-5	13	8
14-18.001					X			X					X															-5	13	8
14-26.001				X									X															-3	13	10
14-99.002				X									X				X											-4	13	9
16-01.001			X										X											X				-3	13	10
16-01.004			X										X											X				-3	13	10

TOTAL COL A	273	188
TOTAL COL B		
B ÷ A = RELATIVE % COMPLETE (CALCULATED ONLY ON LAST SHEET)	69%	

- HAD THIS BEEN THE TOTAL REQUIREMENTS SCORED, IT WOULD HAVE YIELDED A PERCENTAGE COMPLETE OF 69%
- IN OTHER WORDS, THIS DOCUMENT WOULD HAVE FLUNKED THE EVALUATION!

Figure 12-5 Scoring summary sheet.

The book refers to this measure as the "criticality factor." One reason for performing this assessment is to concentrate IV&V resources where they are most needed and, second, this information is quite valuable when developing test plans to slant the testing toward the more critical requirements.

Man-rated systems such as the Space Transportation System (Shuttle), to which this particular scheme was first applied, require a different mix of weighting factors than would a weapon or communication system. For example, safety is a very high-priority factor in a great number of space system requirements because of the nature of the software and the high risk to human life; in a weapon system, safety is still an important factor (although not as universal) because one does not want to destroy one's own troops or equipment. In communication systems, security is likely to be a higher priority than safety. Thus, some tailoring is required to determine what the critical factors are in your particular system and then how to weight them in respect to each other. Absolute values do not mean as much as the ratios among the factors.

Thus, the application of requirements criticality assessment is very dependent upon the ability to recognize, select, and appropriately define and scale the weighting factors. Broadly speaking, the criticality assessment methodology consists of several related elements:

- A numerical figure of merit called the criticality factor (CF) for gauging the relative criticality of each software requirement
- The computation of CF for each of the requirements by IV&V analysts in terms of a criticality assessment matrix
- A set of precise and unambiguous instructions supplied to each IV&V analyst for determining appropriate entries to the criticality matrix for each of the components of CF
- A set of CF component weighting factors established by IV&V and approved by the customer
- A categorical ranking of the CFs, performed by consensus, ordered by the potential for high project payoff leverage when compared to the amount of project resources to be expended
- Concentrated verification through the specification analysis phase of software development of each highly ranked software component in a test configuration thread
- Critical concurrency analysis of each subfunction within each functional data flow.

Two issues—risk and complexity—form the essence of system criticality. Risks are managed in part by a requirement-by-requirement determination of the adequacy of the automation decisions and of the software/hardware interfaces. Another part of the risk management is a judgmental evaluation of the type and degree of potential for described categories of failure contingencies. In some cases a failure mode effects analysis (FMEA) approach is necessary to provide additional depth to the quantification. Analysis of the effects that failures, including software errors, can have on the system often requires in-depth study. Thus, FMEA and criticality assessments can work together to provide a good yardstick on how to get the best leverage from the available IV&V resources.

Complexity concerns primarily the cumulative nature of implementing multidisciplinary software requirements. That is to say, various software requirements may call for interfaces with many subsystems at the same time. There needs to be a measure to describe the degree to which a given software requirement may impact the baseline system performance requirements if problems occur during program executions. That measure should reflect the concept that criticality is directly proportional to the number of connectivities to different subsystems, and that certain subsystem disciplines potentially affect the system performance more than do other disciplines.

Balancing these system-related criticality issues is a set of functional issues. These issues require analysis of the adequacy of pertinent aspects of single point control, system interlocks, error control, and man/machine interaction. Of special concern is the identification of those modules (hardware, firmware, or software) with real-time implications. In the software regime, real-time critical components are known to consist of system software (the operating system), the applications software, and support software, which spans system and applications software execution.

It should be noted that the sample shown in Figure 12-6 includes typical examples from a launch vehicle. Both the subsystems (columns) and criticality factors (rows) require tailoring to individual system parameters.

12.3.1 Proposed Criticality Figure of Merit

Originally, the matrix developed for the DOD Space Shuttle was a little more complicated than the more straightforward one now used. It multiplied portions of the matrix, where this one simply adds across and down to get the total CF for the requirement. The old one acknowledged the effects of interfaces as criticality multipliers; however, since all modern development paradigms stress interface management much more effectively than was the case in the mid-to-late 1970s, it is my opinion that this is no longer necessary and the simplification of the matrix is well-justified and gives satisfactory results.

A noteworthy point is the relative nature of the CFs. There has been no attempt to pursue criticality in any sort of global, multisystem sense. Consequently, the CFs are useful only when compared to each other. The intent is to establish a set of values for the risk components and the subsystem "importance" weights by community-wide consensus. While there would be consensual agreement on the values, their use would have to be bracketed strictly within a specific software development context. The CF is elegant enough to focus adequately on critical issues but remains simple enough to use in guiding the ensuing requirements and design analyses.

12.3.2 Criticality Assessment Activities

The initial step in criticality assessment is for each analyst to compute CF for each software-oriented requirement. He or she does this by first studying all lower-level requirements that trace from each requirement, and then posting entries into the criticality matrix, as shown in Figure 12-6.

The figure shows that each risk component has been subdivided into four or five categories, with separate values associated with each category. The values shown in the figure are established by the IV&V team and discussed with and agreed to by the customer. The analysts will be provided with a set of precise and unambiguous instructions for determining which categories they should apply to each requirement. Using the matrix, the analysts will then post the entries based on their

REQUIREMENT NO._____DOCUMENT NO._____

DESCRIPTION (SHORT OR LONG)_____

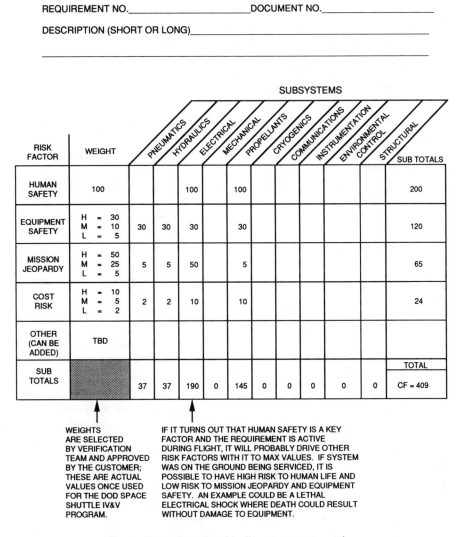

Figure 12-6   Sample criticality assessment matrix.

analysis activities. This analysis will be conducted on a requirement-by-requirement basis until the complete set is processed and assigned a CF.

Step two in the criticality assessment methodology is to rank-order the CFs, and then partition the ranking into three groups by payoff potential:

- *Priority I Requirement Criticality.* IV&V resources must be expended
- *Priority II Requirement Criticality.* Expend IV&V resources after satisfying all Priority I requirements
- *Priority III Requirement Criticality.* Low payoff if IV&V resources are spent.

Community consensus would establish the numerical threshold boundaries separating the priority groups. One recommendation of the book is to set the thresholds after the distribution of CFs is known so that the three groups are divided into approximately equal quantities. If this forces a break point that looks incorrect, vary the threshold up or down a little to break the groupings at an appropriate point.

The third step in the methodology is to develop a set of test configuration threads for each Priority I requirement. A "test configuration thread" is considered to be a unique control path in a program element from the man/machine interface, through computer hardware, through software, through hardware interface modules, to the output. Identified along each of these threads is each individual component of software or hardware to be utilized in performing the real-time test sequence execution. The possibility of conditionals within a given thread implies that multiple threads may exist for each Priority I requirement.

After identifying each unique thread, step four begins, which is a detailed specification analysis on each component of hardware and software discovered in step three that lies along a test configuration thread. All levels of specifications for each of these components would be checked. Each specification would be evaluated for correctness, preciseness (completeness, consistency, nonambiguity), traceability, and testability (input requirements, processing requirements, output requirements) in the same fashion used for metrics in Section 12.2. The dynamic analyzer discussed in Chapter 8 is an excellent tool for exercising these threads.

The culmination of step four is a sort of partial certification for the most critical real-time modules of software and hardware. The execution of the thread indicates that nothing in the specifications for each component would preclude satisfactory performance of that program element.

The fifth and concluding step in the methodology involves an analysis of the data flow of each CSCI. The analysis would be at the CSC level. It would determine if any critical concurrencies exist. The criticality figures (CF) from step one can be encoded into the requirements tracing matrix (RTM) database record for each requirement, or maintained as a separate document. Each CF would be mapped to its subfunction(s). A linear combination of the CFs for each subfunction would be computed. The highest-valued subfunctions represent functional areas within a system element in which highly critical requirements had been concentrated. A proper risk-management approach would then be to separate each of these critical concurrencies into nonoverlapping subfunctions. The risk within that system element would then have been minimized.

12.4 AREAS OF INTEREST FOR FUTURE INDEPENDENT VERIFICATION AND VALIDATION PROGRAMS

Areas of study that appear to offer the most promise to the customer are summarized in the following list:

- Qualification of relative efficiency and effectiveness of the alternative IV&V methods, tools, and techniques. For example, how many undetected program errors will a dynamic analyzer reveal as compared to those discovered through manual inspection techniques. In addition, what are the cost, training, and resource implications of both?

- Determination of the extent to which automated IV&V tools (models, simulators, test tools, and analyzers) can be transferred from one IV&V contract to another. (By the way, Ada has helped this situation a great deal.) How much modification will they require and how much will it cost compared to the development or acquisition of a new tool?

- Studies to determine the relative user satisfaction with the contribution of IV&V on large software system development programs. What are the customer's views, recommendations, and conclusions?

- Development of algorithms for determining a general breakout of IV&V costs, i.e., computer, development of models and simulators, training and acquisition of key personnel, and administrative costs.

- Development of more generic IV&V testbeds, which offer a library of tools, documents, analysis aids, and simulations with general application. These are a reality today but tend to be language-specific. Larger companies can afford these; small ones may not.

- Carefully conceived contracts, which consider IV&V as a more integral part of the development process without violation of the rules that define IV&V as a unique discipline (Chapter 1).

- Development of a government or military standard for IV&V. This would clear up much of the folklore that now exists. The IV&V community has been waiting a long time for this one.

12.5 CHAPTER SUMMARY

- There are 25 guidelines to follow when planning and executing an IV&V program that help optimize the program.

- The use of metrics to determine the relative completeness and apparent quality of key specifications is a good way to estimate when phase transitions should be allowed to occur. When these key documents are below a threshold, the developer should be forced to improve them before being allowed to continue along the development process path, regardless of the paradigm being used.

- The book offers evaluation methods and metric checksheets for the system specification, software requirements specification, and software design document. These are the primary documents of interest.

- The IV&V metrics focus for the most part on the requirements and design phases, because that is where the developer's status data are the most suspect. Code and test status data are much more self-quantifying and accurate. IV&V will probably report on these phases also, but it amounts to bean-counting more than in-depth analysis.

- IV&V metrics are not intended to replace or be substituted for the developer's metrics.

- Requirements criticality assessment is an IV&V mechanism used to determine where to allocate IV&V resources and can also be used to alert the customer and developer of the potential risk and problem areas.
- Programs with high risk to human life, equipment, and mission will require special emphasis on thoroughness in the IV&V approach. This assessment shows how to proportion the effort.
- Future trends in IV&V center mostly on automation, improved tools, and more realistic testbeds.

12.6   WHAT COMES NEXT

Chapter 13 deals with estimating the cost as well as the value of an IV&V program. A set of curves is included to help in estimating the cost of IV&V as a percentage of the development cost. Studies have shown that full, in-phase IV&V can earn up to twice its cost in savings to the development effort.

13

ESTIMATING THE COST AND VALUE OF INDEPENDENT VERIFICATION AND VALIDATION

A frequently asked question is, "What will IV&V cost me and what will it be worth?" Naturally, the answer depends on a number of factors. This chapter will first present a series of discussions based largely on empirical data with as many indicators and qualifiers as possible to help both the customer (procurer) and potential IV&V contractor to develop cost-estimating guidelines. Second, case histories will be discussed in detail that concern the net worth of typical IV&V programs.

Anyone considering an IV&V effort should be aware that the historical evidence collected in the periodic analysis and monthly "progress" or "status" reports and within the configuration status accounting system (CSAS) will enable an adequate appraisal of what the IV&V effort saved. Although it is not always possible to directly equate a savings to a cost, general conclusions can be reached. For instance, if the IV&V contractor's proposed solution to a technical problem saved the purchase or lease of additional hardware, then the hardware cost minus the cost of implementing the fix proposed by the IV&V contractor represents the savings. These collectively are subtracted from the IV&V contract cost to produce the net worth figure. More about this in Section 13.2.

13.1 ESTIMATING THE CONTRACT COST OF INDEPENDENT VERIFICATION AND VALIDATION

As stated in Chapter 1 (Section 1.3.2), there are four generic types of IV&V:

- *Full, in-phase IV&V*, which begins before or during the requirements phase of the development cycle and continues until at least the acceptance of the software.

269

- *Partial IV&V,* which begins anywhere during the design or early coding phases and has little effect upon system and software requirements, except retrospectively.
- *Endgame IV&V,* which is defined as focusing primarily on the test and integration phase.
- *Audit-Level IV&V,* which is a minimal effort wherein the customer calls in an IV&V "tiger team" to determine the adequacy of the customer's development process and practices or to assist in a specific problem area. Audit-level IV&V can occur anytime in the development cycle.

The more comprehensive the IV&V effort, the greater the cost. There is also a direct correlation to potential savings, as discussed in Section 13.2. That section presents a family of cost-estimation curves (Figure 13-1), which require further explanation and definition but which offer a first-order approximation of typical historical costs. The reason the curves slope downward as the size of the software package (number of instructions) increases is largely based on the following factors:

- All IV&V efforts have certain overhead costs that do not increase linearly as the size of the software package increases.
- The thoroughness of the testing effort normally falls off sharply as a function of size. It is a fair statement to say that very large systems (especially real-time weapons, or space systems that cannot expend live rounds, or boosters and space vehicles in testing) are never exhaustively tested; that is, all paths for all conditions are not exercised. Small systems in the order of 10,000 to 50,000

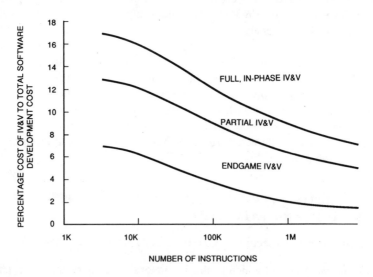

Figure 13-1 Independent verification and validation (IV&V) family of cost-estimation curves.

instructions can conceivably be completely tested. Thus, the effort per instruction generally decreases as a function of size.

- The amount of IV&V analysis generally spent on any one activity falls off as the size of the software increases. Sometimes the difficulty of problem isolation offsets this factor.

- The data derived from testing can generally be shared by a greater number of analysts as the size of the software increases.

The curves shown on Figure 13-1 are the average of all of the efforts that I could identify, then qualify as true IV&V efforts, and for which funding levels were available. There were a few programs that were well beyond the expected standard deviation and, when these were analyzed, it was discovered that the customer had specified unusual tasks for the IV&V contractor. In one case, IV&V had to build a very comprehensive simulation, which would normally have been built by the developer. In another case, the IV&V contractor built a large-scale testbed and acquired significant commercial-of-the-shelf (COTS) software, which was eventually transitioned to the government. Therefore, these anomalies were disregarded since their inclusion would have disturbed the curves. Otherwise, the remaining data were within the acceptable limits and were used to build the curves. This book advocates estimating IV&V costs as a percentage of the software cost. This technique seems to work very nicely and has been widely accepted as the preferred way to estimate the cost of IV&V programs.

13.1.1   Full, In-Phase Independent Verification and Validation

Figure 13-1 shows the average costs of full, in-phase IV&V by percentage of the total software costs. There may be few scattered samples that fall beyond plus or minus 10% of this curve. The real drivers above or below the average curve are the collective effects of the discrete number of options and activities defined in the contract, statement of work, proposal, and IV&V plan. Table 13-1 presents the concept of IV&V program options and provides a general checklist for determining if a given program should be above or below the average cost.

High-cost items such as duplicates of target hardware for the testbed and large simulation and emulation programs can drive the cost up many percentage points. Therefore, it behooves the procurer (customer) of IV&V services to attempt to share the cost of such items with the software developer or purchase them for the operation and service (O&S) period, where their cost can be amortized. Having the majority of such items as either government or contractor-furnished equipment (GFE or CFE) usually drives the program costs below the average.

13.1.2   Partial Independent Verification and Validation

Depending upon the starting point and how much difficulty is involved in going back to verify the requirements, the partial IV&V effort can come very close in cost to full, in-phase IV&V or can fall well below it in cost if the emphasis is only placed

TABLE 13-1. Possible IV&V Program Options

High Cost	Medium Cost	Low Cost
	Programmatic Support	
Perform status monitoring & reporting	Perform status monitoring & reporting	Perform status monitoring
Perform resource monitoring & reporting		
Apply metrics to rqmts & design doc.	Apply metrics to rqmts & design doc.	
Perform key event testing & reporting (selected test results)	Perform key event testing & reporting (selected test results)	Perform key event testing & reporting (selected test results)
Produce comprehensive IV&V reports on:	Produce comprehensive IV&V reports on:	Produce comprehensive IV&V reports on:
Requirements	Requirements	Requirements
Design	Design	Design
Implementation	Implementation	Implementation
Algorithms		
Test planning	Test planning	
Test execution (key event tests)	Test execution (key event tests)	
Configuration management	Configuration management	Configuration management
Adherence to software development plan	Adherence to software development plan	Adherence to software development plan
Perform criticality assessment of software		
Participate in reviews	Participate in reviews	Participate in reviews
Build & maintain requirement tracing matrix (RTM)	Build & maintain requirement tracing matrix (RTM)	Build & maintain requirement tracing matrix (RTM)
Perform open item tracking		
Maintain software library	Maintain software library	Maintain software library
Maintain project library	Maintain project library	Maintain project library
Collect/evaluate error statistics		
Ensure adherence to standards	Ensure adherence to standards	Ensure adherence to standards
Evaluate contractor's SQA program		

	Technical Support	
Participate in FCA	Participate in FCA	Participate in FCA
Participate in PCA	Participate in PCA	Participate in PCA
Aid in transition to operational status		
Use I-CASE tools	Use I-CASE tools	Use I-CASE tools
Build and operate IV&V testbed	Build and operate IV&V testbed	
Build and use simulations	Use simulations	Use simulations as required
Generate IV&V test data	Generate IV&V test data	
Perform timing and sizing analysis	Perform timing and sizing analysis	Review timing and sizing
Analyze support software		
Analyze developer's software tools	Analyze developer's software tools	Review developer's software tools
Evaluate external system interfaces	Evaluate external system interfaces	Review external system interfaces
Conduct independent data flow analysis	Conduct independent data flow analysis	Conduct independent data flow analysis
Evaluate system architecture	Evaluate system architecture	Review system architecture
Perform risk analysis		
Participate in walk-throughs		
Evaluate algorithms	Evaluate algorithms	
Evaluate database structure & elements	Evaluate database structure & elements	Review database structure & elements
Use automated testing tools	Use automated testing tools	Use automated testing tools
Perform independent test analysis	Perform independent test analysis	
Perform error handling study	Perform error handling study	
Build independent models		
Special tests for high risk threads		
Conduct IV&V testing	Conduct IV&V testing	
Participate in system exercises	Participate in system exercises	
Help conduct user training	Serve as initial users	

rqmt., requirement.

on code verification and validation. Table 13-1 can be useful in helping to estimate this type of IV&V program.

On the average, partial IV&V efforts tend to run 20–30% below full, in-phase IV&V in cost, since a great deal of the system and software requirements verification activity is not included or performed in a much less comprehensive manner.

13.1.3 Endgame Independent Verification and Validation

This type of IV&V has virtually no impact on the quality of the design, only its observed accuracy and correctness as represented by the successes or failures of the testing program. In this type of IV&V, the spread is largely a function of the amount of independent testing performed. Typically, the endgame IV&V test activity is centered around monitoring contractor tests, running IV&V tests to gather additional data and retest fixes, tracking problem reports, and perhaps independently analyzing critical algorithms and code. It can also include participation in the functional and physical configuration audits as well as the final qualification (acceptance testing) review of the system (FQR). The bottom curve on Figure 13-1 shows the average cost for endgame IV&V.

13.1.4 Audit-Level Independent Verification and Validation

It is not necessary to produce a curve or set of curves for audit-level IV&V since most of these efforts are between 1 and 2 man-months of effort ($10,000 to $25,000). Most of these efforts involve a "tiger team," who spend a week or two at the customer's facility performing the audit and then prepare and present a dual briefing. Part of the briefing is given to the entire development team and the other just to the manager (and his or her key people). The technical staff briefing is usually focused on overall deficiencies and recommendations to correct them; the manager's part is a no-holds-barred discussion, which could be embarrassing to certain individuals. It is then up to the manager to initiate whatever corrective actions he or she feels are necessary. IV&V can return at some later date and perform another audit to see how well the customer has remedied the deficiencies in his or her organization and development process.

Audit-level IV&V can also serve as a precursor to starting a Software Engineering Institute (SEI) evaluation (described in Chapter 15) to get a quick idea of where the company ranks in the maturity level rating and what remedial actions are necessary before bothering to spend the money and resources on the SEI effort.

13.2 ESTIMATING THE VALUE OF AN INDEPENDENT VERIFICATION AND VALIDATION PROGRAM

The example chosen for this analysis comes from an actual system that had IV&V applied toward the end of the design phase; thus the program can be categorized as a "full, in-phase or partial IV&V program." The IV&V contract had options and attributes similar to those shown in the high-cost (left) column of Table 13-1.

The system in question had a real-time military application and would be considered a large software development effort since it consisted of well over 1 million lines of code.

13.2.1 Error Classification

Error statistics were collected toward the end of the test and integration effort, which tends to disregard the "noise" at the front end of the test program in favor of the "cleaner" data available during this period when status-accounting practices were fairly stable and the problem reports (PRs) were reasonably representative of the system problems. Of the 5100 PRs generated during this time, the IV&V group carefully analyzed 4400, a sample of 86%. The remainder were considered inadequate for inclusion in the study for a number of reasons. A significant effort was then undertaken to type-classify all errors in a very specific manner that consisted of 76 error classes. From this very large sample, it was determined that 62.5% of all the contractor's errors discovered during this testing period were latent requirement and design errors. Further, it was noted that within the requirement faults 89% existed in only five error types, as specified below:

Major Contributors to Requirement and Design Faults

- Operating rules information inadequate or partially missing (largest contributor)
- Performance criteria/information inadequate or partially missing
- Requirement was incompatible with other requirements
- Environmental information inadequate or partially missing
- System mission information inadequate or partially missing.

Then within the design faults, it was noted that 85% existed as "processing" errors, and 89% existed as "data" errors within the following ten error types:

Processing

- Erroneous logic or sequencing (largest contributor)
- Required processing results inaccurate
- Routine does not expect or accept a required parameter
- Routine will not accept all data within stated allowable range limits
- Validity checks are not made for I/O data
- Error handling procedures are not implemented or are not adequate
- Required processing is missing or inadequate.

Data

- Erroneous or ambiguous values (largest contributor)
- Erroneous or inadequate storage
- Missing variables

Major Contributions to Coding Faults

As a point of additional information, the analysis also determined that 76% of all coding faults fell into the following four types:

- Erroneous or inadequate decision logic or sequencing
- Erroneous or inadequate arithmetic computations
- Erroneous branching
- Branching or other test done incorrectly.

13.2.2 Error Cost Analysis

The IV&V contractor then undertook to develop a cost profile. This work consisted of the following steps:

1. The total cost of the test and integration effort was derived from the contractor's productivity data and cost reports.
2. Computer and facility costs were determined and backed out of total costs to derive software costs.
3. Error statistics were compared to configuration management statistics on changes made to the software. These numbers matched very closely, so the assumption was made that 5100 changes was a good number for estimating change costs.
4. Knowing the production rates, costs, and number of lines of code changed (137,000) provided several numbers. The average change involved 27 lines of code. These changes accounted for approximately 40% of the cost of test and integration.
5. Taking 62.5% of 40% = 25%. This number represents the total percentage of cost of latent requirement and design errors that were detected and corrected during test and integration (see Section 13.2.1).
6. The average cost of a change during this phase was over $7,000. Average cost of a line of code changed was therefore about $260. (7000 ÷ 27 = 259.3)
7. Similar calculations were performed on the coding phase, wherein it was estimated that 257,000 instructions were redone, or approximately 24.6% of the total cost of code was the result of changes. Again, this number reflects the adjustment of costs to include the data-processing burden. Average cost of these changes was $977 each, and the average cost per line of code changed was $36.
8. The percent of errors originating from latent requirements and design errors was calculated at 15.4% of the total cost of code. Figure 13-2 graphically depicts the determinations made in the first eight steps.
9. The average costs of changes occurring during the design and requirements phases were estimated from a variety of sources and scaled to the same dollar value used in the other two determinations. These costs have no doubt in-

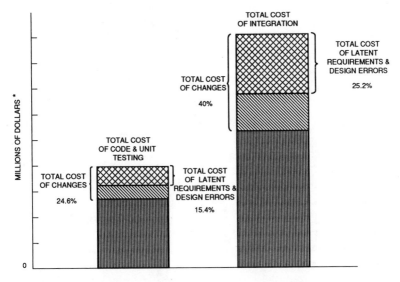

* THE SCALE IS INTENTIONALLY LEFT OFF THIS CHART. THE IMPORTANT ASPECT
OF THIS ANALYSIS IS NOT ABSOLUTE DOLLAR COSTS, BUT RATHER THE
PERCENTAGE COSTS OF CHANGES AND ERRORS TO TOTAL COST. THESE
NUMBERS CAN THEREFORE BE APPLIED TO ANY SIMILAR PROJECT
REGARDLESS OF ACTUAL DOLLAR VALUE.

Figure 13-2 · Code and integration change and error statistics.

creased, but again remember the important aspect is the ratio of costs between
the phases. A requirement change during the requirements phase had an
average cost of $200. A design change during the design phase had an
average cost of $500.

Figure 13-3 shows the significant cost data points plotted against their respective
development phases. A faulty requirement can cost as much as 36 times more to
correct if it is not caught until test and integration. In retrospect, had more time and
resources been spent on requirements and design (especially design, wherein the
number of faults is as high as 10:1 over requirements), dramatic reduction in costs
could have resulted. How great a reduction is the subject of the next topic.

13.2.3 Verification of the Study

To become totally convinced that the numbers were valid, two methods of verification were used. The data just reviewed were used as a base of 100%. Then:

- Approximations of cost impacts that occurred during the program were estimated and then totaled. This number was the same as the first estimate within
0.25%.
- Gross approximations based on code schedule extensions occurring during the
period were used and were within 2%.

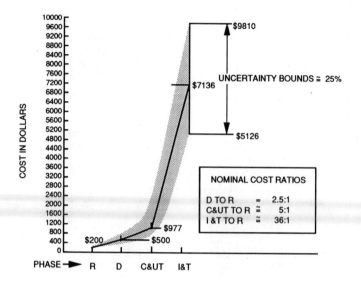

Figure 13-3   Average cost of discovering a requirement error, in various phases of development

13.2.4   Assumptions About the Worth of Independent Verification and Validation in Error Detection

The following assumptions are based on extrapolation of real values discussed in an earlier part of this section. Knowing now where the concentration of errors originates and how much they cost, the following premises could indeed be proven to be true:

Premise 1: If 62.5% of all errors caught during testing and integration were latent requirement and design errors, then early emphasis (precode) on their correction should have significantly reduced total cost of program.

Premise 2: If the developer and IV&V contractor had concentrated on the 15 out of 76 error types that caused 85% of all latent requirement and design errors discovered during integration, this effort could have saved over 50% of the total cost of integration changes (85% of 62.5% = 53%).

Premise 3: If typical integration changes account for 40% of total cost of integration, then this emphasis should save 50% of 40%, or about 20% of the total cost of integration.

Premise 4: In this case integration costs accounted for almost 50% of total program costs. This emphasis could have saved 9% to 11% of the total cost of the program from early detection of possible latent errors alone. This would have more than paid for the IV&V contract.

Without question, this study and analysis revealed where increased emphasis must be placed. In addition, it strongly indicated the specific types of problems that account for the vast majority of errors. A responsive IV&V methodology should address itself to these particular error types through carefully selected tools and manual analysis.

13.2.5 Calculating Other Factors in Independent Verification and Validation Net Worth

Besides a reduction in embedded errors, which is the ultimate concern of IV&V, there are a number of other areas that can produce significant savings:

- By reviewing and assessing each engineering change proposal (ECP) proposed by the software contractor, IV&V can provide second-source opinions and alternatives that are often more cost-effective. (This area usually has the highest cost impact.)
- By providing objective reports that enhance visibility into the development process, IV&V can enable better decision-making by the developer and customer.
- By providing documentation, IV&V can augment contractor's documents.
- By providing data and training, IV&V can aid the transition to government in-house maintenance.
- IV&V can provide tools and analysis aids, which cost-effectively revalidate software after changes.
- IV&V can provide improved algorithms.
- IV&V can produce problem reports (PRs) in a timely fashion.
- IV&V can independently develop models and simulations that address parameters not included in the software contractor's effort.

Adding several quantitative data points to this discussion will help the reader appreciate the kinds of savings that have been obtained in a number of past IV&V efforts:

- The IV&V contractor developed and tested a fix to a radar system for about 10% of the software contractor's ECP estimate, saving over $2 million.
- IV&V contractor saved the purchase of an additional large mainframe computer by developing an online resource manager for local and remote terminal users, enabling the existing development computer to satisfy all users and saving over $2 million.
- The IV&V contractor developed higher fidelity nuclear models than the software contractor and supplied these to the contractor, saving at least $400,000.

- The IV&V contractor documented and verified all critical algorithms. This task was combined into the verification process and did not have to be redone by the software contractor, saving at least $250,000.
- The IV&V contractor developed roughly 10% of the total number of PRs on the equivalent of 6% of the contractor's resources, thus bettering the average efficiency of the contractor by 67%. The savings are difficult to calculate, but could easily represent up to 1% of the total software costs.

Usually the combination of early detection of errors, reduction in unnecessary ECPs, and improved performance can at least equal the cost of the IV&V program. Several examples have indicated that partial IV&V can yield a savings of 1½ times its cost; full, in-phase IV&V can yield savings up to 2 times its cost. Whether or not there is universal agreement that these numbers are totally accurate does not matter as much as the fact that they substantiate the premise that IV&V can invariably pay for itself. This, coupled with the improved visibility on behalf of the developer, should convince even the diehard skeptics that IV&V is a worthwhile investment.

Anyone contemplating a IV&V effort or already involved in one should estimate the implied savings of each significant IV&V contribution.

13.3   CHAPTER SUMMARY

- Most past IV&V programs have cost between 2% and 18% of the software development cost, with less than half exceeding 10%. The higher-cost programs invariably had hardware and/or software development costs like simulations and tools embedded in them, so they were not the normal case.
- For beginning IV&V cost estimates, try to begin between 8% and 10% of the software development cost estimate and add or delete from the specific task list to tune the estimate. This amount should adequately fund a full, in-phase IV&V program, at least of the medium cost range as shown in Table 13-1.
- IV&V programs that are funded at less than 4% to 5% of the development cost will have to begin to delete some routinely performed tasks in order to accomplish the high-payoff ones. Here a trade study will have to be conducted to determine which tasks to sacrifice. Retain automated tools as long as possible since most are not labor-intensive and have a good output-per-labor-hour investment ratio.
- The set of cost curves (Figure 13-1) indicates that the larger the software development effort, generally the lower the percentage IV&V will be of that cost.
- An extensive study conducted several years ago by the author and two of his staff revealed that latent requirement and design errors can cost up to 36 times more to detect and fix during test and integration than if caught in the phase in which they were generated.
- The IV&V effort studied in Section 13.2 was seriously impacted by a late start.

The study concluded that the cost and time required to fix the software during test and integration would have more than paid for an earlier initiation of the IV&V program.

- That study also concluded that a large percentage of the errors detected during testing and integration were latent requirement and design errors (62.5%).

- Through error classification, it became obvious what kinds of errors were most frequently being committed and therefore what kind of development and IV&V tools and methods should have been used to catch them earlier or eliminate them from occurring in the first place. Unfortunately the analysis was after the fact, but you can benefit from the analysis of the error data given in this chapter on your next program.

- Other cost savings and value-added advantages of IV&V include ECP evaluation, improved algorithms, better documentation, easier-to-maintain software, reduced hardware needs, improved models and simulations, etc. The case studies in Part IV point out many others.

13.4 WHAT COMES NEXT

The next chapter presents a comparison between software quality assurance and IV&V. It then discusses how new quality initiatives like total quality management (TQM) and others may affect IV&V in the future. It wraps up with a summary of the benefits of IV&V across the life cycle.

14

INDEPENDENT VERIFICATION AND VALIDATION COMPARED WITH QUALITY ASSURANCE

14.1 A QUICK COMPARISON

Chapter 1 briefly discussed the ideas of internal (quality assurance) and external (IV&V) rigor from the point of view that both reinforce the development process, but in very different ways. It is hoped that by this point that the reader appreciates that IV&V is much more of a life-cycle methodology than quality assurance (QA) is; IV&V also has the inherent flexibility to do many things that software quality assurance (SQA) can never do.

The chief role of SQA is that of internal watchdog; whereas, IV&V participates in the highly technical mainstream as part of the workforce. Traditionally, SQA appears to monitor and regulate the flow of products from the builder to the customer; IV&V analyzes, tests, experiments, and helps manage the development effort. The SQA group reviews documents largely for adherence to published standards; IV&V reads these same books for consistency, traceability, accuracy, technical content, and completeness. Figure 14-1 compares these and other attributes of both traditional SQA and IV&V by major activity groupings. The figure is not intended to be all-inclusive, but rather summarizes the major distinctions.

Of the 32 IV&V activities listed in the figure, almost 70% are unique to IV&V. The remainder are those that have a name match in SQA, shown with an "M." When these sound-alike activities are analyzed, however, it becomes obvious that the activities have far different perspectives and orientations. Thus, IV&V and SQA have virtually no technical overlap. For example, if the SQA task "Evaluation of Software Plans" is compared to IV&V "Review Software Development Plan," you will find the following:

The IV&V review of the software development plan (SDP) requires a procedure

BASED ON DOD-STD-2168

TYPICAL THINGS IV&V DOES vs. **THINGS SQA DOES**

THINGS IV&V DOES	UNIQUE TO IV&V	MAINTAIN SQA RECORDS	MAINTAIN SOFTWARE PROBLEM REPORTS	SOFTWARE QUALITY EVALUATION RECORDS	OTHER SOFTWARE QUALITY RECORDS	SOFTWARE CORRECTIVE ACTIONS	CERTIFICATION	EVALUATION OF SOFTWARE	EVALUATION OF SOFTWARE DOCUMENTATION	EVALUATION OF SOFTWARE PLANS	EVALUATION OF SOFTWARE MANAGEMENT	EVALUATION OF SOFTWARE ENGINEERING	EVALUATION OF SOFTWARE QUALIFICATION	EVALUATION OF SOFTWARE CM	EVALUATION OF SOFTWARE CORRECTIVE ACTIONS	EVALUATION OF DOCUMENTATION & MEDIA	EVALUATION OF STORAGE, HANDLING & DELIVERY	EVALUATION OF OTHER PROCESSES	EVALUATION OF SOFTWARE DEVELOPMENT LIBRARY	EVALUATION OF NON-DEVELOPMENTAL SOFTWARE	EVALUATION OF NON-DELIVERABLE SOFTWARE	EVALUATION OF DELIVERABLE ELEMENTS OF SOFTWARE ENGINEERING AND TEST ENVIRONMENTS	EVALUATION OF SUBCONTRACTOR MANAGEMENT	EVALUATION OF ASSOCIATED WITH ACCEPTANCE & PREPARATION FOR DELIVERY	PARTICIPATION IN REVIEWS AND AUDITS
VERIFY KEY SOFTWARE DOCUMENTATION									M																
PERFORM CRITICALITY AND RISK ASSESSMENT	U																								
REVIEW USER INTERFACE NEEDS	U																								
REVIEW I/O DATA REQUIREMENTS	U																								
REVIEW TRADE STUDIES FOR SYSTEM	U																								
REVIEW TEST RQMTS, PLANS, ETC.													M												
PARTICIPATE IN REVIEWS																									M
PRODUCE PROBLEM REPORTS	U																								
GENERATE REQUIREMENT TRACING MATRIX	U																								
VERIFY DATA FLOW	U																								
VERIFY BEHAVIORAL ASPECTS	U																								
VERIFY DB STRUCTURES & ELEMENTS	U																								
REVIEW DESIGN RISKS	U																								
REVIEW TIMING & SIZING FIGURES	U																								
REVIEW SOFTWARE DEVELOPMENT PLAN										M															
VERIFY CONSISTENCY BETWEEN CODE & SDD	U																								
VERIFY THAT STANDARDS ARE FOLLOWED								M																	
VERIFY TOOLS BEING USED	U																								
VERIFY CODE	U																								
VERIFY ALGORITHMS	U																								
VERIFY VARIOUS OS, UTIL., ETC.																				M					
EVALUATE SOFTWARE LIBRARY																			M						
SELECT KEY EVENT TESTS	U																								
MONITOR DEVELOPER'S TESTS	U																								
EVOLVE IV&V TEST STRATEGY	U																								
RUN INDEPENDENT TESTS	U																								
VALIDATE SPS	U																								
VALIDATE USER & OPS MANUALS	U																								
TRACK CCB ACTIONS															M										
TRACK OPEN ITEMS	U																								
PARTICIPATE IN AUDITS																									M
VERIFY DEVELOPER'S CM SYSTEM														M											

LEGEND:

CCB	= CONFIGURATION CONTROL BOARD
CM	= CONFIGURATION MANAGEMENT
OPS	= OPERATIONS
OS	= OPERATING SYSTEM
RQMTS	= REQUIREMENTS
SDD	= SOFTWARE DESIGN DOCUMENT
SPS	= SOFTWARE PRODUCT SPECIFICATION
SQA	= SOFTWARE QUALITY ASSURANCE
UTIL	= UTILITIES

HOW TO INTERPRET THIS FIGURE

U = UNIQUE TO IV&V

M = MATCH; THESE TASKS SOUND ALIKE BUT ARE GENERALLY COMPLEMENTARY EFFORTS PERFORMED BY SQA AND IV&V. THERE IS NO REAL DUPLICATION OF EFFORT, SINCE THE EVALUATION PERSPECTIVES ARE QUITE DIFFERENT.

Figure 14-1 Comparison of independent verification and validation (IV&V) and software quality assurance (SQA).

several pages long, as described in Section 9.2.1. The SQA evaluation requires the following, excerpted from DOD-STD-2168 [25]:

- All software plans required by the contract have been documented.
- The software plans comply with the contract.
- Each software plan is consistent with other software plans and with system-level plans.

The usual SQA approach is to (1) see that the plan exists, (2) review it to ensure that any specific contract issues are included, and (3) review it for consistency with other plans. There is not much technical depth in this procedure. IV&V, on the other hand, evaluates the implications of the engineering and development management, tools and environments, reviews the testing approach and facilities, reviews how the developer plans to evaluate software products, evaluates configuration management (CM), and much more. Then IV&V periodically audits the developer's adherence to the plan. IV&V is much more thorough than SQA.

The other side of the coin finds SQA in a much better position to evaluate the procedure for distribution of documentation and media than IV&V. SQA is better able to examine nondeliverable software, look at subcontractor management, and maintain quality records.

Thus, there is actually a good complementary balance between the functions performed by SQA and IV&V. <u>Neither is at risk of being replaced by the other</u> since the efforts are so different. Even when total quality management (TQM) is fully embraced by the contractor, there will still be a need for IV&V. Granted IV&V's job may get a little easier in a TQM environment, but TQM will never match the multiple perspectives of IV&V at the detailed technical level. The two things are simply different enough to provide a very synergistic solution to software quality.

14.2   NEW HORIZONS IN INDEPENDENT VERIFICATION AND VALIDATION AND QUALITY ASSURANCE

In all fairness to the subjects of both IV&V and SQA, there are several nontraditional and emerging concepts that must be discussed to get the most complete picture possible:

- IV&V as an integral part of a TQM philosophy
- The large-scale product assurance (PA) organization that combines IV&V with more traditional forms of SQA
- Integrated IV&V
- New paradigms that incorporate verification and validation concepts without the independent component.

14.2.1   Independent Verification and Validation as Part of Total Quality Management

Total quality management (TQM) is the quality management philosophy of the early 1990s. It is based on work conducted by W. Edwards Deming both in the United States and in Japan. TQM has been widely embraced by the U.S. Department of Defense (DOD) as high as the Office of the Secretary of Defense (OSD) as a means of lowering weapons costs and reducing the time required to field new technology. Because TQM is a paradigm shift, it is not instantly accepted by everyone who attempts it, nor can it be introduced and immediately flourish; it takes time, indoctrination, and often an attitude adjustment. In addition, the implementations vary widely depending upon the corporate culture, types of products, and level of technologies involved. Thus, TQM is not easy and it requires redirection at all levels of the organization. It must be remembered that TQM is a philosophy that will require some very interesting relationships in the marketplace. There are very important TQM issues that revolve around how the government and the industrial base will interact in the future to share technology and innovation. Perhaps TQM can be the catalyst to improve that relationship.

The following are the 14 steps in Deming's process, in a slightly abbreviated form:

1. Create and publish a statement of purpose
2. Learn and adopt the new philosophy
3. Cease dependence on inspection to achieve quality
4. End the practice of awarding business on the price tag alone
5. Improve constantly and forever the system of production and service
6. Institute training
7. Adopt and institute leadership
8. Drive out fear. Create trust and a climate for innovation
9. Break down barriers. Optimize teams toward the aims and goals of the company
10. Eliminate slogans, exhortations, and targets for the workforce
11. Eliminate numerical quotas for the workplace
12. Remove barriers that rob people of the pride of workmanship
13. Encourage education and self-improvement for everyone
14. Take action to accomplish the transformation.

At the nucleus of the Deming's approach is the concept of continuous process improvement. This idea requires (1) a thorough understanding of the product requirements, (2) a means to assess the product against those needs, (3) understanding what causes a less-than-perfect product, (4) improvement to the process to eliminate the problems, and (5) continuing the improvement process forever.

IV&V has always sought the goals of improving the process, reducing wasted effort, eliminating errors wherever possible, and improving management visibility. Thus, IV&V can be integrated into an overall scheme of process improvement that receives its stimulation from outside the development organization. When you take the definition and goals of IV&V, they mesh very strongly with the Deming goals of understanding and improving the development process on a continuous basis.

IV&V will not do a lot of things that TQM can. Since IV&V is essentially external, it does not initiate or institutionalize a change in corporate culture or mindset. It will, however, strongly influence and ultimately change the development process for the better. Thus, TQM and IV&V can coexist very nicely, both benefiting from the other.

It is a Deming credo that when a company embraces TQM it must throw away the old and obsolete quality-assurance and control programs. This may be well and good for the overall company, but what is you have a contract that requires the older QA or SQA program? DOD will have to reckon with this potential problem in the near future. So do not throw away or abandon your old SQA program just yet, unless you have figured out a way to remain responsive to all the original requirements. I do not see an easy answer in the Deming philosophy. What I do expect to see is a new set of regulations and standards that are more attuned to TQM than to the old SQA way of doing business. Since DOD has already made a strong commitment to TQM, expect to see the first of the new standards in the 1993–1994 timeframe that will help to make it more of a reality in the contractor world.

14.2.2 Product Assurance

There are a number of product assurance (PA) groups in the military services and a few in other government agencies that operate as omnibus organizations in that they support a number of program and project offices simultaneously in both IV&V and QA-related support activities. These support functions, however, have nothing to do with the contractor's QA activities, so one should not attempt to draw parallels between PA in this sense and the traditional role of QA inside the developer's organization.

One of the very important roles played by this type of PA group is that it can supply continuous support from concept through demonstration/validation (Dem/Val) and/or full-scale engineering development (FSED) into production. In fact, it will still be there when product improvement proposals (PIPs) are funded years after a system becomes operational. This is synonymous to the early-phase discussions of IV&V presented in Chapters 2 and 3, in which the needs for and uses of IV&V prior to FSED were discussed.

These farsighted PA organizations can be funded appropriately to match the level of need at any particular period and therefore can be highly cost-effective. The same military services that have created these broad-based PA programs steadfastly avoid funding IV&V until the full-scale engineering development program. This dichotomy is very hard to understand. The contracting red tape and funding uncertainties are probably as much to blame as anything, but as long as technical support contracts can be awarded during the early phases (concept and Dem/Val), there is no logical reason why IV&V cannot start early, too. Just because it has not been done very often so far should not discourage the prospective procurer of IV&V services. As a matter of fact, a good number of systems engineering and technical assistance (SETA) contracts turn into early IV&V programs without being so named. Hopefully, the stigma that IV&V now suffers in this respect can be cleared up as innovative customers seek better solutions to the numerous problems associated with software development and more is understood concerning the enormous benefits of starting IV&V early.

14.2.3   Integrated Independent Verification and Validation

Integrated IV&V is a concept whereby large companies or government organizations like the U.S. National Aeronautics and Space Administration (NASA) and the U.S. Social Security Administration form their own internal organizations to perform IV&V-like functions. Whether this form of software quality management is really IV&V or a sort of super QA is really a matter of speculation. Suffice it to say, it has to lack the objectivity of a separate contractor or outside organization. The only prayer it has to work effectively is that it must report to upper management through separate channels and not rely on the developing organization for funds, because as soon as the criticism begins, the budget will begin to shrink. My personal view is that this form of support is IV&V as long as it provides alternative technical solutions and augments the mainstream development process in a more or less classical IV&V manner. In other words, it has to essentially satisfy the rules given in Chapter 1.

This form of IV&V can even share the testbed, computers, libraries, support software, I-CASE tools, etc., but should offer some unique added quality-assessment mechanisms, e.g., different software tools, aids, proofs, and analysis aids. The Hawthorne effect may make it work for a little while, but the risk of these programs failing is significantly greater than occurs with separate (outside) groups. The developer may not even be aware of the shortcomings of this type of IV&V, because he or she will be too close to it to appreciate the advantages of having an outside organization perform the work.

14.2.4   Audit-Level Independent Verification and Validation

Audit-level IV&V has only been touched on in this book so far, and it deserves more attention. It is defined as a short-term, high-impact effort wherein the customer calls in a small "tiger team" of IV&V experts to audit his or her software development process. It is very similar to the Software Engineering Institute's (SEI) contractor evaluation process, which will be discussed in Chapter 15. Unlike the SEI evaluation, audit-level IV&V is available whenever the customer feels the need. It can be invoked in a week or two with a purchase order since the dollar amount is usually under $25,000. The SEI evaluation typically runs $75,000 (in 1991–1992 timeframe).

The major payoff to the customer of audit-level IV&V is that he or she can augment the program with outsiders who can often make significant contributions in helping a program avoid many common pitfalls. SEI does not perform this type of function.

The only risk that the customer runs in audit-level IV&V is that it is difficult to ensure that the best personnel will be available when needed. Good people are invariably fully employed and cannot always break away for the time required to perform this type of effort. Nonetheless, these programs have proven to be highly effective and offer a very economical solution to the IV&V issue. Companies with high-risk, complex programs should, however, be discouraged from attempting to use audit-level IV&V in place of a more comprehensive IV&V effort since serious and therefore costly problems could go unattended. Audit-level IV&V looks more at the symptoms than at hands-on correction of the underlying causes.

14.3   SUMMARY OF BENEFITS OF INDEPENDENT VERIFICATION AND VALIDATION

Perhaps one of the most difficult tasks is to reduce the attributes of IV&V to the ten most significant benefits. These will probably vary somewhat depending upon the application, methodology emphasis, and type of system, but the experience of many programs points to the following listing as the consensus:

1. Improved software and system performance
2. Early detection of errors
3. Life cycle cost savings
4. Easier maintenance throughout the operational life of the system
5. Much higher level of user satisfaction
6. Reduced reaction time and better evaluation of proposed changes
7. Systems that don't break when stressed
8. Reduced development risk
9. Improved documentation
10. Improved communication and project visibility.

In conclusion, IV&V is a sort of chameleon that takes on many of the attributes of the system to which it is applied. Any attempts to prestructure it or confine it more than to define the logical processes and the many options available will no doubt lead to frustration and less-than-optimal results. It is my sincere hope that this book leaves the reader with an awareness of the great potential that IV&V offers and an appreciation for how to procure and apply it. Any technique that can offer so much benefit surely has a place in the future of software development; the skeptic need only try it to like it.

14.4 CHAPTER SUMMARY

- When compared to software quality assurance (SQA), IV&V offers an entirely different perspective—SQA is internal whereas IV&V is external to the development process. Thus, there is virtually no overlap in defined tasks.

- SQA's emphasis is largely on adherence to standards and the regulation of the flow of products from the developer to the customer. IV&V's focus is on engineering and analytical issues.

- Total quality management (TQM) is the quality management philosophy of the early 1990s. It is based on work conducted by W. Edwards Deming, both in the United States and in Japan, and is widely endorsed at the highest levels of government and industry. It will eventually have a profound effect on how SQA is performed.

- IV&V and TQM are quite compatible and although they offer different perspectives, this should be considered a strength.

- We recommend that IV&V be considered as a part of any comprehensive TQM philosophy and implementation plan since TQM in no way supplants the functions performed by IV&V.

- Evolving new ways to use IV&V more effectively may couple it more closely to the developer in the future, but the basic tenets should remain unchanged.

- The benefits of IV&V include improved software and system performance, early detection of errors, life cycle cost savings, easier maintenance, and better overall user satisfaction, to name a few. If you have a software-driven system that must work correctly in a stressing situation, then invest in IV&V; you won't be sorry!

14.5 WHAT COMES NEXT

Chapter 15 presents the Software Engineering Institute (SEI) software evaluation methodology for contractors. Through examination of this material, the reader can get a fairly good idea of how his or her company ranks and can help influence the decision-makers in deciding what to do next.

15

HOW THE SOFTWARE ENGINEERING INSTITUTE'S ASSESSMENT OF CONTRACTORS INTERACTS WITH INDEPENDENT VERIFICATION AND VALIDATION

The author wishes to thank the Software Engineering Institute (SEI) at Carneige–Mellon University in Pittsburgh, Pennsylvania, for making it possible to include in this chapter portions of its assessment process for software development contractors. The use of this material (1) promotes its dissemination to the non-Defense software community, (2) enables IV&V practitioners to better understand the differences between the SEI process and audit-level IV&V, and (3) makes it possible for those who are interested to perform a limited self-evaluation of the maturity and adequacy of their software development process. The reader is cautioned to draw only tentative conclusions from such a self-examination since the actual SEI evaluation requires trained analysts and a well-defined and controlled process. It will, however, serve to point out obvious deficiencies as well as strengths in any software development program and therefore can be very valuable to any who exercise this option. Lastly, it can be very effective in preparing for the actual SEI assessment.

There are several important issues that affect IV&V that stem from the Software Engineering Institute (SEI) assessment of software development contractors. Briefly, this assessment is used to determine the maturity level of the contractor's software engineering process. As the reader must be aware by now, this book stresses the importance of a formal, well-defined and structured development process as the foundation for good software products, one upon which IV&V can be efficiently applied. That is one reason why I devoted so many pages to enhancing the reader's understanding of both the commercial and DOD life cycles. If the contractor's process is poorly defined and haphazardly followed, the quality of the products always suffers and IV&V has a terrible time both in its program execution and in the institution of remedies and improvements. It is soft of like trying to nail Jello to the wall. IV&V does not have enough resources or influence with the developer to fix a really poor development process.

This chapter is presented to give the reader an appreciation of the SEI assessment process and how it determines the development process maturity level. Section 15.2 then compares the relative IV&V resource needs to the contractor maturity level. The assumption here is that the better the process, the less waste of IV&V resources will occur. The reader will also find that many of the questions asked during the SEI assessment are directed at the same issues that IV&V addresses. There is an interesting parallel between the SEI methodology and the types of things an audit-level IV&V effort looks for. Both are very interested in how refined, mature, and progressive the development contractor's software process is and how well it is being followed.

15.1 OVERVIEW OF THE SOFTWARE ENGINEERING INSTITUTE'S ASSESSMENT METHODOLOGY

The stated goal of the SEI's assessment methodology is "to facilitate objective and consistent assessments of the ability of potential DOD contractors to develop software in accordance with modern software engineering methods." Because it is the ultimate goal of the government to allow only contractors qualified to a specific level or above to compete on certain procurements, it is in the best interest of the contractor community at large to become knowledgeable of the methodology and get evaluated as early as possible. In so doing, if a contractor finds out that its development process is deficient, remedial steps can be taken before facing disqualification during source selection, when time is too limited to initiate fixes. The remainder of Section 15.1 is based on and excerpted directly from the Technical Report by W. S. Humphrey and W. L. Sweet, *A Method for Assessing the Software Engineering Capability of Contractors*, CMU/SEI-87-TR-23, Pittsburgh, Carnegie–Mellon University, Software Engineering Institute, 1987. [5]

15.1.1 Technical Approach

The assessment process is focused on defining and clarifying the positive attributes of good software engineering practices. It is further recognized that the state-of-the-practice of software engineering is steadily advancing and additional criteria and a higher level of expectation will be appropriate for judging software engineering capability in the future.

Assessment questions are based on the following premises:

- The quality of a software product stems, in large part, from the quality of the process used to create it.
- Software engineering is a process that can be managed, measured, and progressively improved.
- The quality of a software process is affected by the technology used to support it.
- The level of technology used in software engineering should be appropriate to the maturity of the process.
- Software products developed by contractors for DOD use are acquired under contracts invoking DOD-STD-2167/A, *Defense System Software Development* [24], as tailored for each contract.

To provide a structure for assessment, five levels of process maturity and two stages of software technology advancement have been postulated.

Process Maturity Levels

1. *Initial:* The initial environment has ill-defined procedures and controls. The organization does not consistently apply software engineering management to the process, nor does it use modern tools and technology. Level 1 organizations may have serious cost and schedule problems.

2. *Repeatable:* At Level 2, the organization has generally learned to manage costs and schedules, and the process is now repeatable. The organization uses standard methods and practices for managing software development activities such as cost estimating, scheduling, requirements changes, code changes, and status reviews.

3. *Defined:* At Level 3, the process is well-characterized and reasonably well understood. The organization defines its process in terms of software engineering standards and methods, and it has made a series of organizational and methodological improvements. These specifically include design and code reviews, training programs for programmers and review leaders, and increased organizational focus on software engineering. A major improvement in this phase is the establishment and staffing of a software engineering process group that focuses on the software engineering process and the adequacy with which it is implemented.

4. *Managed:* In Level 4, the process is not only understood but it is quantified, measured, and reasonably well controlled. The organization typically bases its operating decisions on quantitative process data and conducts extensive analyses of the data gathered during software engineering reviews and tests. Tools are used increasingly to control and manage the design process as well as to support data gathering and analysis. The organization is learning to project expected errors with reasonable accuracy.

5. *Optimized:* At Level 5, the organization has not only achieved a high degree of control over its process, it has a major focus on improving and optimizing its operation. This includes more sophisticated analyses of the error and cost data gathered during the process as well as the introduction of comprehensive error cause analysis and prevention studies. The data on the process are used iteratively to improve the process and achieve optimum performance.

Software Technology Stages

A. *Inefficient:* Multiple implementations may be available and the practice may be in widespread use, but the technology is no longer effective. An organization that primarily employs inefficient software development technology is likely to be ineffective in developing software. Moreover, at this technology stage some important software engineering practices are not practical in large, complex developments.

B. *Basic:* Multiple implementations are available, and they have been demonstrated to be effective. An organization that primarily employs basic software development technologies is likely to be moderately effective and, depending upon the maturity of its process, reasonably consistent in its performance.

15.1.2   Assessment Process

The following is a partial listing from the SEI technical report of Humphrey and Sweet [5] that pertains to the contractor. I have added a few clarifying remarks in brackets. Items **1** through **5** pertain to the evaluators and are deliberately excluded here.

6. *Contractor Preparation for Assessment.* While making advance arrangements, the assessment team should ask each contractor to provide a listing of the major software development projects at the location, together with a brief indication of their status (e.g., design, implementation, development test, acceptance test). Projects recommended for assessment should also be noted. The assessment team and the contractor should agree in advance on several projects, in different stages of development and indicative of the standard practice in the organization, so that representatives of these projects can be available for participation in the assessment. [Three representative projects are considered sufficient for an evaluation.]

7. *Conduct of the Assessment.* An onsite assessment begins with a briefing explaining the assessment process to the local management and the assessment participants and confirming the planned support for the assessment. The assessment team then goes through the SEI questionnaire [see Section 15.3] with the project representatives as a group, ensuring consistent interpretation of the questions and obtaining an initial set of answers for each project. Based on these initial results, the team makes a preliminary assessment of the organization's process maturity level and technology stage and then requests backup materials and tool demonstrations to support the affirmative answers that determine the highest likely level and stage. For example, if the preliminary evaluation results indicate that an organization is at maturity level 3, the major focus should be directed to probing the affirmative responses to the maturity level 2 and 3 questions. In each case, the team should request evidence for a specific project at an appropriate phase of development. [After the guidelines were written, it was realized that this expectation was difficult to achieve especially in smaller companies, so the minimum of three projects was adopted.]

8. *Assessment Conclusion.* At the end of the assessment, the local management should be informed of the findings and given an opportunity to offer evidence to refute any disputed findings and to explain their [the contractor's] plans for process improvement. Where such plans are material to the procurement, they should be documented and made part of the contract. It is important that the process be completely open because the complexity of the subject matter and the lack of common terms for many of the process elements could lead to confusion and misunderstanding.

9. *Utilization of Results.* The results of the assessments will be made available to the government's Source Selection Advisory Council for consideration prior to final source selection. [As I stated earlier, it is a good idea to prequalify instead of waiting until late in the procurement cycle. It takes considerable time to schedule and conduct the evaluation process, and much more time to modify the process.]

15.1.3   Guidelines for Evaluation of Results

The questions that are asked by the evaluators [included here as Section 15.3] have been designed to require only a "yes" or "no" answer. The method of evaluation incorporates all the questions answered in this document except those in Addendum A. The questions in Addendum A are provided to assist in the assessment of a contractor's experience relevant to a particular procurement.

Level of Process Maturity. To determine a contractor's level of process maturity, the following procedure is used. This procedure requires successive qualifications at each level.

1. Determine the percentage of affirmative answers to all Level 2 questions and to the asterisked (*) questions for Level 2. If the percentage of affirmative answers to all questions is at least 80% and the percentage of affirmative answers to asterisked questions is at least 90%, the organization has qualified at Level 2; otherwise, it is at Level 1. If Level 2 is achieved, go on to the next step.

2. Determine the percentage of affirmative answers to all Level 2 and Level 3 questions combined and to the asterisked questions for Level 2 and Level 3 combined. Again, if the percentage of affirmative answers to all questions is at least 80% and the percentage of affirmative answers to asterisked question is at least 90%, the organization qualifies at Level 3; otherwise, it is at Level 2. If it qualifies at Level 3, this procedure is repeated combining Level 2, 3, and 4 answers, again requiring 80% for all questions and 90% for asterisked questions. If the organization qualifies at Level 4, the assessment for Level 5 combines Level 2, 3, 4, and 5 answers, again using 80% and 90% as the criteria.

3. Determine the level for the organization as a whole by averaging the levels of the projects assessed.

Software Technology Stages. To determine the technology stage of an organization, a similar procedure is used.

1. Determine the percentage of affirmative answers to all Stage B questions and to the asterisked questions for Stage B. If the percentage of affirmative answers to all questions is at least 80% and the percentage of affirmative answers to asterisked questions is at least 90%, the organization has qualified at Stage B; otherwise, it is at Stage A.

2. Determine the level for the organization as a whole by averaging the levels of the projects assessed.

Combined Process and Technology Evaluation. By placing the levels of process maturity and the stages of technology in a two-dimensional matrix, an evaluation can now be made that combines both of these measures. Figure 15-1 presents process levels on the x-axis and technology stages on the y-axis, and indicates the target region toward which an organization should progress.

Qualifying Considerations. As previously noted, the practice of software engineering is not only complex but is still evolving and is not yet fully defined. In using a specific procedure to assess software engineering capability, some qualifying factors should be considered.

It is recognized that there may be alternative methods to address a given prob-

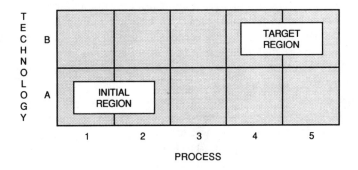

Figure 15-1 Process/technology matrix.

lem, and it is possible that there may be acceptable alternatives to some of the positions taken in this [the SEI] document [5]. Therefore, it is essential that this instrument be used by a competent and adequately trained assessment team if meaningful results are to be obtained. The SEI intends to provide, on a continuing basis, training and/or training materials to facilitate the training of assessment teams.

[Since the technical report was written in 1987, the SEI has trained and authorized nine companies throughout the U.S. to perform evaluations. Because the list will probably change over time, I felt it inappropriate to include their names. The current list can be obtained by calling the SEI at Carneige–Mellon University, Pittsburgh, Pennsylvania, at (412) 268-7630.]

The process activities and data referred to in the questions [in Section 15.3] are used as indicators of software engineering capability and are assumed to be of value to the internal operations of an organization that develops or maintains significant amounts of DOD software. It is not intended that either the process activities or data be identified as deliverable items in a procurement contract solely because they are referenced in the SEI document. The cost-effectiveness of these activities may vary with different organizations; but available evidence clearly indicates that in the context of total life cycle cost and performance, investment in these activities is well-justified. To SEI, the capability is assumed to include the ability to perform large and complex software developments; therefore, the assessment process may not be fully applicable to small projects. [This marks the end of the excerpt from the SEI report except for the questions found in Section 15.3.)

15.2   HOW MATURITY LEVELS AFFECT INDEPENDENT VERIFICATION AND VALIDATION

Figure 15-2 illustrates the idea that IV&V on an effort in which the developer is at Level 1 is going to have so much uncertainty that the outcome becomes somewhat unpredictable. Major concerns to the project center on the inability to effectively plan and consequently execute the process, the project's tendency to be crisis-managed, and large amounts of wasted effort from rework and throwaway designs and code. These factors invariably result in cost overruns, schedule slips, poor design, inadequate testing, all sorts of defects, and general user dissatisfaction. (Your typical software nightmare!) If the developer does not know where he or she is going, IV&V cannot plan its own methodology, select tools, or estimate the size or complexity of the software and will spend an inordinate amount of time working on management issues. IV&V seldom has enough force and weight to change the course of the project, although I have seen some Herculean efforts where IV&V really made an impact on a job that was heading for the scrap heap. In these cases, the developer was sort of bootstrapped to Level 2 through a concerted effort on the part of the developer, the customer, and IV&V. The key thing is understanding the development process enough to instigate essential controls and direction. Some-times it is as simple as finding the right manager, but that assumes that the staff is

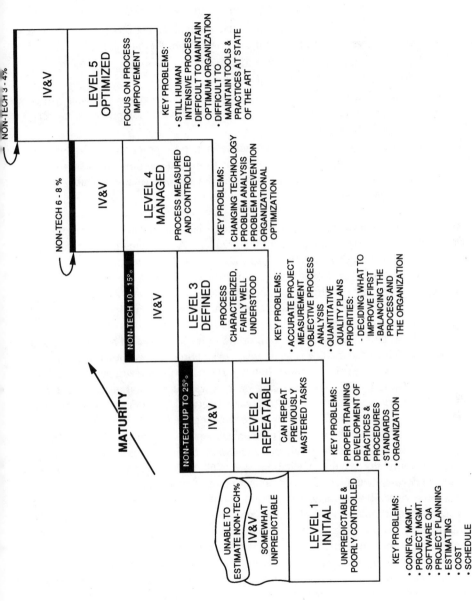

Figure 15-2 How maturity levels affect IV&V.

willing to take direction and be taught a better way. Most of the time, getting out of Level 1 requires:

- Management awareness and a strong desire for improvement
- Willingness to provide training to virtually the whole staff
- Recognition and definition of an acceptable development process for the type of products involved (usually with assistance from the outside)
- Willingness to institutionalize essential things like project management, configuration management, and quality assurance
- Willingness to provide a stable and adequate development environment, which includes appropriate computer(s) and support software (compilers, debuggers, editors, utilities, operating system, etc.)
- Willingness to begin a systematic acquisition of appropriate software tools, staged to support the worst problem areas first. You can only go so far so fast, so do not rush out and buy a trunk full of software tools (that is probably where they will stay if you do).

As you can see, most of the decisions are managerial, not technical. Most organizations follow the attitudes and beliefs of their leaders. Am I saying that it is management's fault when a contractor finds itself at Level 1? Right you are!

Looking at Figure 15-2 once again, notice that once Level 2 is reached and the development process is defined and most essentials are in place, IV&V becomes much more predictable in its behavior and can pretty well anticipate and plan its effort. Because the process may still be a little flaky and the tools and methods are not optimized, IV&V will still find itself doing some unplanned ad hoc analyses and evaluations. These can include such things as evaluating and benchmarking competing operating systems and compilers, helping to write example sections of specifications, evaluating CASE tools, advising on hardware configurations and features, helping to select communications protocols and network configurations, and a myriad of other things normally done by the developer. In addition, IV&V will likely spend some of its time and resources on management-related things like determining project status, auditing configuration management records, tracking things that the developer normally would, evaluating how well the developer is following the software development plan, and participating more than normally expected in meetings and reviews. It is estimated that up to 25% of the IV&V program budget will be spent on nontechnical issues when the contractor is at Level 2. As you go up the evolutionary chain, the amount of nontechnical IV&V effort continues to shrink; however, it should never reach zero since there are still some management-related activities required no matter how efficient the software development process becomes. There can be exceptions to these percentages based on expressed direction from the customer, so treat these figures as nominal values.

Level 3 is considered the minimum threshold to qualify for some procurements; therefore, all U.S. Department of Defense contractors should consider this achievement as the ground floor and seek to improve beyond that point as soon as is reasonable. When the development contractor is at Level 3, chances are that the use of metrics and other management and technical performance indicators is either absent or is not widespread. In addition, the mechanisms to define and collect the appropriate data are probably lacking. IV&V will usually need to support the customer in quantifying the key precode products (requirement and design specifications) so that an objective measure of percent complete can be established (refer to Section 12.2 for more information on metrics) on a periodic basis (usually monthly). Next there usually are some noticeable deficiencies in the area of CASE tools. Sometimes it is a matter that somewhat obsolete practices and tools are being used or that the tools do not cover the entire process adequately. Here IV&V can fill noticeable gaps, but the developer will eventually have to improve the application of tools to advance to the next level. Another area that often represents a weakness in Level 3 involves the organization and how much continuous training is provided to keep the staff current and to enhance the overall skill level. Overspecialization in specific software skills is not always a good thing and cross-training is very beneficial, especially if staff turnover is a problem. Loss of key personnel with critical skills can quickly reduce the maturity level of the process. Very often, Level 3 contractors do not benefit much from the lessons learned on previous projects and continue to do a poor job at estimating and detailed planning for each new project. There is a tendency to collect data at the wrong levels and not know how to recognize and react to adverse trends or pinpoint faults.

Level 4 contractors have identified and collected data on the detailed factors through which their development process is controlled and managed. Through the use of metrics and other performance indicators, this level effectively quantifies the development process, enabling much better understanding of cause-and-effect relationships, greatly improving estimating and planning, and enabling corrective actions to be applied efficiently. Level 4 contractors will typically recognize the critical paths in the software project and will focus resources based on known organizational capabilities—skills, experience, productivity rates, and other measurable data. Extensive use of automated tools can be expected based on cost-effectiveness analysis and return on investment, *not* individual programmer preference. Level 4 will include an active training program wherein all levels of the organization are kept abreast of the current technology and development trends. Thus, Level 4 will have an active program to assess and replace aging technology on a periodic basis. IV&V will find working with a Level 4 contractor allows a strong concentration on the technical issues together with expectations of good-quality specifications, design, and code. Even when working with a Level 4 contractor, however, IV&V can expect to continue to find deficiencies in requirements and design, poorly expressed algorithms, errors in the code, and testing shortcomings. You must remember that the development process, no matter how well understood or refined, is a human-intensive activity and thus prone to errors, interpretations, and misunderstanding.

Level 5 contractors spend a good bit of energy using and exploiting the data collected and processed at Level 4. The goal at this level is to continuously improve and adapt the process to each new development effort in an optimum manner. This requires a focus on continuous training and infusion of the latest technology that suits the development process. This means that tool selection is based on key factors that pertain to the developer's type of business and software products. The Level 5 contractor is able to use the data collected at Level 4 to initiate preventive actions directed at the known problem areas. Perhaps the greatest challenge at Level 5 is staying there. It requires continuous effort on behalf of the entire staff, graceful introduction of new methods and tools, and a strong desire at all levels to continue to become more efficient and skilled at handling the day-to-day activities. IV&V can still expect to find plenty of technical issues, because as I said about Level 4, the process cannot do it all. There will be errors and deficiencies as long as people develop software. Tools are only as good as the input, so you can expect to need IV&V for a long time into the future, even when the developer is at Level 5.

15.3   QUESTIONS FOR ASSESSING A CONTRACTOR

The following section contains the questions and instructions that are used by the evaluation team when assessing a contractor. This extract is taken directly from pages 13–30 of the technical report by Humphrey and Sweet [5] with the permission of the SEI.

QUESTIONS*

In order to achieve clarity in the questions, many of the terms used have been given specific explanatory definitions in the glossary at the end of this document. Each use of a glossary term in the Questions section is italicized. Adherence to these definitions is essential for proper and consistent assessments. There is no significance to the order of the questions.

1. Organization and Resource Management

This section deals with functional responsibilities, personnel, and other resources and facilities. Its purpose is to define the magnitude, quality, and structure of the software engineering organization. The questions focus on responsibilities and the quality and quantity of resources.

The major responsibility concerns relate to quality assurance, process management, and configuration control. The intent is to ascertain whether these functional responsibilities are clearly delineated and assigned, not necessarily that an individual is assigned full time to each.

1.1. Organizational Structure

1.1.1. For each project involving software development, is there a designated software manager?

*The answers to the questions should reflect standard organizational practice.

1.1.2. Does the project software manager report directly to the project (or project development) manager?

1.1.3. Does the Software Quality Assurance (SQA) function have a management reporting channel separate from the software development project management?

1.1.4. Is there a designated individual or team responsible for the control of software interfaces?

1.1.5. Is software system engineering represented on the system design team?

1.1.6. Is there a software configuration control function for each project that involves software development?

1.1.7. Is there a software engineering *process group* function?

1.2. Resources, Personnel, and Training

The questions on resources concern software engineering training, process training, and adequacy of the support facilities.

1.2.1. Does each software developer have a private computer-supported workstation/terminal?

1.2.2. Is there a required training program for all newly appointed development managers designed to familiarize them with software project management?

1.2.3. Is there a required software engineering training program for software developers?

1.2.4. Is there a required software engineering training program for first-line supervisors of software development?

1.2.5. Is a formal training program required for design and code *review leaders?*

1.3. Technology Management

The questions on technology management relate to the mechanisms used to introduce and control new technologies.

1.3.1. Is a *mechanism* used for maintaining awareness of the state-of-the-art in software engineering technology?

1.3.2. Is a *mechanism* used for evaluating technologies used by the organization versus those externally available?

1.3.3. Is a *mechanism* used for deciding when to insert new technology into the development *process?*

1.3.4. Is a *mechanism* used for managing and supporting the introduction of new technologies?

1.3.5. Is a *mechanism* used for identifying and replacing obsolete technologies?

2. Software Engineering Process and its Management

This section concerns the scope, depth, and completeness of the software engineering process and how the process is measured, managed, and improved. The major topics are standards and procedures, metrics, data management and analysis, and process control.

2.1. Documented Standards and Procedures

The standards and procedures questions address the scope and usage of conventions, formats, procedures, and documentation during the various software development phases, i.e., requirements, design, code, and test.

2.1.1. Does the software organization use a standardized and documented software development *process* on each project?

2.1.2. Does the standard software development *process* documentation describe the use of tools and techniques?

2.1.3. Is a *formal procedure* used in the management review of each software development prior to making contractual commitments?

2.1.4. Is a *formal procedure* used to assure periodic management review of the status of each software development project?

2.1.5. Is there a *mechanism* for assuring that software subcontractors, if any, follow a disciplined software development *process?*

2.1.6. Are *standards* used for the content of software development files/folders?

2.1.7. For each project, are independent audits conducted for each step of the software development *process?*

2.1.8. Is a *mechanism* used for assessing existing designs and code for reuse in new applications?

2.1.9. Are coding *standards* applied to each software development project?

2.1.10. Are *standards* applied to the preparation of unit test cases?

2.1.11. Are code maintainability *standards* applied?

2.1.12. Are internal design review *standards* applied?

2.1.13. Are code review *standards* applied?

2.1.14. Is a *formal procedure* used to make estimates of software size?

2.1.15. Is a *formal procedure* used to produce software development schedules?

2.1.16. Are *formal procedures* applied to estimating software development cost?

2.1.17. Is a *mechanism* used for ensuring that the software design teams understand each software requirement?

2.1.18. Are man-machine interface *standards* applied to each appropriate software development project?

2.2. Process Metrics

The process metrics questions focus on the degree to which the software engineering process is quantified and measured. Typical metrics concern software quality, the amount of code developed, resources used, and such progress indicators as review coverage, test coverage, and test completion.

2.2.1. Are software staffing profiles maintained of actual staffing versus planned staffing?

2.2.2. Are profiles of software size maintained for each software configuration item, over time?

2.2.3. Are statistics on software design errors gathered?

2.2.4. Are statistics on software code and test errors gathered?

2.2.5.   Are design errors projected and compared to actuals?

2.2.6.   Are code and test errors projected and compared to actuals?

2.2.7.   Are profiles maintained of actual versus planned software units designed, over time?

2.2.8.   Are profiles maintained of actual versus planned software units completing unit testing, over time?

2.2.9.   Are profiles maintained of actual versus planned software units integrated, over time?

2.2.10. Are target computer memory utilization estimates and actuals tracked?

2.2.11. Are target computer throughput utilization estimates and actuals tracked?

2.2.12. Is target computer I/O channel utilization tracked?

2.2.13. Are design and code *review coverages* measured and recorded?

2.2.14. Is *test coverage* measured and recorded for each phase of functional testing?

2.2.15. Are the action items resulting from design reviews tracked to closure?

2.2.16. Are software trouble reports resulting from testing tracked to closure?

2.2.17. Are the action items resulting from code reviews tracked to closure?

2.2.18. Is test progress tracked by deliverable software component and compared to the plan?

2.2.19. Are profiles maintained of software build/release content versus time?

2.3. Data Management and Analysis

Data management deals with the gathering and retention of process metrics. Data management requires standardized data definitions, data management facilities, and a staff to ensure that data is promptly obtained, properly checked, accurately entered into the database, and effectively managed.

Analysis deals with the subsequent manipulation of the process data to answer questions such as, "Is there a relatively high correlation between error densities found in test and those found in use?" Other types of analyses can assist in determining the optimum use of reviews and resources, the tools most needed, testing priorities, and needed education.

2.3.1.   Has a managed and controlled *process database* been established for *process metrics* data across all projects?

2.3.2.   Are the *review data* gathered during design reviews analyzed?

2.3.3.   Is the error data from code reviews and tests analyzed to determine the likely distribution and characteristics of the errors remaining in the product?

2.3.4.   Are analyses of errors conducted to determine their *process* related causes?

2.3.5.   Is a *mechanism* used for error cause analysis?

2.3.6.   Are the error causes reviewed to determine the *process* changes required to prevent them?

2.3.7.   Is a *mechanism* used for initiating error prevention actions?

2.3.8.   Is *review efficiency* analyzed for each project?

2.3.9.   Is software productivity analyzed for major *process* steps?

2.4. Process Control

The process control questions concern the definition of the development process and the mechanisms for identifying process problems, correcting process deficiencies, and preventing their recurrence.

2.4.1. Does senior management have a *mechanism* for the regular review of the status of software development projects?

2.4.2. Is a *mechanism* used for periodically assessing the software engineering *process* and implementing indicated improvements?

2.4.3. Is a *mechanism* used for identifying and resolving system engineering issues that affect software?

2.4.4. Is a *mechanism* used for independently calling integration and test issues to the attention of the project manager?

2.4.5. Is a *mechanism* used for regular technical interchanges with the customer?

2.4.6. Is a *mechanism* used for ensuring compliance with the software engineering *standards?*

2.4.7. Do software development first-line managers sign off on their schedules and cost estimates?

2.4.8. Is a *mechanism* used for ensuring traceability between the software requirements and top-level design?

2.4.9. Is a *mechanism* used for controlling changes to the software requirements?

2.4.10. Is there a formal management *process* for determining if the prototyping of software functions is an appropriate part of the design *process?*

2.4.11. Is a *mechanism* used for ensuring traceability between the software top-level and detailed designs?

2.4.12. Are internal software design reviews conducted?

2.4.13. Is a *mechanism* used for controlling changes to the software design?

2.4.14. Is a *mechanism* used for ensuring traceability between the software detailed design and the code?

2.4.15. Are formal records maintained of unit (module) development progress?

2.4.16. Are software code reviews conducted?

2.4.17. Is a *mechanism* used for controlling changes to the code? (Who can make changes and under which circumstances?)

2.4.18. Is a *mechanism* used for configuration management of the software tools used in the development *process?*

2.4.19. Is a *mechanism* used for verifying that the samples examined by Software Quality Assurance are truly representative of the work performed?

2.4.20. Is there a *mechanism* for assuring that regression testing is routinely performed?

2.4.21. Is there a *mechanism* for assuring the adequacy of regression testing?

2.4.22. Are formal test case reviews conducted?

3. Tools and Technology

This section deals with the tools and technologies used in the software engineering process. It aims at ascertaining the degree to which the contractor's process employs basic tools and methodologies. (In subsequent revisions of this document, this section will be expanded as the applicability and effectiveness of advanced tools and methodologies become more fully established.)

3.1. Is automated configuration control used to control and track change activity throughout the software development *process?*

3.2. Are computer tools used to assist in tracing software requirements to software design?

3.3. Are formal design notations such as PDL used in program design?

3.4. Are computer tools used to assist in tracing the software design to the code?

3.5. Is the majority of product development implemented in a high-order language?

3.6. Are automated test input data generators used for testing?

3.7. Are computer tools used to measure *test coverage?*

3.8. Are computer tools used to track every required function and assure that it is tested/verified?

3.9. Are automated tools used to analyze the size and change activity in software components?

3.10. Are automated tools used to analyze software complexity?

3.11. Are automated tools used to analyze cross references between modules?

3.12. Are interactive source-level debuggers used?

3.13. Are the software development and maintenance personnel provided with interactive documentation facilities?

3.14. Are computer tools used for tracking and reporting the status of the software in the software development library?

3.15. Are prototyping methods used in designing the critical performance elements of the software?

3.16. Are prototyping methods used in designing the critical elements of the man-machine interface?

ADDENDA

Addendum A: Software Engineering Experience

A complete assessment of a contractor's capability to produce quality software at a particular facility should include an evaluation of the experience level of the software development personnel at that location. The experience level of the development staff significantly and directly influences the cost of software development projects. Information about experience level is normally obtained during source selection from proposals or from review team interviews. However, for the purpose of this evaluation, suggested questions are listed below.

A.1. What is the median number of years of applicable experience of software development managers?

A.2. What is the median number of years of applicable experience of software integration and test managers?

A.3. What percentage of the software development staff has a bachelor degree or higher in computer science or software engineering?

A.4. What is the median number of years of software development experience of the software staff?

A.5. What percentage of the software staff has at least one year of development experience with the design and implementation languages to be used?

A.6. Of those with such experience, what is the median number of years of experience with those languages?

A.7. What is the median size, in source lines of code, of software development projects completed in the last five years? The size of the smallest project? The largest?

A.8. What is the total size of the software development organization, including direct professionals, management, and support personnel?

A.9. What is the total number of software engineers in the organization?

Addendum B: Software Engineering Process Maturity Levels

Five levels of process maturity have been defined for the assessment of software engineering organizations.

- Level 1 Initial
- Level 2 Repeatable
- Level 3 Defined
- Level 4 Managed
- Level 5 Optimized

Level 1   Initial Process
The initial environment has ill-defined procedures and controls. While positive responses to some of the organizational questions are likely, the organization does not consistently apply software engineering management to the process, nor does it use modern tools and technology.

Level 2   Repeatable Process
At Maturity Level 2, the organization uses standard methods and practices for managing software development activities such as cost estimating, scheduling, requirements changes, code changes, and status reviews. The organization will provide positive responses to most of the following questions.

1.1.1. For each project involving software development, is there a designated software manager?

1.1.2. Does the project software manager report directly to the project (or project development) manager?

*1.1.3. Does the Software Quality Assurance (SQA) function have a management reporting channel separate from the software development project management?

*1.1.6. Is there a software configuration control function for each project that involves software development?

1.2.2. Is there a required training program for all newly appointed development managers designed to familiarize them with software project management?

1.3.1. Is a *mechanism* used for maintaining awareness of the state-of-the-art in software engineering technology?

*2.1.3. Is a *formal procedure* used in the management review of each software development prior to making contractual commitments?

2.1.4. Is a *formal procedure* used to assure periodic management review of the status of each software development project?

2.1.5. Is there a *mechanism* for assuring that software subcontractors, if any, follow a disciplined software development *process?*

2.1.7. For each project, are independent audits conducted for each step of the software development *process?*

2.1.9. Are coding *standards* applied to each software development project?

*2.1.14. Is a *formal procedure* used to make estimates of software size?

*2.1.15. Is a *formal procedure* used to produce software development schedules?

*2.1.16. Are *formal procedures* applied to estimating software development cost?

2.1.17. Is a *mechanism* used for ensuring that the software design teams understand each software requirement?

2.2.1. Are software staffing profiles maintained of actual staffing versus planned staffing?

*2.2.2. Are profiles of software size maintained for each software configuration item, over time?

*2.2.4. Are statistics on software code and test errors gathered?

2.2.7. Are profiles maintained of actual versus planned software units designed, over time?

2.2.8. Are profiles maintained of actual versus planned software units completing unit testing, over time?

2.2.9. Are profiles maintained of actual versus planned software units integrated, over time?

2.2.10. Are target computer memory utilization estimates and actuals tracked?

2.2.11. Are target computer throughput utilization estimates and actuals tracked?

2.2.12. Is target computer I/O channel utilization tracked?

2.2.16. Are software trouble reports resulting from testing tracked to closure?

2.2.18. Is test progress tracked by deliverable software component and compared to the plan?

2.2.19. Are profiles maintained of software build/release content versus time?

*2.4.1. Does senior management have a *mechanism* for the regular review of the status of software development projects?

2.4.5. Is a *mechanism* used for regular technical interchanges with the customer?

*2.4.7. Do software development first-line managers sign off on their schedules and cost estimates?

*2.4.9. Is a *mechanism* used for controlling changes to the software requirements?

*2.4.17. Is a *mechanism* used for controlling changes to the code? (Who can make changes and under which circumstances?)

2.4.20. Is there a *mechanism* for assuring that regression testing is routinely performed?

Level 3   Defined Process

At Maturity Level 3, the organization not only defines its process in terms of software engineering standards and methods, it also has made a series of organizational and methodological improvements. These specifically include design and code reviews, training programs for programmers and review leaders, and increased organizational focus on software engineering. A major improvement in this phase is the establishment and staffing of a software engineering process group that focuses on the software engineering process and the adequacy with which it is implemented. In addition to the questions for Level 2, organizations at Level 3 will respond "yes" to most of the following questions.

1.1.4. Is there a designated individual or team responsible for the control of software interfaces?

1.1.5. Is software system engineering represented on the system design team?

*1.1.7. Is there a software engineering *process group* function?

1.2.1. Does each software developer have a private computer-supported work-station/terminal?

*1.2.3. Is there a required software engineering training program for software developers?

1.2.4. Is there a required software engineering training program for first-line supervisors of software development?

*1.2.5. Is a formal training program required for design and code *review leaders?*

1.3.2. Is a *mechanism* used for evaluating technologies used by the organization versus those externally available?

*2.1.1. Does the software organization use a standardized and documented software development *process* on each project?

2.1.2. Does the standard software development *process* documentation describe the use of tools and techniques?

2.1.6. Are *standards* used for the content of software development files/folders?

2.1.8. Is a *mechanism* used for assessing existing designs and code for reuse in new applications?

2.1.10. Are *standards* applied to the preparation of unit test cases?

2.1.11. Are code maintainability *standards* applied?

2.1.18. Are man-machine interface *standards* applied to each appropriate software development project?

*2.2.3. Are statistics on software design errors gathered?

*2.2.15. Are the action items resulting from design reviews tracked to closure?

*2.2.17. Are the action items resulting from code reviews tracked to closure?

2.4.3. Is a *mechanism* used for identifying and resolving system engineering issues that affect software?

2.4.4.   Is a *mechanism* used for independently calling integration and test issues to the attention of the project manager?

*2.4.6.   Is a *mechanism* used for ensuring compliance with the software engineering *standards?*

2.4.8.   Is a *mechanism* used for ensuring traceability between the software requirements and top-level design?

2.4.11.   Is a *mechanism* used for ensuring traceability between the software top-level and detailed designs?

*2.4.12.   Are internal software design reviews conducted?

*2.4.13.   Is a *mechanism* used for controlling changes to the software design?

2.4.14.   Is a *mechanism* used for ensuring traceability between the software detailed design and the code?

2.4.15.   Are formal records maintained of unit (module) development progress?

*2.4.16.   Are software code reviews conducted?

2.4.18.   Is a *mechanism* used for configuration management of the software tools used in the development *process?*

*2.4.19.   Is a *mechanism* used for verifying that the samples examined by Software Quality Assurance are truly representative of the work performed?

*2.4.21.   Is there a *mechanism* for assuring the adequacy of regression testing?

2.4.22.   Are formal test case reviews conducted?

Level 4   Managed Process

At Maturity Level 4, the organization typically bases its operating decisions on quantitative process data, and conducts extensive analyses of the data gathered during software engineering reviews and tests. Tools are used increasingly to control and manage the design process as well as to support data gathering and analysis. The organization is learning to project expected errors with reasonable accuracy. In addition to questions for Levels 2 and 3, organizations at Level 4 will respond "yes" to most of the following questions.

1.3.3.   Is a *mechanism* used for deciding when to insert new technology into the development *process?*

*1.3.4.   Is a *mechanism* used for managing and supporting the introduction of new technologies?

2.1.12.   Are internal design review *standards* applied?

*2.1.13.   Are code review *standards* applied?

*2.2.5.   Are design errors projected and compared to actuals?

*2.2.6.   Are code and test errors projected and compared to actuals?

*2.2.13.   Are design and code *review coverages* measured and recorded?

*2.2.14.   Is *test coverage* measured and recorded for each phase of functional testing?

*2.3.1.   Has a managed and controlled *process database* been established for *process metrics* data across all projects?

*2.3.2.   Are the *review data* gathered during design reviews analyzed?

*2.3.3.   Is the error data from code reviews and tests analyzed to determine the likely distribution and characteristics of the errors remaining in the product?

*2.3.4.   Are analyses of errors conducted to determine their *process* related causes?

*2.3.8.   Is *review efficiency* analyzed for each project?

2.3.9.   Is software productivity analyzed for major *process* steps?

*2.4.2.   Is a *mechanism* used for periodically assessing the software engineering *process* and implementing indicated improvements?

2.4.10.   Is there a formal management *process* for determining if the prototyping of software functions is an appropriate part of the design *process?*

Level 5   Optimized Process

At Maturity Level 5, organizations have not only achieved a high degree of control over their process, they have a major focus on improving and optimizing its operation. This includes more sophisticated analyses of the error and cost data gathered during the process as well as the introduction of comprehensive error cause analysis and prevention studies.

*1.3.5.   Is a *mechanism* used for identifying and replacing obsolete technologies?

*2.3.5.   Is a *mechanism* used for error cause analysis?

*2.3.6.   Are the error causes reviewed to determine the *process* changes required to prevent them?

*2.3.7.   Is a *mechanism* used for initiating error prevention actions?

Addendum C: Technology

This section defines a method for evaluating the software engineering technology of a contractor. The quality of a software process is affected by the stage of software technology employed. Two stages for describing the level of software technology have been defined.

Stage A   Inefficient Technology

An organization that primarily employs inefficient software development technology is likely to be ineffective in developing software. Many different implementations may be available and the practice may be in widespread use, but the technology is no longer effective. Moreover, at this technology stage some important software engineering practices are not practical in large, complex developments.

Stage B   Basic Technology

An organization that primarily employs basic software development technologies is likely to be moderately effective and, depending upon the maturity of its process, reasonably consistent in its performance. Multiple implementations are available, and they have been demonstrated to be effective. Organizations at Stage B will respond "yes" to most of the following questions.

*3.1.   Is automated configuration control used to control and track change activity throughout the software development *process?*

3.2.   Are computer tools used to assist in tracing software requirements to software design?

3.3. Are formal design notations such as PDL used in program design?

3.4. Are computer tools used to assist in tracing the software design to the code?

*3.5. Is the majority of product development implemented in a high-order language?

3.6. Are automated test input data generators used for testing?

3.7. Are computer tools used to measure *test coverage?*

3.8. Are computer tools used to track every required function and assure that it is tested/verified?

3.9. Are automated tools used to analyze the size and change activity in software components?

3.10. Are automated tools used to analyze software complexity?

3.11. Are automated tools used to analyze cross references between modules?

*3.12. Are interactive source-level debuggers used?

*3.13. Are the software development and maintenance personnel provided with interactive documentation facilities?

*3.14. Are computer tools used for tracking and reporting the status of the software in the software development library?

3.15. Are prototyping methods used in designing the critical performance elements of the software?

3.16. Are prototyping methods used in designing the critical elements of the man-machine interface?

15.4 CHAPTER SUMMARY

- The SEI has developed a comprehensive way to evaluate contractor's software engineering process in terms of five levels of maturity.

- The five levels cover the complete spectrum from ill-defined and flawed (Level 1) to highly optimized (Level 5); Level 3 is considered just adequate.

- The U.S. Department of Defense intends to limit some procurements to companies that are at Level 3 and above. Certainly, less proposal space would have to be devoted to proving each company's software engineering capabilities if all the bidders are prequalified.

- Audit-level IV&V and the SEI evaluation process look at many of the same factors in determining how well the contractor has evolved and formalized the development process in accordance with modern software engineering methods.

- SEI evaluations typically cost $75,000 (as of 1991) and require several levels of interaction between SEI and contractor personnel. The time span for the complete evaluation will take several months.

- Companies with known (or even unknown, but suspect) deficiencies may want to use audit-level IV&V for a quick assessment and for initiating remedial actions prior to beginning an SEI evaluation. This could save considerable time and money in the long run.

- Some amount of self-evaluation is possible by using the guidelines and questions found in this chapter.

15.5   WHAT COMES NEXT

Part IV of the book, which contains eight IV&V case studies, follows. These examples were taken from a wide range of experience to illustrate the comprehensiveness, flexibility, and adaptability of IV&V to work cost-effectively on virtually any type of development effort.

PART IV

CASE STUDIES IN INDEPENDENT VERIFICATION AND VALIDATION

The following case studies are based on actual systems and projects. They are, however, somewhat disguised to protect the interests of all three parties—the customer, the software development contractor, and the IV&V contractor. All examples of program idiosyncrasies, IV&V methods and approaches, and summary results came from actual experiences and are, therefore, an effective basis for the study of applied IV&V.

Case studies offer an excellent opportunity to profit from lessons learned and afford the serious student of IV&V insight into the myriad of approaches and problems that can and do arise in the development of software. The case studies are divided into the four basic types of IV&V programs, as were defined in Chapter 1:

Full, In-Phase IV&V

A. Very Large Realtime Weapon System
B. Large Data Acquisition System
C. Large Instrumentation System

Partial IV&V

D. Very Large Manned Space Vehicle Ground System
E. Commercial Information Storage and Retrieval System

Endgame IV&V

F. Small Experimental Missile System

Audit-Level IV&V

G. ABC Missile Program
H. Very Large Federal ADP Operation

CASE STUDY A

A VERY LARGE
REAL-TIME WEAPON SYSTEM

FULL, IN-PHASE IV&V

A.1 SYSTEM DESCRIPTION

This system consisted of radars; large-scale multiprocessor computers; interceptor missiles; and communications, command, and control (C3) systems both local to the radar and missile sites and remote to the U.S. National Command Authority (NCA). Live target intercept testing occurred using the Pacific Test Range, and the hardware and software were developed separately at several locations. This was one of the largest and most sophisticated one-of-a-kind software-controlled weapon systems ever undertaken in the U.S. Department of Defense (DOD). It evolved over an almost 20-year period with several prototype predecessor systems being developed to prove the feasibility, reduce the program risk, support the near-continuous testing, and push the technology to a more advanced state of the art.

A.2 CHARACTERISTICS OF THE SYSTEM OR PROGRAM THAT AFFECTED INDEPENDENT VERIFICATION AND VALIDATION

Some time after the system entered full-scale engineering development, the sheer magnitude of the effort, with its highly complex and probabilistic nature, made the government customer aware that help was needed to ensure better visibility, especially in the area of software development. The result was the largest IV&V effort that had ever been funded by DOD up to that time.

The IV&V program began in the middle of the design phase (some coding and process testing were also occurring on deliveries needed early in the program, e.g., system exercisers, early versions of the operating system, installation and test software, test range software, data reduction packages, etc.). Because the system was using an incremental build approach to code development, there was not a clean break between the end of the design phase and start of code phase; rather it was a very complex series of interactive processes. The testing network program evaluation and review technique (PERT) charts were, therefore, representative of this building-block process and contained literally thousands of discrete tests; far too many for IV&V to monitor or evaluate.

Almost three million lines of real-time software were eventually baselined, which probably means that double that figure was produced when one considers the throwaway from interim releases, test drivers, and temporary prototype implementations that had to be done over. The development process methodology was thus neither purely top-down nor bottom-up. Perhaps "middle-out" would be a good way to describe it (see Section 2.1.3 for definitions of these methods), since the idea was to build a functional process thread that would cycle on the computer and then incrementally add capabilities. The major deficiency with this approach was twofold: (1) it was very difficult to determine overall program status accurately at any point in time and (2) the hardest problems (most complex code) were put off until last. With this concept, progress looked great in the beginning and then began to waiver even to the extent that in a particular month one could find less code done than two or three months earlier. Negative growth or progress is a reality of large systems, but high-level managers invariably cringe at the idea. This phenomenon results in part from a certain amount of code being thrown away as new capabilities are added because the designers and programmers cannot always see far enough ahead to build something that will support or even tolerate the new growth. This is especially true in interrupt-driven, real-time processes wherein adding functional capabilities often destroys the timing sanity, which in turn requires algorithm retuning and, at times, even rethinking of entire subprocess designs. At one point the software in this case study got too big for the hardware system and had to be sharply reduced. This is a problem that occurs all too frequently in embedded computer systems in which memory is severely limited.

Because the requirements and many of the design documents were already written when IV&V began, the IV&V contractor had to go back into these documents to attempt to verify the requirements and design baselines. That is, the IV&V group had to know with confidence where the detailed design was coming from before trying to verify code. A large number of deficiencies were found in building the requirements and design tracing database. But, as discussed in Chapter 13, it was largely too late to avoid the high cost of repairing these errors, because coding was by then well underway.

During this period, the IV&V contractor undertook algorithm analysis on everything that appeared firm enough for scrutiny. Because of the weakness in documentation on many of the key algorithms, the IV&V contractor undertook a threefold effort: (1) analyzing and documenting the existing algorithms, (2) recommending improvements or corrections as required, and (3) testing the basic and improved versions in the IV&V testbed. This proved very fruitful in many of the highly probabilistic equations including such things as target detection during nuclear

CHARACTERISTICS OF THE SYSTEM OR PROGRAM

events, reentry vehicle (RV) identification and discrimination, waking targets, RV impact prediction, intercept, kill assessment, which targets to attack first, etc.

This case study is not intended as a criticism of the developer in any way; rather, it brings to light that added analytical resources (i.e., IV&V) can invariably aid in the discovery of deficiencies and suggestions for improvement. At the same time, it speaks well of the IV&V contractor, whose dedication to the goal of quality enabled him to make significant contributions to the software system.

Testing was mentioned earlier as a very complex network of many partial builds of interim capabilities. Software testing began using an all-digital emulation of the tactical computer that resided on a big mainframe (IBM 370). When the actual hardware was finally available, the IV&V contractor picked up this all-digital emulation, improved it to run in a dual mode (exerciser and weapons processes), and used it for independent testing. It was much slower (at least 100:1) than the target hardware and ran hours for the same test that would take minutes at the development or tactical site. Nevertheless, it was 100% repeatable with the actual system and enabled the IV&V contractor to record and test changes independent of the software contractor. Because the testing program was so complex and immense, the government, with IV&V consultation, identified and selected a series of key mid- and end-point tests for preliminary and formal qualification tests (PQT and FQT). It was agreed with the development contractor that these tests would have significant data collection and be monitored and analyzed by the IV&V contractor. These key-event tests averaged about one per month per major process (of which there were five); thus about five tests per month were run for these purposes until the final system test series, wherein all were witnessed and evaluated. This concept was highly successful and made something efficient and manageable out of a potentially difficult if not impossible task.

Most of the configuration management functions went smoothly except for the configuration status accounting system (CSAS). The contractor did not recognize the need for a single consolidated software CSAS early enough in the program and allowed each major design group to operate its own manual hard-copy forms and file systems for some time (several years). Finally, about the middle of the program, the software contractor "overdeveloped" an automated CSAS that attempted to be "all things to all people," offering almost one hundred separate reporting formats and variations, in response to a user survey. In retrospect, the user community should have been educated on how to use a half-dozen unique types of reports that would have contained all of the needed information. Largely because of its complexity, the CSAS was very late in becoming operational and therefore missed the peak problem report (PR) load period, causing manual techniques to be used instead. The new system was difficult to use, involved extensive training, and, in effect, was not very effective. Meanwhile, at the government's request, the IV&V contractor developed several automated reports and databases that tracked program status while all this CSAS problem was occurring. These reports were so informative that the software developer requested to be placed on distribution.

Another area in which IV&V performed was to supply on-site test personnel to participate in several national exercises which could be considered part of Operational Test III. Near the end of the program, the customer tasked IV&V to prepare a comprehensive series of technical reports on the lessons learned throughout the development effort.

A.3   INDEPENDENT VERIFICATION AND VALIDATION PRODUCTS AND MAJOR ACTIVITIES

There were eight major activity areas, as listed below with their approximate percentage of effort:

- (58%)   Design and code verification coupled with monitoring and analyzing the contractor's tests
- (15%)   Independent IV&V tests and testbed operation
- (8%)   Algorithm analysis and documentation
- (5%)   System and software requirements verification and tracing
- (5%)   Special studies and analysis, including ECP evaluation
- (4%)   Software maintenance and data reduction and archival
- (4%)   Management support and status monitoring
- (1%)   Operational experience (lessons learned)

There are numerous ways to evaluate an IV&V program, but one of the most effective and quantifiable methods is to look back over the amount of data, analysis results, and documentation produced in the performance of the contract. In this case, IV&V:

- Wrote 84 classified reports and well over 100 unclassified reports
- Monitored over 100 key-event tests at both the development and operational sites
- Performed in-depth analysis of over 50 key-event tests
- Performed design and code verification of well over 2 million lines of code
- Ran several hundred independent tests of all types (regression, algorithm modeling, simulations, special functions, system tests, etc.)
- Developed and maintained an independent status accounting and reporting system for customer
- Generated over 500 problem reports (PRs) which equates to 3 times the nominal output if based on IV&V's percent of the software budget
- Refined and documented the operation of a large number of algorithms including a significant number that the developer ended up incorporating into the final system
- Verified acceptance test requirements and defined the pass/fail criteria

- Developed and participated in operational exercises (including those for joint services)
- Developed a requirements tracing database for all requirements and design specifications and referenced these to the test program
- Participated in design review board and CCB actions
- Provided the customer with analysis and alternatives to engineering change proposals (this turned out to be a very big cost-saver for the government)
- Developed, evaluated, and used a significant number of software tools and testing aids
- Maintained both classified and unclassified document, software, and data libraries jointly for the customer and IV&V.

CASE STUDY B

A LARGE
DATA-ACQUISITION SYSTEM

FULL, IN-PHASE IV&V

B.1 SYSTEM DESCRIPTION

This system consisted of two VAX computers, a multichannel front-end telemetry processing and recording subsystem, displays and controls subsystem, and related hardware and software. The system was designed to collect and process all the data from a heavily instrumented high-energy laser test range. When such devices are being tested, the data-acquisition system has to record all sensor inputs in real time, provide immediately available quick-look data, and allow playback in various modes for detailed frame-by-frame analysis. Since such tests typically only occur for a few seconds and it is necessary to collect hundreds of kilobytes of data, the system had to have extremely high bandwidth and recording and playback fidelity.

B.2 CHARACTERISTICS OF THE SYSTEM OR PROGRAM THAT AFFECTED INDEPENDENT VERIFICATION AND VALIDATION

In this case, IV&V was initiated during preliminary design of the system and, therefore, was classified as a full, in-phase effort. One of the big problems early in the program was that the government did not invoke a full military standard (MIL-STD) development effort, but rather chose to require selected deliverables that were supposed to be prepared in the spirit of MIL-STD documents. Thus, this effort looked much more like a typical commercial software development effort than a Department of Defense (DOD) program.

The software was subcontracted to a medium-sized, high-tech developer. Upon analyzing that subcontract, the software developer was not required to generate a B-level software functional specification (equivalent to the software requirements specification). Thus, the software developer began by attempting to go from a system-level description and hardware configuration directly to the software design. Did they have problems because of skipping a step? You bet they did!

As the hardware system evolved, there was no fixed baseline for the software (or hardware) since the allocated baseline normally provided by approving and freezing the B-level specification never occurred. Thus, the software developer was at the mercy of the prime contractor's hardware team who pretty much ran open loop. In addition, the software team had no document to validate the code against at the computer software configuration item (CSCI) level, only down at the discrete function level. Therefore, it was just about impossible to write a comprehensive test plan since that document typically has to point back to the B-level or software requirements specification (SRS) for test criteria, capabilities, and objectives.

Another very interesting requirement levied by the prime contractor on the software developer was that every time a test as to be run, a new software build would have to be compiled, linked, and loaded on the system. The alternative would have been to test with exactly what was running immediately prior to the test. Unfortunately and quite predictably, many of the tests failed not because of bad software, but because the new untested build had problems. This caused much frustration and wasted significant time and resources. Worst of all, this caused serious hard feelings between team members that remained until the end of the program. (This was one of the most unreasonable requirements I ever discovered in any IV&V effort.)

A comment about the development environment is also necessary. The software developer first worked at his own facility, remote from the hardware integration site. Not until early hardware integration began did the software team move across the country to the prime's facility. At that point, the design was still evolving, together with some mixture of prototype and final code. It was anticipated that the completion would only take a few months, but because of lack of formal baselines, poor hardware configuration management and reliability, lack of B-level specifications, generally overly optimistic planning, and Murphy's law,* the job dragged on and on.

Because of the somewhat fluid nature of the software design and consequently more rework of code than normally would have been expected, the IV&V contractor sought a way to optimize its effort, considering these circumstances. The solution was to use a comprehensive automated test tool, which provided both static and dynamic analysis of the code. The approach was two-phased: When code was considered ready for integration, it was first shipped to IV&V for static analysis and the results were returned to the lead programmer for that part of the system. Corrections were incorporated, reverified by IV&V, and sent to integration and test (I&T). Once combined into executable threads, that portion of code was supplied to the I&T team for functional testing and evaluation and to IV&V for dynamic analysis. This concept was very cost-effective and shifted much of the burden from manual code inspection and labor-intensive testing to an automated environment. IV&V also witnessed most of the major tests including those that did not run because of setup and build problems.

---

*"Whatever can go wrong will go wrong."

IV&V was handicapped somewhat by the lack of adequate documentation, but despite that was able to help define pass/fail criteria for the more important tests and conduct comprehensive evaluations of both hardware and software. One thing that eventually helped was that the software developer was finally convinced that it was essential to have a B-level specification so one was written retrospectively about the middle of the I&T phase, which at least gave the testers something tangible to look at. The formal test plan and procedures evolved together and in synch with the B-level specification so at least they were all compatible. IV&V played a significant role in the review and evolution of that set of documents.

In retrospect, the IV&V program was a very effective, low-budget effort that accomplished the primary goal of enhancing the quality of the software through significant design and code verification and validation efforts. The software requirements verification came as an afterthought and had some positive influence on test definition and stability. The worst problems encountered were lack of hardware stability, absence of formal hardware and software baselines, and the "new build before test" rule.

B.3   INDEPENDENT VERIFICATION AND VALIDATION PRODUCTS AND MAJOR ACTIVITIES

The IV&V contractor produced and participated in the following:

- Verified software design using available sources focused on the software design specification
- Applied static analysis tool to 100% of the code, finding a large number of construction faults prior to any attempt to integrate the code
- Evaluated the test plan and procedures and user documentation
- Applied a dynamic analysis tool to much of the code, finding a significant number of performance, functional, and logical deficiencies
- Was instrumental in defining test pass/fail criteria and in assessing the adequacy of the test program
- Witnessed the more significant tests
- Worked closely with the software developer to reduce frequently committed errors
- Advised the program manager on technical issues
- Participated in design reviews and CCB-type actions.

CASE STUDY C

A LARGE INSTRUMENTATION SYSTEM

FULL, IN-PHASE IV&V

C.1 SYSTEM DESCRIPTION

This system consisted of a large number of digital and analog sensors, front-end processors, data collection and analysis computers, consoles, and related hardware and software. Development occurred at a location remote from the operational site under a fixed-price contract. Once the data-processing system was installed at the site, the software subsystem integration began, followed by full-up system testing.

C.2 CHARACTERISTICS OF THE SYSTEM OR PROGRAM THAT AFFECTED INDEPENDENT VERIFICATION AND VALIDATION

Initial definition and design of this system were performed by an architectural and engineering (A&E) contractor, who used the engineering services of several companies that later became the IV&V subcontractors. This IV&V effort is an example of an engineering services contract that became an IV&V contract as the system transitioned into full-scale engineering development. This particular example is not as clear-cut as it could be since the A&E contractor was given the responsibility to set up the IV&V and put together a team of five companies to do the job. The customer, fearing that the arrangement would not work efficiently, put its own IV&V program manager in charge, who directed the effort via detailed work packages and very specific job assignments.

Thus, the IV&V group consisted of key personnel from several companies and had a government program manager. It was unorthodox, but all along this book has reminded the reader that IV&V is adaptive, flexible, and has to shape itself to the environment. I know of no better example of complexity, as far as contract configuration goes, than this effort. To the credit of everyone involved, it worked very nicely.

Aside from the unorthodox organizational structure, this IV&V effort was a full, in-phase program with formal IV&V planning, requirements verification, a requirements tracing database, full design and code verification, and participation in the development contractor's test program.

One problem that had to be solved by the customer was that the development contract was fixed-price and did not include any cost provisions for the data, code, and documentation required by the IV&V organization in advance of the period when the software and DP system was to be installed at the site. This shortcoming adversely affected the IV&V activities during early phases since the development contractor had no obligation to supply these artifacts without adding the cost impact. The customer tried to provide copies for some time, but eventually found it easier to modify the contract to include these things as part of the routine deliveries.

The instrumentation system was used in the real-time monitoring and control of a very expensive testing complex in which certain types of failures could seriously damage or destroy the facility. Therefore, IV&V participated in the failure mode effects analysis (FMEA) and criticality assessment that determined where redundant sensors, circuits, and control loops were required. They also allocated additional IV&V resources to these parts of the system to ensure algorithm optimization, fail-safe design, and exhaustive code analysis. Modeling and independent evaluations were used to predict behavior of the system when certain types of inputs were denied. IV&V analysis results were then fed into the test design to ensure adequate and safe testing of the critical parts of the system. IV&V had hands-on participation throughout the test effort and was able to check out the user documentation at the same time that test procedures were being verified. IV&V also participated in the final acceptance testing of the system and in the functional configuration audit (FCA) and the physical configuration audit (PCA) of the system.

Because of the nature of the system, a great deal of circuit and sensor loop verification took place long before any attempts were made to run the first live test. This effectively debugged the system at the discrete-function level and built confidence that the subsystem and system level tests would not be plagued by minor errors and deficiencies. This strategy worked very nicely.

There were few automated IV&V tools used, most of the effort was spent evaluating the developer's products and determining the adequacy of the algorithms, design, code, and interfaces. Since this was a MIL-STD development effort, IV&V spent a good bit of its effort enforcing the various standards and practices on the developer.

C.3 INDEPENDENT VERIFICATION AND VALIDATION PRODUCTS AND MAJOR ACTIVITIES

The IV&V contractor produced or participated as follows:
- Created a formal IV&V plan
- Performed system and software requirements verification and tracing

- Performed in-depth design verification with emphasis on critical parts of the software
- Performed failure mode analysis and criticality assessment of software with respect to the hardware
- Reviewed and evaluated all documentation
- Performed independent algorithm analysis and modeling
- Verified test requirements and acceptance criteria
- Participated actively in the test program
- Participated in all design reviews and audits
- Participated in CCB actions and open-item tracking
- Generated numerous problem reports (PRs)
- Performed special studies as requested by the customer for risk reduction and to gain technical insight into potential problem areas
- Advised the program manager on technical issues.

CASE STUDY D

GROUND SYSTEM FOR A VERY LARGE MANNED SPACE VEHICLE

PARTIAL IV&V

D.1 SYSTEM DESCRIPTION

This overall system consisted of the many ground-based systems and equipment to support the preparation and servicing of a reusable space vehicle, a large number of minicomputers for the control and checkout of the ground systems and space vehicle up to the moment of launch, several large mainframe computers used for a variety of purposes, and all the associated hardware and software. The software system in question was highly distributed and modular with a large amount of independent control over the discrete processes involved. Because a human simply could not digest the throughput of the system, it was divided into functional areas with supporting (reprogrammable) consoles that could assume an appropriate configuration for the type of activity being tested or monitored and it used "exception monitoring" and operator-called sequences as the method of allowing a human to interact with the system. The exception-monitoring concept was one in which a high-speed, computer-driven test sequence was initiated and monitored by a scheme that only alerted the operator when an anomalous value (out of pre-established range) was detected. The operator (or test engineer) could then call up any particular part of the test and pace slowly through it on a step-by-step basis or take another form of action based on the response of the system. Thus, the software in question involved the automation of testing functions and sequences as well as the support system that operated the entire network. It was in effect a very large, distributed real-time processing network.

D.2   CHARACTERISTICS OF THE SYSTEM OR PROGRAM THAT AFFECTED INDEPENDENT VERIFICATION AND VALIDATION

In this case, IV&V was initiated during the requirements phase of the software development; thus, it had all the earmarks of a full, in-phase IV&V effort. The biggest problems facing the IV&V contractor initially were obtaining and analyzing the documentation, which was being written at the same time. The software specifications first available for analysis were not based on military standards and represented a format compromise between segmented system specifications and software requirements documents. The contractor had gone to extensive effort making the documents trace to each other and the computer system requirements specifications, but something was lacking. At that time, even the contractor admitted that these books should not be baselined and that a second series of specifications would be produced. A key problem was that the automation decisions were difficult to trace and it was not immediately apparent whether a function was software, hardware, or a manually invoked procedure.

In any case, the IV&V contractor was faced with a monumental task unless some assessment could be made concerning where to concentrate his resources. The first major activity was to build a requirements tracking database. This was accomplished and gave light to the fact that many of the references already traced were too vague and high level to be of any benefit. Second, a system of metrics (as discussed in Section 12.2) was applied to each key station set specification and the results indicated a general weakness in several areas:

- Missing values, so the requirements were not quantifiable as written
- Many requirements could not be tested as written
- Vagueness to the extent that the requirements were inadequate
- Impossible-to-trace sources of many (in fact, most) requirements
- Many types of inconsistencies.

Third, a criticality assessment was conducted to assist in the allocation of IV&V resources to those sets of requirements considered to be most critical to safety, mission, cost risk, etc. (per Section 8.3). Over 100 critical safety-related issues were surfaced by this analysis that were briefed to the customer.

Thus, the major goal of the IV&V effort initially was to verify requirements in the classic sense, use metrics to estimate the percentage of completion of various specifications, and determine which requirements were most critical.

An interesting pilot program was conducted to assess the cost-effectiveness of one of the popular software requirements analysis tools. This effort surfaced several interesting things:

- To apply the tool to all major processes on the first analysis level would require several hundred thousand dollars of effort and computer time that was not in the IV&V plan or budget.

- The processes involved were easily diagrammed and could be analyzed manually as the diagrams were generated, instead of running the automated analyzer.
- The tool offered no capability to assess timing, resource conflicts, or interface constraints—several of the major concerns of the system.
- The tool required moderate-to-high user training and significant data input effort. In short, it is determined that the tool simply would not be cost-effective in this application.

The major thrust of the IV&V activity became one of specification quality assessment and forecasting where the system design would likely have trouble spots. The IV&V contractor was able to advise the customer on a large number of technical issues and ways to improve the documentation and development process.

The IV&V contractor also designed and developed a special-purpose simulation of the ground support monitoring and checkout facility to assist in analytical studies of the expected loading and throughput, performance bounds, functional allocation, hardware and software architecture, data handling, data structures, human in the loop, etc.

D.3 INDEPENDENT VERIFICATION AND VALIDATION PRODUCTS AND MAJOR ACTIVITIES

The government eventually decided not to complete the development of this system. However, I felt it significant enough to include because most of the space systems today have been verified and validated by NASA's own people, which takes away the independence. This was not a NASA program; it was a DOD program. In this case study, the IV&V contractor performed the following before the entire effort was cancelled:

- Generated a complete set of formal IV&V planning documents
- Performed a comprehensive requirements tracing procedure
- Applied criticality assessment to the requirements to help allocate IV&V resources effectively
- Performed cost-effectiveness analysis of a CASE tool
- Performed detailed review and verification of all available documentation
- Applied metrics to the specifications to determine their relative quality and percentage of completion
- Developed a special-purpose analytical simulation
- Advised the government program manager on many technical issues
- Originated problem reports on deficiencies in the documentation
- Participated in design reviews and CCB-type actions.

CASE STUDY E

INFORMATION STORAGE AND RETRIEVAL SYSTEM

PARTIAL IV&V

E.1 SYSTEM DESCRIPTION

This commercial system involved a single large mainframe computer with a large number of terminal users networked over a medium-sized state. The online database was quite large, requiring a large number of disc drives and an extensive tape library.

E.2 CHARACTERISTICS OF THE SYSTEM OR PROGRAM THAT AFFECTED INDEPENDENT VERIFICATION AND VALIDATION

Since this was a commercial procurement, the usual rigor of military standard (MIL-STD) development was missing. There were no formal requirements specifications, just a couple of meetings to discuss what the system was supposed to do. The contractor began by producing partial flowcharts and loosely defined algorithms and then began coding. The customer had little or no confidence in this development scheme and, having no expertise in software engineering, decided to procure an IV&V contractor to help look after the system development contractor. Thus, IV&V began somewhere in the middle of the effort.

The first IV&V effort was to construct a "strawman" system specification which contained all of the operational requirements, assumptions, and constraints. This was followed by a definition of software requirements, which were mapped first to the system requirements and then to the incomplete set of detailed design flowcharts. During this same period, the proposed database architecture was analyzed and found to be totally inappropriate for typical user data-request sequences.

A traffic study was conducted and a series of operational priorities were established. The schema and subschemas were redefined to better organize and depict the appropriate relationship database model.

Code analysis consisted of checking the listings and writing problem reports (PRs) as errors were uncovered. Validation was basically a combined IV&V and systems development contractor effort, since the contractor was by that time depending upon the IV&V group to perform a large portion of the systems engineering function. There was no independent testing and no automated test tools were used. Testing was largely a series of attempts by the test group to initiate all the report formats and responses from typical user requests and debug as problems occurred. Although this technique was far from optimal, it seemed the only workable solution to this totally bottom-up development. With a little better understanding of rapid prototyping, the developer could have reoriented the effort to his advantage by developing the core user interface and data retrieval software first. The user documentation eventually grew out of the validated test procedures and all the flowcharts were completed and corrected to complement the "as-built" code. A combined functional and physical configuration audit (FCA/PCA) was held and the system was accepted by the customer approximately on schedule.

This case study is an example of how a small IV&V level of effort properly focused on the critical shortcomings of the development effort had a profound influence on the successful delivery of the system.

E.3   INDEPENDENT VERIFICATION AND VALIDATION PRODUCTS AND MAJOR ACTIVITIES

The IV&V contractor produced or participated in the following:

- Developed "strawman" system specification
- Developed the equivalent of a software functional requirements document
- Assisted in redeveloping numerous algorithms
- Developed a requirements tracing database
- Performed extensive systems engineering
- Optimized the database architecture and schema
- Conducted a traffic study to help establish processing priorities
- Participated in code verification
- Participated in testing and development of user documentation
- Structured and conducted a combined FCA/PCA and assisted in system acceptance.

CASE STUDY F

A SMALL EXPERIMENTAL MISSILE SYSTEM

ENDGAME IV&V

F.1 SYSTEM DESCRIPTION

The system involved an integrated booster, a maneuverable target, an interceptor with autonomous guidance and control, and telemetry to the ground. The IV&V focused on the interceptor, which had sophisticated on-board processing performed by multiple central processing units (CPUs).

F.2 CHARACTERISTICS OF THE SYSTEM OR PROGRAM THAT AFFECTED INDEPENDENT VERIFICATION AND VALIDATION

The system had been under development for a couple of years and had an active test program when IV&V was initiated. The test program was spread over a long period of time so that performance of all subsystems could be evaluated following each test and then changed to accommodate evolving requirements and be made ready for the next test. Therefore, IV&V was a series of evaluations to help ensure success by catching deficiencies before each major release of the software was approved for live testing. This meant that a lot of verification and validation activities had to take place in a short time with results fed back rapidly to the developer for action.

The code was written in three different computer languages, which caused the IV&V contractor to have to acquire appropriate tools to match each one. The decision was made to use both static and dynamic code analyzers (refer to Sections 7.4 and 8.5.1, respectively) as the primary IV&V software tools. The size of the software was such that these tools easily handled the amount code and worked very efficiently to uncover errors, inconsistencies, and poor design and coding practices.

Another area that the government customer was extremely interested in was error handling and the effects of undetected or uncontrolled error propagation on mission success. The developer had performed a failure mode effects analysis (FMEA) and had incorporated a reasonably comprehensive error control scheme in the software. Despite this, IV&V was able to detect several vulnerabilities and recommend improvements.

IV&V worked closely with the systems engineering staff who were performing detailed algorithm analysis and six-degree-of-freedom (6DOF) simulation which included hardware-in-the-loop (HWIL) testing in a government-owned facility. Thus, IV&V and the system engineering staff were able to effectively share analysis results and assisted each other in detailed evaluation of the software. An attempt was made to forecast where the system might expect to have processing problems and then during testing the actual results were compared to the predictions.

During the interval between tests, IV&V performed limited requirements analysis and developed a tracing database despite somewhat dated documentation. This helped assure that the primary test objectives were being addressed by the test program.

F.3   INDEPENDENT VERIFICATION AND VALIDATION PRODUCTS AND MAJOR ACTIVITIES

The IV&V contractor produced or participated as follows:

- Did formal IV&V planning
- Performed requirements-tracing function and database preparation
- Performed static analysis of software
- Performed limited dynamic analysis of software
- Performed limited design evaluation
- Reported on analysis results to government customer
- Shared analysis results from independent 6DOF and HWIL tests
- Reviewed all documentation
- Performed error control and propagation evaluation
- Participated in reviews and meetings
- Monitored developer's test program.

CASE STUDY G

ABC MISSILE PROGRAM

AUDIT-LEVEL IV&V

G.1 SYSTEM DESCRIPTION

This system involved acquisition and tracking radars, surface-to-air missiles, mobile launchers, a command and control system, and associated hardware and software. The radars were not included in the IV&V program as they were non-developmental items (NDI). The customer was a large aerospace company that wanted a very low budget audit-level IV&V effort because the program manager, who was new to the company, felt uneasy about how the program was progressing. He had been a military program manager before retiring and had expected a more formal and disciplined approach than he found. The project was in preliminary design when the IV&V audit occurred.

G.2 CHARACTERISTICS OF THE SYSTEM OR PROGRAM THAT AFFECTED INDEPENDENT VERIFICATION AND VALIDATION

In this case, it was more the development methodology and environment that was being examined in detail than the missile system itself. The effort was funded for a one-man-month level of effort. The customer agreed to make any of the development and support staff available and gave access to all procedures, practices, tools, etc. that IV&V might wish to evaluate. IV&V was given a private work area and whatever support services were necessary.

This effort was performed a couple of years before the Software Engineering Institute (SEI) produced its structured evaluation methodology (discussed in Chapter 15), but it encompassed similar objectives and addressed many of the same issues. Audit-level IV&V probed how well the customer's software development methods and team compared to what IV&V considered to be an adequate methodology, environment, and organization.

Three IV&V analysts took part in an intensive week long fact-finding investigation and then presented their results and recommendations to the program manager and other interested parties in a two-part meeting. The various organizations within the customer's shop that were affected by the audit were present in the second session and given the opportunity to refute the findings, although very little rebuttal occurred.

The effort was divided into three groups of disciplines so that each IV&V analyst had a manageable set of things to evaluate. The groups were as follows:

1. *Management Practices and Support Systems.* Questions and assessments centered on formal plans and policies, methods and practices, databases and archived information, libraries, cost models, budgeting and scheduling systems, MIS, and especially how well everything was integrated around a work breakdown structure (WBS). Major disciplines included: program management, configuration management, data management, and quality assurance.

2. *Software Development Practices and Environment.* Questions and assessments focused on the adequacy of the overall development methodology and process model for the type of system being developed by the group. Significant attention was given to how up-to-date the paradigm was and how well the tools being used fit the paradigm. Also of interest was whether the group retained and analyzed quality and productivity data project to project. Major categories included: development process paradigm and practices, software tool selection and coverage, active technology insertion program, and statistics and metrics collection and dissemination.

3. *Organization.* Questions were asked up and down the organization to determine how well everyone understood his or her job and its relationship to the group and to this particular project. Each interviewee was profiled by resumé data and assigned responsibilities. Then the amount of training, its currency, and whether cross-training occurred was evaluated. Despite the lack of individual productivity data, some ranking of skills vs. job assignment was made to determine the degree of specialization found in the organization. Major areas of interest included: roles and responsibilities, on-the-job training and cross-training, and training for new technology including such things as classes in Ada, C, UNIX, etc., and skill assessment and productivity ratings.

G.3   INDEPENDENT VERIFICATION AND VALIDATION PRODUCTS AND MAJOR ACTIVITIES

IV&V found a significant number of shortcomings that included some real surprises for the program manager as well as group managers. I have included the first six issues, which were presented at the end of the IV&V effort, in priority order.

1. *Findings*   The software development methodology was ill-defined, not based on a modern paradigm, did not insist on design before coding, paid lip service to documentation especially in requirements, and did not have effective CASE tools. In essence, they had an obsolete and inadequate process not well-suited to critical real-time systems.

Recommendations   Adoption of a modern real-time paradigm and appropriately matched set of automated software tool; extensive in-house training; and addition/reassignment of key personnel to establish, maintain, and train on the software engineering environment to continuously stay abreast with the state of the practice.

2. *Findings*   Technical staff members tended to be expert in one small software area and lacked both the incentive and desire to learn other skills or to cross-train. Several were expert in obsolete techniques and systems and badly needed to be reassigned and/or retrained.

Recommendations   Begin with extensive training program in Ada, C, and UNIX to generally elevate capabilities of entire group. Then, as new technology is introduced, broaden areas of involvement to include modern CASE tools, DBMSs, new operating systems, and new user interfaces (e.g., X-windows).

3. *Findings*   Configuration management (CM) practices were being only partially followed. The most glaring problem was lack of formal baselines. The programmer or designer was allowed to change requirements if he or she thought it was a "good idea." Configuration status accounting was not consistently applied, especially in problem reporting. Some of the staff verbally reported problems and never wrote formal problem reports, saying that to write them was too time-consuming. There were no CM audits so recordkeeping was inconsistent or nonexistent.

Recommendations   Establish a comprehensive CM plan and program to include strict baseline control, comprehensive automated status accounting, and a notion of an internal development configuration to help control design changes. In addition, bring in an outside CM expert to audit the program periodically to ensure adequacy and adherence to the plan.

4. *Findings*   The program had scheduling and budgeting software but it was not well-integrated around the contract work breakdown structure (WBS). Cost modeling was not used to predict the cost of the software because the company had insufficient historical data from previous efforts.

Recommendations   Develop an integrated program management information system (PMIS) structured around the WBS that will enable tracking of any item so that adequate visibility can be provided. It is important that this system be usable from the proposal effort forward for graceful transition into the development phase. Plans must be included to collect productivity data so that cost estimating can be enhanced in future programs.

5. *Findings*   Quality assurance (QA) was always a last-minute sign-off of documents and software releases wherein the QA personnel were never given time for an adequate review or evaluation.

Recommendations   Get QA involved much earlier and allow time for in-process reviews and evaluations. Make QA responsible for the quality of the products, not just for another signature. This company was a good candidate for a major quality enhancement program. Today, TQM would be appropriate; at that time it was urged that they integrate the quality organization into their day-to-day activities, give QA more of a role in product evaluations, and elevate QA's authority in the organization.

6. *Findings*   The group did not collect productivity statistics, so it never knew where it stood relative to national statistics or even to other parts of the company who did similar projects. There were no metrics used to evaluate the completeness or quality of development products, so passage from one phase to the next was not based on quantitative measures.

Recommendations.   Incorporate a minimal number of metrics, sufficient to quantify at least the critical products such as requirements and design specifications, code, and testing. These data must be used by management to help control the project and must be retained for future estimating purposes. Since this group was part of a much bigger company, IV&V urged the manager to elevate this problem to the corporate level so that some consistent set of objectives and a systematic approach could be developed where the whole company could participate. We further urged that the company could save enormous amounts of money if it began a coordinated effort to develop a unified software engineering environment (SEE) and focused its CASE tool acquisition and training program around a common set of products.

CASE STUDY H

A VERY LARGE
FEDERAL AUTOMATED
DATA-PROCESSING
OPERATION

AUDIT-LEVEL WITH TRANSITION TO FULL, IN-PHASE IV&V

H.1 SYSTEM DESCRIPTION

The system consisted of a very large network of big mainframe computers, peripherals, data archives, a national telecommunications network, and software development and operations personnel that numbered in the thousands.

H.2 CHARACTERISTICS OF THE SYSTEM OR PROGRAM THAT AFFECTED INDEPENDENT VERIFICATION AND VALIDATION

Because this was a federal agency that was not part of the Department of Defense, standards and practices from the then National Bureau of Standards were used for the development process. These standards represent a middle ground between good commercial practices and military standards (MIL-STDs). The software organization was divided into three major software functional operations—requirements, development, and operations.

The IV&V effort began as part of a government-funded modernization program to enhance and upgrade overall operation of the agency as related to software.

IV&V started as an intensive audit-level program oriented at finding out where the deficiencies were and planning a comprehensive methodology and time-phased modernization program tailored to fit the needs of that agency. Once the institutionalization of modern technology and practices was complete, IV&V transitioned to in-phase operation to support new higher-order language (HOL) software developed to replace the difficult-to-maintain and seriously out-of-date assembly language programs. This case study concentrates mostly on the initial phase of the effort, when the deficiencies were first discovered, and on what was proposed to remedy them. The main reason for this perspective in the case study is that once the modernization program set up all of the mechanisms and ran a series of pilot and training programs, newly created organic groups within the agency took over and began autonomous operation.

H.3   INDEPENDENT VERIFICATION AND VALIDATION PRODUCTS AND MAJOR ACTIVITIES

The audit-level IV&V was part of the team effort that included experts in configuration management, software development methodology, management information systems, databases, telecommunications, quality assurance, etc. IV&V was given one of the most challenging and interesting tasks, that of defining the complete life cycle models. This resulted in two large wall charts—one depicting the product model and the other the process model. Early versions of the charts were color-coded to identify items that would remain essentially unchanged, items that required redefinition and reconstitution, and new items that were necessary to satisfy the infusion of modern development practices. Many management and technical personnel were surprised to see the "big picture" for the first time. IV&V ran a series of in-house training seminars to promote better understanding of the total development process. The life cycle models were also used to show a "before" and "after" characterization of the process. These charts proved to be very popular training, management, and communication aids.

After some investigation, it was found that modern configuration management (CM) practices did not exist. A typical operational scenario went something like this: Operator calls programmer about midnight to say the program run abnormally ended. Programmer suggests a fix from home or goes in, assembly code is patched and never documented, program runs, everyone is happy until next fatal run. This process was repeated thousands of times for years and there were no baselines, no clean code, very little documentation, etc. It was a form of job security, but after a while began to border on collapse. That was when the modernization effort was initiated. The team established a comprehensive CM program that closely controlled and monitored every facet of the development process from that point forward.

The problem of CM was complicated also by the fact that certain classes of changes resulted from congressional actions and, therefore, were mandatory and urgent. Another class of changes resulted from routine updates to hardware systems, operating systems, and support services and were likewise both mandatory and urgent. Other classes of changes included a typical spread of requested changes—new features, error fixes, improvements, etc. The result was that several levels of configuration control and review boards were established to coordinate the change control problem in the most appropriate fashion.

It was discovered that various development organizations had bought the same software tool upward of 20 times without knowledge that the agency already had copies on the system. It appeared to us that a station license and only the latest copy would make a lot more sense. When we reworked the tools, there was a 70% reduction in the number on the development system. Most important, we purged all the obsolete versions. Remember too, that most of these tools would soon go away and be replaced by more modern and comprehensive CASE tools as the HOL code (COBOL) replaced the assembly code.

Through the years over a half-million 2400-ft. magnetic tapes had been archived. After our investigation, we recommended purging a large number of them, freeing up an enormous amount of physical storage space and reusable tapes.

One of the most significant additions to the day-to-day operation of the total organization was the establishment of a nerve center or as some called it, "the war room". This was a dedicated area from which all development projects would be monitored. It had numerous status displays with color graphics, projection systems, and network access to various databases for data collection and tracking. It was the first time the agency ever attempted to centralize and focus project management so that high-level managers could have all the essential information available immediately in a highly useful form. Production statistics, trend data, problem reporting, CM status, and open-item tracking were all supported by this system. A few years earlier, this same approach was used very successfully on a very large defense project (discussed in Case Study A). At that time, we defined a new type of management analyst, who would collect and help interpret the data for the program managers to aid them in the decision process. We passed this concept on to the federal agency in hopes that if it recognized the need for this specialty that it would have a precedent to go by in creating this new job classification.

In-house training programs were initiated in virtually every discipline so that all levels of management would better appreciate and understand how the greatly enhanced development process would work and make their roles more efficient and effective. As new software was introduced, tailored in-depth training with the technical personnel was provided so that transition to organic maintenance and support would occur smoothly.

If this effort had been assessed by the Software Engineering Institute (SEI) evaluation methodology, the modernization program would probably have resulted in a solid Level 3 with most of the Level 4 criteria satisfied. The real issue becomes one of staying abreast with the state of the practice—infusing technology and training as needed to keep the organization at its peak and continuing coordinated investment in the appropriate software tools and the development and engineering environment. These problems are often enormous in a very large organization. Hopefully continued modernization and technology infusion will not become the first targets of the budget cutters.

REFERENCES

1. Boehm, B. W., *Software Engineering Economics*. Englewood Cliffs, N.J.: Prentice-Hall, 1981, pp 39–41.

2. Cooper, John D. and Fisher, Matthew J., ed., *Software Quality Management*. Princeton, N.J.: Petrocelli Books, 1979, pp 150–151.

3. Deutsch, Michael S., *Software Verification and Validation*. Englewood Cliffs, N.J.: Prentice-Hall, 1982, pp 52–59.

4. Dickson, W. J. and Roethlisberger, F. J., *Management and the Worker*. Cambridge: Harvard University Press, 1946.

5. Humphrey, W. S. and Sweet, W. L., *A Method for Assessing the Software Engineering Capability of Contractors*. CMU/SEI-87-TR-23. Pittsburgh: Software Engineering Institute, Carnegie-Mellon University, 1987.

6. Lewis, R. O., *An Approach to Software Verification and Validation*, 3rd ed. Huntsville, AL: Science Applications International Corporation, 1976.

7. Lewis, R. O., "Seminar to Social Security Software Managers." Baltimore: 1983. (Unpublished)

8. Lewis, R. O., *The Cost of an Error: A Retrospective Look at Safeguard Software*. Huntsville, AL: Science Applications International Corporation, March 1977.

9. McClure, Carma, *CASE is Software Automation*. Englewood Cliffs, N.J.: Prentice-Hall, 1989, pp 196–198.

10. Schindler, Max, *Computer-Aided Software Design*. New York: John Wiley & Sons, 1990, p 193.

11. Stevens, Roger T., *Operational Test and Evaluation*. New York: John Wiley & Sons, 1979.

12. U.S. Air Force Military Standard MIL-STD-499A (USAF), "Engineering Management," May 1, 1974.

13. U.S. Air Force Military Standard MIL-STD-1521B (USAF), "Technical Review and

Copies of listed federal and military standards, specifications and handbooks are available through the DOD Single Stock Point, Commanding Officer, U.S. Naval Publications and Forms Center (Attn: NPFC 1032), 5801 Tabor Avenue, Philadelphia, Pennsylvania 19120. Telephone (215) 697-2667.

Audits for Systems, Equipment, and Computer Software," June 4, 1985 (supersedes MIL-STD-1521A, June 1, 1976).

14. U.S. Department of Defense Directive DODD 5000.1, Major and Non-Major Acquisition Programs," February 23, 1991.

15. U.S. Department of Defense Handbook DOD-HDBK 286/287, "Guide for Application and Tailoring of Requirements for Defense Material Acquisitions."

16. U.S. Department of Defense Instruction DODI 5000.2, "Defense Acquisition Management Policies and Procedures," February 23, 1991.

17. U.S. Department of Defense Manual DOD 5000.2-M, "Defense Acquisition Management Documents and Reports," February 23, 1991.

18. U.S. Department of Defense Military Specification MIL-S-83490, "Specifications, Types, and Forms," October 30, 1968.

19. U.S. Department of Defense Military Standard MIL-STD-480B, "Configuration Control—Engineering Changes, Deviations, and Waivers," July 15, 1988 (supersedes DOD-STD-480A, April 12, 1978).

20. U.S. Department of Defense Military Standard MIL-STD-481A, "Configuration Control–Engineering Changes, Deviations, and Waivers (Short Form)," October 18, 1972.

21. U.S. Department of Defense Military Standard MIL-STD-482, "Configuration Status Accounting Data Elements and Related Features," December 31, 1970.

22. U.S. Department of Defense Military Standard MIL-STD-490A, "Specification Practices," June 4, 1985 (supersedes MIL-STD-490, October 30, 1968).

23. U.S. Department of Defense Military Standard MIL-STD-881A, "Work Breakdown Structures for Defense Materiel Items," April 25, 1975 (supersedes MIL-STD-881, November 1, 1968).

24. U.S. Department of Defense Standard DOD-STD-2167A, "Defense System Software Development," February 29, 1988 (supersedes DOD-STD-2167, June 4, 1985).

25. U.S. Department of Defense Standard DOD-STD-2168, "Defense System Software Quality Program," April 29, 1988.

26. U.S. Department of the Air Force Regulation 800-14, Volume I, "Management of Computer Resources in Systems," September 12, 1975.

ABBREVIATIONS

A&E	architecture and engineering (company)
ACAT	acquisition category (e.g., ACAT I, ACAT ID)
ACI	allocated configuration identification (allocated baseline)
AD	advanced development (obsolete term still in limited use)
Ada	(a U.S. Department of Defense standard programming language)
ADP	Automated data processing
APB	acquisition program base
BCD	binary-coded decimal
C	Coding; a computer language
C3	communications, command, and control
CAD	computer-aided design
CAE	computer-aided engineering
CAM	computer-aided manufacturing
C&UT	code and unit test
CASE	computer-aided software engineering
CCB	configuration control board
CD	concept definition (was also "concept development," now called CE&D)
CDR	critical design review
CDRL	contract data requirements list
CE&D	concept exploration and definition
CF	criticality factor
CFE	contractor-furnished equipment
CI	configuration item
CIS	critical item specification
CISE	computer-integrated software engineering
CM	configuration management

COTS	commercial off-the-shelf (hardware or software)
CRLCMP	computer resource life-cycle management plan
CRMP	computer resource management plan
CSAS	configuration status accounting system
CSC	computer software component
CSCI	computer software configuration item
CSU	computer software unit
CV	code verification

D	design
DAB	Defense Acquisition Board
DB	database
DBDD	database design document
DBMS	database management system
DCDS	Distributed Computing Design System
DD	data dictionary
DDL	data definition language (also distributed design language)
Dem/Val	demonstration and validation phase (same as advanced development)
DFD	data flow diagram
DIAG	diagram
DID	data item directive
DML	data manipulation language
DOC	document
DOD	U.S. Department of Defense
DODD	Department of Defense Directive
DODI	Department of Defense Instruction
DOD-STD	Department of Defense Standard (equivalent to MIL-STD)
DP	data processing
DRM	data resource management
DT or DT&E	developmental test and evaluation
DV	design verification

E&MD	engineering and manufacturing development (same as ED, FSD or FSED)
ECO	engineering change order
ECP	engineering change proposal
ED	engineering development (same as FSD, FSED or E&MD)
ENG	engineering
EPROM	erasable permanent read-only memory
ERR	engineering release record
EV	effectiveness value

F	fabrication of hardware
F_NET	Functional Network (a diagram in DCDS)
FCA	functional configuration audit
FCI	functional configuration identification (functional baseline)
4GL	fourth-generation language
FMEA	failure mode effects analysis
FQR	formal qualification review
FQT	formal qualification tests
FSCM	Federal Supply Code for Manufacturers
FSD or FSED	full-scale engineering development (E&MD or ED)
FUE	first units evaluation
FUNCT	function or functional
GFE	government-furnished equipment
GFP	government furnished property
HOL	higher-order language
HV	hardware verification
HW	hardware
HWCI	hardware configuration item
HWIL	hardware in the loop
I&T	integration and testing
I-CASE	integrated CASE
IDD	interface design document
I/F	interface
INIT	initialization or initial
INTEG	integration
I/O	input/output
IORL	input/output requirements language (TAGS by Teledyne Brown Engineering)
IPSE	integrated project support environment
IRS	interface requirements specification
IV&V	independent verification and validation
JSD	Jackson System Development
LCD	liquid crystal display
LCM	life cycle model
MAINT	maintenance
MCCR	mission-critical computer resources
MDL	module development language (in DCDS)
MIL-STD	military standard (of U.S. DOD) (equivalent to DOD-STD)
MIS	management information system

MNS	mission need statement
MS	milestones (MS0, MSI, MSII, MSIII)
NASA	National Aeronautics and Space Administration (U.S.)
NCA	National Command Authority
NDI	nondevelopmental items
O&M	operation and maintenance (same as O&S)
O&O	operation and organization
O&S	operation and support (also operation and service)
OMA	operation and maintenance activity
OOD	object-oriented design
ORD	operational requirements document
OS	operating system
OSD	Office of the Secretary of Defense
OT or OT&E	operational testing and evaluation
P	primary user
PA	production activity or product assurance
PCA	physical configuration audit
PCI	production configuration identification (product baseline)
PD	preliminary design
PDL	program design language
PDR	preliminary design review
PDSS	postdeployment software support
PERT	program evaluation and review technique
PIP	product improvement proposal (or program)
PIS	prime-item specification
PM	program manager or program management
PMIS	program management information system
PQT	preliminary qualification test
PR	problem reports
PRELIM	preliminary
PROC	procedure
PROCED	procedure
PROG	program
PROM	programmable read-only memory
PSL/PSA	problem statement language/problem statement analyzer
P3I	preplanned product improvement
PU	percent of use
QA	quality assurance
R	requirement(s)
RDD	Requirements Driven Development (by Ascent Logic)

REVAL	revalidation
RFP	request for proposals
RQMT	requirement
R_NET	Requirements Network (a diagram in DCDS)
RSL	Requirements Specification Language (in DCDS)
RTM	requirements tracing matrix
RV	reentry vehicle
SAC	Strategic Air Command (U.S. Air Force)
SAM	surface-to-air missile
SCCS	a code management system for UNIX-based systems
SCN	specification change notice
SDD	software design document
SDDD	software detailed design document
SDDS	Strategic Defense Development System (a CASE tool)
SDLC	system development life cycle
SDP	software development plan
SDR	system design review
SEE	software engineering environment
SEI	Software Engineering Institute (at Carneige-Mellon University)
SETA	systems engineering and technical assistance (contract type)
6DOF	six degrees of freedom
SLC	system life cycle
SLCSE	software life cycle support environment (a CASE tool)
SOW	statement of work
SOOD	structural object-oriented design
SPEC	specification
SPS	software product specification
SQA	software quality assurance
SQL	standard query language
SQPP	software quality program plan
SREM	Software Requirements Engineering Methodology (in DCDS)
SRR	system requirements review
SRS	software requirements specification
SSDD	system/segment design document
SSL	System Specification Language (in DCDS)
SSR	software specification review
STD	software test description
STLDD	software top-level design document
STP	software test plan
SUM	software user's manual
SV	system verification
SW	software
SYS	system
SYSREM	System Requirements Engineering Methodology (in DCDS)

TDP	technical data package
TEMP	test and evaluation master plan
TRR	test readiness review
TSL	test support language (DCDS)
TTY	teletype
UDF	unit development file (folder)
UTIL	utility (software)
VAL	validation
VHDL	very high density (design) language
WAN	wide area network
WBS	work breakdown structure

INDEX